Watercolor Cabinet of Curiosities

Paint Perfectly Peculiar Insects, Antiques & Other Oddities

Nassybah Touriño

Creator of Nussay Art

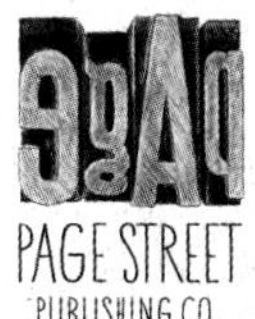

PAGE STREET
PUBLISHING CO.

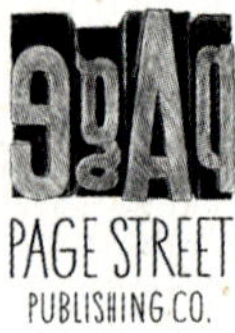

PAGE STREET
PUBLISHING CO.

First published in 2025 by

Page Street Publishing Co.

27 Congress Street, Suite 1511

Salem, MA 01970

www.pagestreetpublishing.com

Distributed by Macmillan, sales in Canada by The Canadian Manda Group.

28 27 26 25   1 2 3 4 5

ISBN-13: 979-8-89003-266-9

Library of Congress Control Number: 2024945198

Edited by Sadie Hofmeester

Cover and book design by Emma Hardy for Page Street Publishing Co.

Photography and photography research by Nassybah Touriño, except for reference photos (see page 218 for full list)

Printed and bound in China

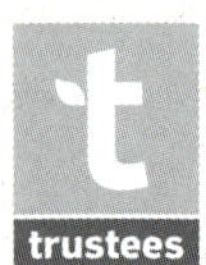

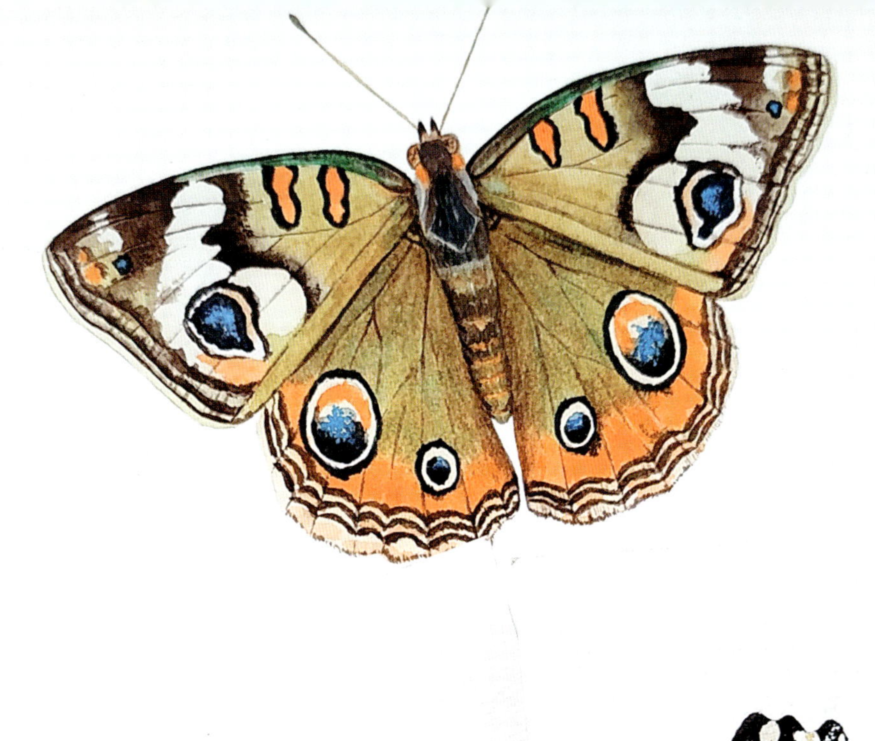

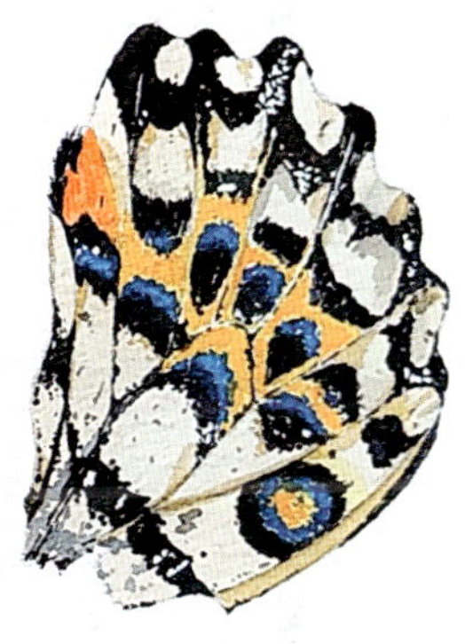

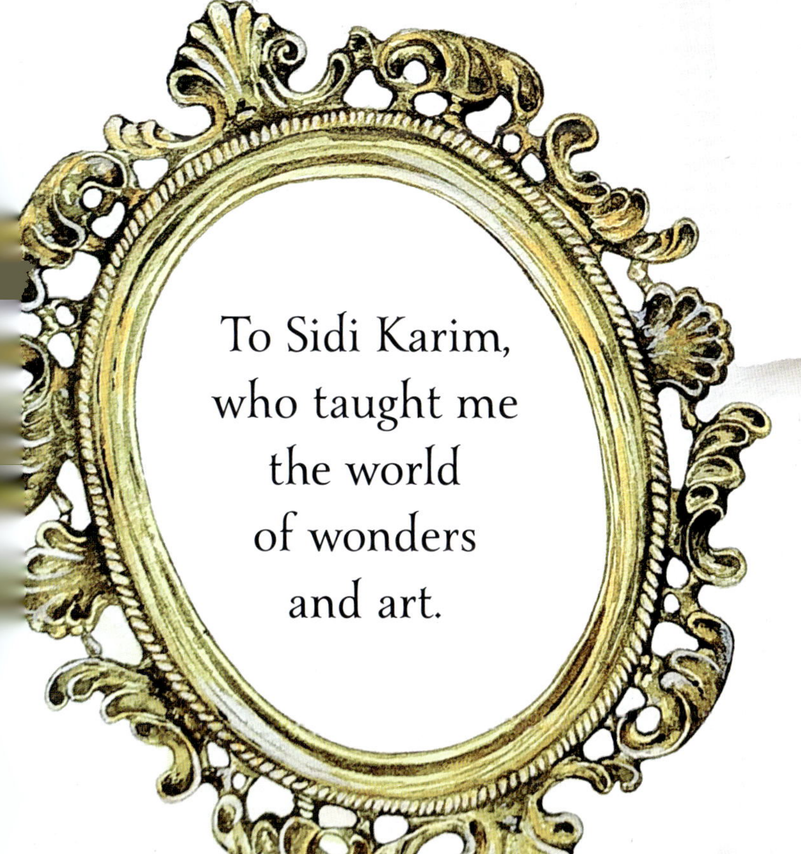

To Sidi Karim,
who taught me
the world
of wonders
and art.

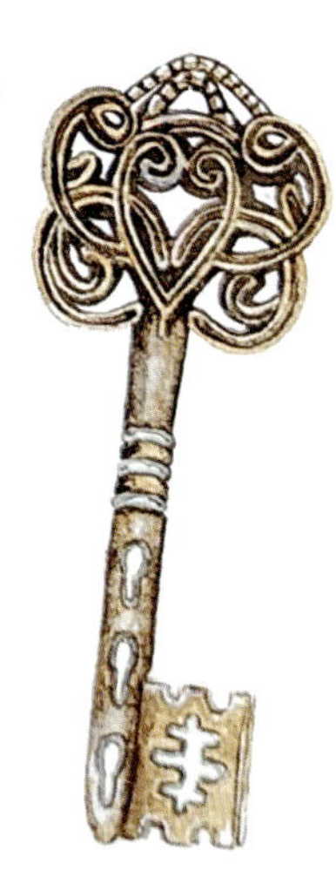

Contents

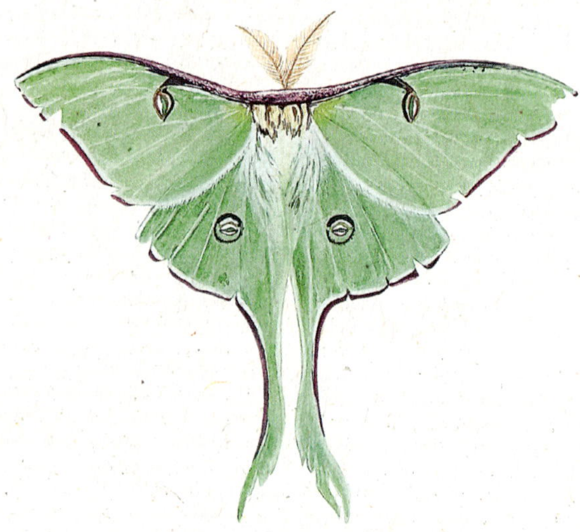

Introduction 7

Tools of the Trade 8

Techniques for Success 12

Nature's Jewelry: Butterflies & Moths 21

Blue Morpho Butterfly 23

Emerald Birdwing Butterfly 27

Tiger Moth 31

Cabbage Butterfly 37

Luna Moth 41

Death's-Head Hawkmoth 47

Monarch Butterfly 51

Sunset Moth 55

Common Buckeye Butterfly 59

Emperor Moth 67

Atlas Moth 73

Orange Oakleaf Butterfly 79

Insectarium 85

Hercules Beetle 87

Flower Chafer 93

Ladybug 97

Stag Beetle 103

Mecynorhina 107

Goliath Beetle 113

Leaf Insect 119

Roly-Poly 127

Cicada 131

Honeybee 137

Peanut-Headed Lantern Fly 143

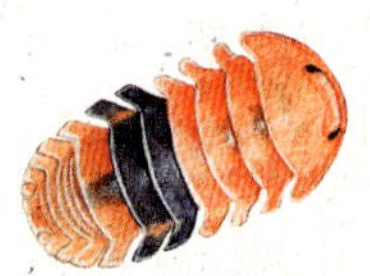

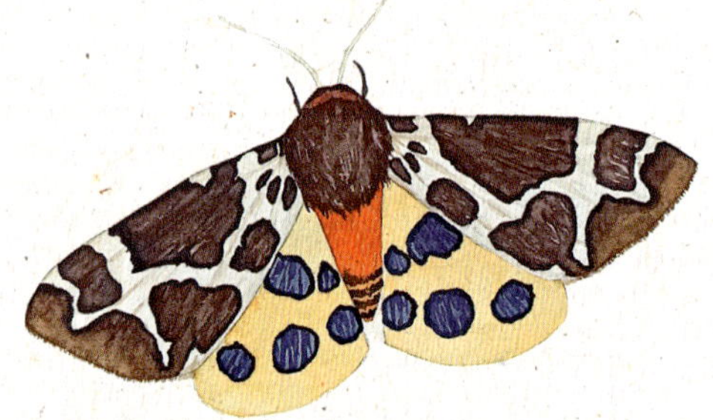

Beautiful Oddities   149

Tarantula   151

Vintage Scissors   155

Cat Skull   159

Vintage Frame   165

Old Key   171

Amanita Muscaria   177

Feather   181

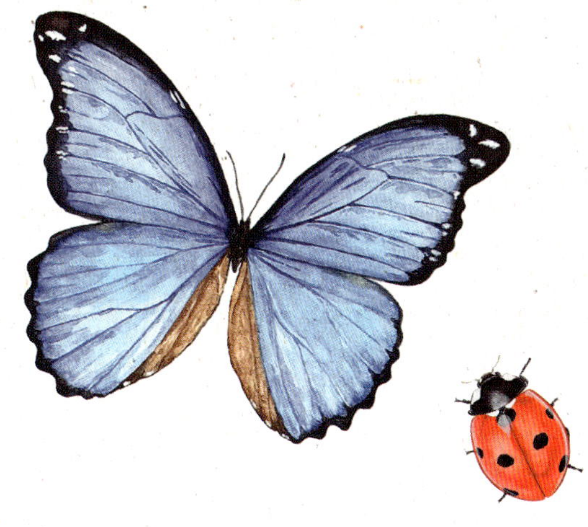

Entomology Drawer   187

Butterfly Wing   189

Antique Magnifying Glass   193

Glass Dome Insect   195

Moth Dust Bottle   199

Insect Taxidermy Box   205

Old Entomology Flyer   215

Reference Image Credits   218

Acknowledgments   219

About the Author   220

Index   221

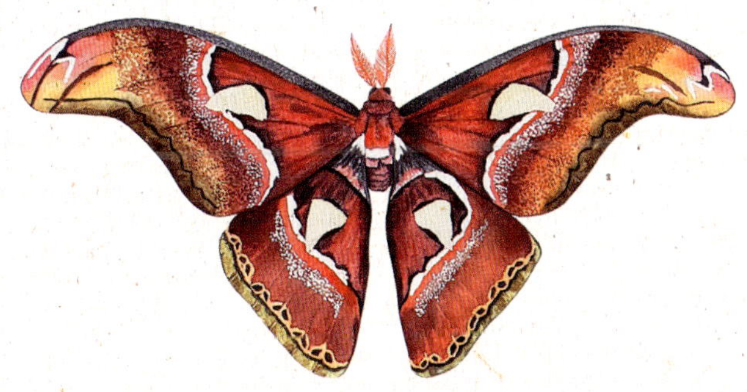

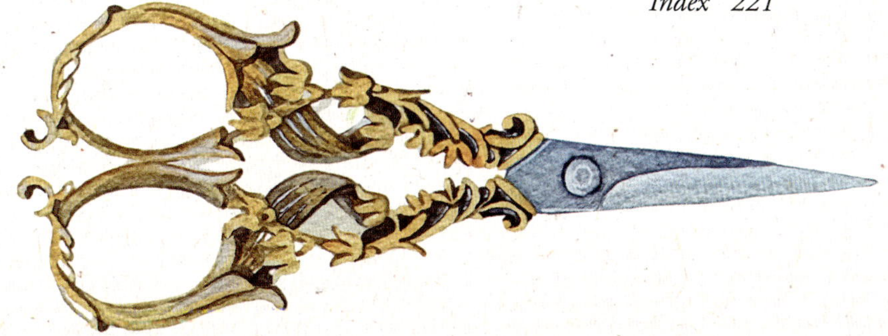

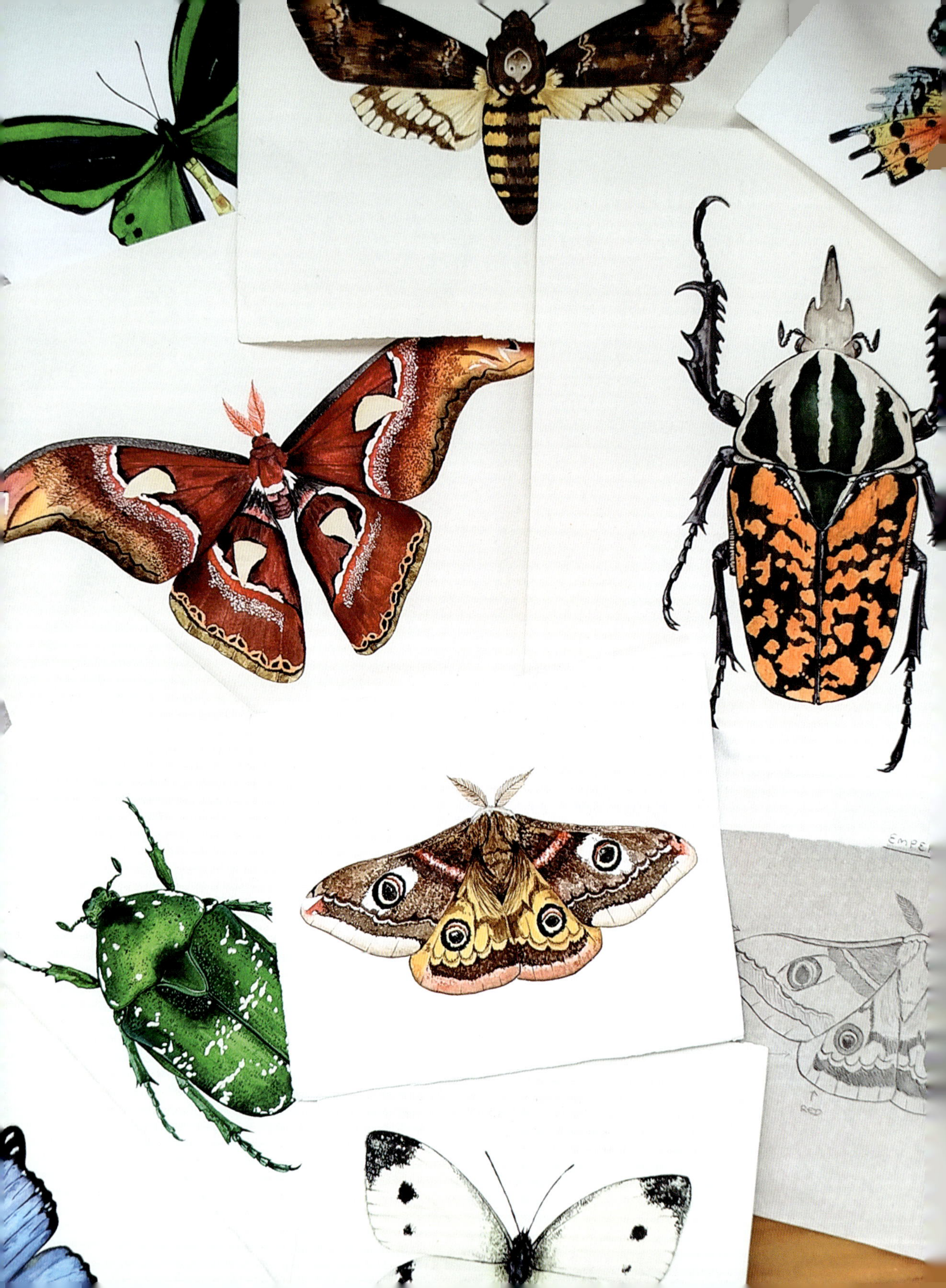

Introduction

Hi! My name is Nassybah, and I'm the illustrator behind all the bugs and oddities in this book! I was born into a family of artisans in Spain, so art has always been a part of my life. But it took a move to Madison, Wisconsin, and a bit of sadness due to the cold weather to get me to pick up my brushes again. And I'm so happy I did! I just started painting with a small set of watercolor paints and the basics on my kitchen counter, but the feeling I got was indescribable. After a while, I then took the chance to quit my job to become a freelance illustrator. I've been fortunate to have my work featured in product design, stationery, and textiles, as well as wholesale and private commissions.

I have always loved vintage things, skulls, and above all else, bugs. I especially feel like illustrating insects allows you to observe the tiniest details, and reproducing these beautiful creatures honors them. What I hope you will get from this book is more than just illustrations—I hope these works also unlock awareness. My illustrations have inspired bug love in over 1,000 homes, leaving a positive impact about these often feared creatures.

Besides my freelance business, I also lead workshops, and I like to do something different from the norm with them. I like to add a bit of a dark swirl to the watercolor world, which hopefully appeals to those who want to learn how to paint with watercolors, but aren't so fond of pastels and flowers. You'll see this tendency on full display in this book.

I'm also here to dispel the belief that you need a lot of supplies to start. What you *do* need, more than super-expensive tools or thousands of brushes and watercolor tubes, is the will to do it . . . to find the time to sit down and create.

Each of the four chapters in this book has projects of different difficulty levels, which are noted for each. Navigate through these projects however you like, but by starting with the easy ones and progressing till you can handle the more challenging ones, you'll learn the basic techniques needed to create beautiful illustrations in no time at all.

Each project contains step-by-step instructions to guide you through the process. I recommend reading the instructions before digging in, because I feel it's always easier to have a complete understanding of the process before starting.

Finally, I want these projects to lead to discussions with the next generation about how important these small dwellers are. Today, the biodiversity of our planet is in danger; my hope for this book is that it not only provides great instruction, but that it also creates more awareness of how important and amazing these small creatures are. In a world crowded by screens and technology, we need to remember how important biodiversity is.

I invite you to unleash your creativity and to learn a bit about insects. And I truly hope you love this book as much as I loved creating it!

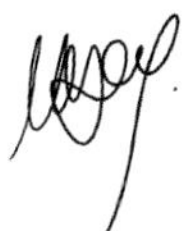

Tools of the Trade

Many beginning watercolor artists don't know where to start when it comes to art supplies. Before jumping into painting, here is a list of the essential tools you need to accomplish any of the projects in this book!

Watercolor Paints

Watercolor paints come in pans and tubes; it's up to you to which one to use. If you use pans, you just need to wet them before painting.

Setting up your watercolor paint collection can feel a bit overwhelming, but it's actually easy to learn how to mix your own colors. If you don't want to make a big investment on buying the Sennelier professional palette, you can start out with a small range of colors, and add to them as your preferences evolve.

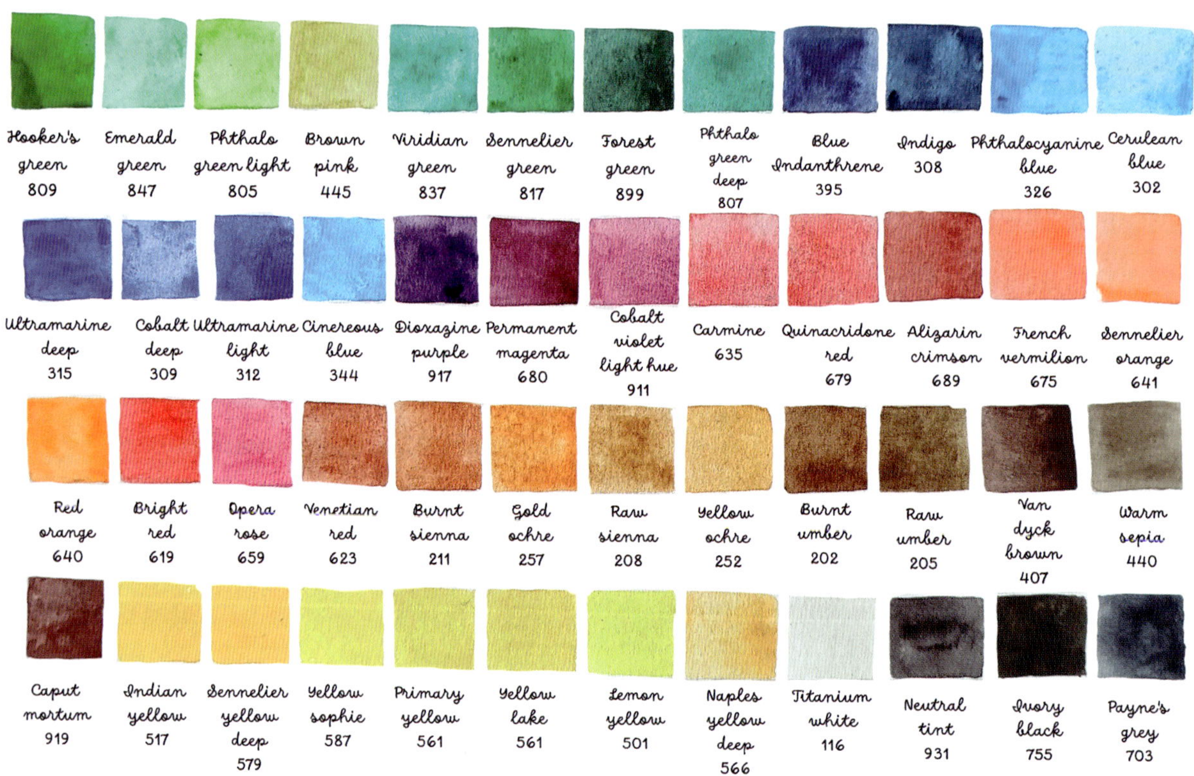

My personal Sennelier palette.

If you have a set of essential colors, you can mix almost any shade. A good beginner's set should include:

* Titanium White
* A neutral gray such as Neutral Tint
* A warm brown such as Van Dyck Brown or Raw Sienna
* A cool brown such as Raw Umber
* A warm red such as Red Orange
* A cool red such as Quinacridone Red or Carmine
* A warm yellow such as Yellow Ochre or Indian Yellow
* A cool yellow such as Lemon Yellow
* A warm blue such as Ultramarine Light
* A cool blue such as Phthalocyanine Blue.

For ease of painting, it can also be nice to have:

* A purple such as Dioxazine Purple
* A selection of greens (my favorites include Hooker's Green, Phthalo Green Deep, and Emerald Green)
* A unique yellow-green color ironically called Brown Pink.

However, remember: If I use a color you don't have, you can always use what you have, and practice your mixing skills!

Paintbrushes

I advise you to invest in natural or good quality synthetic hair brushes if possible, but these can be quite expensive. I really like Panart brushes because they're good quality brushes at a reasonable price.

If you can afford a few brushes, get:

* A size 0 to 2 round detail brush
* A size 6 to 12 round medium brush
* A 10/0 liner brush.

You can do any of the projects in this book with just these three brushes.

Note: You will also need an old small brush to apply masking fluid. I used a round size 2, but anything smaller than a size 6 will work.

Watercolor Paper

In my opinion, if there's a tool that's the most important to invest in, it's the paper. Why? Well, choosing the right watercolor paper can make or break your artwork—especially in the beginning. Paper is a factor in the appearance of colors and how water and pigments pool, blend, and dry. Painting can be really frustrating without a good surface to work on. There are a few different things I look for when shopping for paper:

* Surface with texture (granulation)
* Cold-press
* A weight of 140 lb (300 gsm)

Cold-press paper is not as smooth as hot-press and has a nice toothy texture, which helps absorb the paint. Heavy paper (140 lb [300 gsm]) is less likely to buckle and can hold more water, making it ideal for heavy washes and multiple layers.

My favorite watercolor paper is 140 lb (300 gsm) 100% cotton cold-press paper with a rough surface. My preferred brands are Arches, Canson®, and Fabriano. Also, it's always best to use acid-free cotton paper, such as archival, if you want to achieve high-quality results.

Pencil or Pencils

If your pencil (or mechanical pencil lead) is too soft, your wash will get dirty, and if it's too hard, the pencil will scratch your paper. For these reasons, the best pencil hardness for watercolor sketching is a graphite drawing pencil, grades F, H, or 2H. Water-soluble graphite and water-soluble colored pencils are also suitable.

Tracing Paper

I use the Blick® Studio Tracing paper pads, but on some occasions (such as when I run out), I use vellum paper, which you can find in any craft store. You can read about my tracing technique under Transferring Sketches (page 14).

White Gouache

White gouache is an opaque water-based medium used to create highlights in your illustrations. My personal choice is Winsor & Newton Designers Gouache™ in Permanent White.

Masking Fluid

Masking fluid is a liquid that artists apply to paper to prevent it from being marked by paint. It's commonly used to preserve fine, light details and highlights that would be difficult to paint around. My personal choice for masking fluid is Winsor & Newton. I haven't had issues tearing the paper when I remove it with an eraser.

To apply masking fluid, use an old brush to add it to dry watercolor paper (either on the plain paper or on a completely dry wash to preserve that color). Then paint as you would like. Once you are ready to reveal the preserved areas, wait until everything is completely dry. Then use an eraser to gently remove the dried masking fluid.

Other Supplies

Outside of your main materials, for each painting in this book, you will also need:

- An eraser (any eraser should do the job)
- A palette (my personal choice is a ceramic palette; you can use an old white plate as well)
- A glass or jar of water
- A spray bottle for misting your paints before use (optional; you can also drip water on them using a brush)
- A clean towel or paper towels

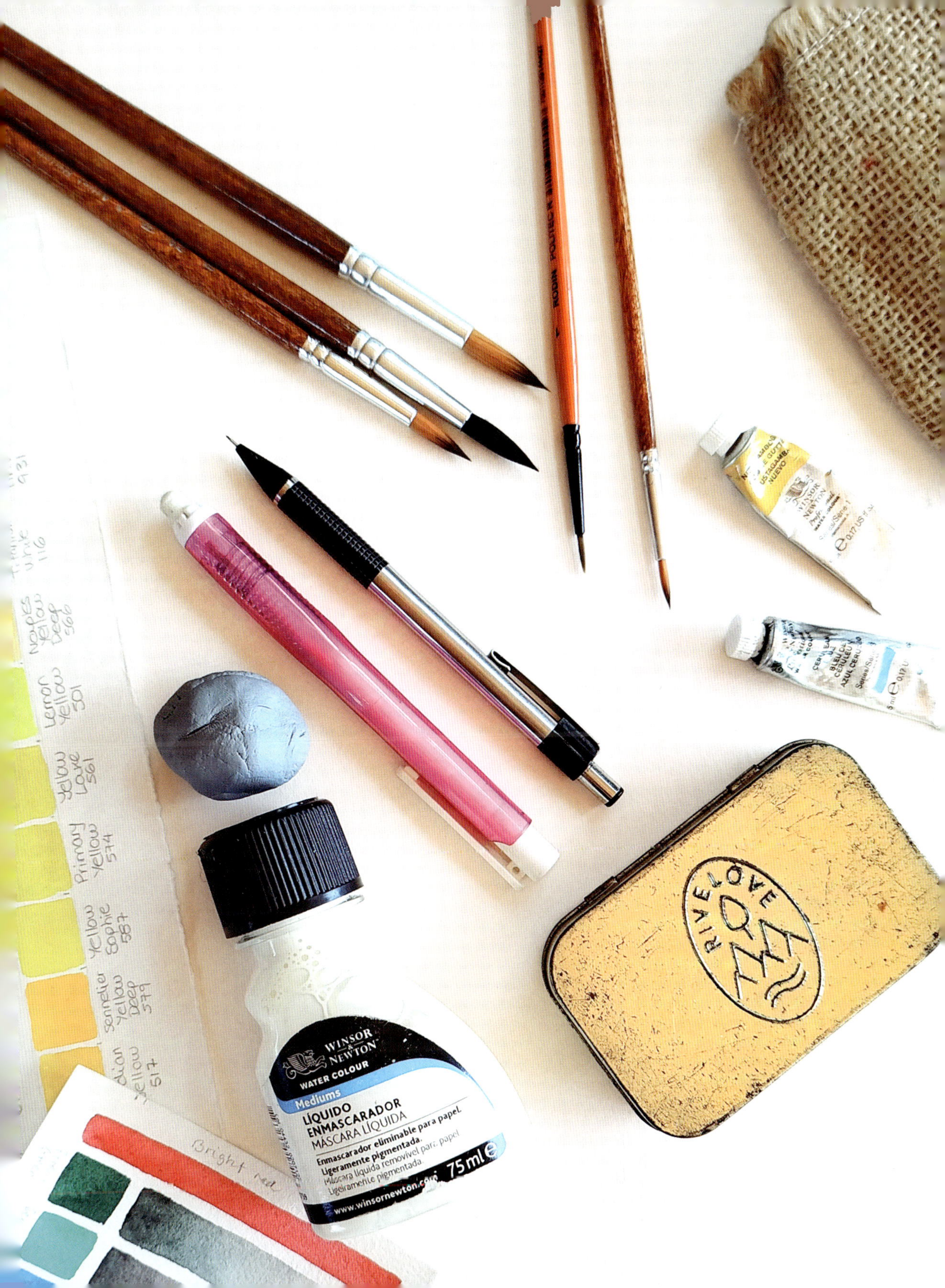
Titanium White 116
931
Naples Yellow Deep 566
Lemon Yellow 501
Yellow Lake 561
Primary Yellow 574
Yellow Sophie 587
Sennelier Yellow Deep 579
Indian Yellow 517
Bright Red
WINSOR & NEWTON
WATER COLOUR
Mediums
LÍQUIDO ENMASCARADOR
MÁSCARA LÍQUIDA
Enmascarador eliminable para papel.
Ligeramente pigmentada.
Máscara líquida removível para papel.
Ligeiramente pigmentada.
75ml
www.winsornewton.com
RIVE LOVE

Techniques for Success

As you're learning about the basics of watercolor painting, you'll come across a few different techniques over and over again. The more familiar you get with watercolor, the easier these techniques will become, and the more effects you'll be able to create in your artwork. You won't need anything beyond your standard watercolor supplies to get started. What follows is a list of techniques you'll use throughout the book.

Tip: If you aren't familiar with the following techniques, I suggest practicing them on scrap paper before diving into the projects.

Washes

A wash is a thin layer of watered-down paint that provides a background for your painting. Washes are generally used to cover large areas of a painting in one go.

Washes are essential for watercolor painting and are often the first thing you'll put on the paper.

Clear Water Wash

A clear water wash involves pre-wetting your paper with clean water for future washes. This technique is most often used with wet-on-wet painting.

Wet-on-Wet

Wet-on-wet watercolor painting is exactly what it sounds like: wet paint applied to a wet surface, such as pre-moistened paper or a still-wet layer of paint.

There are a lot of benefits to painting wet-on-wet with watercolors, particularly in terms of the ethereal effects that you can create. In many cases, you'll combine both wet-on-wet and wet-on-dry techniques in a single painting, so it's important to have a full understanding of both practices and what they can help you achieve.

There is also technical value to wet-on-wet painting. It is ideal for when you want to blend colors, and it can be used to layer hues for color mixing, background washes, and ombrés (smooth gradients).

Wet-on-Dry

Wet-on-dry painting requires a little more patience. For this technique, you need to wait for the first layer of paint to dry before you paint over it.

With wet-on-dry painting, you can add fresh details to your work, and the colors beneath will still shine through due to the translucent nature of the paint. You can also achieve crispier layers by allowing each one to dry before applying the next.

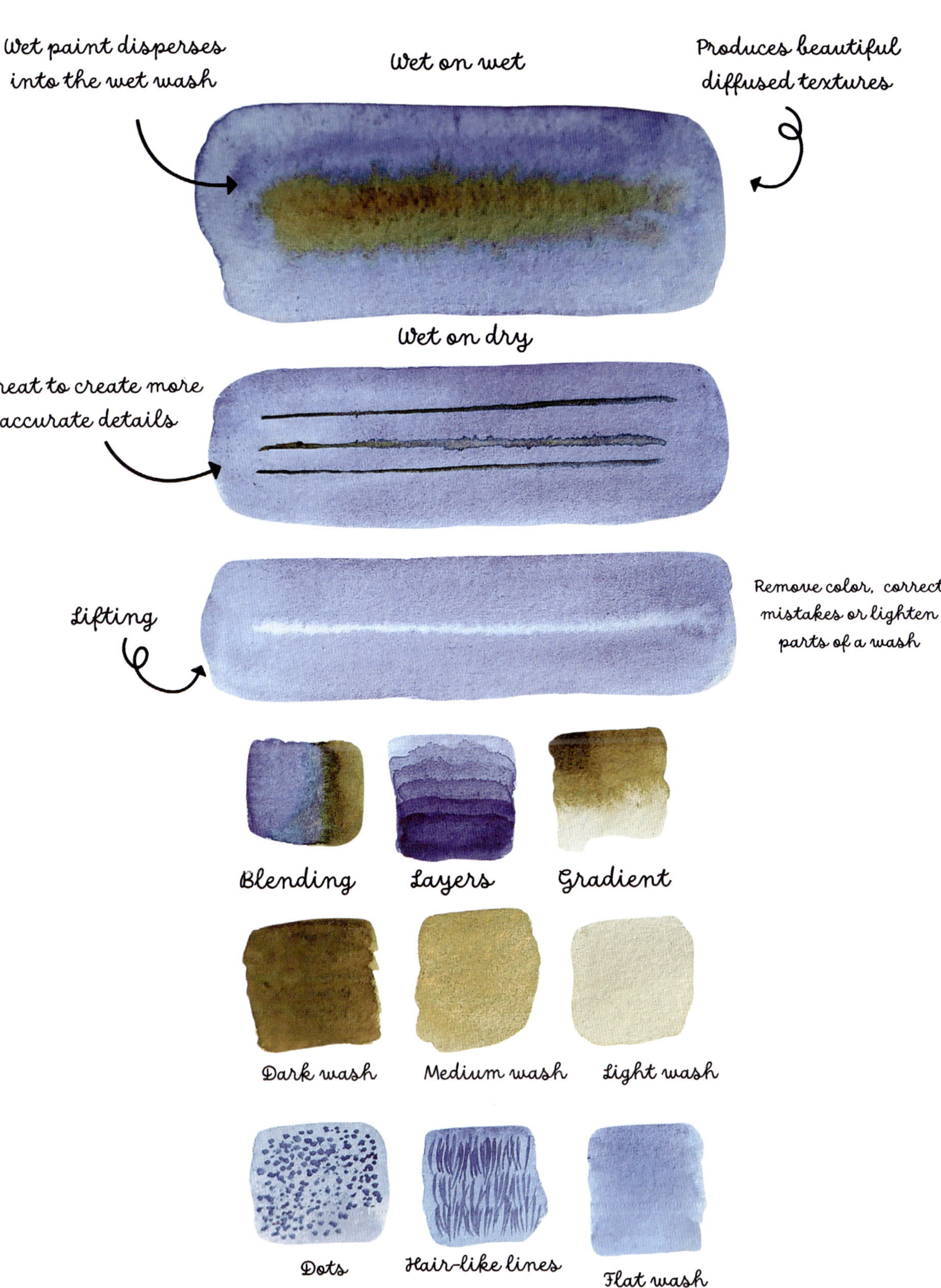

Wet paint disperses into the wet wash
Wet on wet
Produces beautiful diffused textures
Wet on dry
Great to create more accurate details
Lifting
Remove color, correct mistakes or lighten parts of a wash
Blending
Layers
Gradient
Dark wash
Medium wash
Light wash
Dots
Hair-like lines
Flat wash

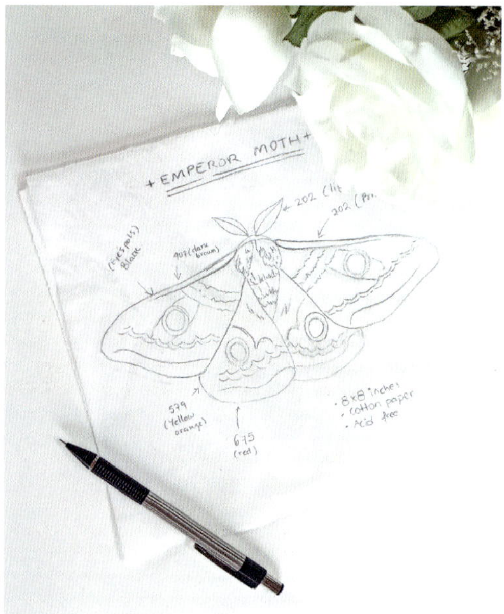

Lifting Color

When you've just applied a layer of paint to your page, it may seem strange to immediately take it off, but that's exactly what you need to do when you're using the lifting technique. Use your clean brush as a mop to take some of the color off your painting to create lighter areas. This is a great technique for adding highlights to your painting.

Transferring Sketches

Trace the reference image or my final painting using a graphite pencil on a piece of tracing paper (pressing down with medium to hard pressure). Then place your tracing paper graphite-side down onto your watercolor paper and rub the back to transfer the image. With this technique, you will be able to create amazing paintings following the steps in this book.

> **Tip:** *If your traced image isn't transferring to the watercolor paper, your graphite is either too hard or you aren't using enough pressure when tracing the image. Try switching to a softer pencil (such as a 4B) or retracing the lines using more pressure to deposit more graphite.*

Basic Color Theory

In color theory, colors are organized on a color wheel and grouped into three categories: primary colors (red, blue, and yellow), secondary colors (green, orange, and purple), and tertiary colors (red-orange, yellow-orange, yellow-green, blue-green, blue-purple, and red-purple).

Mix the primary colors together, and you'll create secondary colors. Mix a primary color with a secondary color and you'll create tertiary colors. You can also experiment with mixing different amounts of each primary color to create various shades and tones.

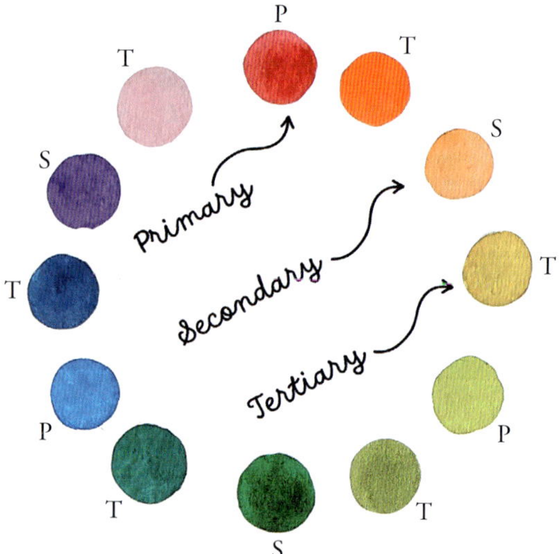

A color wheel showing primary, secondary, and tertiary colors.

Complementary colors are opposite to each other on the color wheel, such as red and green or blue and orange. When mixed together, complementary colors can create a neutral color (such as gray or brown) or a muted version of the original colors.

Color mixing is an important skill to learn in painting because it allows you to create a wide range of colors and tones and to achieve the desired hue and saturation for your artwork. Here are some basic steps to learn color mixing in painting.

Complementary

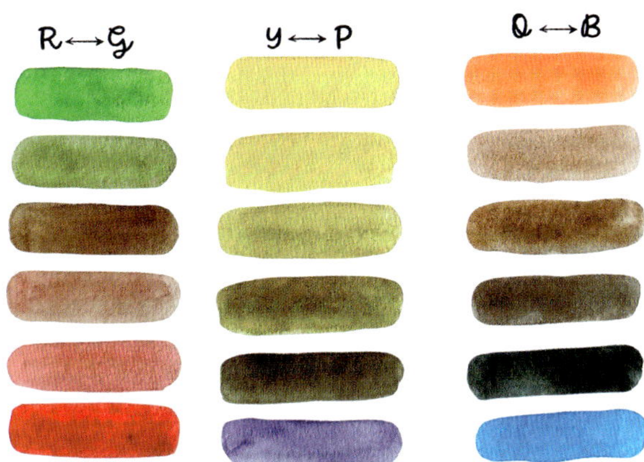

The complementary color columns above show how mixing complementary colors (red with green, yellow with purple, and orange with blue) can create organic shaded tones.

Bright Red

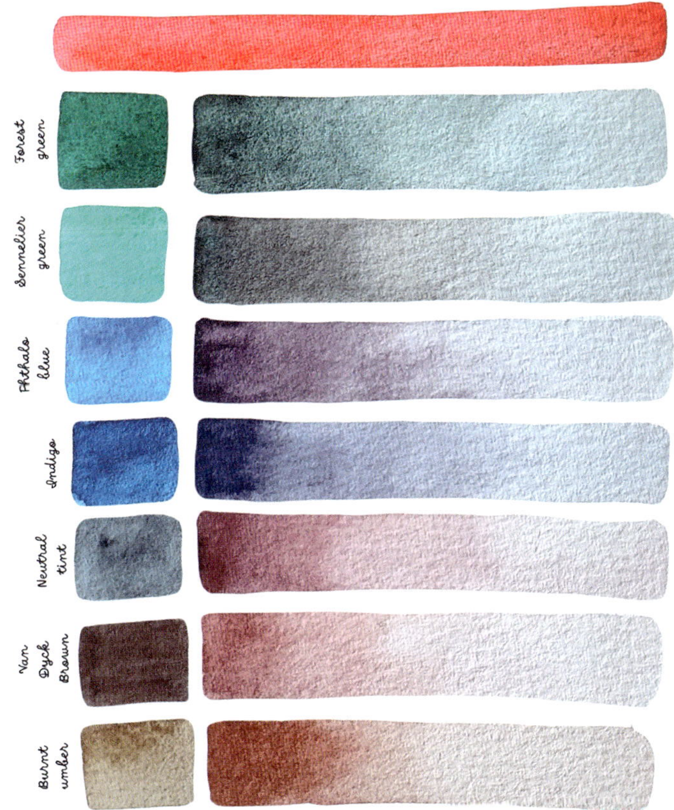

Here you can visualize how to use a primary color base (in this case, red) to create several other shades and hues.

Making Colors Darker

Add More of the Same Color: Adding more of the same color you are using (or adding less water) can make it more saturated.

Use a Complementary Color: Adding a small amount of the complementary color (the color opposite on the color wheel) can darken a color without making it too dull. For example, adding a touch of green to red can darken it while maintaining its richness.

Use a Darker Shade: Use a premixed darker shade of the same color (like navy for blue or burgundy for red).

Add Gray: Mixing gray into your color can darken it while keeping its saturation and hue relatively intact.

Add Black: Mix a small amount of black paint (or pigment) into the color. This method is straightforward but can quickly overpower the original color, so add it gradually. It can even make the color look dirty.

Making Colors Lighter

Add Water: Mix in water to achieve a lighter value.

Add White: Mix in white paint to lighten your color, but be cautious, as too much white can wash out the color.

Add a Lighter Shade: Use a pre-mixed lighter shade of the same color. This keeps the hue consistent while lightening the overall appearance.

Tips for Both Methods

Test on a Palette: Always test your mixtures on a separate palette or piece of paper to see how the colors interact before applying them to your main work.

Small Adjustments: Make small adjustments gradually to avoid overshooting the desired shade.

> ***Tip:*** *Don't forget to wash your brush thoroughly between colors, as complementary colors will create dull, muddy colors if allowed to mix. Having two jars of water, one with clean water to add to the pigments and another to clean your brush, will make this much simpler.*

Anatomy Guide

If you are not familiar with the names of the different parts of the subjects you are going to work on in this book, I've provided a little guide.

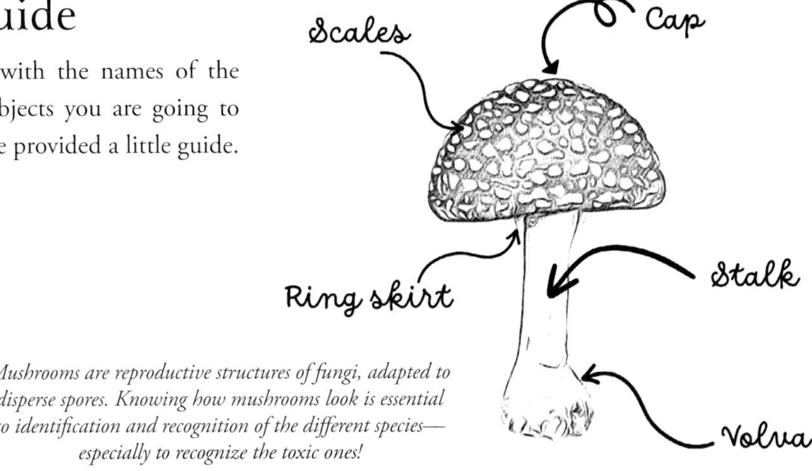

Mushrooms are reproductive structures of fungi, adapted to disperse spores. Knowing how mushrooms look is essential to identification and recognition of the different species— especially to recognize the toxic ones!

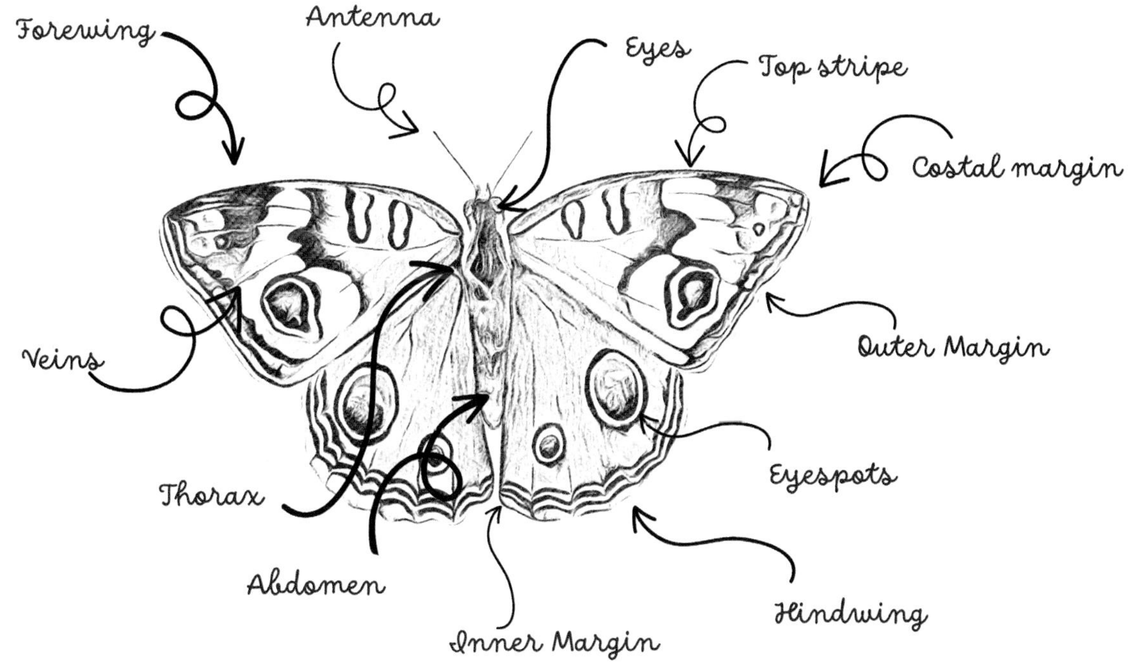

Lepidoptera is the order of insects that includes butterflies and moths. Their anatomy is specialized and adept for flying, feeding in flowers, and reproducing.

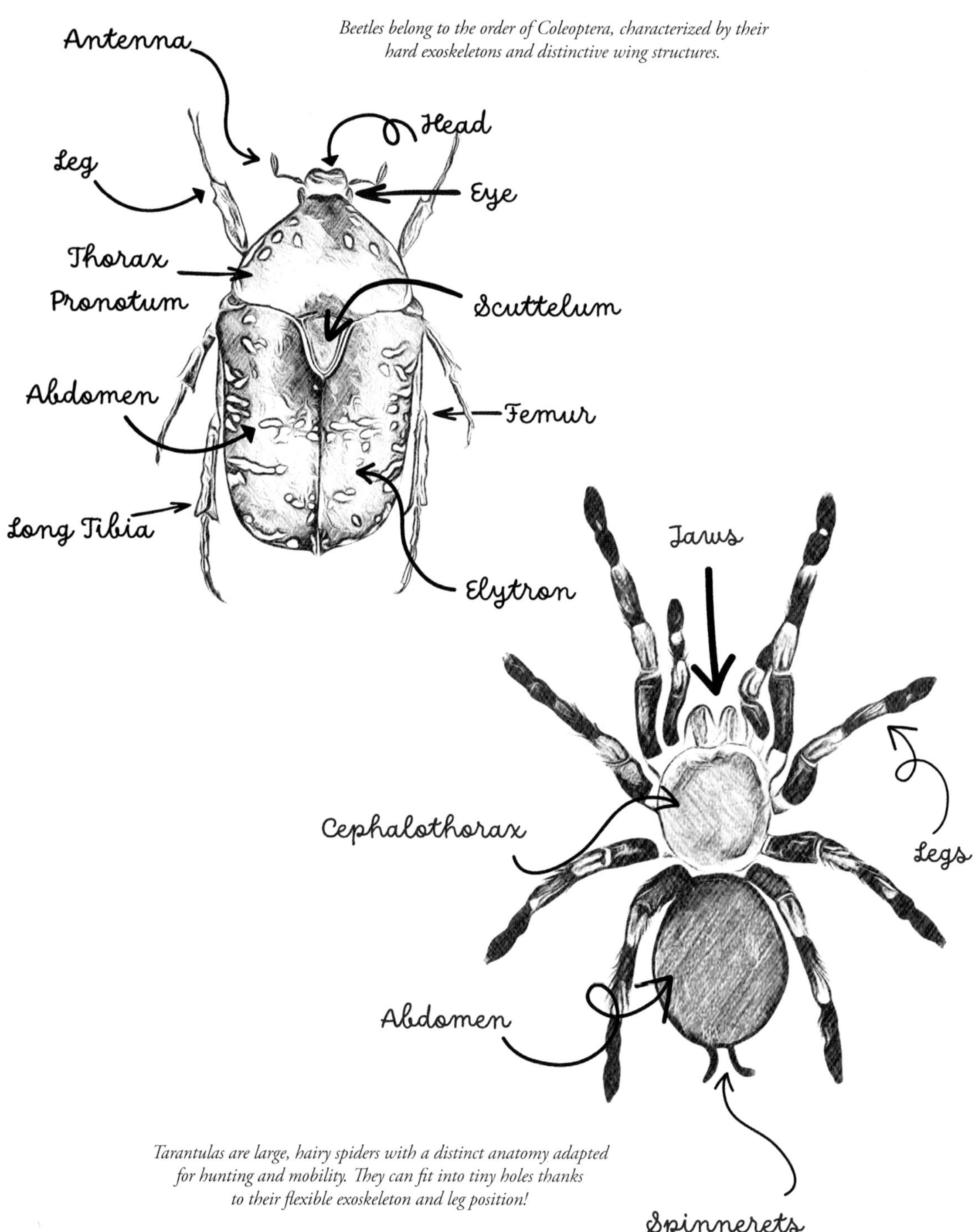

Beetles belong to the order of Coleoptera, characterized by their hard exoskeletons and distinctive wing structures.

Tarantulas are large, hairy spiders with a distinct anatomy adapted for hunting and mobility. They can fit into tiny holes thanks to their flexible exoskeleton and leg position!

Skill Levels

Each project has been assigned a difficulty level depending on the amount of detail and time you will need to accomplish the illustration, as well as the difficulty of the techniques you have to use.

Easy

Easy projects like the Ladybug (page 97) or the Emerald Birdwing Butterfly (page 27) have just a few washes of watercolor and easy details to paint; they are great to start with.

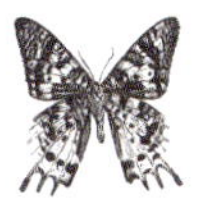

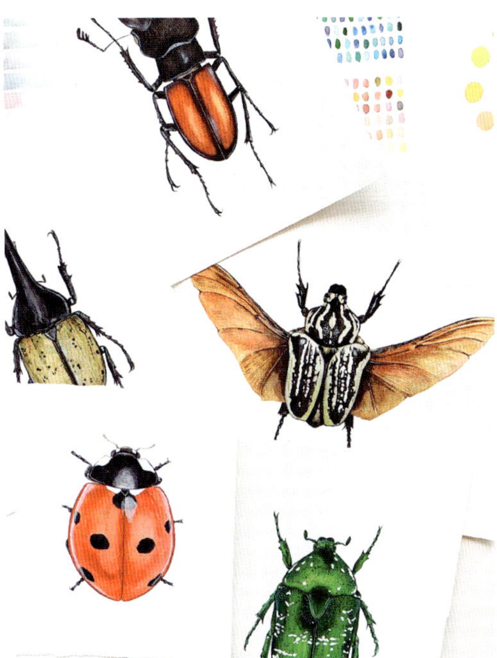

Easy projects like the Ladybug (bottom left; tutorial on page 97) are great warm-ups for difficult projects like the Goliath Beetle (center right; tutorial on page 113), which uses similar techniques with more layers and greater attention to detail.

Medium

Medium-difficulty projects are meant to get you into the mood of learning some new skills and challenging yourself while still being comfortable. The Cicada (page 131), for example, has lots of veins on its wings, though painting them shouldn't be an issue!

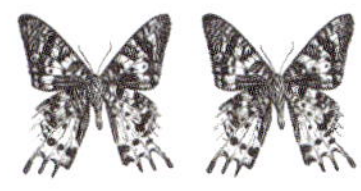

Difficult

The big projects in this book are labeled under this category because of the attention to detail you'll need and the number of different techniques you'll be using. The Atlas Moth (page 73) is a good example where you'll use different types of washes and textures, and it will probably take you a few hours to finish. Once again, however, there's nothing to be scared of!

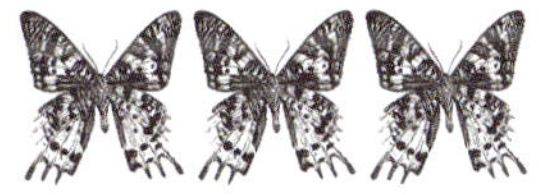

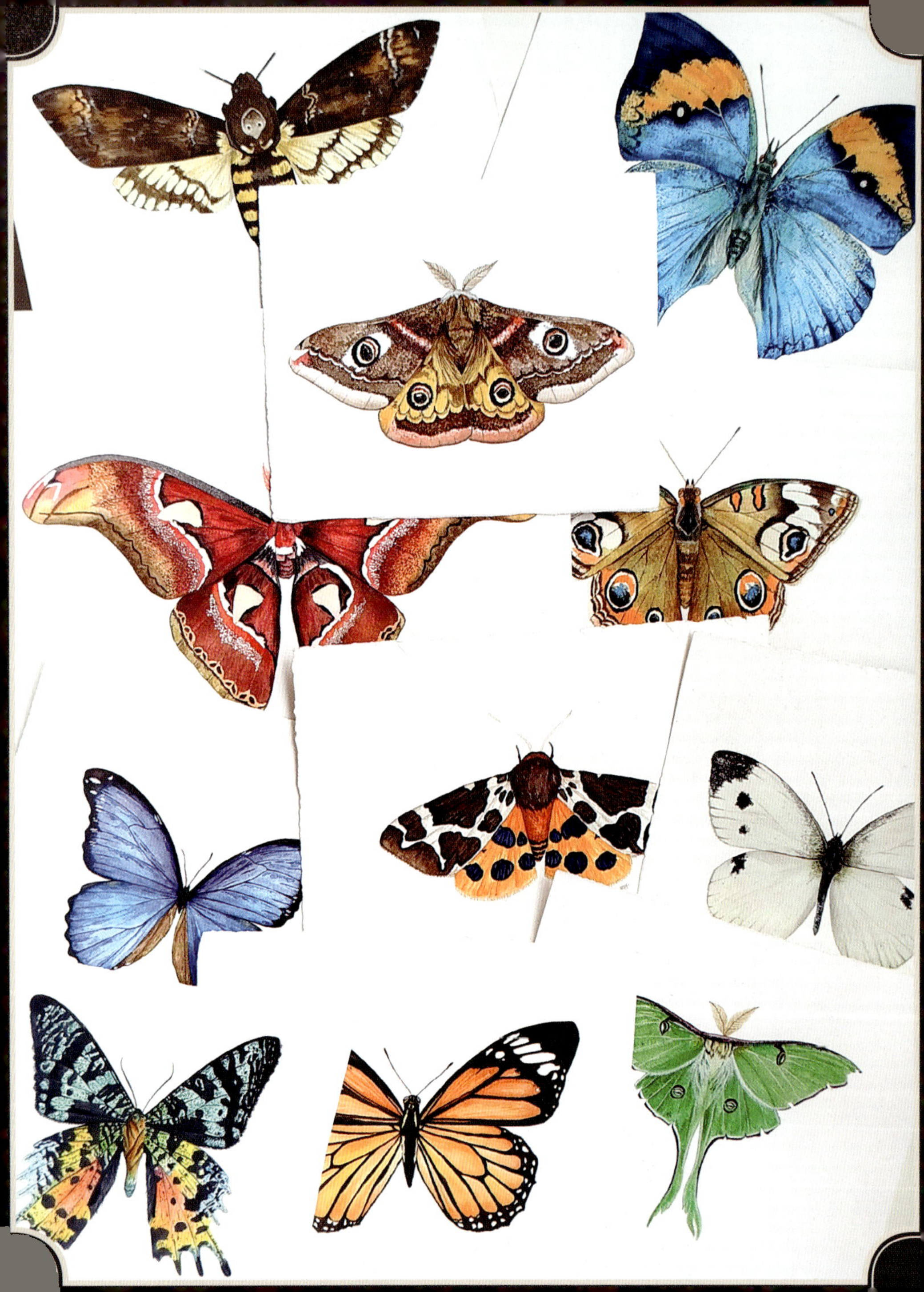

Nature's Jewelry: Butterflies & Moths

Butterflies and moths are an order of insects known as Lepidoptera, which means "scaly wings." It is these overlapping scales that give them their spectacular colors and patterns.

This might actually be the most intimidating chapter of all. After all, these insects have intricate patterns and iridescent or transparent wings, among other characteristics. While painting a watercolor butterfly is not as complicated as you might think, it does take time, so patience is essential throughout the process. But once you are done, you'll be able to create your own Lepidoptera collection! Learning how to paint butterflies and moths can be very rewarding, as it can enhance many watercolor techniques.

I recommend using at least an 8 x 8–inch (20 x 20–cm) square piece of paper for each of these paintings. That size should give you enough room to create all the details.

If you want to warm up first, the Blue Morpho Butterfly (page 23) is an easy project to start with as it only has a few colors and no patterns on the wings. Once you feel adventurous, you can go chase the stunning Atlas Moth (page 73), one of the largest Lepidoptera on Earth. Or if you like spooky things, the Death's-Head Hawkmoth (page 47) is the rebel of the moth world. Strikingly large, with a skull-like marking on its thorax along with the ability to squeak when alarmed, this moth was traditionally seen as an omen of death.

If you are ready, grab your supplies and let's dig into the world of these beautiful, delicate creatures!

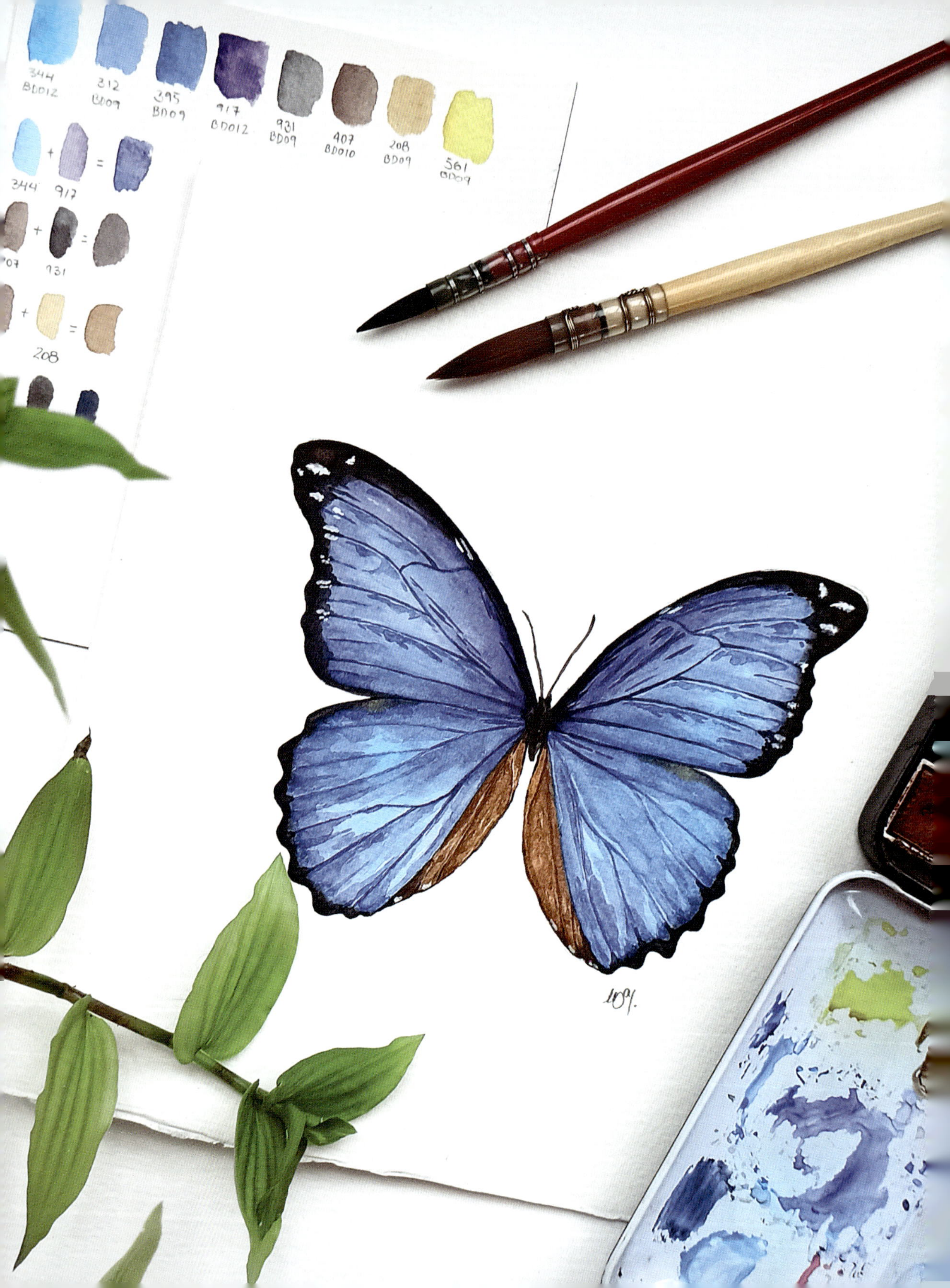

344 BD012
312 BD09
395 BD09
917 BD012
931 BD09
407 BD010
208 BD09
561 BD09
344 + 917 =

Blue Morpho Butterfly

Blue morphos are among the largest butterflies in the world. Their vivid, iridescent blue coloring is a result of the microscopic scales on the backs of their wings, which reflect light. These insects live in the tropical forests of Latin America, from Mexico to Colombia.

This project is a great way to start getting familiar with these delicate creatures and practice your techniques. In this painting, you will learn how to blend colors (wet and dry), make seamless transitions, and create the stunning texture of a butterfly's wings.

- Watercolor paper of your choice
  - I used an 8 x 8–inch (20 x 20–cm) sheet
- Paints
  - Cinereous Blue, Blue Indanthrene, Ultramarine Blue Light, Neutral Tint, Raw Sienna, Van Dyck Brown, Dioxazine Purple
  - White gouache
- Brushes
  - Medium round brush (I used size 8)
  - Detail round brush (I used size 0)

Difficulty: Medium

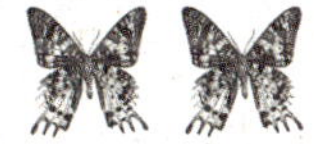

Sketch

Draw the butterfly freehand or trace the reference image and transfer it to the watercolor paper of your choice, focusing on the shape of the wings, body, and antennae. Spray your paints with water to moisten them.

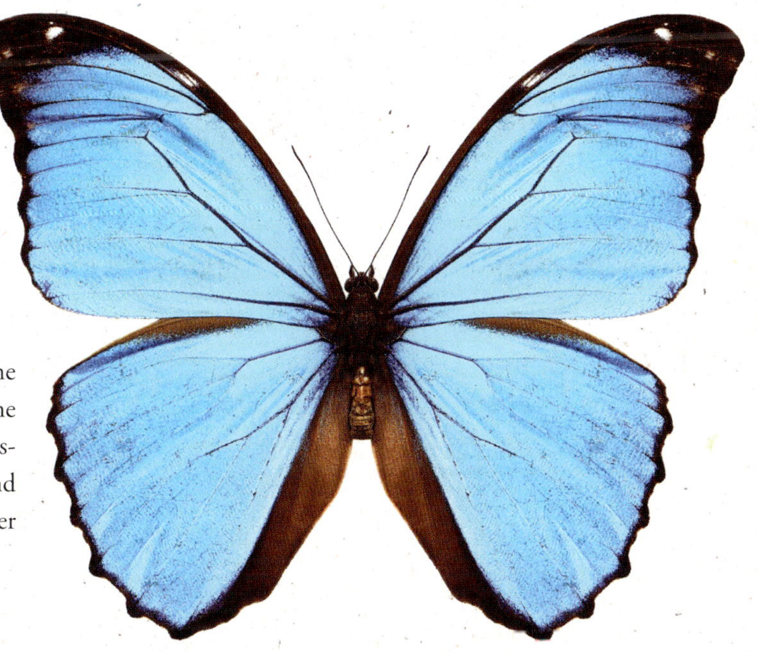

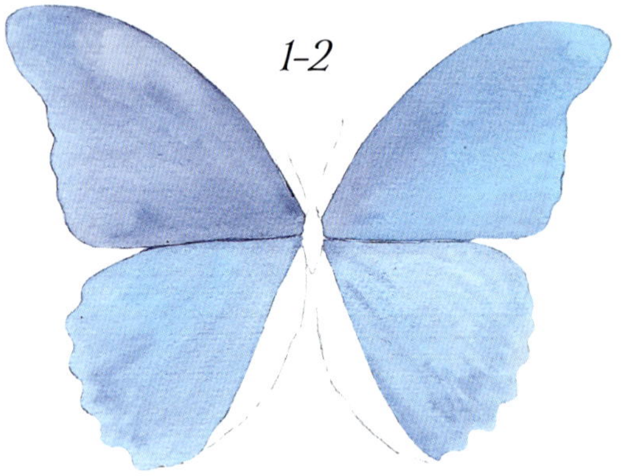

Step 1

First, with your medium brush, create a clear water wash by wetting one hind wing with water (avoiding the inner edge). Then, brush a transparent Cinereous Blue tone across that hind wing, focusing on the outer and lower edges.

Wait until this is partially dry, and then add some brushstrokes along the wing with Blue Indanthrene. We want to have a slightly damp surface so the colors will blend a bit but still keep the shape of the brushstrokes along the wings to create shadow-like lines. Don't overthink these lines; let it flow. Do the same with the other hind wing.

Step 2

Now let's move to the forewings. Keep using your medium brush and wet one forewing with clear water. After this, paint a light wash of Cinereous Blue—just make sure the hind wings are completely dry first in case you rest your hand on them while painting the forewings!

While the surface is still damp, load your brush with Indanthrene Blue, and add brushstrokes along the wings towards the body.

Immediately pick up the Ultramarine Blue Light, and brush it on the top edges of the forewing. Now do the same thing for the remaining forewing.

Tip: To make sure you don't bleed your colors all over your painting while using the wet-on-wet technique, I always have a paper towel next to me, and I dab it on the tip of my brush to unload the excess water. This will give you more control over the amount of water that comes out of your brush.

Step 3

One wing at a time, use your clean, damp medium brush to prepare the surface of the wing you are going to work on with a very light clear water wash.

Use your detail brush to add gentle curves of dark—nearly black—Neutral Tint paint along the bottom edges one hind wing. With each stroke, the dark paint will bleed into the blue, creating a beautiful gradient effect.

Outline the upper edge of the forewings too. Repeat on the other wings until complete.

Once the wings are dry, use your detail brush and the same saturated value of Neutral Tint to paint a line separating the forewings from the hind wings. We want to create a clean line that doesn't blend with the background.

Once that is dry, load your medium brush with Raw Sienna, and paint a wash on the bottom, inner part of the hind wings. Before it dries, grab your detail brush and Van Dyck Brown to add a little bit of contrast to the lower edge.

Keep using your detail brush loaded with saturated Van Dyck Brown, and paint some veins (inside the brown area), from top to bottom. Then, before it dries, add a saturated

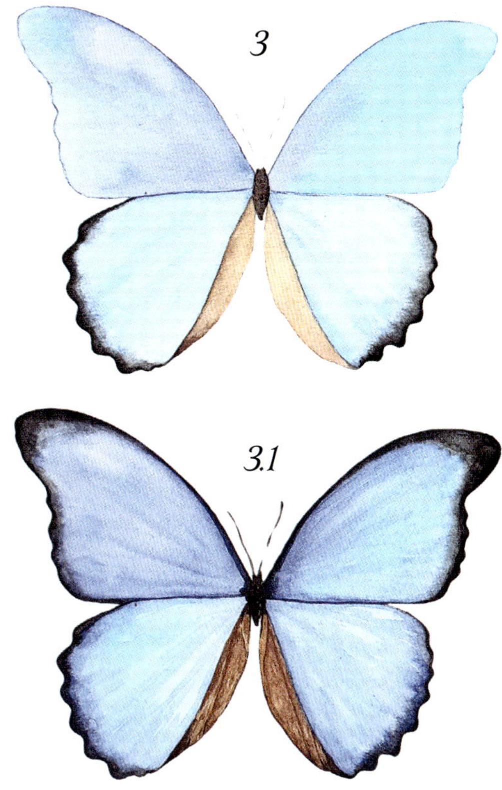

tone of Neutral Tint to the bottom edge and the butterfly's body, and extend it out to the wings a bit. You can mix the Neutral Tint and Van Dyck Brown and use it to create more contrast on the bottom corner. Lastly, grab your detail brush, and paint the antennae with Neutral Tint.

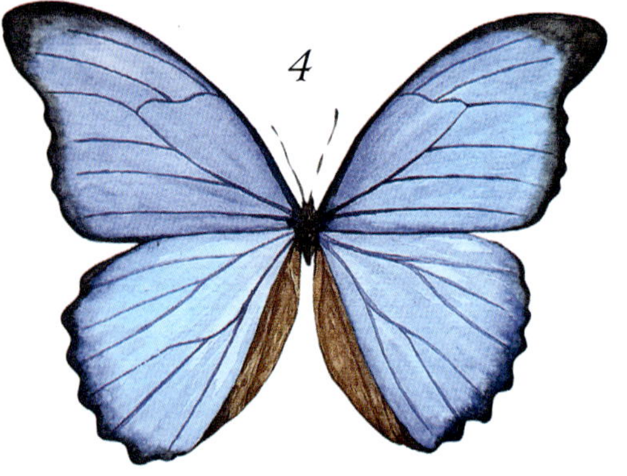

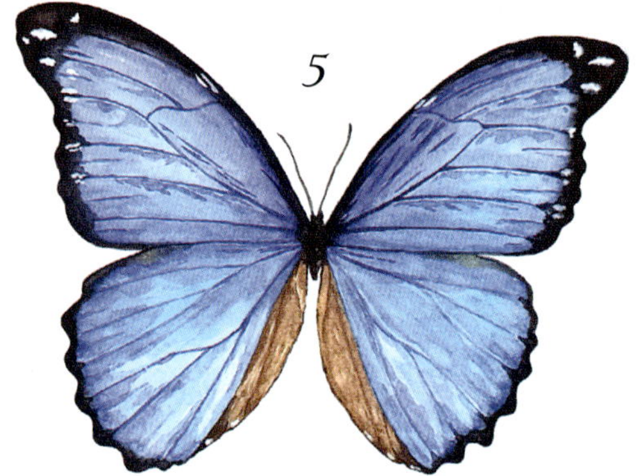

Step 4

Mix Blue Indanthrene with a bit of Neutral Tint, and use your detail brush to paint thin veins across the butterfly's forewings and hind wings, following the pattern shown on the photo reference. Don't worry if these lines are not perfect; we will work on it later.

We are almost there! Rest your hand and get ready to make this butterfly more lifelike!

Step 5

Mix Cinereous Blue with Dioxazine Purple (same amount of each), and with the detail brush, add thin lines across the wings. Vary the brush pressure to paint thicker and finer lines; the point here is to create shadows. We are also refining the wings' creases. If you didn't like some of the veins you painted before, now's the time to add some lines to hide them. Once it dries, use the gouache diluted with water to paint the white markings on the wings.

Now your blue morpho butterfly is ready to fly!

Emerald Birdwing Butterfly

This amazing emerald birdwing butterfly is also known as the common green birdwing. Birdwing butterflies are named for their exceptional size, angular wings, and bird-like flight. They are among some of the largest butterflies in the world.

Using black watercolor to darken areas is a bit of a controversial subject among artists. If you want to use black, I suggest you don't use it straight out of the pan or tube. Instead, carefully mix small amounts at a time into the color of your choice. If you prefer to create your own darker shades, keep reading, because with this project, I'll teach you a bit of color theory.

Difficulty: Easy

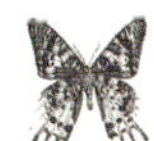

Sketch

Draw the butterfly freehand or trace the reference image and transfer it to the watercolor paper of your choice, focusing on the shape of the wings, body, and markings. Spray your paints with water to moisten them.

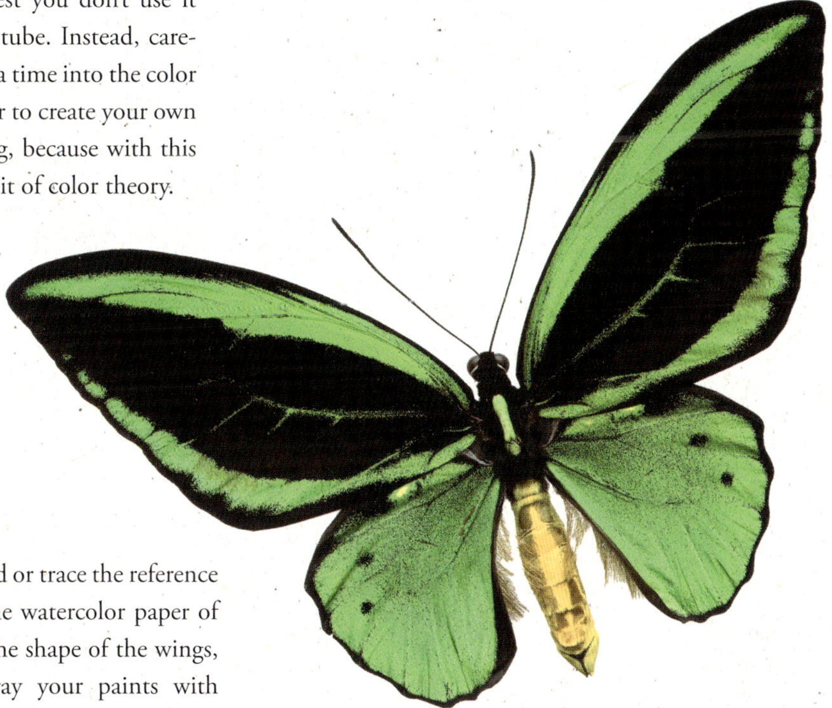

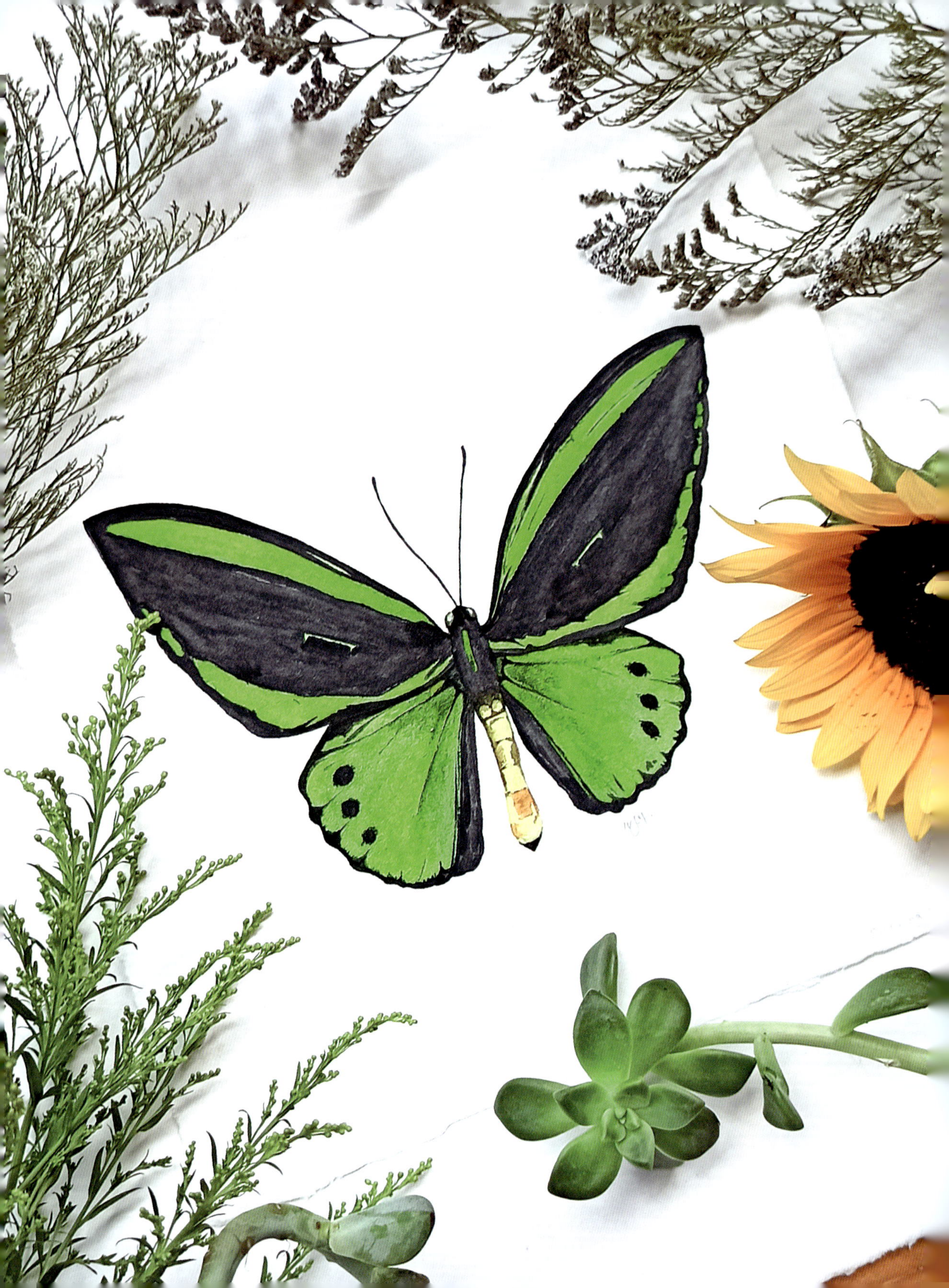

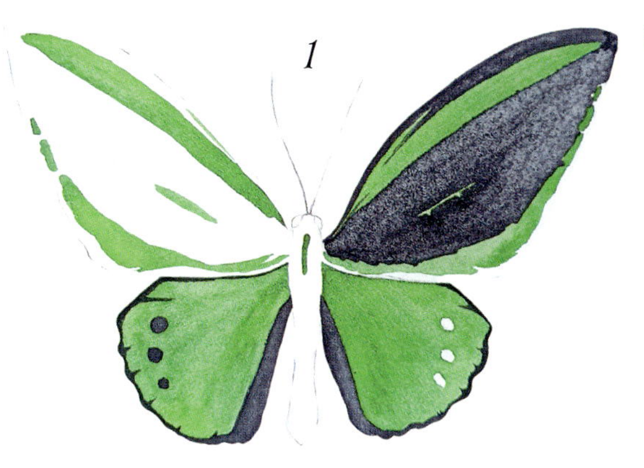

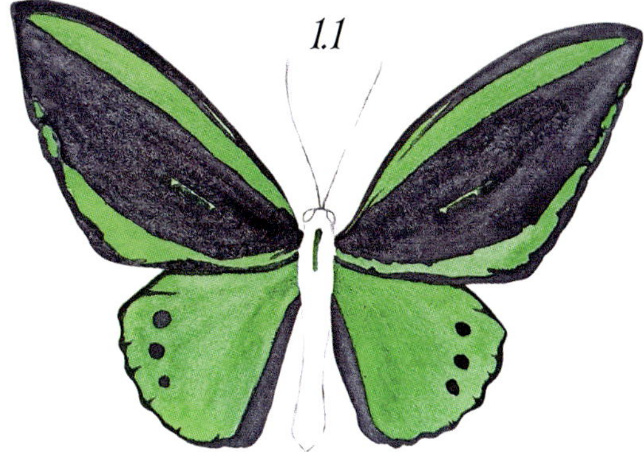

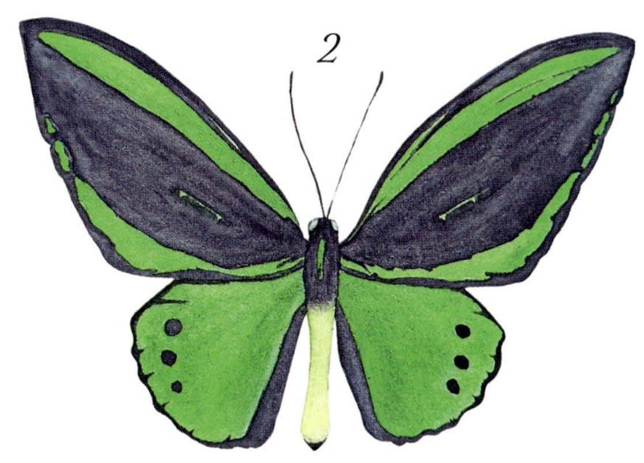

Step 1

Load your medium brush with Hooker's Green and paint both hind wings, save the three circular markings and the bottom edges. Before it dries, add a bit of Yellow Sophie to the green in your palette, and paint two larger brushstrokes near the edges of the forewings and one thin one in the center. This will make the wings look brighter in some spots, creating a light-like effect. Wait for the hind wings to dry.

Move to the forewings, and with the medium brush, paint strokes in the middle of the forewings with Hooker's Green. Add a bit of the Hooker's Green and Yellow Sophie mixture while still wet and let dry. Once the green on both wings is completely dry, paint around the hind wings, the circles, and the inside of the forewings with Payne's Grey, shaping up the green mark you painted before. With your detail brush, paint a straight line down the body with Hooker's Green.

Step 2

Load your detail brush with Payne's Grey and carefully paint the antennae. Use a very light value of the same color to paint the eyes.

Move to the body, clean your medium brush and paint a light wash of water. Load the brush with Yellow Sophie, and paint a light wash from the middle of the body to the bottom. Immediately change colors to Payne's Grey and paint the other half, leaving the green marking in the middle intact. Let dry and then use a dark value of Payne's Grey to paint the last pointed segment of the abdomen.

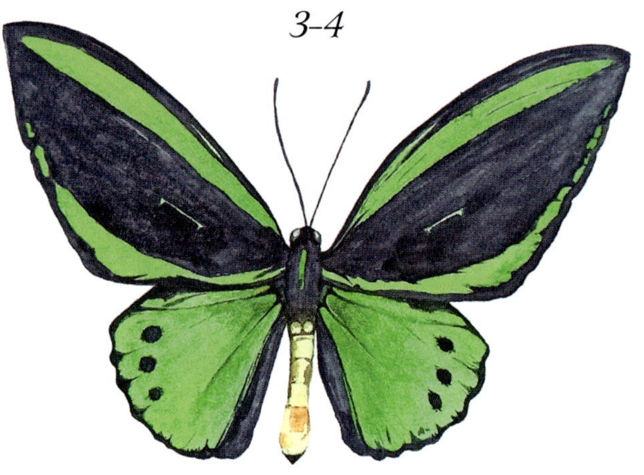

Step 3

Let's work on the hind wings. It's a natural instinct to want to use black to darken the green color we used for the first layer of painting. But black watercolors have a high tinting strength, meaning they are very pigmented. Black paint is also opaque and tends to hide underlying colors when layered over the top, modifying the original hue in a rather harsh way.

So I'm going to show you how to use color theory to darken the color green without using black. In general, this can be done by mixing any given color with a complementary color on the opposite side of the color wheel.

Because the complementary color of green is red, to darken the Hooker's Green, we'll use Carmine. On your palette, mix just a bit of Carmine with Hooker's Green. Load your medium brush with this mixture and darken the areas close to the body.

Once it's dry, change to your detail brush and use Payne's Grey to paint the veins on the hind wings. Use light brush pressure to let the lines become thinner as they go further into the wing. Also paint lines on the bottom edge, up to the black circles.

Finally, using the same brush and a light value of Payne's Grey, paint over the green area on the top edge of the forewings with a few more lines to create texture. Let it dry.

Step 4

Use the same color theory technique to darken the Yellow Sophie. Add a bit of Dioxazine Purple, and use this mixture for the body. Load your detail brush to paint the section lines and add shadow by painting the edges of the body.

Once it's dry, load the same brush with Payne's Grey, and paint the circular markings where the black and the yellow colors meet on the middle of the body. Also paint the bottom tip of the body with the same color.

Lastly, load your brush with Gold Ochre, and paint a square section on the bottom of the body, kind of like a smudge. And your beautiful birdwing butterfly is done!

Tiger Moth

The tiger moth is most notable for its brightly colored wings. Their wing design can include a pattern of red, orange, green, white, and black. These moths live in gardens, meadows, and woodlands across North America, Europe, and Northern Asia.

Difficulty: Medium

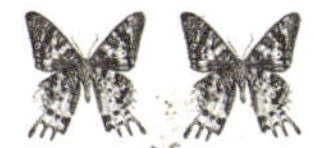

Sketch

Draw the moth freehand or trace the reference image and transfer it to the watercolor paper of your choice, focusing on the shape of the wings, markings, and antennae. Spray your paints with water to moisten them.

- Watercolor paper of your choice
  - › I used an 8 x 10–inch (20 x 25–cm) sheet, landscape orientation
- Paints
  - › Van Dyck Brown, Raw Sienna, Indian Yellow, Red Orange, Sennelier Orange, Naples Yellow Deep, Bright Red, Blue Indanthrene, Payne's Grey, Yellow Ochre
- Brushes
  - › Medium round brush (I used size 6)
  - › Detail round brush (I used size 0)
  - › Liner brush (I used size 10/0)

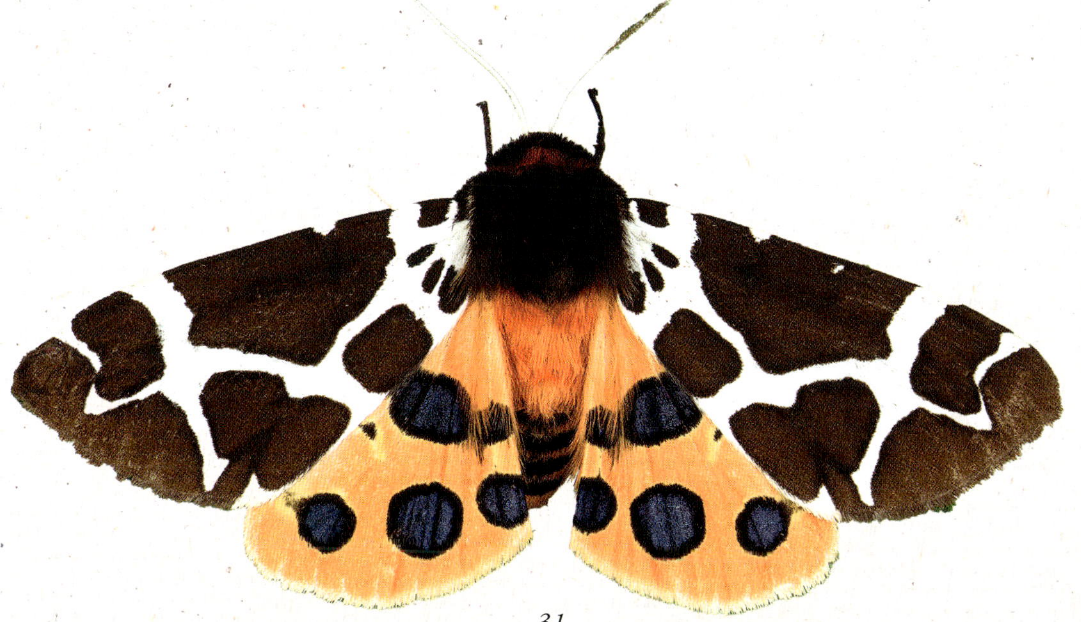

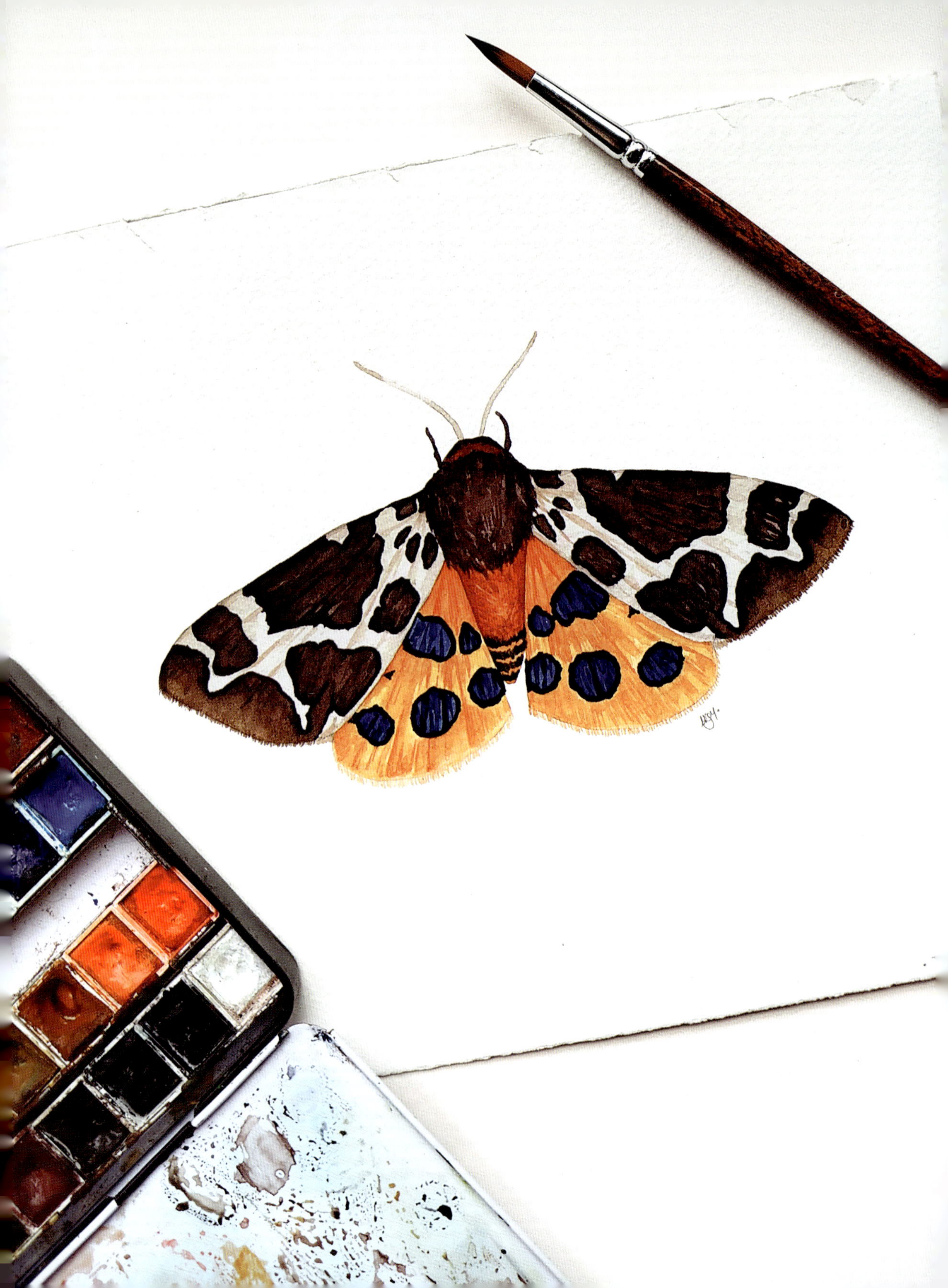

Step 1

Apply the first wash of Van Dyck Brown to the forewings with your medium brush. Keep some of the wing details white as shown in the reference photo. Before this wash dries, load the same brush with Raw Sienna, and towards the bottom of the hind wings, dot a bit of this color to create a gradient. Wait until this dries completely before continuing.

Now moving to the hind wings. To create the perfect hue, mix Indian Yellow with a bit of Red Orange, and paint the first smooth wash with the mixture, saving the round spots for later.

> **Tip:** *Practice your color mixing, and use some scrap paper to test your colors before you apply them to your painting.*

Step 2

Once the wings are dry, mix Sennelier Orange with a bit of Naples Yellow Deep. Use this mixture to paint the lower section of the body with your medium brush.

To create the fluffy texture of the upper body, paint a clear water wash over this area. While still wet, use your medium brush loaded with a saturated value of Van Dyck Brown, start dabbing the tip of your brush into the water wash we painted, and let the colors do their thing. (We're using a saturated value of the color so as not to lose all the pigment in the water surface we created on the paper.) When we use the wet-on-wet technique, we will lose a little bit

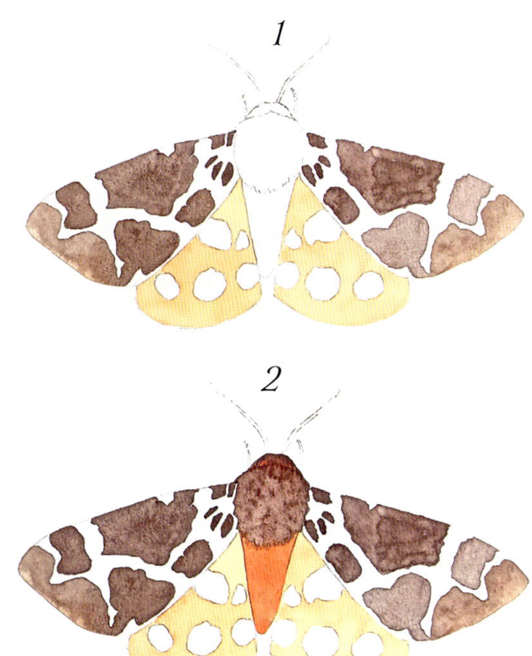

of control over what's going to happen, but the texture that we create is beautiful.

Wait a little bit, and when it's almost dry, add a line of Bright Red with your detail brush to keep control of how much paint comes out over the head area. (If you end up having a lot of red in the painting, don't worry. You can always lift part of the color with a clean brush, using it like a mop, and then correcting it by adding the brown back where it should be.)

> **Tip:** *The bigger the brush, the less control you are going to have when it comes to how much water will come out of it. So if you are new to watercolors, it's always better to use a small brush to avoid having a puddle all over your painting.*

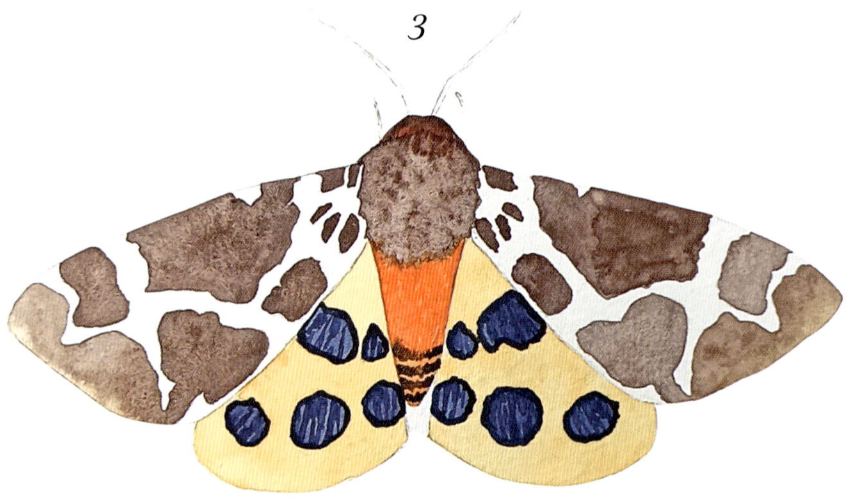

Step 3

Let's start making this moth more life-like. With your detail brush loaded with Blue Indanthrene, paint all the circular markings on the hind wings with a light value of the color. After you're finished, use a saturated value of the same color to add lines along these circles, like the wings' creases. For this step, you don't need to wait till it's dry. In fact, it's actually better if it's a little damp and the lines blend a bit with the background.

Once your painting is dry, clean your detail brush and change to Payne's Grey. Carefully outline the blue markings. When everything is dry, move to the body again, grab your medium brush, and prepare the surface by painting a light wash with clear water just to dampen the paper a little. (Don't use a lot of pressure with your brush or you might lift the pigments off the paper.) With your liner brush, add short, thin lines along the third part of the moth body to create a hairlike texture. Then paint four lines across the tail end of the body, and add little brushstrokes across these lines to make them look fuzzy.

Step 4

Moving to the forewings again, work with one wing at a time. With your medium brush, add a clear water wash over the brown you painted before. Then, using a saturated value of Van Dyck Brown and your detail brush, paint lines along the brown markings to create the creases. Repeat the process for the other wing. While the wings are still damp, load your detail brush with Payne's Grey, and outline the brown areas. Don't worry if it bleeds a bit over the brown—it'll give the wing a more realistic look.

Step 5

Once dry, paint the Yellow Ochre lines along the forewings with your liner brush. Play with your brush pressure to create thinner and thicker lines from the top edge to the bottom, skipping the brown parts, to prevent dragging the darker color over the white part of the wing.

Once dry, paint more hairlike lines on the abdomen. Load your detail brush with Van Dyck Brown and make lines from top to bottom, finishing a bit inside the orange. With your detail brush, paint the very tip of the head with a saturated value of the same color, saving the red area. Use the same color and brush for the front legs.

Load your detail brush with a light value of Yellow Ochre, and paint the antennae. Use a more saturated value on the tips and bottom.

Then with the same brush, mix equal amounts of Van Dyck Brown and Raw Sienna and paint tiny lines across the bottom edge of the forewings. Paint a few of these lines with just

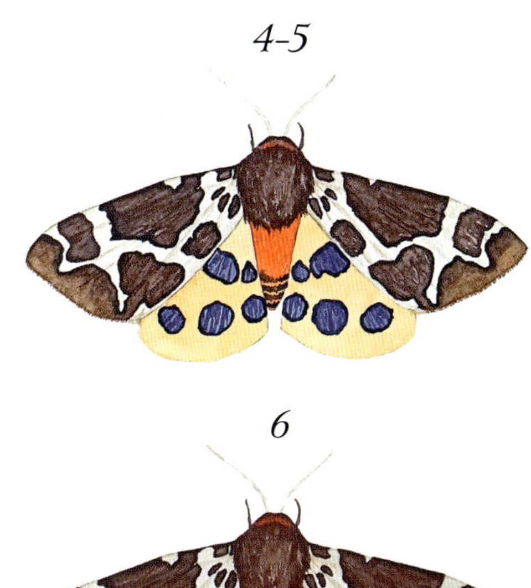

4-5

6

Raw Sienna or just Van Dyck Brown to create additional texture and depth.

Step 6

With the liner brush, use a saturated value of Sennelier Orange to paint thin lines across the hind wings. Add more water as you go down to make the value lighter. Don't overthink these lines or try too hard to get them straight. By using quick, bold movements, you will achieve an organic, realistic effect.

Finally with your detail brush, paint the little hairs all across the bottom edge of the hind wings using Naples Yellow Deep, and add some darker one with Sennelier Orange. Just be intuitive with these lines, painting the orange ones where the creases of the wing meet. With that, your tiger moth is ready to be framed!

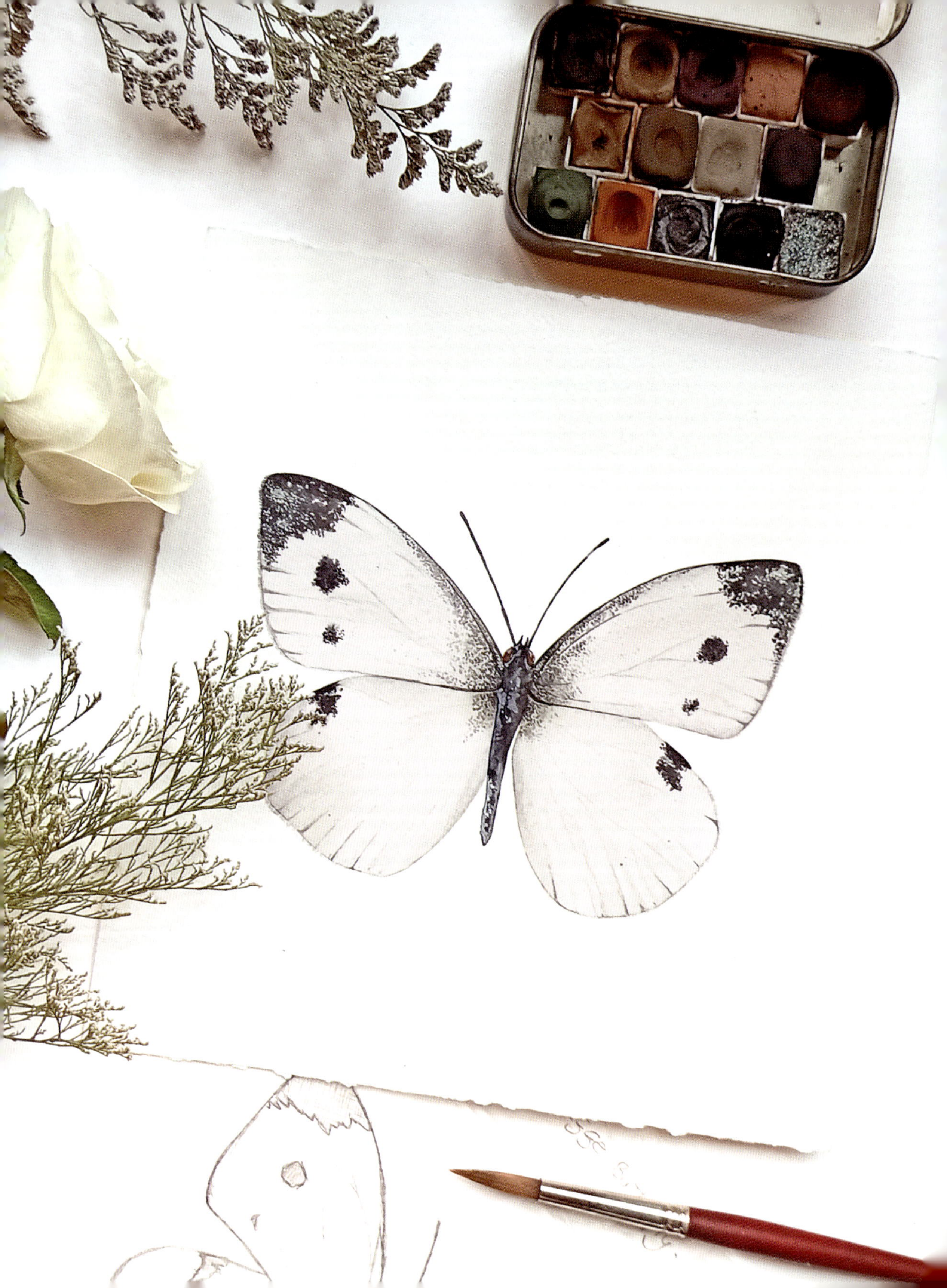

Cabbage Butterfly

Pieris brassicae, also known as the cabbage butterfly, is one of the most common butterflies seen flying around urban and suburban America. Their host plants are leafy garden vegetables such as broccoli, cauliflower, and cabbage, hence the name.

These butterflies are white or creamy white with grayish/black wing tips. You can tell the males from the females by looking at their forewings. Males have a single black spot, and females have two black spots. Female wing coloration is also slightly yellower than in males. This is another great project to start with since this butterfly doesn't have intricate patterns.

Difficulty: Easy

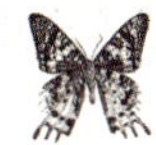

Sketch

Draw the butterfly freehand or trace the reference image and transfer it to the watercolor paper of your choice, focusing on the shape of the wings, body, and antennae. Spray your paints with water to moisten them.

MATERIALS

- Watercolor paper of your choice
  - I used an 8 x 10–inch (20 x 25–cm) sheet, landscape orientation
- Paints
  - Raw Sienna, Titanium White, Primary Yellow, Neutral Tint, Raw Umber, Sennelier Green
- Brushes
  - Medium round brush (I used size 8)
  - Detail round brush (I used size 1)

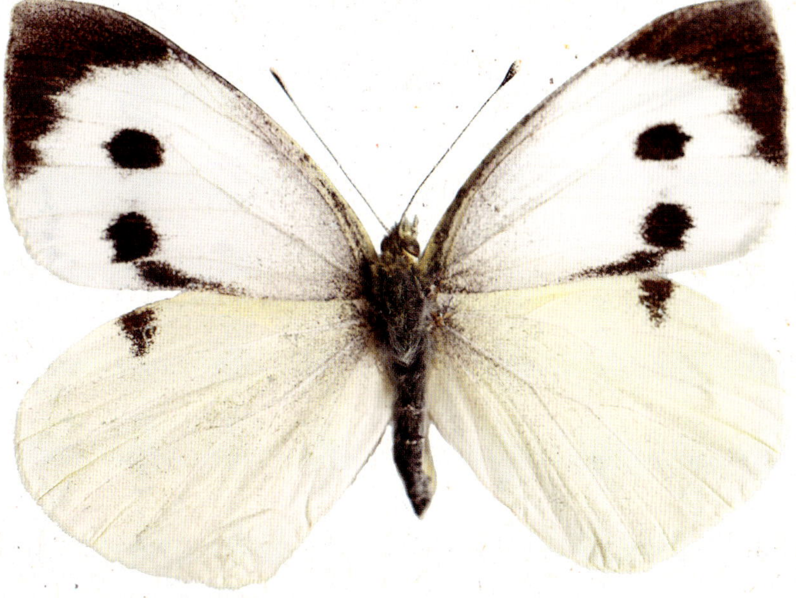

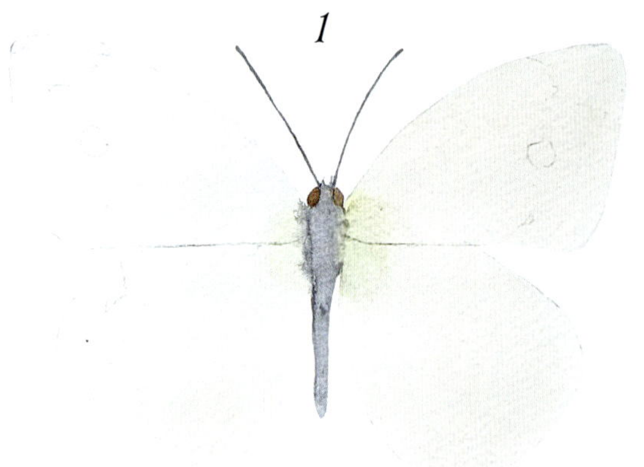

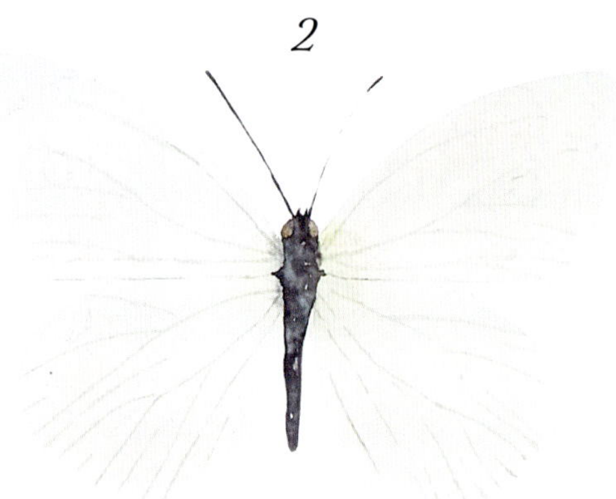

Step 1

Mix Raw Sienna with a bit of Titanium White. For the first layer of color, use your damp medium brush to paint the entire butterfly with a clear water wash. Then, brush a transparent wash of the mix we just made across the wings (both hind wings and forewings). Immediately pick up a saturated value of Primary Yellow, and dab it down the center of the butterfly, where the wings meet with the body. Once the yellow is dry, load your medium brush with a light value of Neutral Tint, and brush it down the center of the butterfly's body.

Wait until dry and change to the detail brush to paint the antennae with Neutral Tint and the eyes with Raw Umber.

Step 2

Use the detail brush to paint the body again, with a more saturated value of Neutral Tint, leaving some spots unpainted. This will make the body look more realistic.

Now on to the butterfly veins. Mix Raw Sienna with just a little bit of Neutral Tint to darken the color. Add enough water to make this mixture very translucent, and start painting the veins using the detail brush. Each vein should stream into the body. It doesn't matter if the body isn't quite dry. It will look good if the veins merge and bleed a bit with each other.

***Tip:** If you feel like it's difficult to paint the veins freehand, use your pencil to trace the lines really lightly, and use these lines as a reference to paint the veins.*

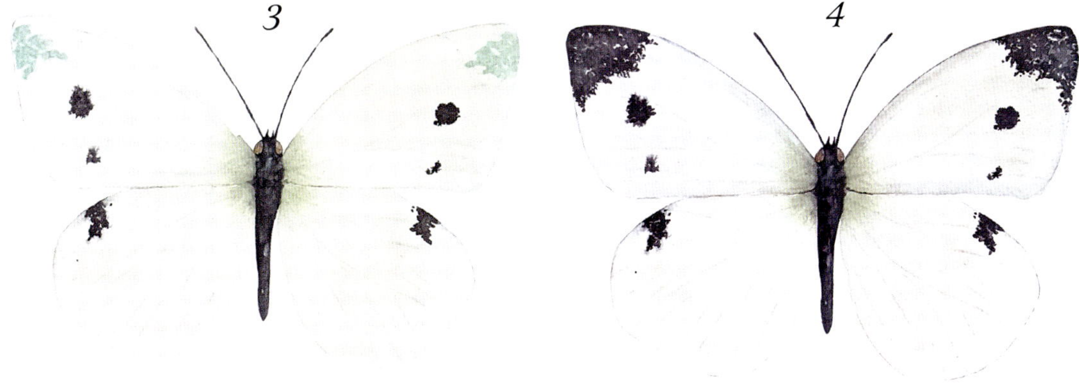

Step 3

To make the vein lines subtler, clean your medium brush and paint a wash with clear water all over the butterfly wings. Don't put pressure on the brush; we just want to make these lines fade a little.

Wait until dry, and then use the same brush loaded with Neutral Tint to paint the black dots on both forewings and hind wings, mirroring them to make them look as similar as possible. With a light value of Sennelier Green, paint the spots in the top forewings' edges.

Step 4

Load your medium brush with Neutral Tint and paint over the green spots, covering the area but leaving some of the green visible. Dab your brush instead of dragging the paint to create the impression of scales. Change to your detail brush and use Neutral Tint to paint a line separating both wings, starting from the body to the middle part of the wings.

With the same brush and a medium value of Neutral Tint, paint a line along the forewings' top edge, starting on the body and going all the way up to the tip of the wings. Then, while the line is still damp, use your damp medium brush to soften the lines by painting a clear wash along the previous lines to make the paint blend with the wing. Let it dry.

5-6

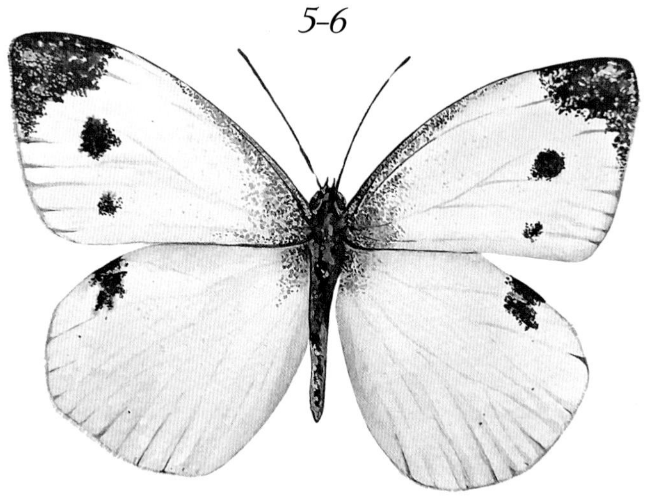

Step 5

Use your medium brush to paint a light wash of Raw Sienna over all four wings. Allow it to fully dry.

Step 6

Now for the best part: all the dots and details that will make your butterfly look alive. Allow yourself to be playful with this part of the painting. The only thing to remember is to be cautious around the veins so they do not smudge.

Mix Primary Yellow with a bit of Neutral Tint and, with the detail brush, use a light value of the mixture to add dots close to the body where the wings meet.

Tip: While the dots are still wet, slightly press the tip of a finger on them. This will make them look less perfect and more organic.

Paint dots along the top edges of the forewings (not too close together) for texture. Change to a medium value of Neutral Tint, and keep adding dots, especially towards the center of both forewings and hind wings. Add more dots around and inside of the black markings. Wait until it dries, and then paint a second line just under the top edge of the forewings.

Lastly, use a mixture of Neutral Tint and Primary Yellow to define the wings' veins, especially towards the bottom of the wings, to create more depth and the little hairs all around the wings' edges.

Now your cabbage butterfly is ready to fly!

Luna Moth

The luna moth (*Actias luna*), with its incredible 3 to 4½–inch (8 to 11–cm) wingspan, seafoam color, and long tails, is one of the most spectacular moths found in North America. The name is derived from Luna, the Roman moon goddess, because of the beautiful moon-like eyespots on their hind wings, which also serve as a clever defense mechanism used to confuse predators.

Difficulty: Easy

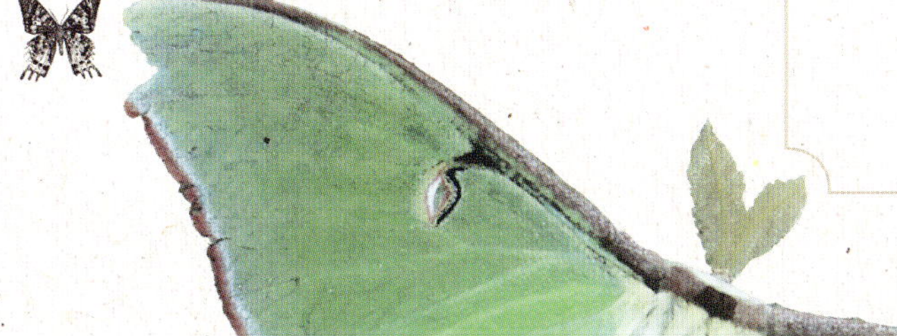

MATERIALS

- Watercolor paper of your choice
  - I used an 8 x 10–inch (20 x 25–cm) sheet, landscape orientation
- Paints
  - Emerald Green, Hooker's Green, Raw Sienna, Lemon Yellow, Permanent Magenta, Payne's Grey
  - White gouache
- Brushes
  - Medium round brush (I used size 8)
  - Detail round brush (I used size 1)

Sketch

Draw the luna moth freehand or trace the reference image and transfer it to the watercolor paper of your choice, focusing on the shape of the wings, body, and eyespots. Spray your paints with water to moisten them.

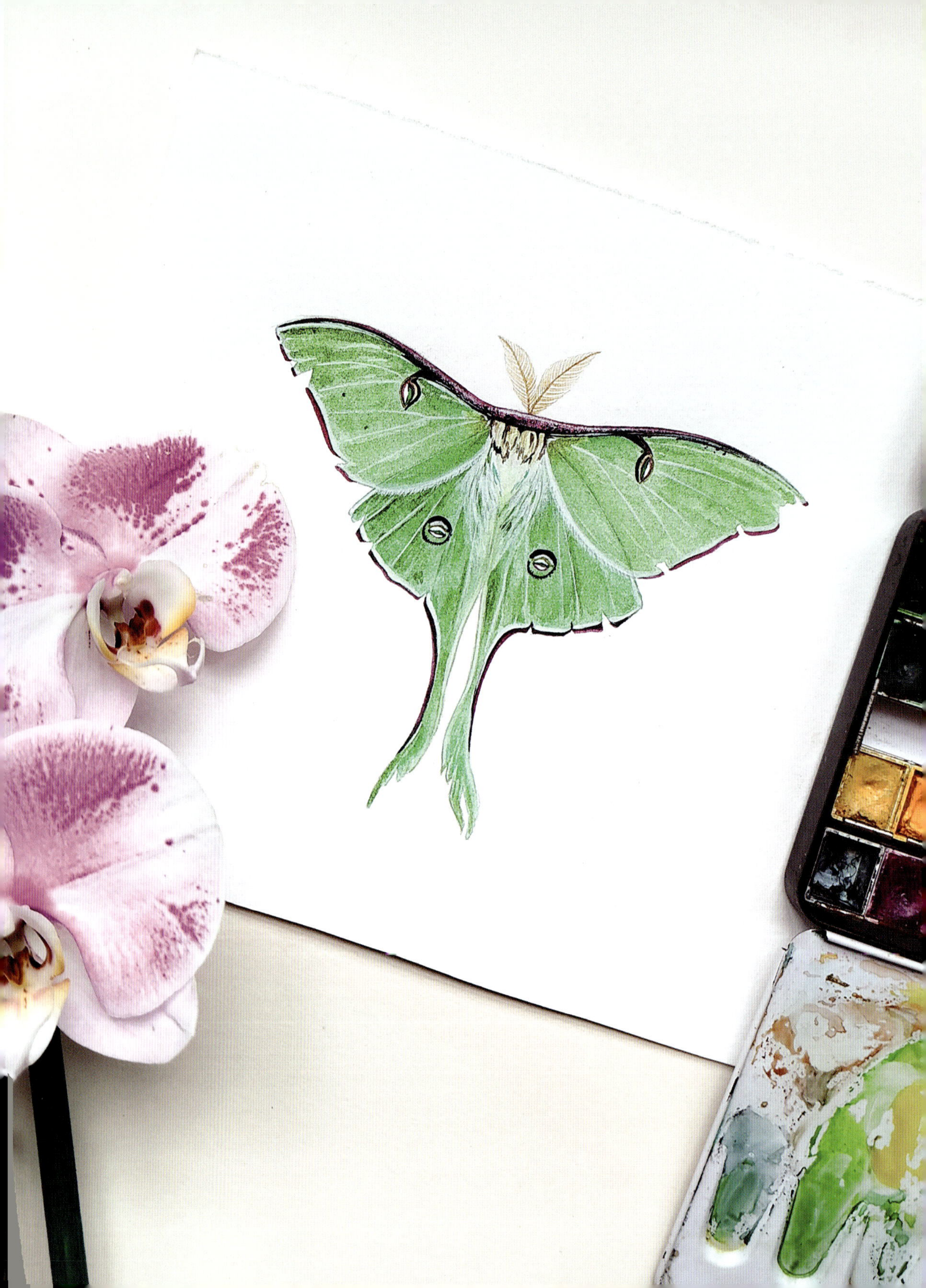

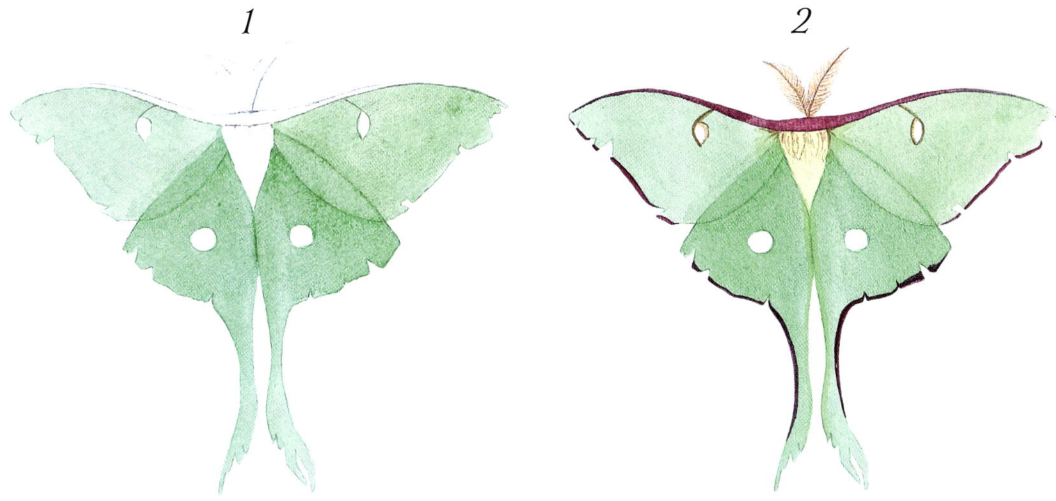

Step 1

Mix Emerald Green with Hooker's Green and a bit of Raw Sienna to create the perfect dusty blue-green color. Swatch before painting to make sure you have the right hue.

Once the colors are mixed, load a very light wash of the mixture to your medium brush and apply it to the wings. Paint one wing at a time, saving the eyespots for later. Allow the wings to dry before moving on to the next one. The reason for painting one wing at a time is that we want to create the effect of the wings being transparent and overlapping.

Step 2

Load your medium brush with Lemon Yellow and paint the body. Once the body dries, very carefully use your detail brush loaded with a dark value of Permanent Magenta to outline the edges of the forewings, over the top of the head stripe, and around the eyespots. Do the same thing on the hind wings' bottom edge. While you wait for this to dry, change to Raw Sienna to paint a few hairlike lines on the body area, starting from the top, towards the middle part of the abdomen.

Once the Permanent Magenta is dry, use your detail brush loaded with Raw Sienna to paint the antennae. First paint a line from the head towards the outside, and then fill it out with thin lines to complete the feather-looking antennae. Use the tip of your detail brush so you can leave spaces between each line. Next, load your brush with Lemon Yellow to add a long line along both hind wings' inner edges.

Load your medium brush with Lemon Yellow, and gently tap a bit of color onto the base of both forewings, where the wings come out of the body.

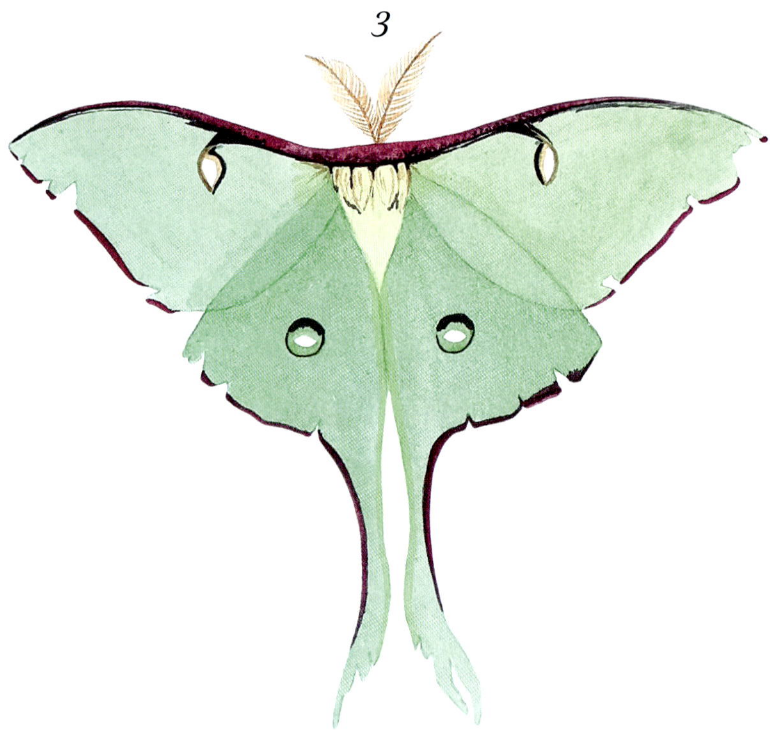

Step 3

Now it's time to add more emphasis and a 3D-effect to the illustration. First, use your detail brush to paint the insides of the hind wings' eyespots with Emerald Green, leaving a white spot in the middle. Do the same on the forewings' eyespots, but with Raw Sienna instcad of Emerald Green.

Load your detail brush with Payne's Grey, and start adding depth to the top edge of the fore-wings, painting a thin line along the top edge of the forewings and the hind wings. Once done, paint another line right underneath, leaving a little space in-between. Add little dots to create a more organic look. Outline all four eyespots with the same color. To finish this step, add a few more lines with Payne's Grey, shaping the fluffy area on the moth's head.

> *Tip: While you want to be careful while painting the lines and dots, you also don't want to create perfect lines. This could create an artificial look. So let your hand flow. Make these lines with just one long brushstroke, and add dots and little lines around to correct if necessary.*

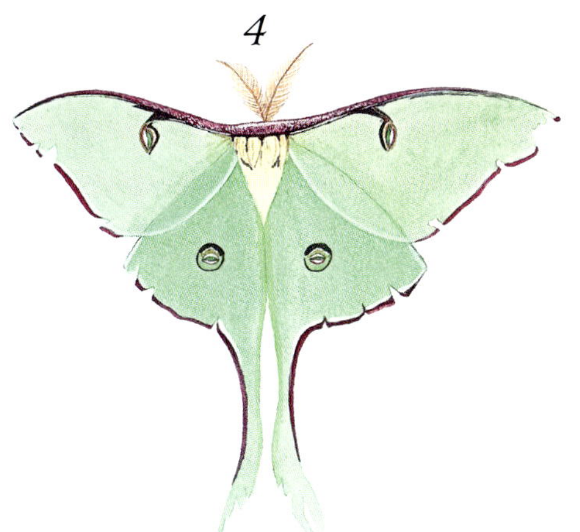

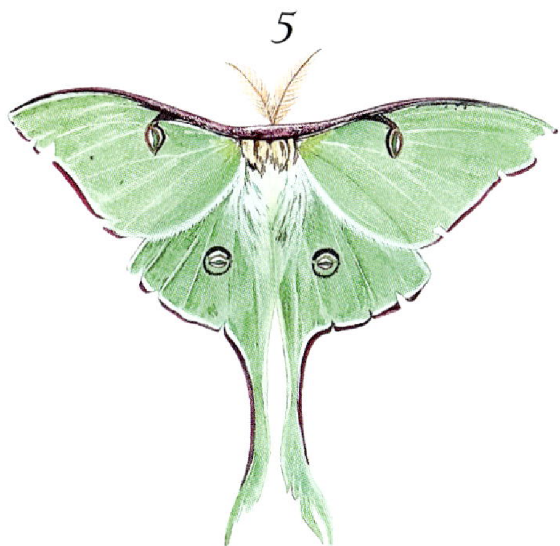

Step 4

Now it's time to paint the inside of the hind wings' eyespots. First, paint a semicircle of Raw Sienna with your detail brush directly below the Payne's Grey you added in Step 3 and over the green part. (It's okay if there's not much space.) Then paint the white part (the little eye-shaped space inside) with Hooker's Green. Outline all the different colors in the inner circle with a thin line of Payne's Grey, and add lines to finish using the gouache. Repeat on the other eyespot.

Let's move on to the eyespots on the forewings. On the side of the eyespot pointing to the edge of the wings, paint a line with your detail brush loaded with Permanent Magenta. Then paint a line with Hooker's Green on the opposite side, and that's it! Go slowly and put the shapes of the eye details together like a puzzle.

Since all those little lines dry really fast, I didn't advise you to wait until each line is dry to paint the next one, and though it doesn't matter if it's a bit damp, be careful not to overload your brush. You can also dab your brush onto a paper towel before going onto the paper.

With your detail brush loaded with watered-down white gouache, add your highlights. Outline all four wings, specifically where the forewings and hind wings overlap. Add a line over the Permanent Magenta area and more dots.

Step 5

Gently wet the moth's body with a clear water wash, and load your medium brush with the dusty blue-green color from Step 1. Slowly build up the next layer, leaving long lines unpainted to create the veins with the negative space. You can also play a bit with the color and add more Raw Sienna or Hooker's Green to the mixture to change the hue a bit.

Switch to your detail brush to add fluffy, hair-like lines on the bottom edge of the forewings using white gouache. Then paint the lines gently joining at the center and fading at the edges, giving the body a rounded look. To finish your beautiful luna moth, highlight the veins with your detail brush loaded with white gouache.

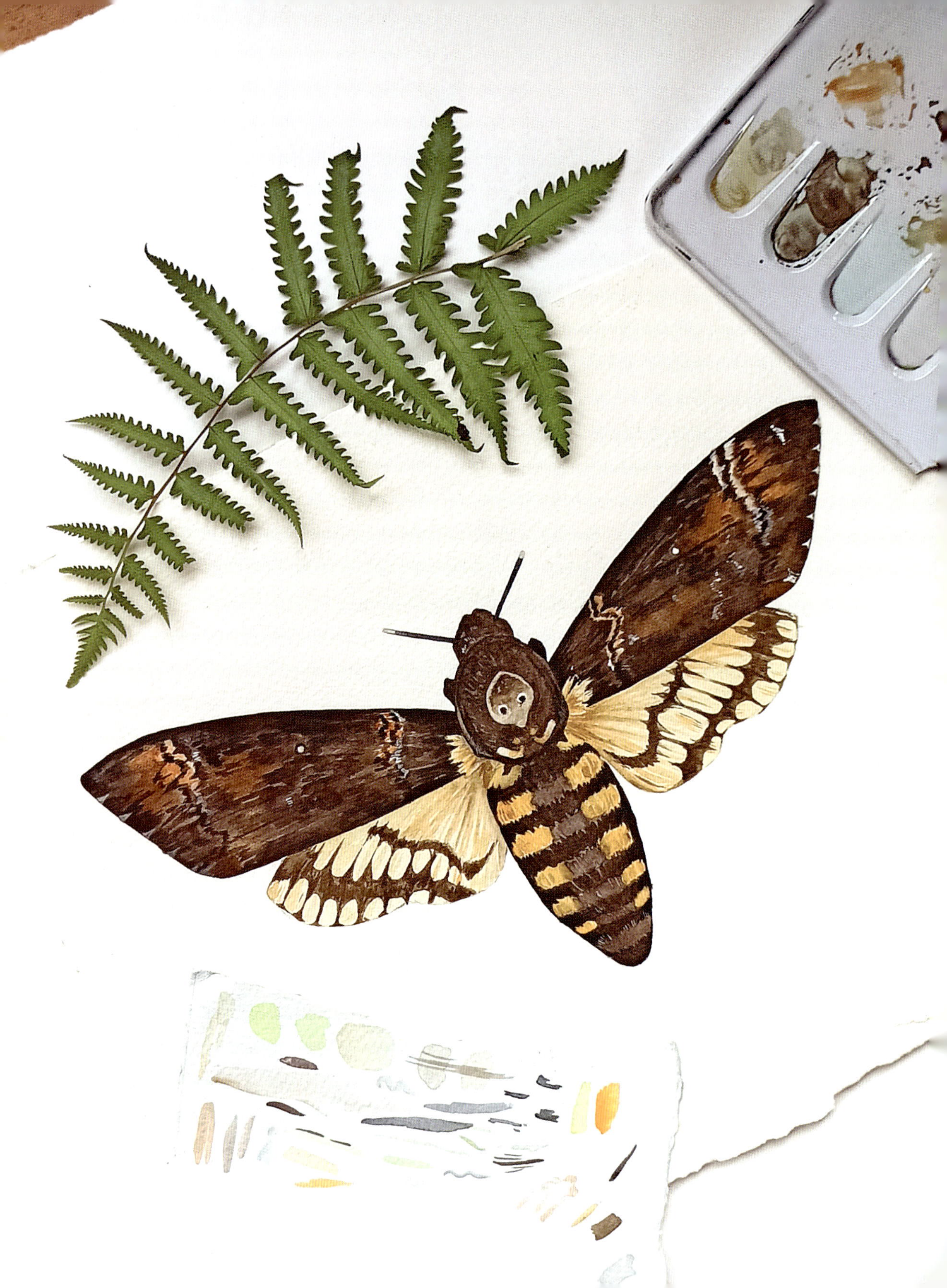

Death's-Head Hawkmoth

The death's-head hawkmoth, also called the bee robber because it is very fond of honey, is a large species of moth found throughout Europe, Africa, and Asia. They can mimic the scent of bees so that they can enter a hive unharmed to get honey. Their tongue, which is stout and very strong, enables them to pierce the wax cells of the beehive and suck the honey out. The identifying "skull" pattern on the top of their thorax has made them very popular and you can probably recognize them from the movie *The Silence of the Lambs*.

This one is a little tricky, so if you struggle the first time you try this tutorial, don't fret! Take a break and try again. Are you ready to paint one of the scariest moths?

- Watercolor paper of your choice
  - › I used an 8 x 10–inch (20 x 25–cm) sheet, landscape orientation
- Paints
  - › Naples Yellow Deep, Gold Ochre, Van Dyck Brown, Warm Sepia, Sennelier Yellow Deep, Raw Sienna, Neutral Tint
  - › White gouache
- Brushes
  - › Medium round brush (I used size 8)
  - › Detail round brush (I used size 1)

Difficulty: Difficult

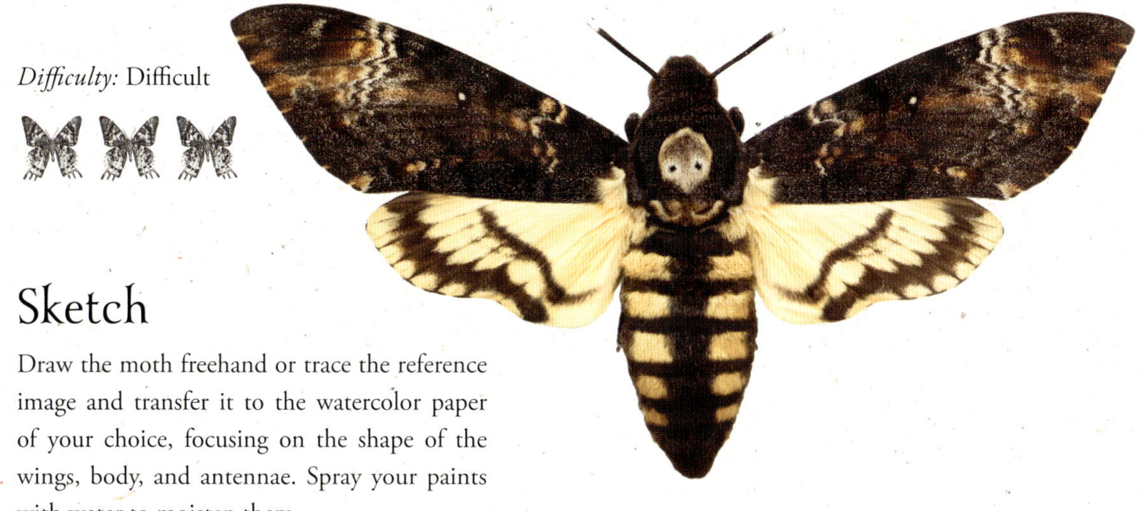

Sketch

Draw the moth freehand or trace the reference image and transfer it to the watercolor paper of your choice, focusing on the shape of the wings, body, and antennae. Spray your paints with water to moisten them.

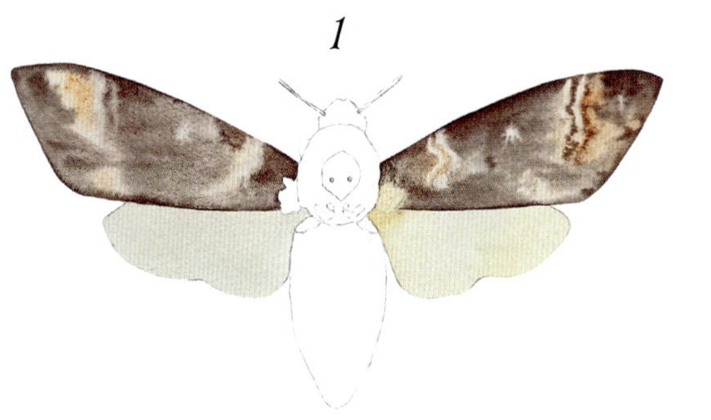

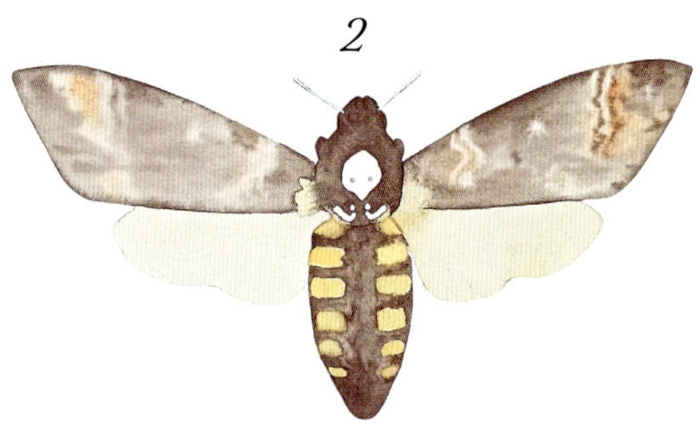

Step 1

Load your medium brush with Naples Yellow Deep and paint a light wash on the hind wings. Let this dry.

Moving to the forewings, work on one wing at a time to avoid them drying during the painting process. Use your clean, medium brush to paint a clear water wash. With the same brush loaded with a saturated value of Gold Ochre, deposit the pigment where there are lighter markings. (Refer to the reference image on page 47 for placement.) Before this dries, paint the rest of the forewing with Van Dyck Brown, being careful to avoid the areas with Gold Ochre. Lastly, clean your medium brush and use it to lift the brown color around the Gold Ochre, making a zigzag line.

Move to the other forewing and repeat the process. Try to get the details as symmetrical as possible, but it's okay if they are not exact—at the end, it won't be so noticeable.

Paint the hair markings at the base of both forewings with your medium brush and a medium value of Naples Yellow Deep. (I've painted the right hair section but not the left in the photo above.)

> ***Tip:*** *If you feel your paper is drying before you're finishing, wait until everything is completely dry. Then add a water wash over the whole area—just don't press too hard with the brush!*

Step 2

Now you are going to focus on the body and head. Load your medium brush with Warm Sepia and paint a wash all over the head area, avoiding the skull markings. Let this dry while you start on the abdomen. With your medium brush loaded with Sennelier Yellow Deep, paint the markings along the body. Once the area is dry, finish painting the body using the same brush with a medium value of Warm Sepia. Wait for this step to dry before starting the next.

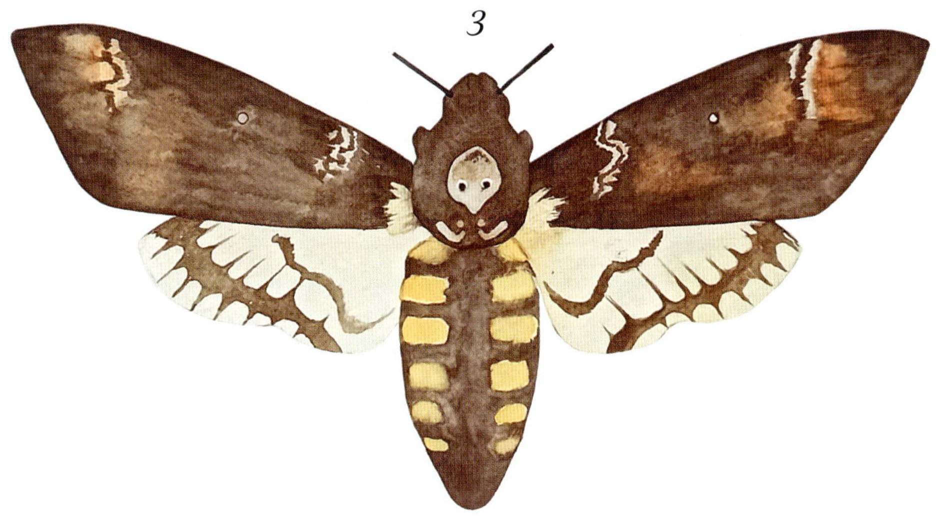

Step 3

Keep using your medium brush to paint the markings on both hind wings. Use a saturated value of Raw Sienna to build up the veins and markings. There's a lot of detail in a moth wing. This is where the moth reference photo comes in super handy. I'm a firm believer in using reference images for artwork.

Load your medium brush with Gold Ochre, and paint another wash on the forewings, over the previous golden markings from Step 1. Before it dries, use your medium brush loaded with Warm Sepia to paint the forewing, starting on the top edge and lightening the value of the color as you go down. Change to your detail brush to paint lines with the same color within the zigzag lines. Try to paint everything before it dries so everything will blend together. Don't forget to keep the little ovals untouched as well as the hairy spots where the wings meet the body. Use your detail brush with Warm Sepia to paint some lines going inside to recreate the fluffy texture of the hairs coming out.

Use a medium value of Van Dyck Brown to paint the top of the skull with the detail brush, lightening the color as you go down. When it's almost dry, paint a few dots on the top part to make it look even darker. Don't forget to paint the skull's eyes with a dark value of Van Dyck Brown! Load your detail brush with Neutral Tint to paint the antennae.

> *Tip:* *When you want colors to blend together, you have to work quickly. One way to make this easier is to work on one wing at a time.*

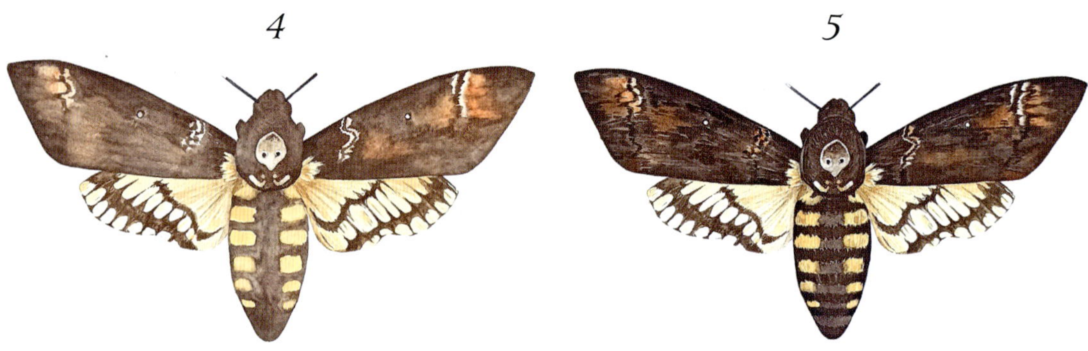

Step 4

Mix Naples Yellow Deep with a bit of Raw Sienna to darken the color, and with this mixture and your detail brush, start painting lines diagonally from the top of the hind wings (where they join the body) down to the bottom. Paint these lines with different thicknesses. Then add a bit more Raw Sienna to darken the mixture and paint thinner lines with it. This will create a more lifelike effect. Use the same mixture for the hairy part coming out of the middle abdomen area. Once dry, paint some lines with Warm Sepia over the brown lines for added depth.

Step 5

Now, back to work on the forewings for some final details. With your detail brush and a saturated value of Warm Sepia, paint small lines, close together, on both forewings. Add more lines close to the body, on the top edge, and where you first painted the Gold Ochre in Step 1. Use your detail brush to paint the tips of the antennae with a very light value of Neutral Tint.

Use your detail brush loaded with white gouache to paint a few highlights. Here you can be more intuitive and add lines where you think it's too dark. Also paint the lines on the edge of both forewings, acting as the end of the veins.

Congratulations! Your moth is finished. Be proud because this is one of the hardest projects in this book.

Monarch Butterfly

Monarchs are large, beautifully colored butterflies that are easy to recognize with their striking orange, black, and white markings. The annual migration of North America's monarch butterflies from Canada to Mexico is a unique and amazing phenomenon. The monarch is the only butterfly known to make a two-way migration as birds do. These international travelers return to the same forests each year, and some even find the same tree that their ancestors landed on. Some estimates say up to a billion butterflies arrive in the mountains of Mexico each year. Of course, this special specimen has to be part of the tutorials in this book!

Difficulty: Easy

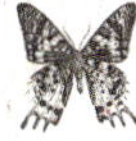

Sketch

Draw the butterfly freehand or trace the reference image and transfer it to the watercolor paper of your choice, focusing on the wing pattern. Spray your paints with water to moisten them.

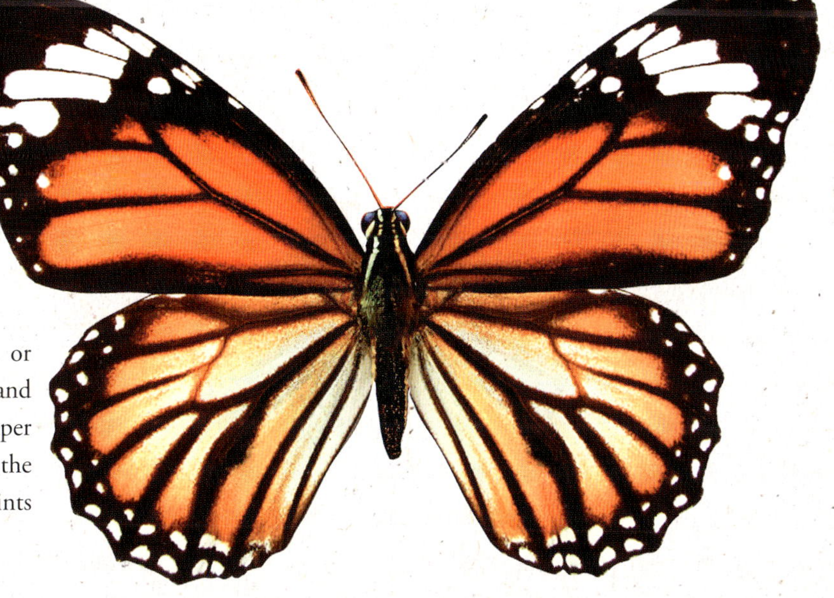

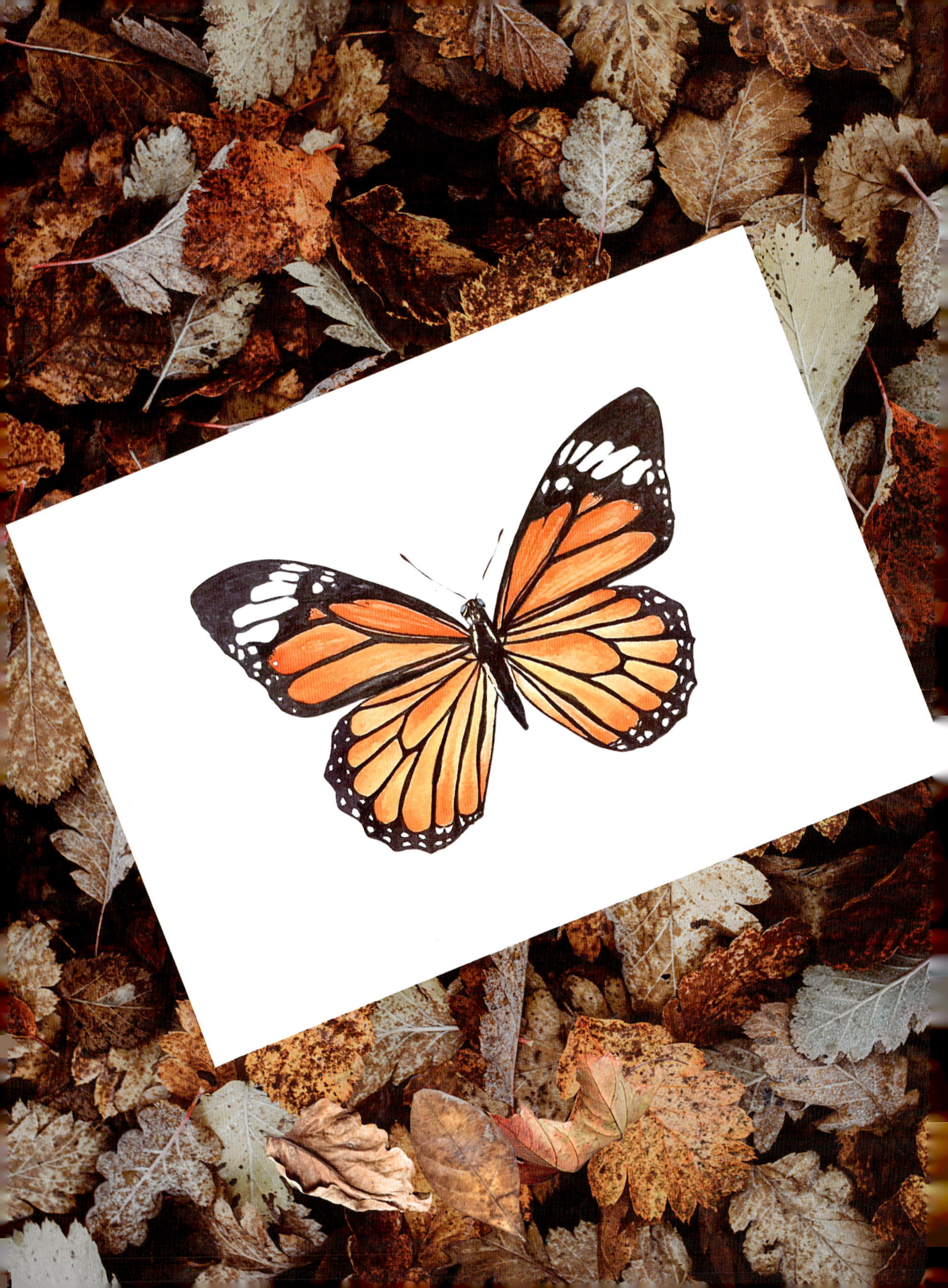

Step 1

Prepare your palette with a light value of Red Orange, Sennelier Orange, and Sennelier Yellow Deep. You have to have the colors ready because you want the painting to stay damp throughout this process. Begin to build color using your medium brush. Start painting the markings on the forewings with the darkest color (Red Orange), and as you go down, add the lighter hues of orange. You don't have to mix them, but paint the spaces of the pattern, adding the colors to create a gradient.

Use the same brush and technique to paint the markings on the hind wings, but skip the Sennelier Orange, because the hind wings are lighter than the forewings. Use Red Orange, Sennelier Yellow Deep, and then Naples Yellow Deep instead, adding the Naples Yellow Deep as you go down. Before it's dry, add a bit of Sennelier Orange to the bottom edge of the markings. Don't worry about trying to get the paint on smoothly and all the same. Variations make the painting more interesting.

Change to your detail brush, load it with a light wash of Sennelier Orange, and add details on the body and around the eyes. Let the washes get lighter as you move down the body. Let this dry.

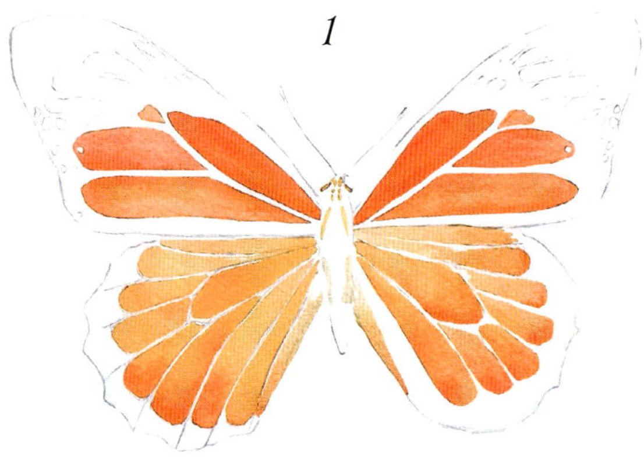

Tip: One thing to keep in mind with watercolors is that you can always go darker, but it is very difficult to go lighter. Start with lighter washes, and if once they are dry you want a darker color, layer a second wash on top.

Tip: If you find it difficult to paint around or avoid small areas, before moving on to this next step, you may want to apply masking fluid with an old brush (page 10) to keep the white markings on the wings untouched. Wait until it's completely dry to begin the painting process.

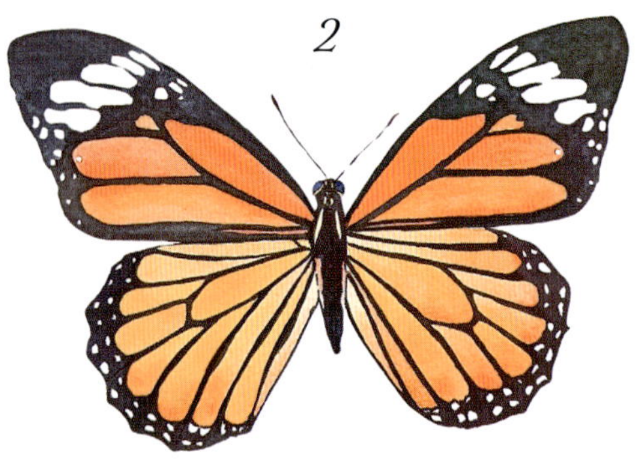

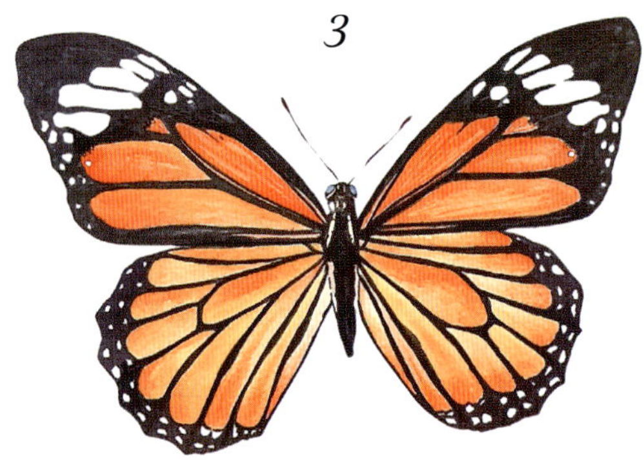

Step 2

To make the painting more harmonic, we are going to create our own black. Black watercolors are carbon-based and tend to look harsh and opaque.

Mix the same amount of French Vermilion, Hooker's Green, and Indigo. Swatch the mixture, and once you are happy with the color, load your medium brush with it and apply a wash on the forewings, leaving the white markings untouched. Use your detail brush to outline small details and spots and paint the veins. Do the same with the hind wings.

Once the wings are dry, use the detail brush to paint the body with the same mixture, outlining the orange markings. Use the Indigo with your detail brush to paint the eyes, and then outline them with the black mixture.

Tip: I advise you to create enough black for the whole process, otherwise you'll have to stop painting to prepare more and the painting will dry, which will give you an uneven layer of watercolor.

Step 3

Almost done now. With the detail brush, add a second layer of orange to the wings. This time, instead of painting the wash evenly, use the brush to paint thin lines of Red Orange and Sennelier Orange inside all orange areas. Also add strokes of Red Orange on the widest part of the orange markings, dragging the color upwards and toward the body of the butterfly.

Lastly, using the same brush but loaded with the black mixture you mixed in Step 2, refine the veins, and add some thin lines to the black area in both forewings and hind wings.

Your Monarch butterfly is now finished!

Sunset Moth

It's easy to see why the Madagascan sunset moth was originally misidentified as a butterfly. Bright colors and daytime activity aren't typical moth traits, but this Madagascan native is anything but ordinary. They have iridescent wings, which are black, red, yellow, blue, and green. The indigenous Malagasy of Madagascar call the sunset moth *adriandolo*, which roughly translates to "noble spirit" or "king spirit."

Difficulty: Medium

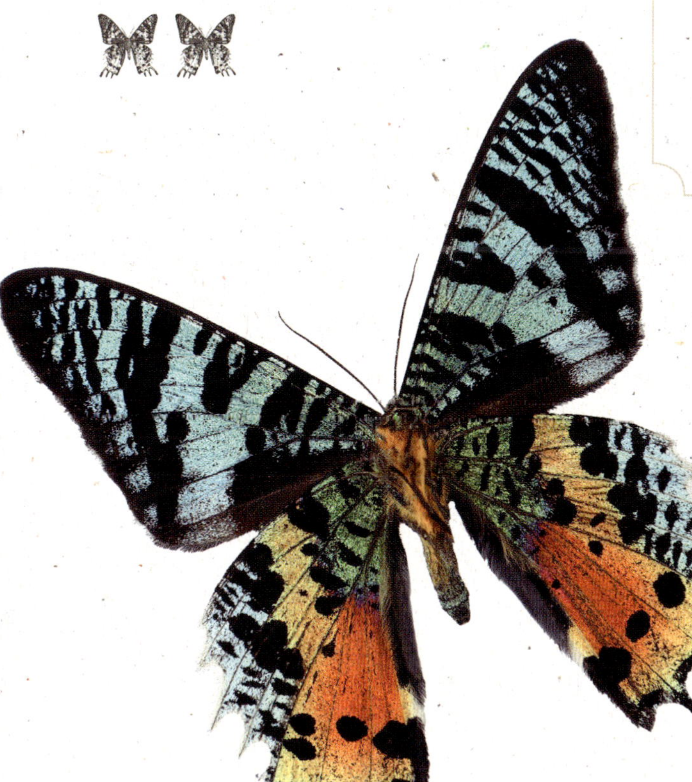

MATERIALS

- Watercolor paper of your choice
  - I used an 8 x 8–inch (20 x 20–cm) sheet
- Paints
  - Light Phthalo Green, Primary Yellow, Cerulean Blue, Gold Ochre, Red Orange, Emerald Green, Ivory Black, Permanent Magenta, French Vermilion, Raw Umber
- Brushes
  - Medium round brush (I used size 8)
  - Liner brush (I used size 0)
  - Detail round brush (I used size 1)

Sketch

Draw the moth freehand or trace the reference image and transfer it to the watercolor paper of your choice, focusing on the wing patterns and veins. Spray your paints with water to moisten them.

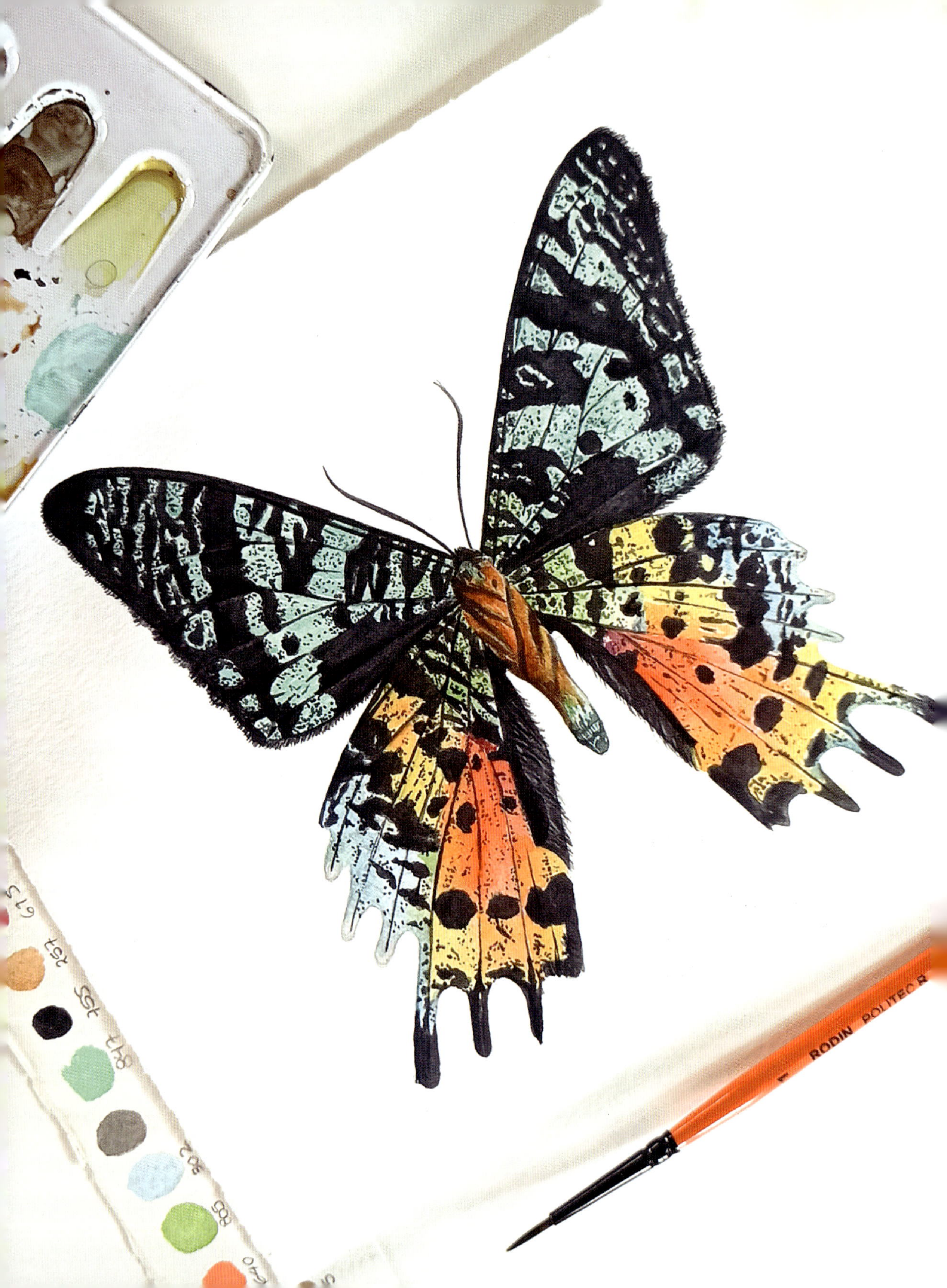

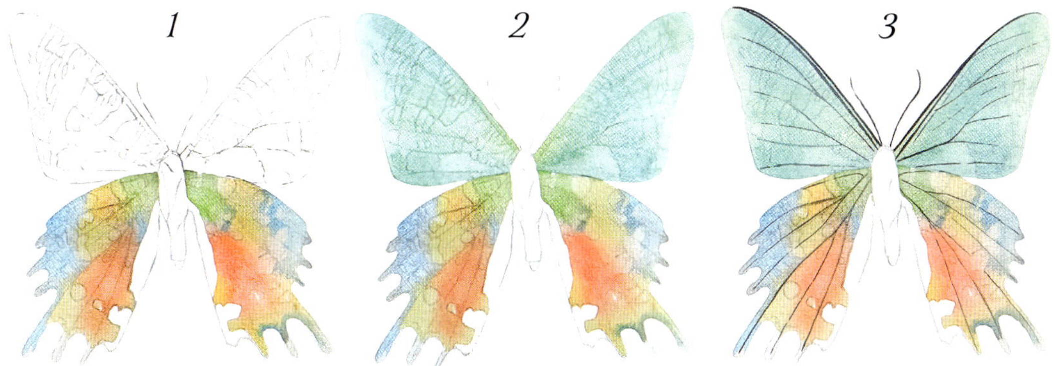

Step 1

First the hind wings. Starting from top to bottom, load your medium brush with Light Phthalo Green, and paint a medium wash where the wings meet the body. Change to Primary Yellow, and paint a wash right next to and a bit below the green color. (The colors should blend a bit, but if they blend too much, let the first color dry a bit longer before adding the next.) Continue painting your way down the hind wings with a wash of Cerulean Blue, Gold Ochre, and then Red Orange. Refer to the reference photo on page 55 as needed. Leave the inner tips of the hind wings unpainted. Don't worry about outlining the black markings while painting— you'll cover it later with the black. Leave it to dry.

Step 2

For the forewings, paint a medium wash of Emerald Green with your medium brush. Before it's dry, add a bit of Light Phthalo Green

fading into the top inner edge of the wings; for this, use the tip of your brush and dot the paint without rubbing it or dragging the pigment. Here you want to add a nice subtle change of hue. Clean your brush and use it to lift a bit of the Emerald Green from the outer edge of the wings for a subtle gradient. Let it dry.

Step 3

Use Ivory Black and your liner brush to paint all the veins and lines in the wings. Start with the forewings. Use the same brush to paint a thin line along the top edge of the wing and another one right underneath, making this one closer to the top at the end. Both lines should be a bit thicker than the veins. Now, when you paint the veins, the brush should only touch the paper lightly! This way you'll get fewer perfect lines but more of a natural look. For the hind wings, paint the veins using the same brush and Ivory Black. Paint the antennae using the same brush and color.

Step 4

This step might look complicated, but it's actu-ally not. It's simply a matter of patience filling out all the black markings. It's a great way to meditate and concentrate on something; let yourself take the chance! Use Ivory Black and your medium round brush to paint these spaces.

You should be able to see the pencil markings through the Emerald Green wash. If you don't, look at the photo reference, and let your intu-ition take over. Start from top to bottom, first painting both forewings. For the inner section of the hind wings, paint a light wash of Ivory Black. Once it's nearly dry, change to your liner brush to add hairlike strokes alongside the inner edges.

Make sure your painting is dry, and then add a second wash with the same colors you used before for the whole butterfly (Steps 1 and 2). For this, keep using the medium brush. Start with Emerald Green, and add color to the forewings area, dabbing your brush to create texture. Avoid the black markings if possible.

Do the same for both hind wings—just add the same color on a more saturated value. Add a bit of Permanent Magenta and French Vermilion in-between the green and the orange and blend it.

Once everything is dry, start painting the body. Load your brush with Light Phthalo Green, and paint a light wash over the head area. Con-tinue with Raw Umber for the middle section and Cerulean Blue for the bottom.

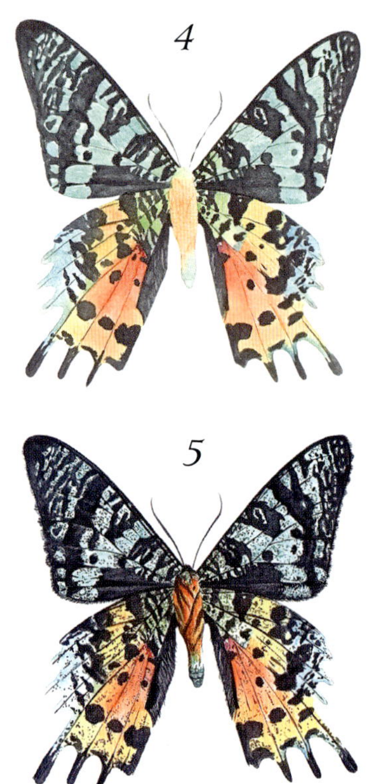

Step 5

It's time to add the details. Use your detail brush and Ivory Black to add dots. With the tip of your finger, smooth the dots as you paint them to make them look less perfect and more organic. Use the photo for reference, but also feel free to play around a bit. Sunset moths are all different, and their patterns vary a bit.

With the same brush, paint more hairlike lines on the inner hind wing section, and paint a thick line to separate this part from the color section. Refine the veins with your liner brush and Ivory Black. Now your sunset moth is ready to take flight!

Common Buckeye Butterfly

Named for its conspicuous target-shaped eye-spots, the common buckeye (*Junonia coenia*) is one of the most distinctive and readily identifiable North American butterflies. This tutorial will teach you to blend similar colors and to add lifelike texture to the wings.

Difficulty: Difficult

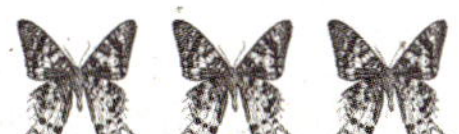

- Watercolor paper of your choice
  - › I used a 6 x 8–inch (15 x 20–cm) sheet, landscape orientation
- Paints
  - › Raw Sienna, Emerald Green, Brown Pink, Red Orange, Van Dyck Brown, Gold Ochre, Phthalocyanine Blue, Payne's Grey, Phthalo Green Deep
  - › White gouache
- Brushes
  - › Old brush for masking fluid (I used a round size 2)
  - › Medium round brush (I used size 6)
  - › Detail round brush (I used size 2)
- Masking fluid and eraser (to remove)

Sketch

Draw the butterfly freehand or trace the reference image and transfer it to the watercolor paper of your choice, focusing on the wing patterns. Spray your paints with water to moisten them.

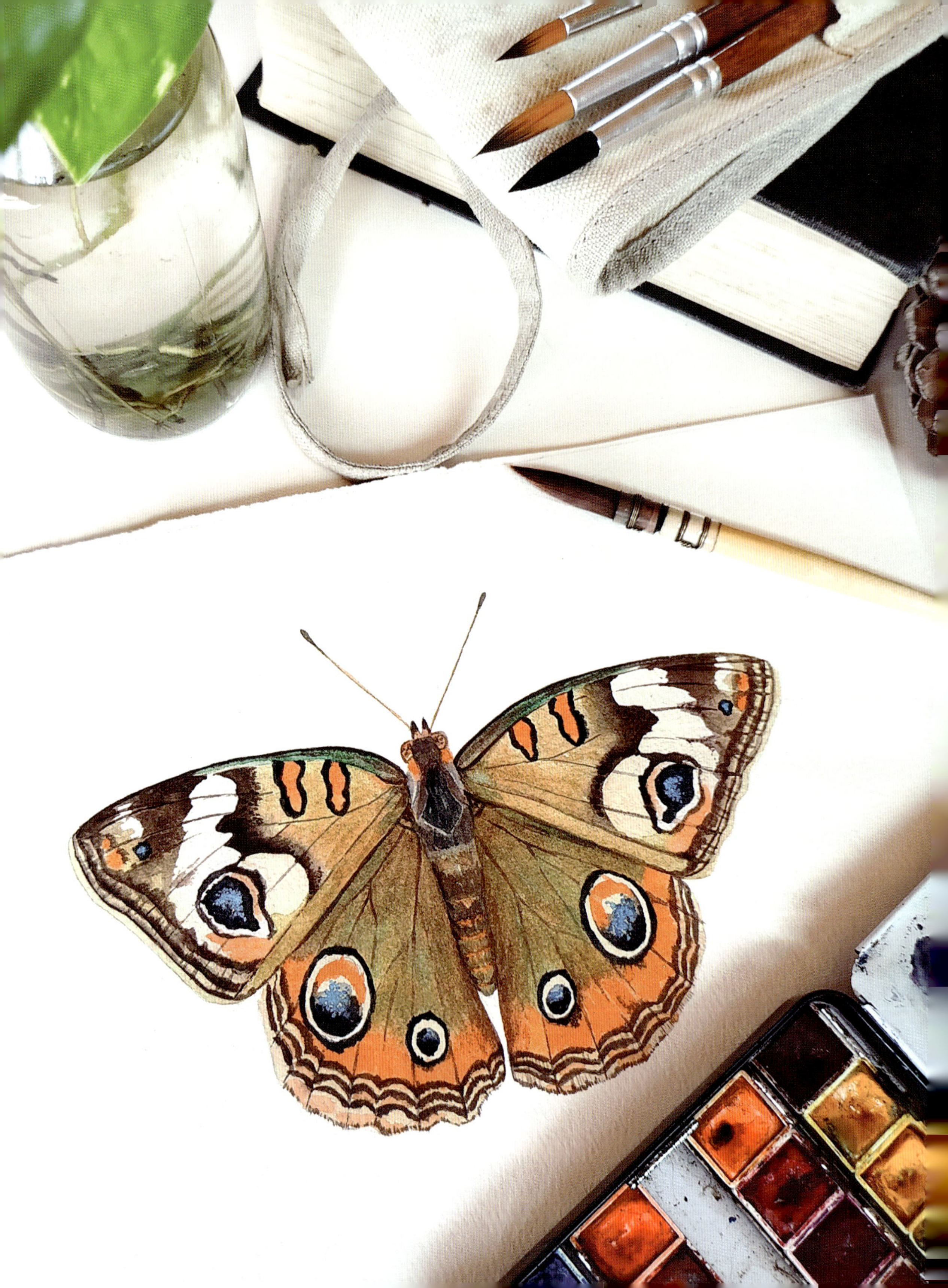

1-2

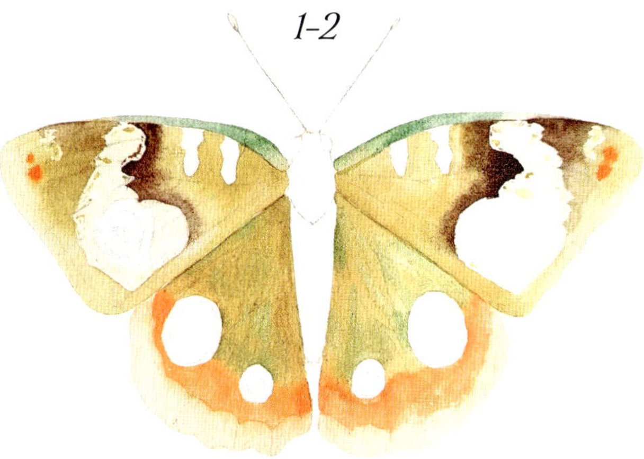

Step 1

Before laying down any paint, use your old brush to apply masking fluid to the forewings' white areas.

Tip: If you don't have an old brush on hand, use a clean brush and wash it right after you're finished.

While you wait for the masking fluid to dry, paint the hind wings. Use your medium brush to paint a light wash of Raw Sienna down until the butterfly eye markings, leaving these untouched for later. While still wet, load the same brush with Emerald Green, and add some strokes, adding some color to the wings' surface, and then switch to Brown Pink and do the same, especially around the body area, creating a darker color on that area.

Use your brush to move the color where you want it to go, and don't worry if it bleeds a bit over the white areas. You can always clean it with a dry, clean brush as if you were using a mop.

Before it dries, add the next wash right at the edge of the Raw Sienna wash, using the same brush and Red Orange. Leave a line right on the bottom edge of the hind wings to paint the last wash of Raw Sienna. Apply the last wash of Raw Sienna when the orange is dry. You don't want them to mix. Let all of this dry.

Step 2

Time for the forewings. Paint them one at a time so the surface stays wet. Start with your medium brush loaded with Raw Sienna, and paint a wash all over the area except for the two vertical markings on the top, right under the top stripe. Then, switch to Brown Pink and add color to the upper section of the wing, except for the top stripe.

Switch to Van Dyck Brown and add color around the area where you painted the masking fluid, and a lighter value around the top of the wing. Switch to your detail brush and load it with Red Orange. Add two dots of color to the tip of the wing. This should be done when the paper is just a bit wet, but not so much so that it completely bleeds into the background.

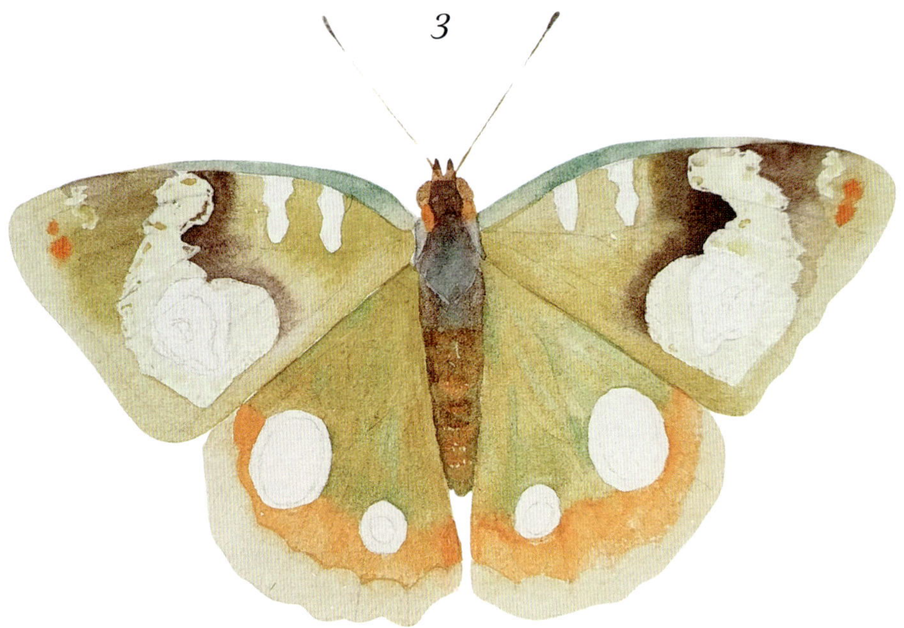

Paint the top stripe with a medium wash of Raw Sienna, and then add Emerald Green in the middle, blending it.

Step 3

Paint the body. Use your medium brush with Van Dyck Brown and paint right down to the triangular mark on the thorax. Switch to Gold Ochre to paint the rest, leaving some areas blank. Switch to Brown Pink and add hairlike strokes defining the sections of the thorax and abdomen. Then switch to Van Dyck Brown, and do the same, but on the edges of the thorax. This is to create depth.

Load the same brush with Phthalocyanine Blue to paint the middle triangular area on the thorax, switching to Van Dyck Brown to paint up to the eyes. Let it dry.

Load your detail brush with a dark value of Raw Sienna, and paint the tips right over the eyes, adding Van Dyck Brown to the top. Use the same value of Raw Sienna to paint the eyes, but wait until this area is dry so it doesn't mix with the rest of the body. Load your detail brush with Red Orange, and paint two dots on the sides of the head, and continue painting this little section with a light value of Phthalocyanine Blue.

Oh! Don't forgot to paint the antennae with your detail brush and a dark value of Raw Sienna, adding Van Dyck Brown right on the top of them.

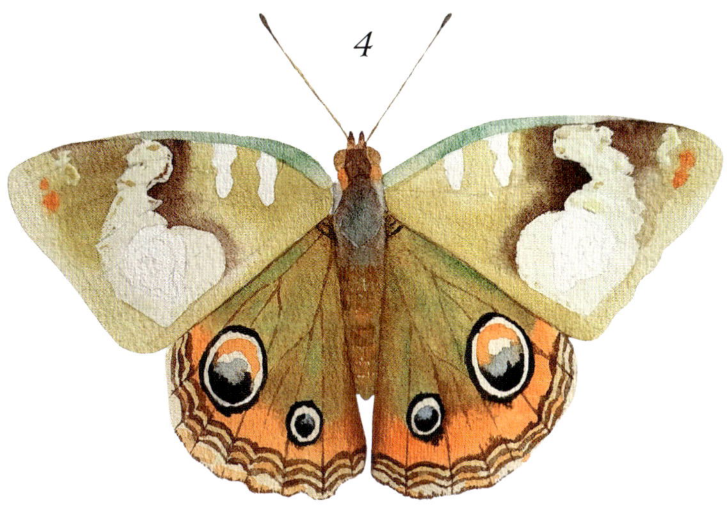

Step 4

Paint the eyespots on the hind wings. With your detail brush, start in the middle of the big ones. Use Red Orange for the top, making a semicircle shape or like a C looking downward, and then add Phthalocyanine Blue in the middle; leave a space between colors, but allow them to mix a bit. Then add Payne's Grey to the bottom. Leave a blank circle around it, and paint the outer circle with Payne's Grey to finish.

For the smaller eyes, use a dot of Phthalocyanine Blue on the top and a semicircle of Payne's Grey on the bottom, again allowing the colors to mix a little. Leave a blank space all around before outlining the eyespot with a Payne's Grey circle.

Add value to the hind wings' color, using the same colors as Step 1 and your medium brush. The only difference is that you'll paint Emerald Green over the part of the hind wing where it touches the forewing, creating a shadow right along the line separating both wings. Also, add Van Dyck Brown to the inner area. Don't worry if the grey of the eyespots bleeds a bit over the area. It will make the painting look more organic.

While still a bit wet, add the veins, using the tip of your detail brush with a medium value of Van Dyck Brown. For the corner section where both wings merge, use Payne's Grey and paint two transverse lines.

Move down to the bottom of the hind wings, and using the same detail brush and Van Dyck Brown, paint three wavy lines across each hind wing. Add some tiny lines right at the bottom of the wings too, to give them some texture.

Once everything is dry, use your medium brush and a medium wash of Red Orange to create smudges over the lined area. Let it flow. This was a lot of work! Rest your eyes and hands while this dries.

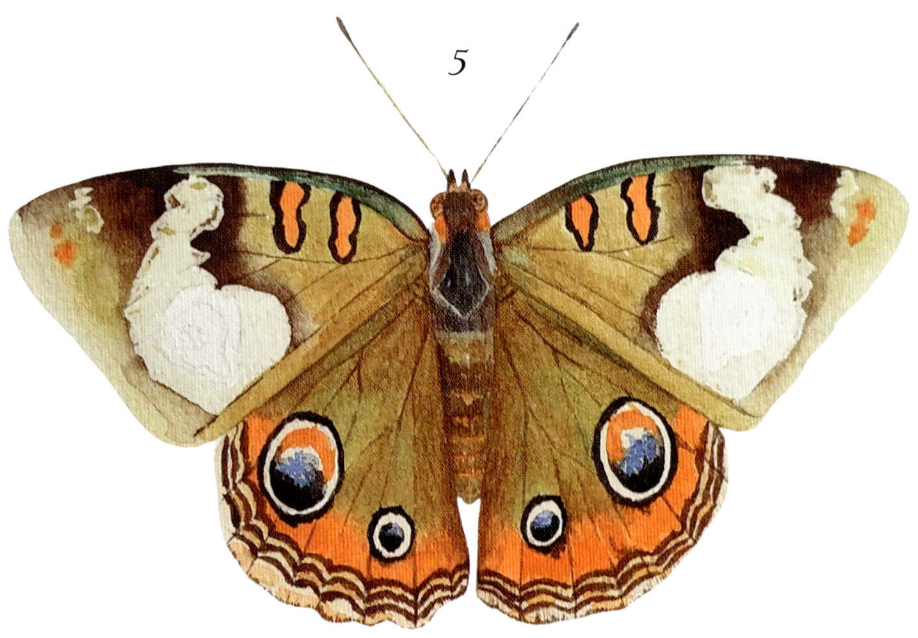

Step 5

Work on the forewings again. Load your medium brush with Van Dyck Brown (medium value), and paint another wash around the masking fluid area. Soften the edges with your clean brush. Paint both markings under the top stripe with Red Orange, and once it's dry, outline them with Payne's Grey.

Switch to your detail brush and Phthalo Green Deep to add another wash over the top stripe. Clean your brush, and soften the paint so it blends with the background. Outline the top of the forewing with Van Dyck Brown.

For the body, keep using your detail brush with Van Dyck Brown to paint hairlike strokes on each ring of the abdomen, and for in-between, switch to Red Orange. Use very little water to keep these lines sharp. On your palette, mix Brown Pink with Van Dyck Brown to soften the value; add this color to the bottom of the abdomen. Moving to the head, use a medium wash of Payne's Grey to paint the middle area, using the same detail brush and hairlike strokes. Switch to Van Dyck Brown again for the area in-between the eyes and add more value to the orange markings using a darker value of Red Orange. Outline the eyes with Van Dyck Brown and paint some dots inside the eyes.

Step 6

Once all the washes are completely dry, use the eraser to gently remove the masking fluid. Load your detail brush with Van Dyck Brown, and continue painting the vein lines over the white area you just uncovered. Switch to your medium brush and a lighter value of Van Dyck Brown to paint some smudges around the veins inside the white area.

Keep using your medium brush and the same color to paint two thick lines at the bottom edge of the forewing. Use your brush to create some smudges above these lines but with a lighter value of Van Dyck Brown. Add more lines across these two lines, using a lighter value and your detail brush. Add two brushstrokes right over the orange markings on the tip of the forewing.

Use your detail brush with a darker value of Van Dyck Brown to outline the forewings and the top stripe. Load your medium brush with a medium value of Red Orange and paint a big smudge right under the eyespots. Switch to Brown Pink, and add a bit of color right over the eyespots, connecting this with the colored part of the wing.

Mix white gouache with a dark value of Phthalocyanine Blue. Use this opaque color and your detail brush to paint a little circle over the two orange markings on the tip of the forewing. Outline it with Payne's Grey.

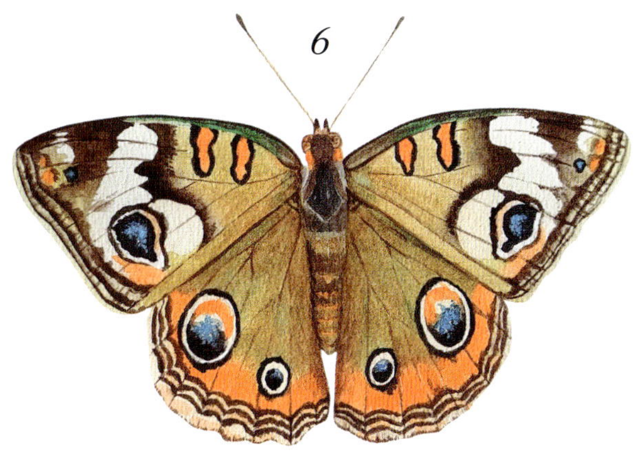

Paint the eyespots in the forewings. First load your detail brush with a dark value of Payne's Grey, and paint the center, leaving some white space around it. Now, create a line all around the entire eyespot spot. Once it dries, use the mixture of white gouache and Phthalocyanine Blue to paint little dots in the center, like scales. To finish, add a light value of Red Orange in the eyespot, in-between the line and the center. Load your detail brush with Emerald Green, and add some wash to the top stripe. Almost done! Use the white gouache and Phthalocyanine Blue mixture to add some dots on the hind wings' eyespots. This butterfly is about to take flight!

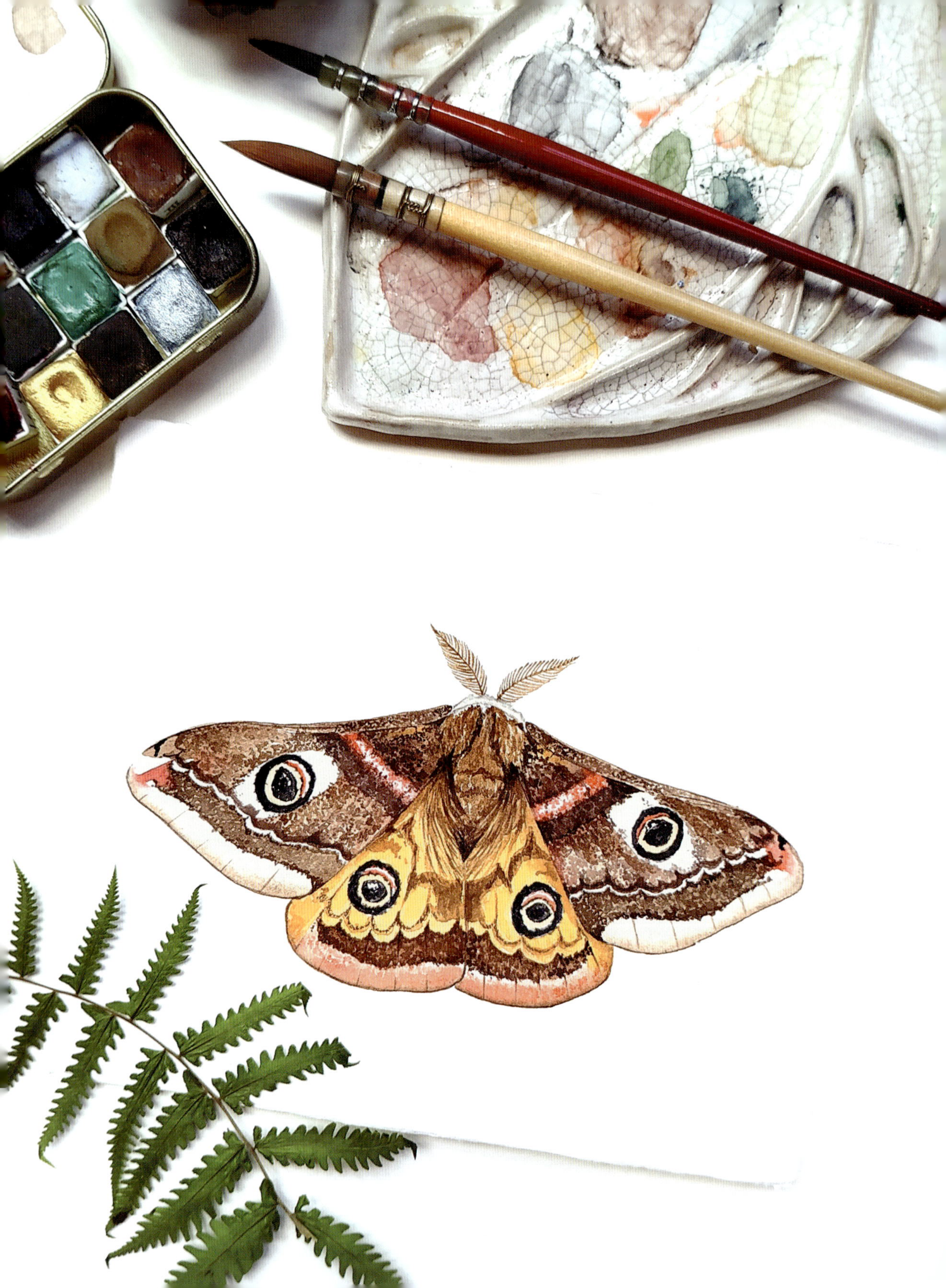

Emperor Moth

Another beautiful moth, the emperor moth (*Saturnia pavonia*) was named after the ringed planet Saturn, as many species have large, ringed spots on their wings. All have larvae, which spin cocoons that we use to produce commercial silk.

Females are gray and only fly at night, and males are more active during the day and more colorful. (You are painting a male for this project.) The eye marks are a warning to predators, portraying the startling face of a much larger creature.

The male antennae are feathered and used to detect the pheromones given off by females. To attract males, the female gives off a potent scent trail of pheromones that can lure males from over a mile away!

Difficulty: Difficult

MATERIALS

- Watercolor paper of your choice
   - I used an 8 x 8–inch (20 x 20–cm) sheet
- Paints
   - Sennelier Yellow Deep, Raw Umber, French Vermilion, Burnt Umber, Alizarin Crimson, Naples Yellow Deep, Van Dyck Brown, Ivory Black, Titanium White
- Brushes
   - Medium round brush (I used size 7)
   - Detail round brush (I used size 1)

Sketch

Draw the moth freehand or trace the reference image and transfer it to the watercolor paper of your choice, focusing on the wing patterns, eyespots, and antennae. Spray your paints with water to moisten them.

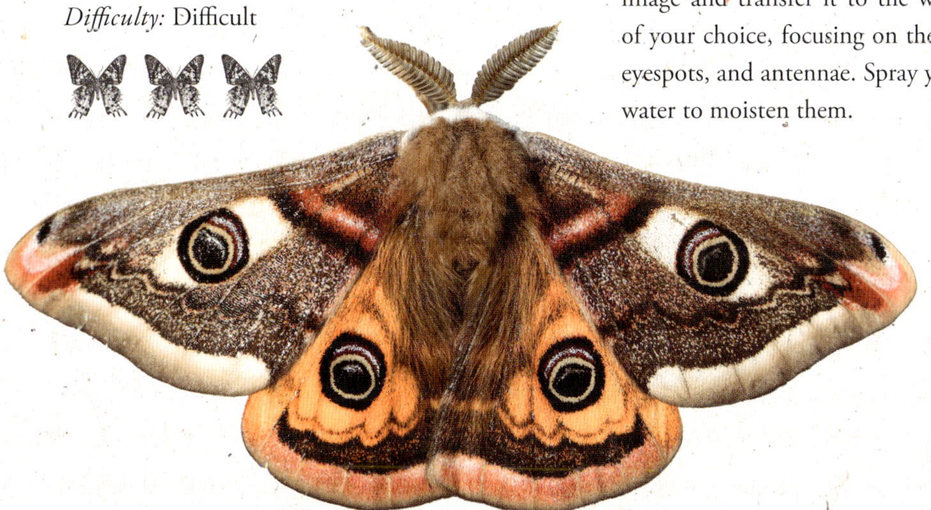

1-2

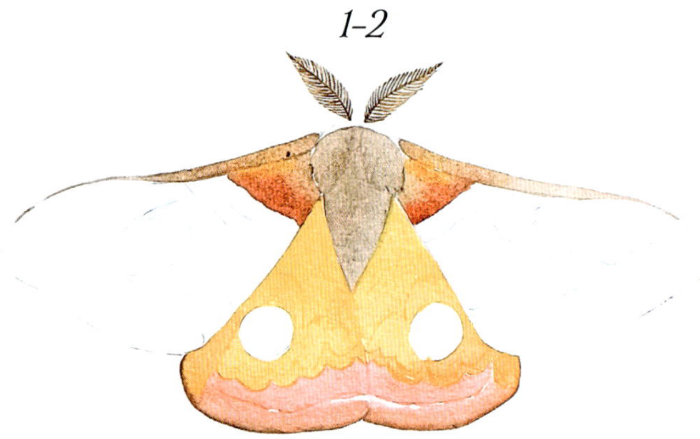

Step 1

Starting with the hind wings, load your medium brush with Sennelier Yellow Deep and paint a medium wash up until the second scalloped line under the eyespots. Don't forget to paint the external scallops on the edges of the hind wings. While you wait for this section to dry, use your detail brush to paint the furry antennae with a mix of Raw Umber and Sennelier Yellow Deep.

Once it's dry, load your medium brush with a very light wash of French Vermilion and paint right below the Sennelier Yellow Deep section, leaving the other half of the bottom edge unpainted for now. Wait until this dries before painting the second half using the same brush and color—letting bits of white peek out between the two washes. Before it dries, outline the bottom edge with your detail brush loaded with Raw Umber. This line should fade into the French Vermilion a little bit. If your painting is dry, smooth the edges with your clean and damp medium brush.

Step 2

Use your medium brush with a light value of Raw Umber to paint the costal margin (the top edges) of both forewings, making the line thinner as you get closer to the edges. With the same brush and Burnt Umber, paint the body section.

Once everything is completely dry, paint the first section of the forewings (connecting the costal margin and the head). Use your medium brush loaded with Alizarin Crimson, and paint the bottom edge of the first section, leaving the part closest to the head white. Before the color dries, change to Burnt Umber and paint the rest of the section. Clean your brush and load it with Naples Yellow Deep. Dot a bit of this color on the upper edge, being careful with the amount of water to make sure it stays where you put it. While it does have to blend with the rest of the colors, you want it to be a clean blending!

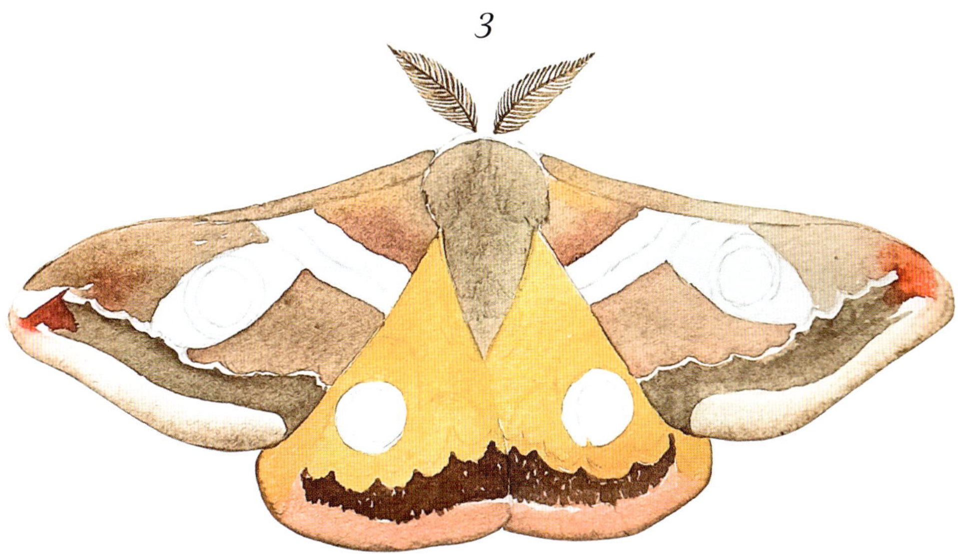

Step 3

Moving to the hind wings, load your medium brush with Van Dyck Brown, and use the tip of your brush to paint hairlike strokes in the middle bottom section of the markings.

While you wait for this to dry, paint the forewings. Load your medium brush with Burnt Umber and paint a light wash over the third section of the wings, saving the eyespots and the two line markings that separate both sections for later. Before it dries, dot a bit of Alizarin Crimson on both external edges of the forewings.

Load the same brush with Raw Umber and paint the next section on the forewings, leaving a blank space between the sections. Once this section is dry, with the same brush loaded with Alizarin Crimson, paint a brushstroke on the tip of the wings pointing inwards. It doesn't have to be perfect—it's just a touch of the brush.

Clean your medium brush and dampen the last section of the forewing with clear water. Then, load your detail brush with Raw Umber and outline the forewings' bottom edge to create a nice gradient. (Your paper should be damp but not with a lot of water so you have a bit of control over where the paint goes!)

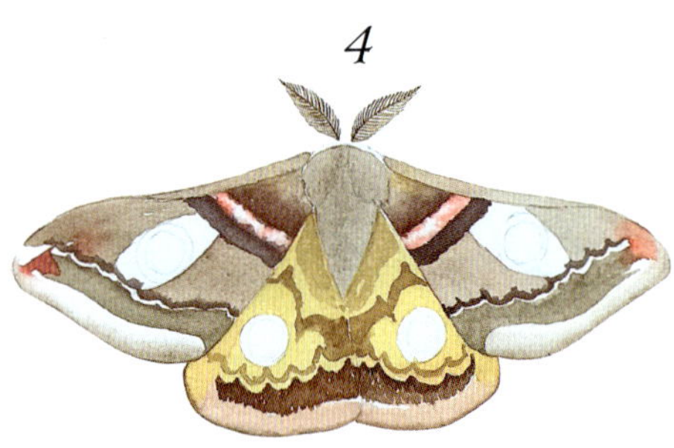

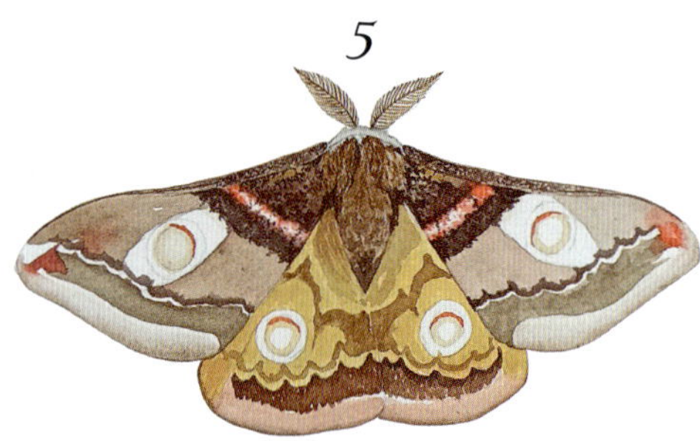

Step 4

Back to the hind wings to build the second layer of color! Load your medium brush with a light wash of Van Dyck Brown and paint the area around the abdomen. Use the same brush with a more saturated value of Van Dyck Brown to paint the first layer of the patterned veins and markings.

While the hind wings dry, use your medium brush to add a wash Van Dyck Brown over the Alizarin Crimson you painted in Step 2. While the colors are still damp, add a light wash of clear water to the first line you left untouched. Blend French Vermilion on both ends of that first line. It's okay if a bit of brown runs over it. Then paint the second line with Van Dyck Brown.

Move down to the bottom of the third forewing section. Add a line of Van Dyck Brown right on top of the blank space you left on the previous step. Let this dry.

Tip: To increase intensity of watercolors, it's always best to add layers rather than painting with a lot of pigment. Watercolors should be always translucent!

Step 5

Once the first layers of paint are dry, we can start to add details. Start with the head. Use a really light value of Ivory Black, and use your detail brush to outline the head to create depth.

Wait until this dries, and then load the detail brush with Burnt Umber to paint the fluffy texture on the abdomen. Create layers of thin strokes along the body with different values of the color from light to dark. Switch to Van Dyck Brown to get the darkest details—especially on the bottom corner of the abdomen. Once this dries, load the brush with Titanium White, and paint a light wash on the head and going a little into the abdomen area.

Keep using your detail brush with Naples Yellow Deep to paint the eyespot circles. Wait until dry, and switch to French Vermilion to paint a semicircle line over the yellow.

Keep using your detail brush and loaded with Van Dyck Brown, paint dots over the brown areas on the top half of the moth. This is a more intuitive step, but start on both forewings, covering the whole area. Use a fingertip to smooth the dots.

6-7

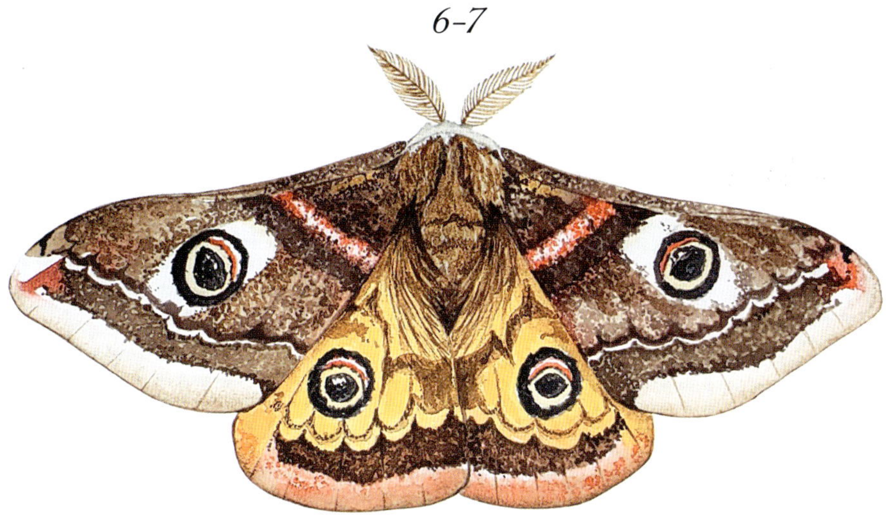

Step 6

Use your detail brush and Ivory Black to paint around and inside the eyespots. Also paint tiny dots between the yellow and the red. Keep using your detail brush to add more dots on the forewings, avoiding the white areas. Paint these dots with the three different shades of brown.

Then use a saturated value of Van Dyck Brown to paint a line of dots right on top of the forewing edge as well around the red marking. Switch to Raw Sienna and paint the veins on this area. Once everything is dry, use a very diluted wash of French Vermilion to paint a light wash to the middle of the forewing. Mix equal amounts of Ivory Black and Van Dyck Brown to paint a few more dots over the upper section of the forewing and to outline the wings with a really thin line.

Step 7

Work with Van Dyck Brown and your detail brush to add depth to the hairy abdomen area with some darker lines around the fluffy areas, the bottom of the abdomen, and the two lines that separate the abdomen sections. Keep using your detail brush to add some long lines on the hind wings' top edges, where the wings merge.

Fill out the markings with your medium brush and Van Dyck Brown, painting bigger dots and brushstrokes to the wider areas and little dots over the markings and veins. (Change to the detail brush, if necessary, for the smaller dots.) You are almost done!

Use Van Dyck Brown and your detail brush to add more dots to the last section of the hind wings. Then paint lines for the veins. Load your medium brush with French Vermilion to add a few more dots over the bottom section of the hind wings, and your emperor moth is done!

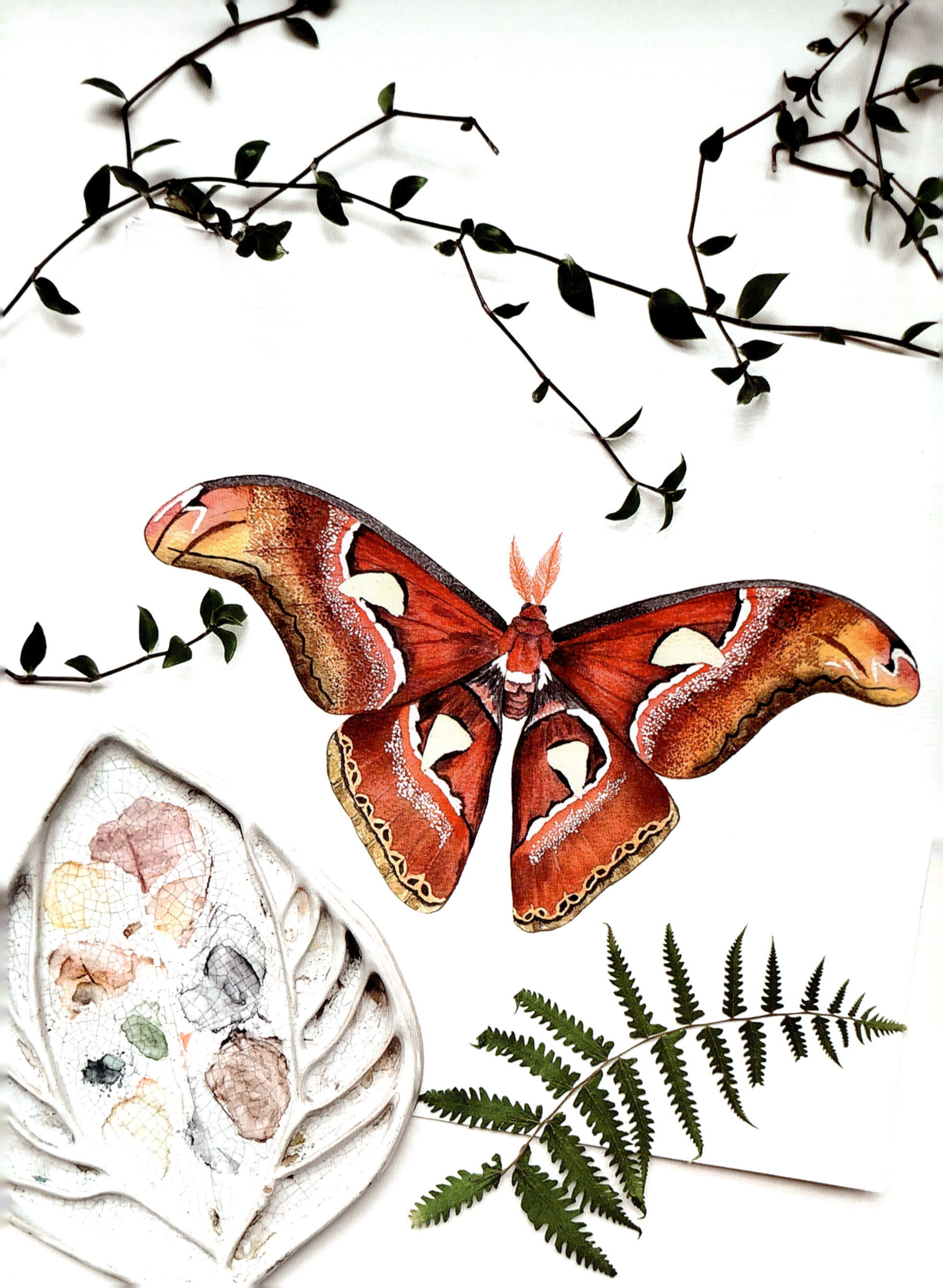

Atlas Moth

The Atlas moth is one of the largest moths in the world. Its massive wingspan is wider than a human hand. But despite their large size, they do not feed at all after they have emerged from the cocoon! Their proboscis, which other butterflies and moths use to drink nectar, is tiny and does not work. Without the ability to feed, Atlas moths only manage between one and two weeks of life before the energy to power their huge wings runs out. Atlas moths are perhaps most famous for the markings on the upper corner of their wings, which bear an uncanny resemblance to cobra heads.

This is one of the most difficult projects in the book, but also one of the most rewarding! Are you ready for it? Let's paint one of the most beautiful moths!

Difficulty: Difficult

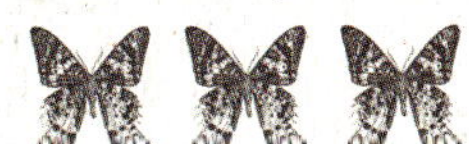

MATERIALS

- Watercolor paper of your choice
    - I used a 12 x 13–inch (30 x 33–cm) sheet, landscape orientation
- Paints
    - Bright Red, Alizarin Crimson, Ivory Black, Carmine, Raw Umber, Sennelier Yellow Deep, Indian Yellow, Opera Rose, Caput Mortuum, Red Orange, Van Dyck Brown, Raw Sienna
- Brushes
    - Old brush for masking fluid (I used a round size 2)
    - Medium round brush (I used size 6)
    - Detail round brush (I used size 2)
    - Liner brush (I used size 0)
- Masking fluid and eraser (to remove)

Sketch

Draw the moth freehand or trace the reference image and transfer it to the watercolor paper of your choice. Spray your paints with water to moisten them.

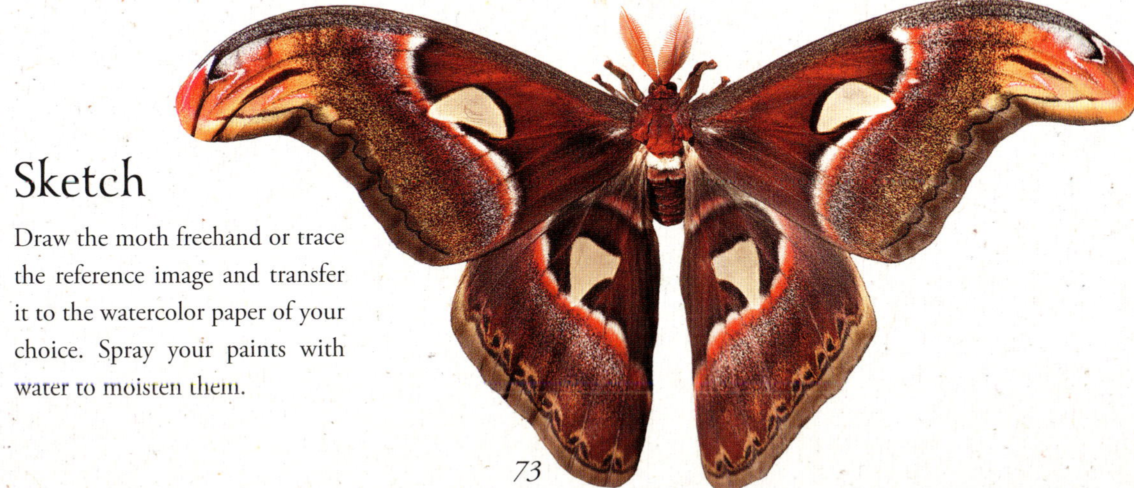

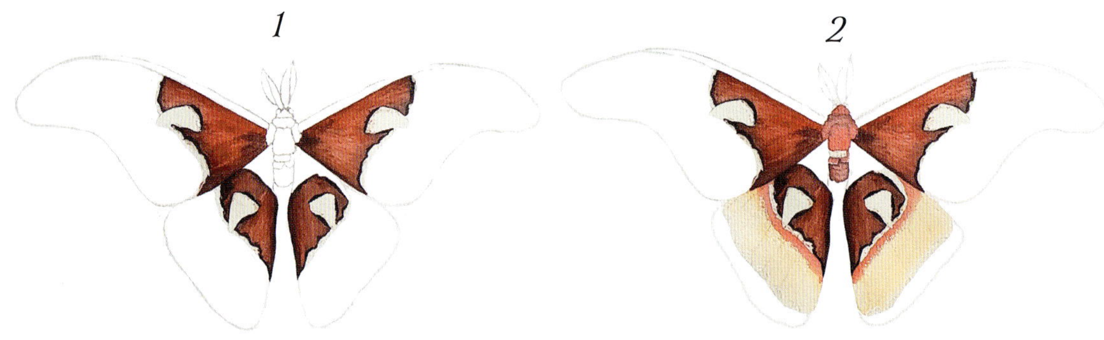

Step 1

Use an old, small brush to apply masking fluid to all of the white areas seen in the finished photo of this tutorial. Mask the white dots on all four wings by applying small amounts of masking fluid in a dotting motion. Then, mask the four eye spots and the four wavy lines just below them. Mask the bottom of both hind wings around each black eye-shaped marking.

Once the masking fluid is completely dry, load your medium brush with Bright Red and paint a medium wash over both forewings. (If you feel like it's drying too quickly, and you can't paint the washes correctly, work with one forewing at a time.) While still damp, use the same brush with Alizarin Crimson to paint lines along the wings, creating texture. Add a bit of Ivory Black to the Alizarin Crimson, and blend a bit of this darker color where the wings join the body. Switch to your detail brush and outline the bottom edges of both forewings with the mixture.

Wait until dry to paint Ivory Black over the white areas (over the masking fluid), using your detail brush. Load your medium brush with Bright Red and paint a medium wash on the middle section of the hind wings.

While still damp, load the same brush with Alizarin Crimson and paint a few brushstrokes along the hind wings. Change to your detail brush and Ivory Black to outline the red area (while still damp), allowing the red to blend a bit with the black. Once the surface is dry, paint the lines around the triangular markings.

Step 2

With your medium brush, paint each section of the body separately with Bright Red, and outline each section with a mix of Bright Red and Ivory Black to create depth. The reason for painting each section separately is to help establish the lines between each section instead of them blending all together.

While the bottom part of the abdomen is still damp, paint some lines with your detail brush and Ivory Black across this section.

Move to the hind wings. Use your medium brush to paint a medium wash of Carmine under the masking fluid line, and before it dries, add a wash of Raw Umber down to the next masking fluid line (where the little eye-shaped circles are). Let it dry.

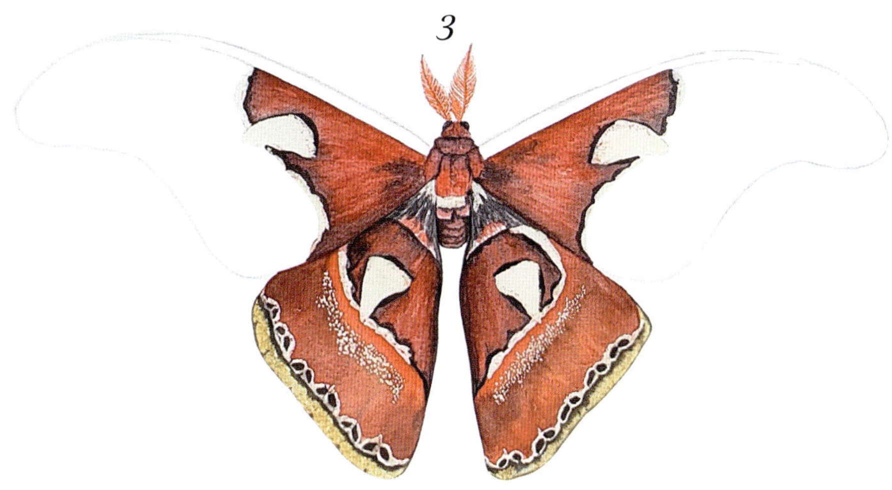

Step 3

Paint the feathered antennae with Bright Red and your liner brush. Change to your detail brush and Ivory Black to paint the eyes. Once these are dry, use the same brush loaded with Alizarin Crimson to paint a second wash over the body area, except for the bottom section. Then, with the detail brush, outline each section with a medium value of Ivory Black. Gently wet the surface of the bottom section of the body with your detail brush, allowing the colors to mix a bit. Paint the previous lines (from Step 2) with a more saturated value of Ivory Black, and also paint the shadows around the body. It doesn't matter if the black runs into the red slightly—it will help make it look more rounded.

Load your medium brush with Alizarin Crimson and paint a medium wash on the hind wings, over the previous Raw Umber color. Use a clean brush with water to soften the part where it transitions with the Carmine, just above the little dots.

Because we have the masking fluid border, you don't need to wait until dry to keep painting. Change to your detail brush and load it with a dark value of Ivory Black to fill in all eye-shaped markings inside the masking fluid. Also paint a line just under the eyespots. While still wet, load your medium brush with Sennelier Yellow Deep and paint the bottom section of the hind wings, allowing the black and yellow to blend a bit. Wait until this section dries to add a bit of texture by dabbing a darker value of the same yellow with the tip of your brush. Use your liner brush to outline the hind wings' bottom edge with Ivory Black, and add a little line upwards to create the end of the veins.

To finish this step, use your detail brush to paint the upper section of the hind wings. Use your brush with Ivory Black with just a little water to paint lines down the section, with different values of the black to create texture. Change to Alizarin Crimson, and paint the part that's closer to the white marking. Use the tip of your brush to paint lines, creating a hairy effect. Let it dry.

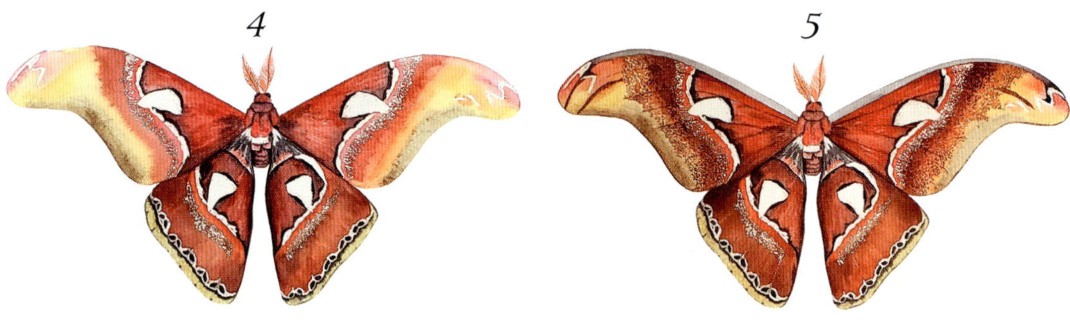

Step 4

Load your medium brush with Carmine and cover the little dots. Then change to Indian Yellow, and continue painting almost to the bottom. Add a dash of Opera Rose to the tip of the wings and a light wash of Raw Umber to the bottom part. Use enough water for the colors to blend, and use a paper towel to ensure that the colors don't bleed too much into each other. Let it dry.

> **Tip:** *Have all the color ready in your palette to avoid the colors drying between transitions.*

Step 5

Use your medium brush and a light wash of Ivory Black for the costal margin of the fore-wings. Add more value at the end of the wings, and paint the black marks at the tips. Next, switch to your liner brush to paint the veins using Ivory Black. To paint these lines, vary the pressure you put on your brush while painting to create a more organic line with parts that are thin (almost disappearing) and parts that are thick and bold. This will give the veins a more realistic look.

Keep working on the forewings, painting all the dots that will make this moth look lively. Load your detail brush with Caput Mortuum, and start adding dots just under the white spots, and then change to Red Orange as you go down, allowing yourself to play a bit in this area by mixing all the shades to create a scale-like texture.

Use your detail brush and Alizarin Crimson to paint the line across the tips of the forewings. While that begins to dry, outline both fore-wings with a light value of Van Dyck Brown.

Load your medium brush with Caput Mortuum to add a third layer of paint down the hind wings to the bottom section. Start with a dark value on the upper edge and lighten the value as you go towards the middle, leaving some spaces unpainted where the veins should go. Work your way to the inner edge of each hind wing, and saturate the color again as you get closer to the end of each wing, creating a nice guradient. Use the reference photo on page 73, if needed.

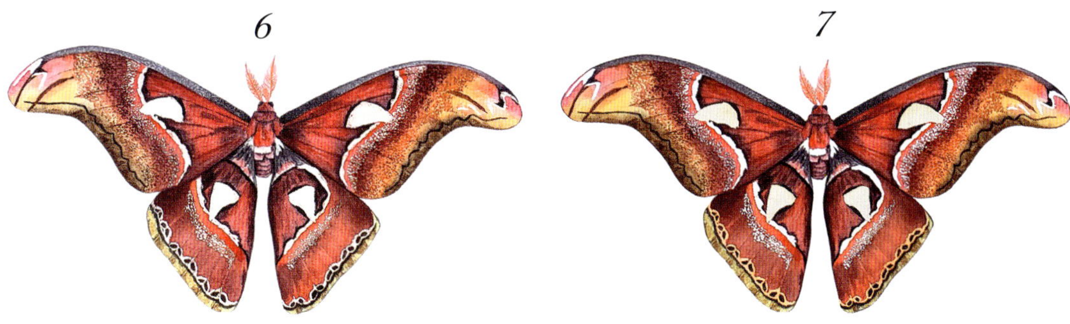

Step 6

Now, let's finish the hind wings. Mix Alizarin Crimson with Ivory Black to create a very dark red, and use your medium brush to add volume to the hind wings' middle section. Use the wet-and-dry technique to add brushstrokes along this part and especially on the side edges of the red section. Load your medium brush with Raw Umber to paint the bottom edges of the hind wings. Add thick, vertical lines in the yellow area, creating the creases of the wing. With the Ivory Black and your liner brush, outline the hind wings with a very thin line. Do the same to the forewings, but with mixing Ivory Black with Alizarin Crimson to paint some darker areas over the middle red section.

Use your medium brush and Van Dyck Brown to darken the bottom edge of the forewings. Let it dry. Switch to your detail brush to paint the zigzag markings on the bottom edge of both forewings. Load the same brush with Alizarin Crimson to paint more veins over the dotted area. Switch to your detail brush to paint the costal margin of the forewings with more dots, using a higher value of Ivory Black and watering down the value as you get closer to the tip of the wings.

Step 7

Once completely dry, use the eraser to gently remove the masking fluid. Load the detail brush with Red Orange and fill in the space around the black eye-shaped markings. Paint a very light wash of Raw Sienna inside the four triangle-shaped markings.

When I was painting this tutorial, a real Atlas moth landed on my desk! So this is one of the most special tutorials because I took that as a good sign!

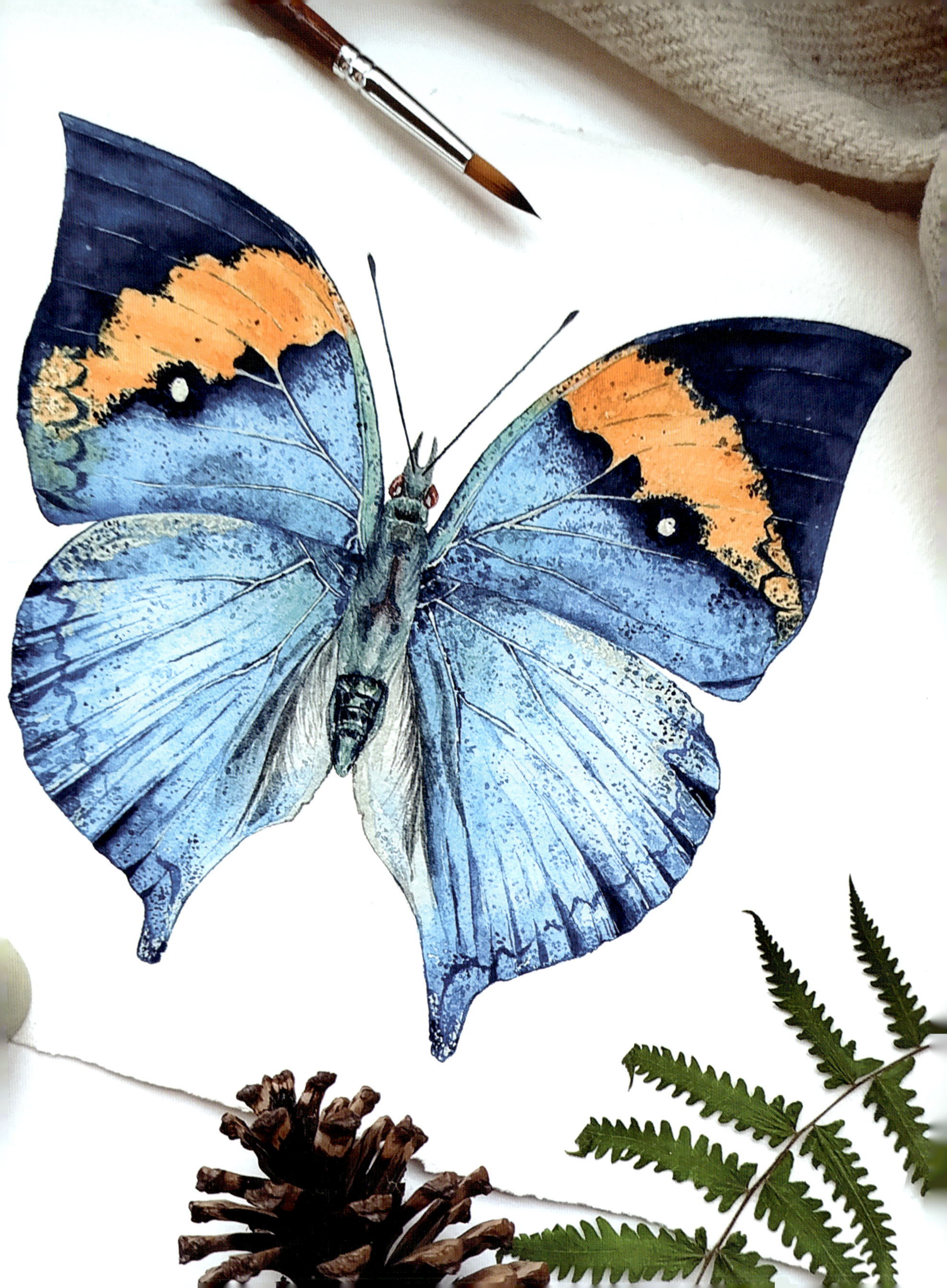

Orange Oakleaf Butterfly

This beautiful butterfly, known as the orange oakleaf butterfly (*Kallima inachus*), is native to Asia. When its wings are closed, it looks exactly like a dried autumn leaf, giving it the cleverest camouflage a butterfly could want. But when its wings are open, it reveals a luminous color pattern that can hold its own against the world's prettiest wings! And what's especially cool about this insect is that it changes its look with the seasons.

An absolutely beautiful specimen.

Difficulty: Difficult

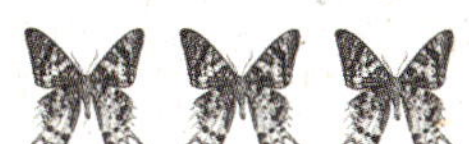

Sketch

Draw the butterfly freehand or trace the reference image and transfer it to the water-color paper of your choice, focusing on the wing patterns, veins, and eyespots. Spray your paints with water to moisten them.

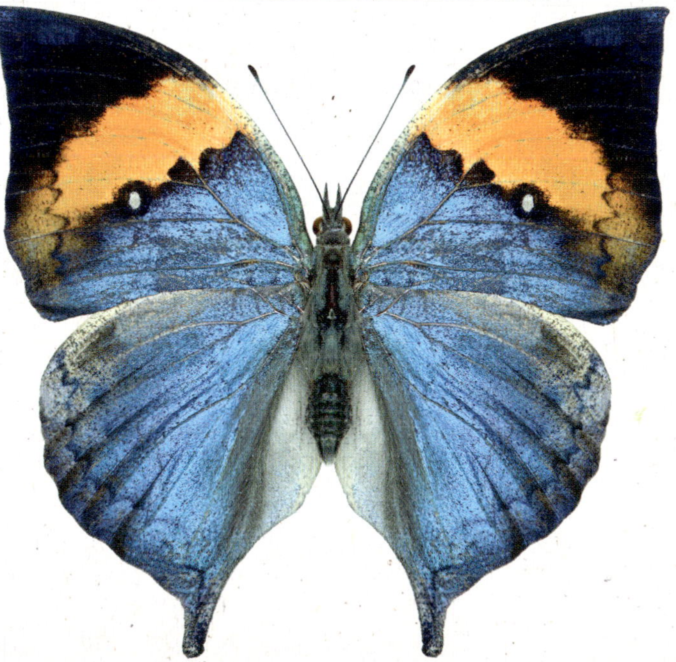

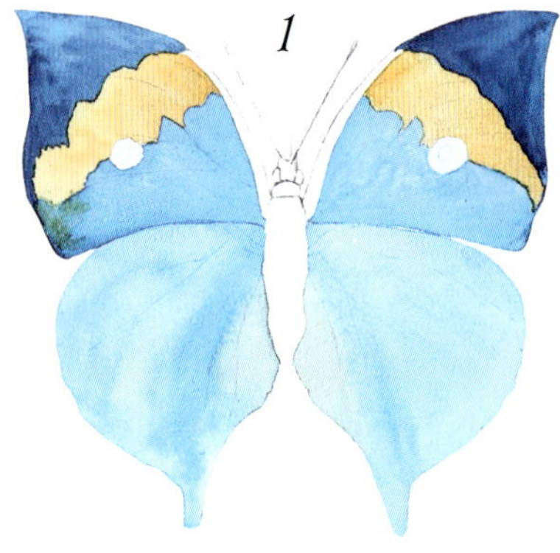

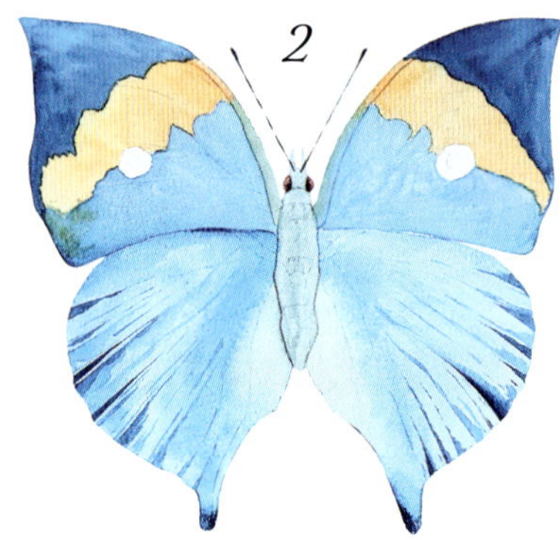

Step 1

Load your medium brush with Phthalocyanine Blue and starting on the left forewing, paint a light wash over the upper section. Skipping over the middle stripe, switch to Cinereous Blue, and continue painting the lower section of the wing. Wait until dry to paint the middle stripe with Red Orange. Save the eyespot for later. Repeat the process for the right forewing.

Once the forewings are dry, load the same brush with Cinereous Blue, and create a light wash over the left hind wing. While the wash is still wet, load your brush with a very diluted Ivory Black and continue painting the inner section of the hind wing. Repeat for the right hind wing. Let it dry.

Step 2

Mix Emerald Green with a bit of Ivory Black to create an ash-blue color for the body. Load your medium brush with this mix and paint a medium wash over the body and head. Once dry, switch to your detail brush and Caput Mortuum to paint the little eyes. Add a bit of shadow to the corner of the eyes with Ivory Black. Load your detail brush with Cinereous Blue and paint the antennae. Switch to Ivory Black and paint over the Cinereous Blue—just a few lines along them and the tips.

Paint the top stripe of the forewings with your detail brush loaded with Emerald Green for the the part closer to the body. Switch to Red Orange at the middle stripe and allow the colors to blend a bit.

Now you're going to start creating the creases of the hind wings. Load your detail brush with a light value of the Cinereous Blue, and start creating lines from the bottom of the hind wings towards the center. For this you need to use the reference photo on page 79, but also allow your creativity to flow! Switch to Phthalocyanine Blue and keep creating lines. The thicker lines should be lighter than the thin ones.

Paint the lower tips of the hind wings with a darker value of Phthalocyanine Blue, and paint a thin line separating both wings. Let this dry. Paint a wash of Emerald Green over the center of both hind wings, and soften the edges with clear water to preserve the color in the middle area. Rest your hand while you wait for this to dry.

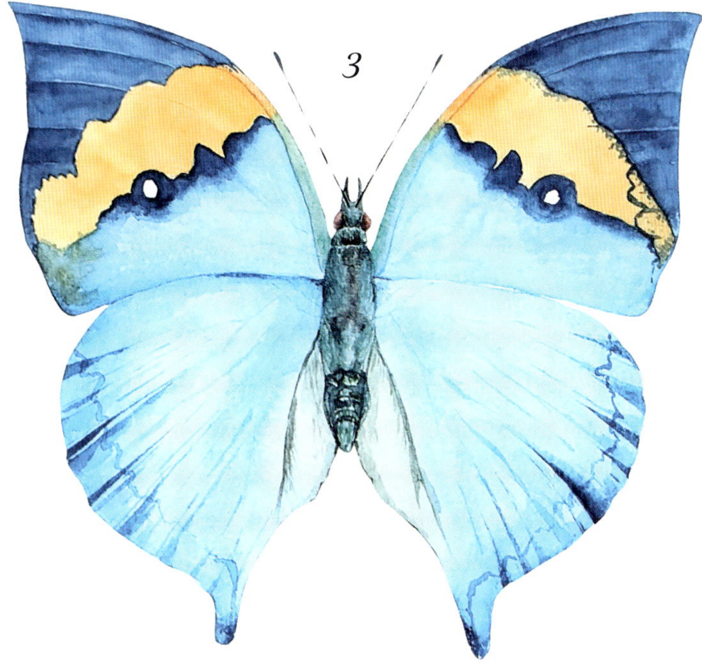

Step 3

Load your medium brush with Phthalocyanine Blue and paint a second wash over the upper section of the forewings. Instead of painting the wash over the whole area, paint in sections, leaving a space between each section to create a line between them.

Create a water wash over the lower section with your medium brush, right under the orange area, and load your brush with a dark value of Phthalocyanine Blue to darken the area around the eyespots and the orange markings.

While you wait for this to dry, work on the body. Switch to your detail brush and mix Emerald Green and Ivory Black on your palette. With this mixture start adding lines around the eyes and the different sections of the body. Paint a line down the middle of the abdomen and soften the edges with a clean brush. Once it's dry, use the same brush to paint hairlike strokes from the body's edge towards the center. Once this is dry, add more darkness to the head with Ivory Black and your detail brush; paint dots and hair-like lines.

Use the mixture of Emerald Green with a bit of Ivory Black and your detail brush to add a line separating both colors on the hind wings (where you painted the light value of Ivory Black on Step 1). Paint hairlike strokes towards the center in different values of the mixture.

Step 4

Repeat the process in Step 3, and add another wash on the upper section of the forewings, adding value especially on the costal margin of the wings and tips. For this, use your medium brush and once again, the Phthalocyanine Blue. The only difference here is that you will be adding dots inside the orange area and the top stripe on the forewings. For these details, switch to your detail brush. Add a line along the top stripe too, from where the wing merges with the body to where the orange starts. Keep adding dots all over the forewing area—even add some inside the orange area. Use a fingertip to soften some of these spots. Make some bigger than others. This will create a nice texture.

Keep using your detail brush to paint the veins with Phthalocyanine Blue. Try to paint these lines very thinly—not even touching the paper with your brush all the time.

Can you see the scalloped markings on the side of the wings? Paint those using your detail brush and Phthalocyanine Blue. It's like a zigzag line across the lower section of the forewing.

Moving down, let's work on the hind wings while we wait for the forewings to dry. Use your detail brush and Phthalocyanine Blue to paint the veins, using your brush the same way as you did for the veins on the forewings, not

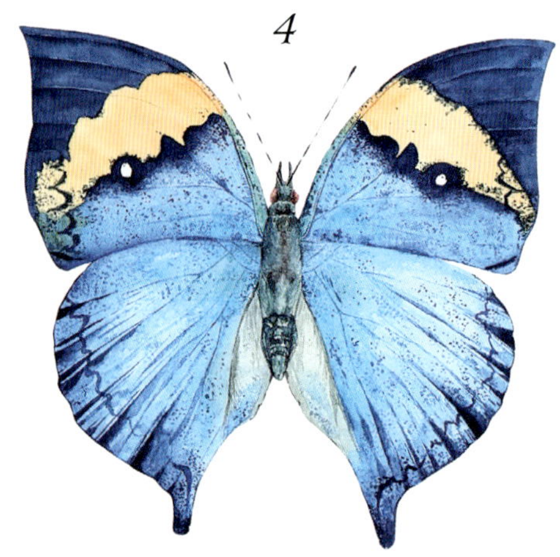

putting so much pressure to get those lines a bit imperfect. Switch to your medium brush to create a light wash of Cinereous Blue over the Ivory Black area (inside area of the hind wings). Let it dry.

Use the tip of your detail brush loaded with Phthalocyanine Blue to paint dots all over the hind wing area. Once the dots are dry, work on the creases again. Use a darker value of Phthalocyanine Blue than before, and paint darker lines on the same area, creating depth.

Using the same brush and color, paint the zigzag lines over the same lines you painted in the previous step, across the lower edge of the hind wings, and add a bit of a darker color in both tips of the hind wings. Also outline the lower section of the hind wings.

Step 5

Paint another wash over the top edge of the forewings with Indigo and your medium brush, respecting the lighter lines.

Under the orange area, add another wash of Indigo, softening the edges with your clean medium brush. Switch to your detail brush and create more dots on both forewings and hind wings using a darker value of Indigo. Keep using your detail brush to paint the veins. Where you already had a line, paint another one parallel to it, with a dark value of Indigo. Use the tip of your detail brush to darken the area where the wings meet the body. To do this, add more dots together instead of painting just one brushstroke. This will make your illustration look more cohesive since you are using dots all over the wing area.

Switch to the previous mix of Emerald Green and Ivory Black to add a long line right above the previous lines you painted in Step 3 on the bottom inner edge of the hind wings. Create a deeper orange by mixing Venetian Red with a bit of Indian Yellow, and use this and your medium brush to add texture and value to the orange markings, extending the sections made on the wing tips. Paint brushstrokes along the area, leaving some spots unpainted, and lightening the value as you get down.

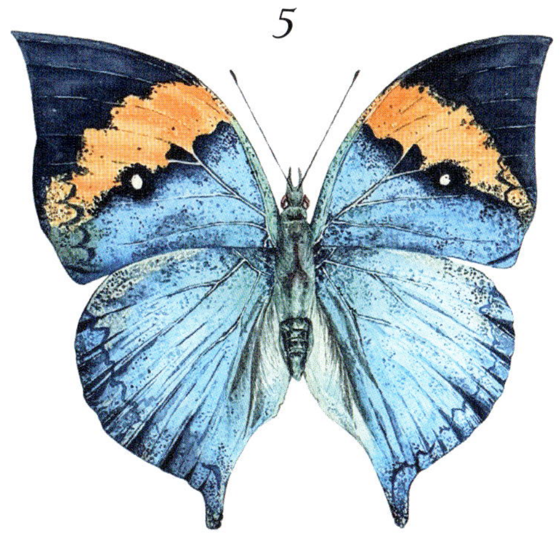

To finish this special butterfly, I'm going to teach you my favorite trick. Add a dash of white gouache to your palette, and then use a bit of the watercolor of your choice to create a pastel color that's not going to be translucent to create the last details on the wings. I used Emerald Green and a bit of Ivory Black with the gouache.

Use your detail brush and paint inside the space you created in the veins. Start close to the body and lighten the value as you get closer to the edges. On the top edge of the hind wings, paint a white shadow. Use your detail brush to make circles around the dots in the area, filling the space. Lastly, add a bright white dot to both eyes. (This will make the eyes come to life.) Fill in the eyespots with white gouache too.

This stunning butterfly is ready to fly, and you should applaud yourself for accomplishing this project!

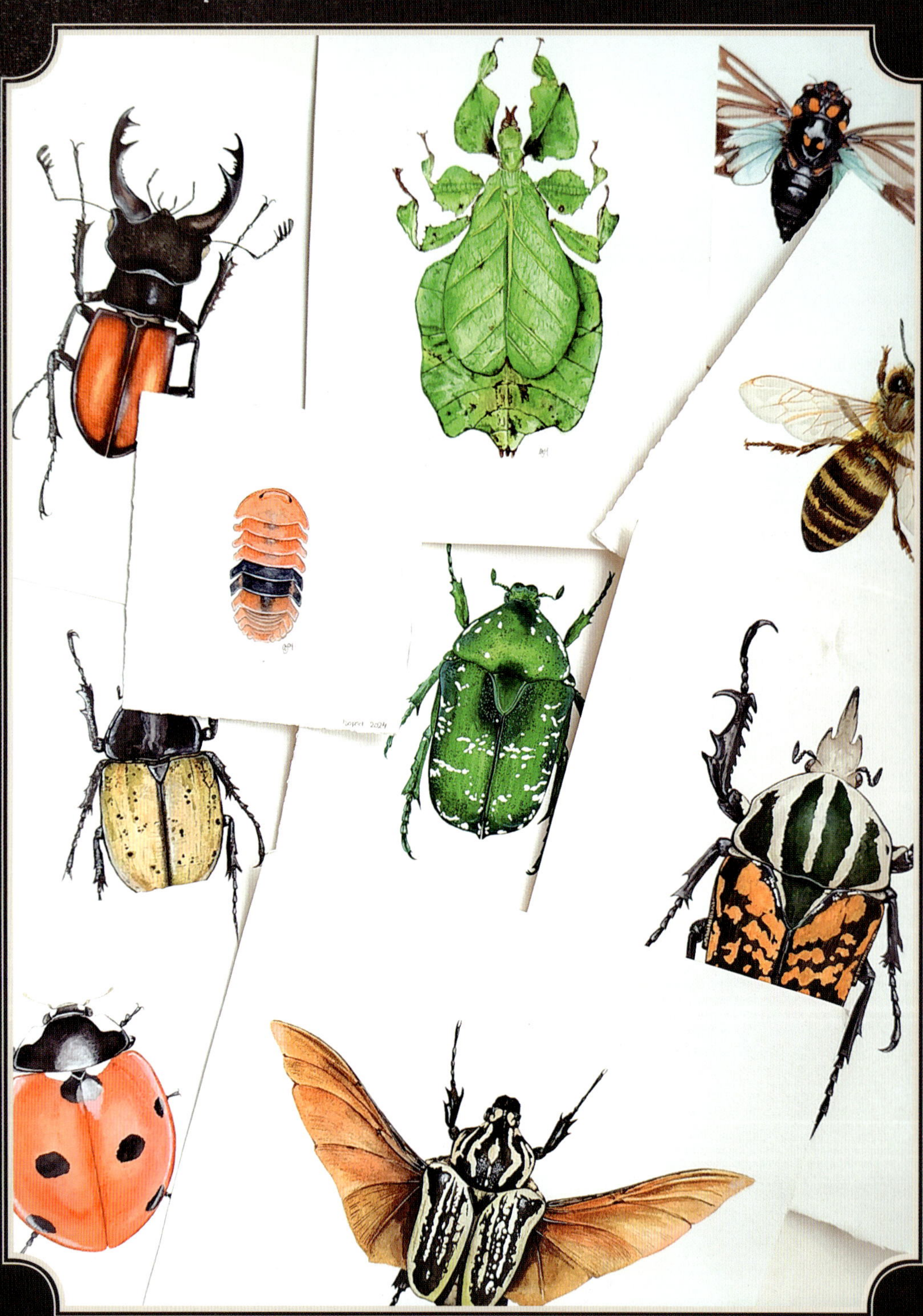

Insectarium

Have you ever sat down on the grass or on a log when you go hiking, and stayed still? Breathing lightly, becoming one with your surroundings? If you manage to stay like this for a while, a tiny hidden world will appear. It's a magical world full of amazing creatures. They have a few more legs than us, as well as wings and armor. I like to call them the little Earth dwellers. Many people dislike these important creatures because we have been told that they are icky or dangerous, but most of these little guys are more afraid of you than you are of them! In this chapter, I introduce you to some of them.

The magnificent Hercules Beetle (page 87), one of the largest flying insects in the world, is a medium difficulty project. Meanwhile the cute Roly-Poly (page 127), which comes in so many more colors than the gray one we all know, is a great project to start with due to the simplicity of its shape.

Once you think you have a bit of control over the techniques used in those tutorials, you can go ahead and paint the Cicada (page 131), which might look easy, but the delicacy of its wings makes it one of the most fun projects on this chapter.

What's great about this chapter (at least for me!), is that once you start painting all these insects, you are going to appreciate them more, pay more attention to their tiny legs, and learn about their curious anatomy.

Get your supplies ready, look for a nice bright spot to set up everything, and let's start!

Tip: I'll be referencing body parts of insects in these instructions. They include the three main divisions of insects: the head, the thorax (the middle), and the abdomen (mostly the wing covers, in terms of painting). Also, the elytra (singular is elytron) are the wing casings; the pronotum is the upper section of the body; and the scutellum, is the triangular-shaped piece between the wing covers.

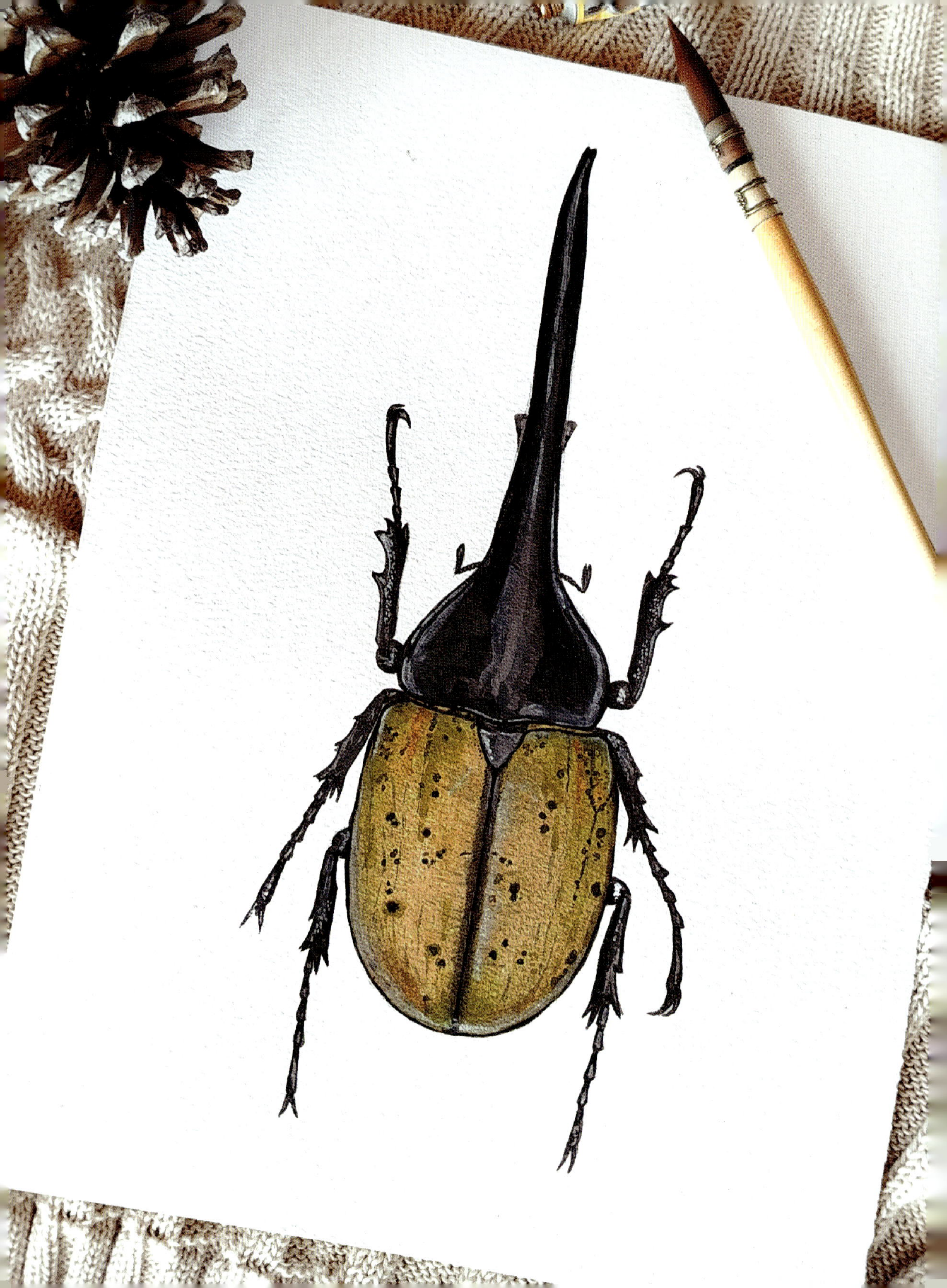

Hercules Beetle

Dynastes hercules is known for its tremendous strength and is named after Hercules, the hero of classical mythology famed for his great strength.

While some say Hercules beetles can carry up to 850 times their bodyweight, more realistic estimates hover around 100 times. Still, this feat is nothing short of Herculean for any insect or animal, regardless of size.

Difficulty: Easy

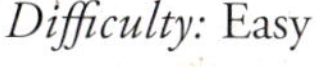

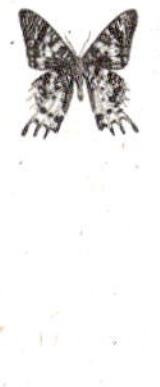

- ♦ Watercolor paper of your choice
  - › I used an 8 x 10–inch (20 x 25–cm) sheet, vertical orientation
- ♦ Paints
  - › Raw Sienna, Brown Pink, Ivory Black, Gold Ochre
  - › White gouache
- ♦ Brushes
  - › Medium round brush (I used size 8)
  - › Detail round brush (I used size 1)

Sketch

Draw the beetle freehand or trace the reference image and transfer it to the watercolor paper of your choice, focusing on the shape of the horn. Spray your paints with water to moisten them.

Step 1

Use your medium brush to paint the first wash of Raw Sienna over the wing covers (the elytra). Switch to Brown Pink and apply some color on the bottom and top and a bit in the middle. This doesn't have to be exact—let the colors blend and do their thing. Next, load your detail brush with a medium value of Ivory Black to outline the wing covers, and then switch to your medium brush to paint two thick lines down the center with the same color.

Paint these lines one at a time, first the right side and then the left. Use the tip of your brush to deposit the color right at the center line, and let the color bleed inside.

> *Tip: If the color bleeds too much into the center, dot a bit of Raw Sienna to stop it from getting into the middle.*

Switch to Gold Ochre and dot some paint, making a line on the top section of the wing covers, creating a thin line and a dot right next to it. Paint a curved line on the bottom too.

Now work on the legs. Paint a medium wash of Ivory Black using your detail brush on all six legs. With the same brush and medium wash of Ivory Black, paint the little antennae, the scutellum, and paint the thorax and head, darkening the value as you get to the horn. Lastly, use a light value to paint the two protuberances (the tiny triangle shapes) coming out of the horn. Let it dry.

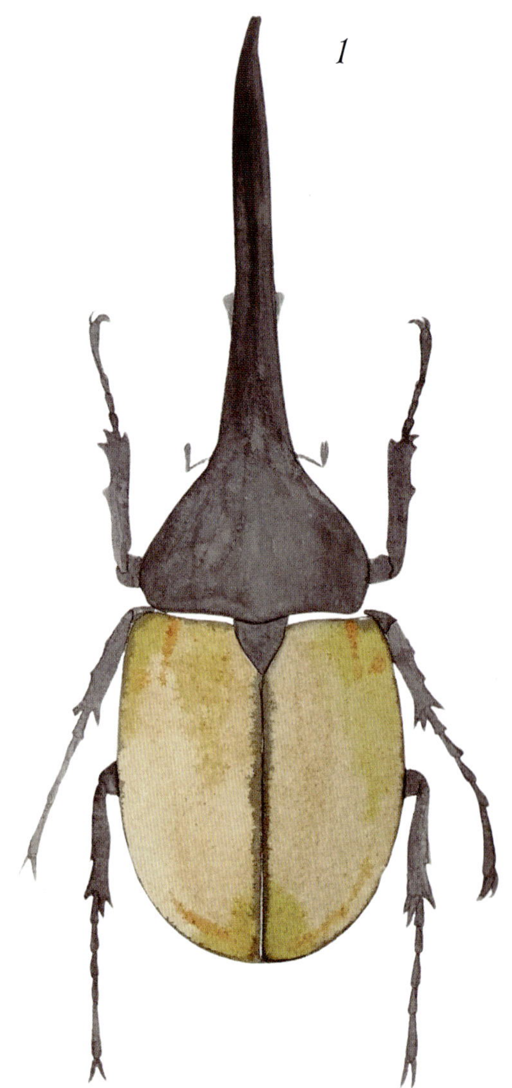

Step 2

Load your medium brush with a darker value of Raw Sienna to paint another wash over the wing covers. While this is still wet, switch to your detail brush and Ivory Black to again outline the wing covers and paint the two lines in the center. It's important to create washes instead of trying to paint everything on the first step! Watercolor requires a lot of patience.

Keep using your detail brush to add dots on the wing covers. Look at the photo reference on page 87 or let your inner artist take care of this step. Each beetle has different freckles, so there's no wrong way to go here. As you paint the surface, it's going to start drying, and this is okay—this way you'll get some faded dots and more accurate ones.

Once you are happy with the number of dots, create creases (painting shaky lines) over the wing covers. If the paper is already dry after you are done with the lines, wait until these lines are dry and paint a water wash over the whole area to soften the lines a bit.

Step 3

Work on the legs' definitions. Load your detail brush with a dark value of Ivory Black, and paint the areas where the light wouldn't hit, for example, the inner edges of the legs and the joints between segments.

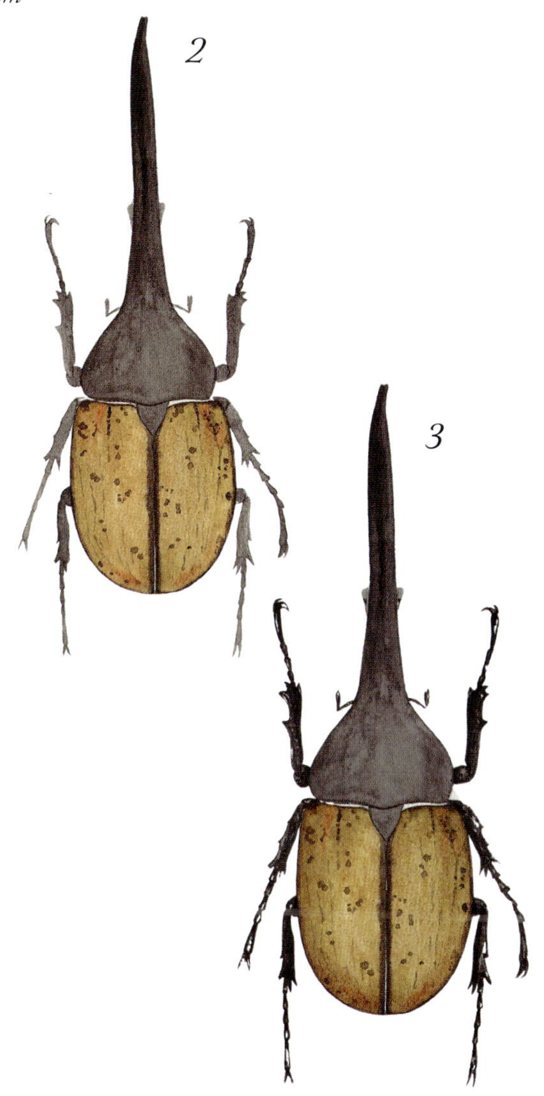

Use the tip of your brush to add dots and create some texture. I added bigger dots on the inner side of the legs and lines imitating the creases of the skin. Do the same with the little antennae. Outline the tip and paint tiny circles over the antennae stalks. Let it dry.

Step 4

Keep using Ivory Black to create some dimension over the thorax and head area (which in this beetle, happen to be together). Load your medium brush with Ivory Black, and paint a dark wash on both the right and left sides, leaving the middle lighter, softening the area with your clean brush.

Move to the abdomen area, outline it again using a darker value of Ivory Black and your detail brush. Repaint some of the dots, making them look bolder, and also paint some of the line creases a bit darker.

Switch to your medium brush, and load it with a medium value of Ivory Black to add value to the center stripes. Use the brush with some pressure to create these thick stripes. First create one, and once it's dry, create the other one. This way, you'll get a more defined line in the middle. When everything is dry, switch to your detail brush to paint a few tiny dots over the stripes.

There's a space between the abdomen and the thorax. Paint a medium wash of Raw Sienna in this area, using your detail brush. Once this is dry, add some dots inside it. For the scutellum, load your detail brush with Ivory Black and outline it, adding some color inside towards the left side, creating the effect that the light is hitting on the right side.

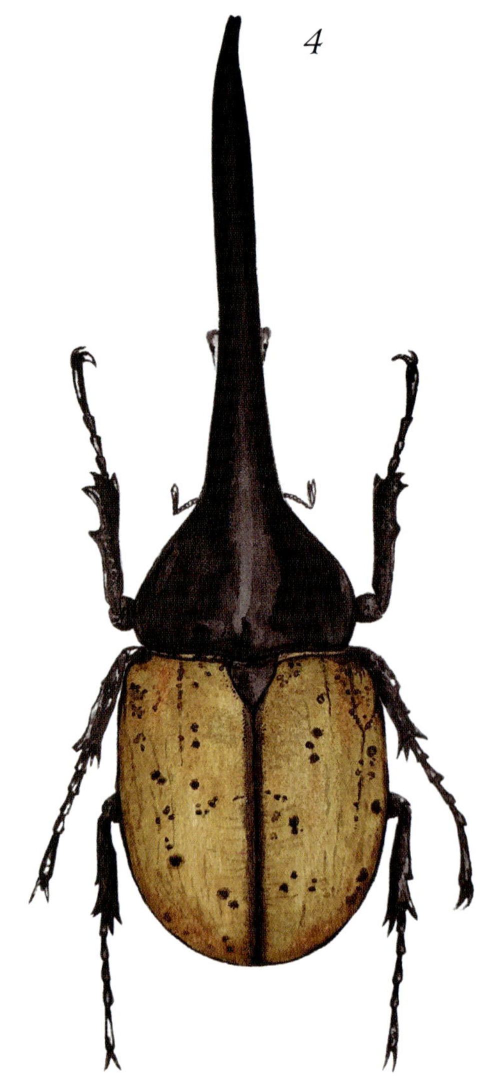

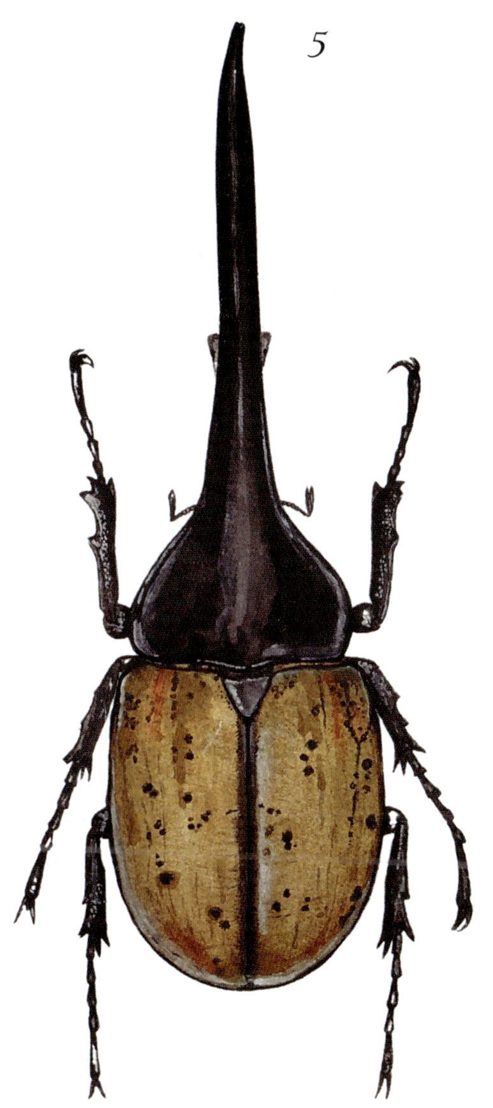

Step 5

Load your detail brush with white gouache diluted with water to start painting the highlights. First over the horn, paint a line right in the middle with your detail brush. Using the same brush, paint a line all around the thorax area, leaving a little black on the edges.

For the legs, use the same method—imagine the light hitting the beetle's legs, and add dots and lines to this area. For the darker shadows, you painted the inner edge of the legs, so for the highlights, you should be painting the outer edges. Over the wing covers, paint a line down the middle right next to the black stripes and on the bottom edge of the wing covers.

All these lines should be softened with water to create the illusion of light. You don't want straight, sharp lines—lean towards faded lines! I really enjoy doing this part of the painting process because it feels like the insect is coming to life. Finally, paint the scutellum with a bit of white gouache diluted with water. This big boy is about to go look for some rotten wood to snack on!

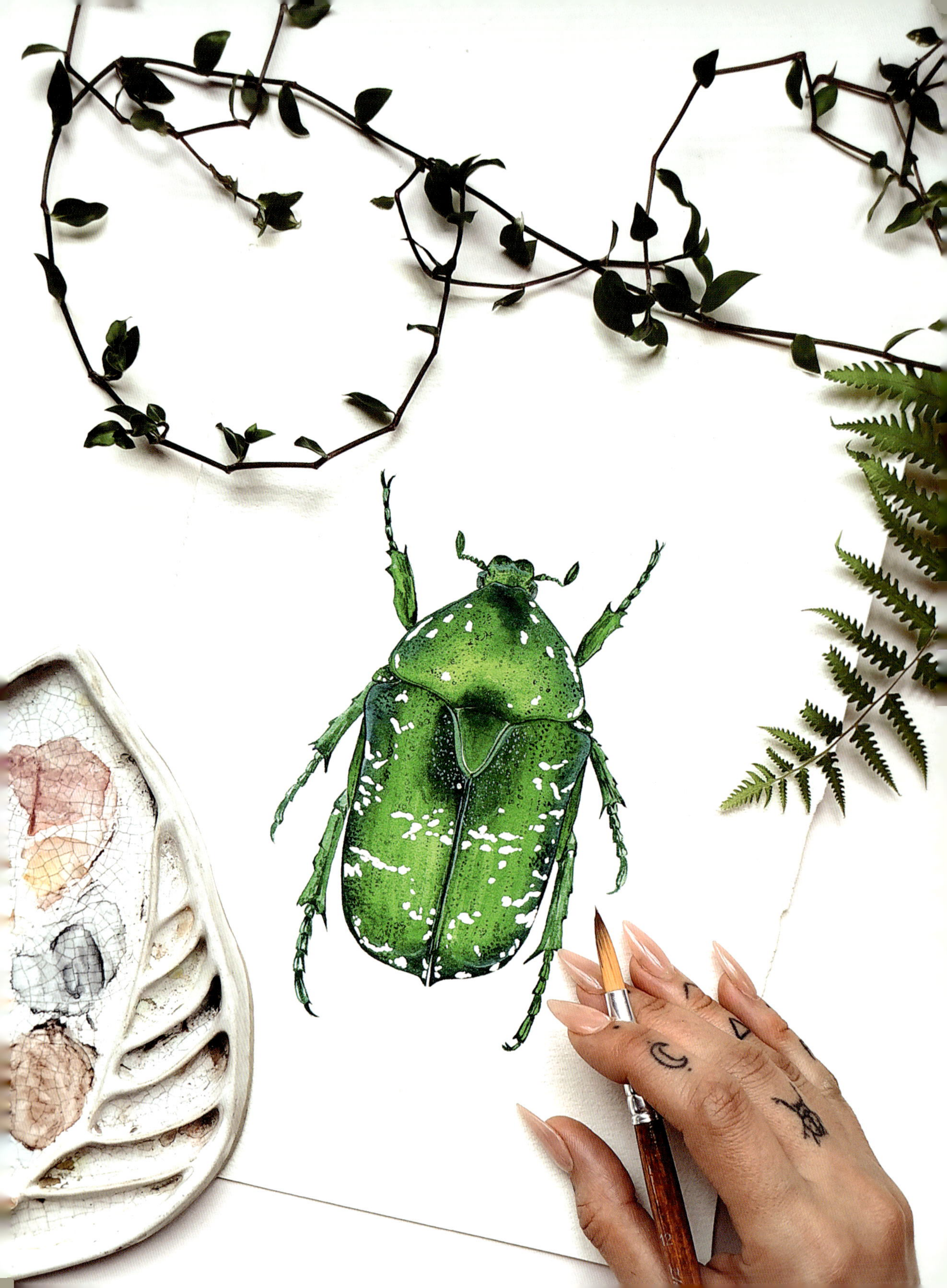

Flower Chafer

Flower chafers are a group of scarab beetles. Many species are diurnal and visit flowers for pollen and nectar. They're important pollinators!

The rose chafer (*Cetonia aurata*) (the exact specimen you'll be creating on this project) really loves roses. On warm, sunny days, these metallic-green beetles can be found among roses, busily and happily eating the nectar and the flowers. They are very pretty, and look like striking emeralds shimmering in the sunlight.

The larvae of rose chafers are unique in that they develop inside decomposing wood, a role crucial for nutrient recycling in their ecosystem. Next time you see a rose, make sure to check for these little habitants!

Difficulty: Medium

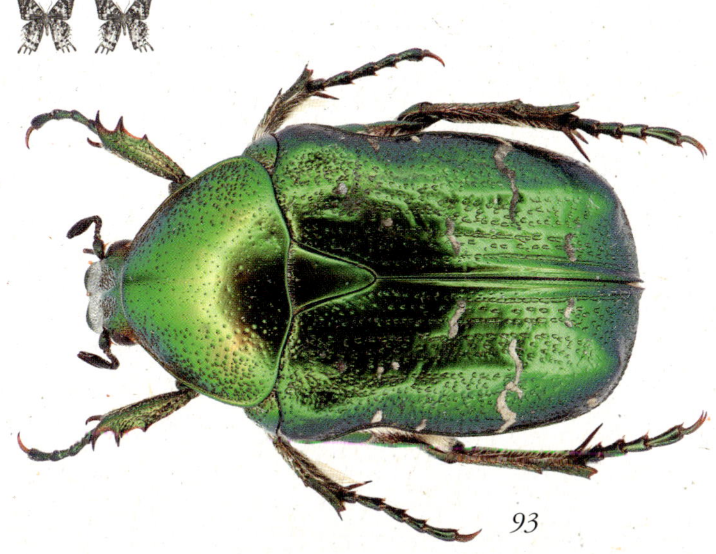

MATERIALS

- Watercolor paper of your choice
  - › I used a 6 x 8–inch (15 x 20–cm) sheet, vertical orientation
- Paints
  - › Primary Yellow, Phthalo Green, Hooker's Green, Phthalo Green Deep, Cobalt Green, Payne's Grey
  - › White gouache
- Brushes
  - › Old brush for masking fluid (I used a round size 2)
  - › Medium round brush (I used size 8)
  - › Detail round brush (I used size 2)
- Masking fluid and eraser (to remove)

Sketch

Draw the beetle freehand or trace the reference image and transfer it to the watercolor paper of your choice, focusing on the markings on the wing covers, legs, and antennae. Spray your paints with water to moisten them.

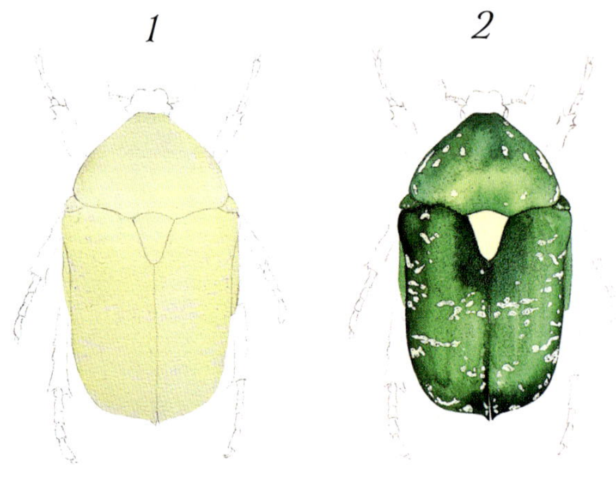

Step 1

Start applying masking fluid to all the markings that will remain white (see the reference photo on page 93). Start with the upper section of the body, applying the masking fluid in all dots, and continue with the lower section, masking all the markings on the wing covers that look like cracks. Make sure the masking fluid is completely dry before painting. Load your medium brush with Primary Yellow and create a light wash over the body, skipping head and legs. Let it dry.

Step 2

Load your medium brush with Phthalo Green, and paint a light wash over the pronotum, lightening the value as you get closer to the middle. Before it dries, clean your brush and add a few drops of clean water to the middle to keep the yellow color brighter. As you do this, the green pigment will run out of the area where you dropped the water, and it'll look as if the light is hitting the beetle. Keep working on the pronotum before it dries, adding a wash of Hooker's Green, starting on the edges and working your way to the middle, lightening the value again as you get closer to the center. Switch to your detail brush to outline with Phthalo Green Deep, and add a bit of color on the edges, especially close to the head. Let it dry.

Once the pronotum section is dry, load your medium brush with Phthalo Green and work on the right elytron, repeating the same technique of adding washes of color, starting with the lighter green and adding Hooker's Green after. Finish outlining the section with Phthalo Green Deep, darkening the value close to the edges and also in the center of the beetle. Before it dries, use your detail brush with Phthalo Green Deep to paint a few lines across the section. This will create a subtle texture. Repeat the process on the left elytron.

Finally, paint the protuberances on both sides of the beetle with your detail brush loaded with Hooker's Green. To finish, use the same brush to paint the protuberances on both sides, right under the pronotum, adding Phthalo Green Deep to the upper edges.

Step 3

Now, work on the pronotum again. Paint a water wash with your medium brush over the area, making sure not to press the paper with your brush—be gentle. In the wet area, dot Cobalt Green with your medium brush. Switch to Phthalo Green Deep, and create another wash, letting the colors blend nicely into each other. When the area is slowly drying but still wet, you will have more control over the colors blending, and it's time to add a darker value of Phthalo Green Deep over the scutellum. Use the same technique of layering colors on the bottom section of the beetle. First one side, and once it's dry, the other.

Create a water wash over the abdomen, and then load your medium brush with Cobalt Green. Paint a wash over the costal margin (top edge), and then switch to Hooker's Green to outline the whole section, letting the colors blend and do their thing. Don't obsess too much about it! Then when it starts to dry, switch to your detail brush loaded with Hooker's Green and add lines along this section. Last, and while still semi-wet, outline the section with Payne's Grey. Repeat on the other side.

Step 4

Load your detail brush with Primary Yellow and create a smooth wash on the head. While you wait for the head to dry, load the same brush with Phthalo Green, and paint a medium wash on both upper legs, and then change to Hooker's Green and paint the other four legs with a medium wash.

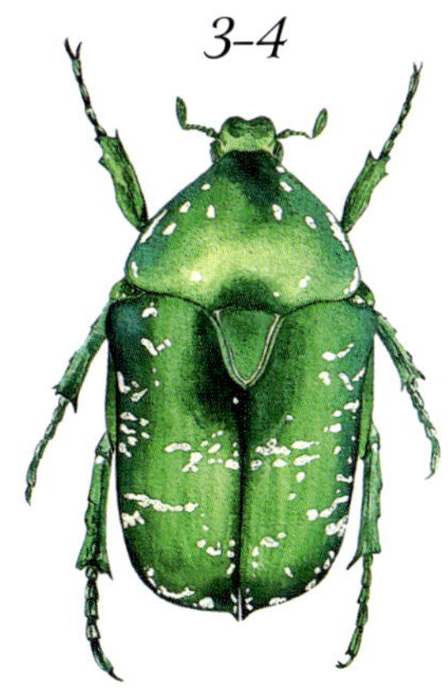

Back to the head: Load your detail brush with Hooker's Green, and create a light wash, darkening value close to the body and the top (leaving a light area in the middle). Let it dry. Use the same brush and color to paint the eyes.

Switch to Phthalo Green Deep to outline the head and darken the top area. Once the eyes are dry, paint the areas around the eyes. Switch to Phthalo Green to paint the antennae, and then switch to Phthalo Green Deep to outline them, and add details (for example: a bit of darkness where the joints of the antennae meet).

Mix Hooker's Green with a bit of Phthalo Green Deep to paint the scutellum, leaving about a millimeter of the yellow wash around it unpainted.

Load your detail brush with a little Phthalo Green Deep to paint the lines and details on the legs using the wet-on-dry technique. Use the tip of your brush to create dots, lines, and shadows on all six legs. (Use the reference photo if needed.) Finally, darken the area under the pronotum and the two protuberances on the sides with the same color and brush.

Step 5

Use the eraser to gently remove the masking fluid. This last step is all about the details. I want you to relax and feel free to play a bit. Load your brush with Phthalo Green Deep and add dots all over the body, although some dots should be like lines while others should be random.

Load your detail brush with white gouache and a dash of Cobalt Green to create more dots and paint the final details: two lines around the scutellum, two lines on the middle section where each wing cover separates, a little smudge on the head, and two semicircular lines on the bottom section of the wing covers. These two lines should be softened with a clean and damp brush. To finish this beautiful beetle, load your brush with Phthalo Green Deep and paint a line in the lower section of the pronotum.

This beetle is ready to pollinate some flowers!

> **Tip:** *Mix a bit of white gouache with the watercolor of your choice to create a pastel color that won't be translucent. It'll be great for creating details that stand out more.*

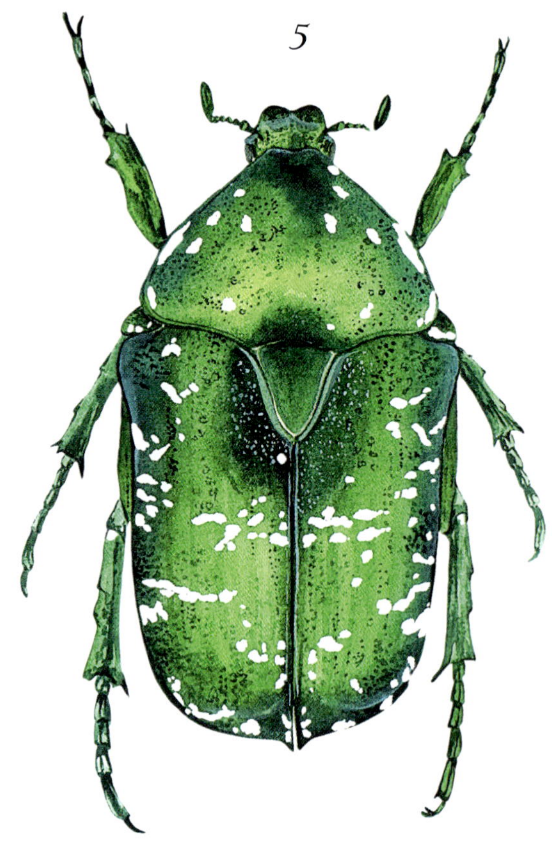

Ladybug

Ladybugs, with their distinctive spots and charming appearance, are often mistakenly called bugs—it's even in their common name! However, the truth is ladybugs are not "bugs" at all! Contrary to popular belief, ladybugs belong to the order Coleoptera, making them beetles rather than bugs.

The name "ladybug" comes from European farmers who prayed to the Virgin Mary when pests began eating their crops. After ladybugs came and wiped out the invading insects, the farmers named them "beetle of Our Lady." This eventually was shortened to "lady beetle" and "ladybug."

Many ladybugs are red for a reason. Their markings tell predators, "Eat something else! I taste terrible." Not all ladybugs are red with black spots. Many are yellow or orange with black spots, and some are black with red or yellow spots. But for this project, I chose to stick with red.

Difficulty: Easy

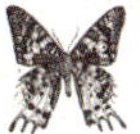

Sketch

Draw the ladybug freehand or trace the reference image and transfer it to the watercolor paper of your choice, focusing on the markings on the wing covers, legs, and antennae. Spray your paints with water to moisten them.

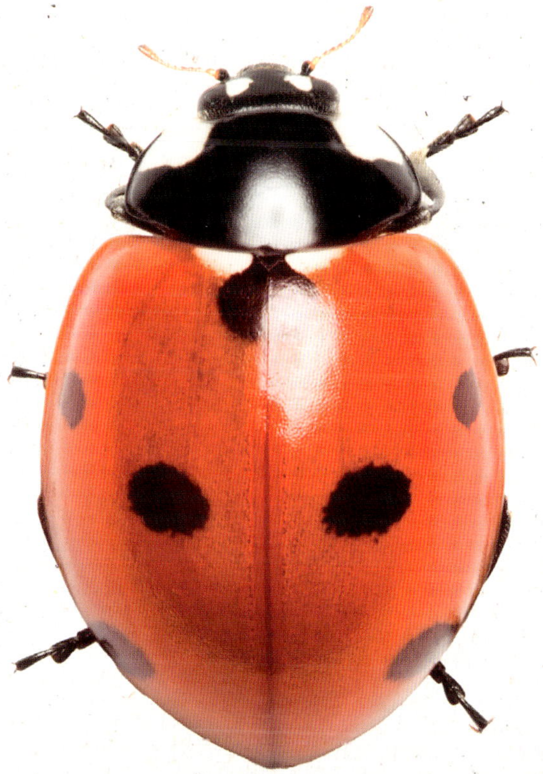

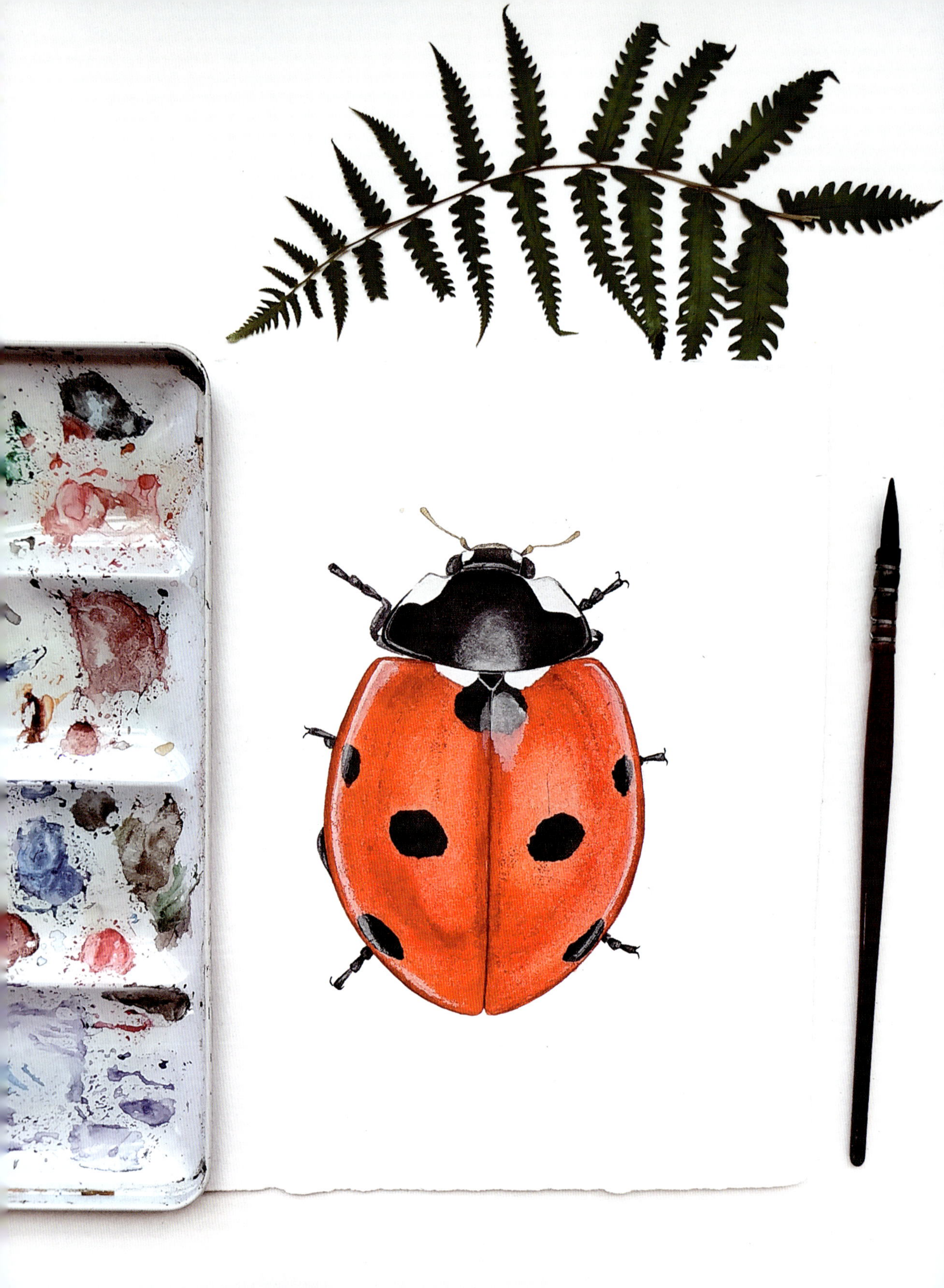

Step 1

Load your medium brush with French Vermilion, and paint the first wash over the wing covers with a medium value of the color. While still wet, add a darker value to both edges, creating a 3D effect. Skip all the markings, leaving them untouched for later. Wait until dry.

Switch to Neutral Tint and paint a medium wash on the pronotum, saving the two white markings on the sides. Once this dries, paint the thorax using the same brush and color. Again, wait until it dries to paint the head area, saving the white spots close to the eyes.

While you wait for the head to dry, use your detail brush to paint the scutellum (the small triangle on top of the wing covers), and all the tiny legs.

Switch to Raw Sienna to paint the little part over the head and the antennae. Add a little bit of Neutral Tint to the Raw Sienna to darken the color, and use this to paint the part where the antennae joins the head to create depth. Let it dry.

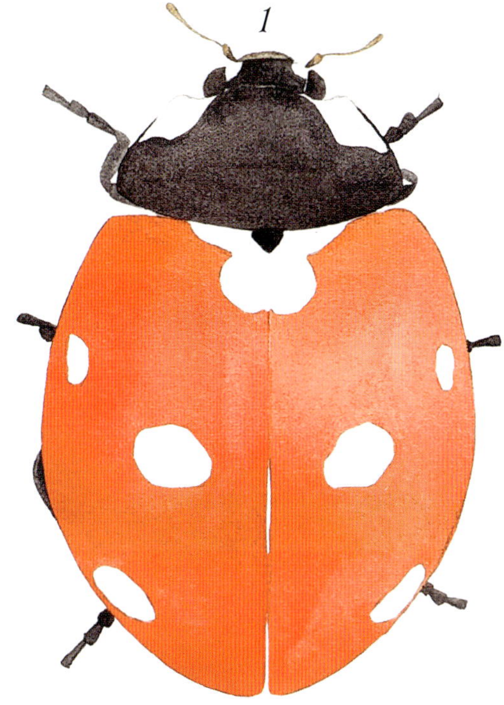

Tip: *Letting each section dry before painting the next helps define the different parts of the body, resulting in a more lifelike painting.*

Step 2

Load your medium brush with Neutral Tint and paint the dots on the wing covers, but not the whites close to the head. Move to the pronotum to paint another wash with a darker value of Neutral Tint, adding more water as you get closer to the middle, creating a light spot.

Switch to your detail brush to paint the shadows on the lower sides of the legs. Use a darker value of Neutral Tint, and add a line of color in all joints, and outline them. Once the pronotum is dry, switch to your medium brush, again using the same Neutral Tint to paint another wash on the head and eyes.

> *Tip: To create dark colors in watercolor, it's always best to layer to achieve the value you are looking for instead of painting a very pigmented layer. The reason is that watercolor should be translucent and never opaque or have residues of the pigments. Layering will always give you a cleaner look!*

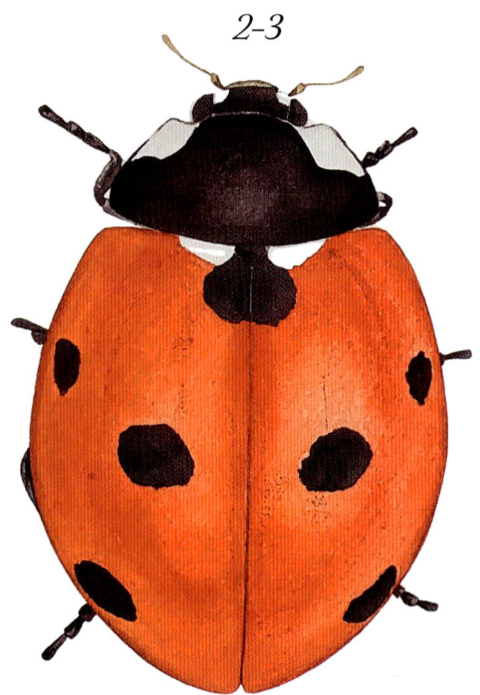

Step 3

Use French Vermilion and your medium brush to paint another wash over the wing covers. Start using a dark value on the edges and lighten the value as you get closer to the middle. You can even add a bit of clean water in the middle of each wing cover to create a lighter spot. Once this dries, switch to your detail brush to add some texture. Paint thin lines across the wing covers and dots. Feel free to play a bit and be intuitive! Switch now to Neutral Tint and paint the line between the two wing covers.

Step 4

Now it's time to paint the highlights on this beautiful ladybug. My favorite part! Load your detail brush with white gouache diluted with some water, and paint a line across the head. Add more water to the white mix, and paint the outer edge of the eyes. For the pronotum, paint a line all around it, leaving a bit of black on the edges. Start from the white marking on the left and work your way to the other white marking. Switch to your medium brush and add more water to paint a big smudge in the middle. Clean your brush and soften the edges with clean water.

Switch to your detail brush to outline the scutellum and the wing covers. Clean your brush with water to soften the inner edge. Use your medium brush to paint another smudge on the upper right section of the wing covers, simulating the light hitting the ladybug, and soften the edges with your clean brush. Use your detail brush add highlights to the legs. Think about where the light would hit the legs, and add dots of white gouache there.

Now your ladybug is ready to protect your garden!

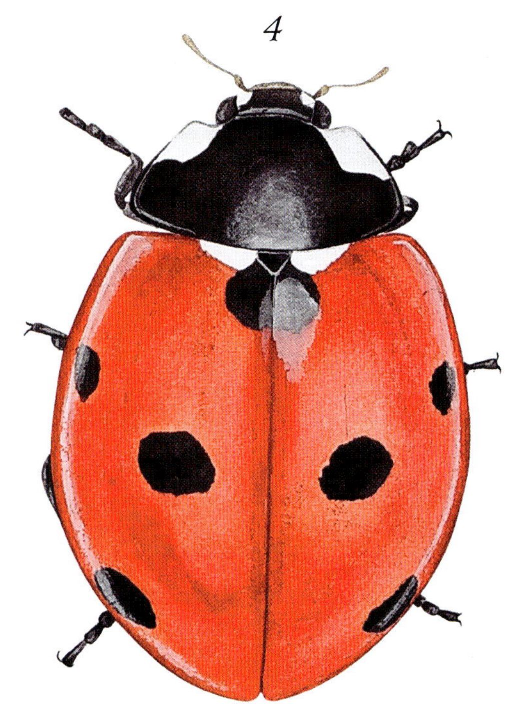

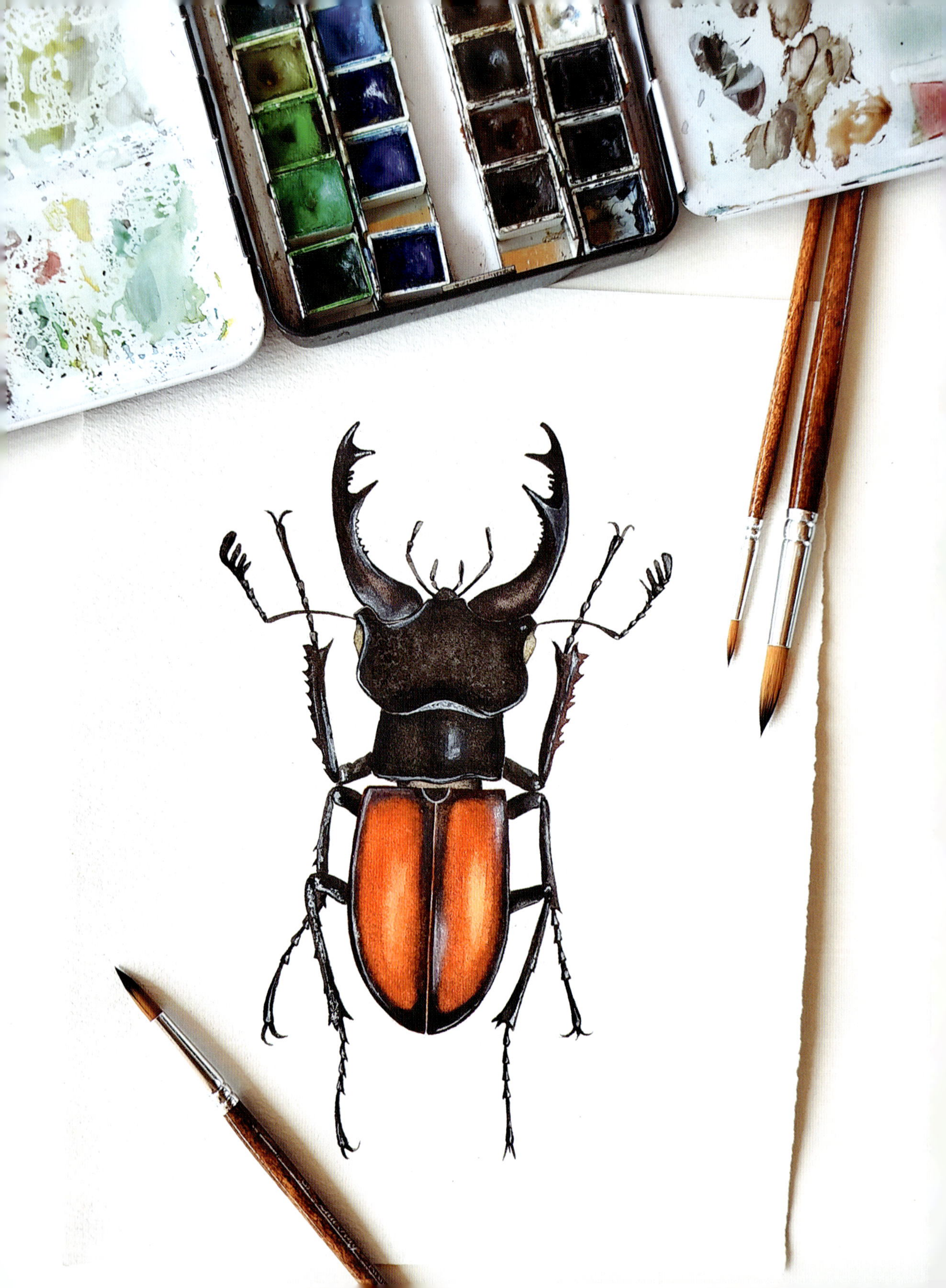

Stag Beetle

Impressive, heavily armed, and a formidable fighter, the stag beetle depends on trees and woods for its survival. Its fat larvae feed on the decaying wood of old broadleaved trees. Stag beetles are a family that, though not very colorful (most are black, brownish, or reddish brown), have prominent pincers. Male stag beetles usually have enlarged, sometimes astonishing jaws.

Difficulty: Medium

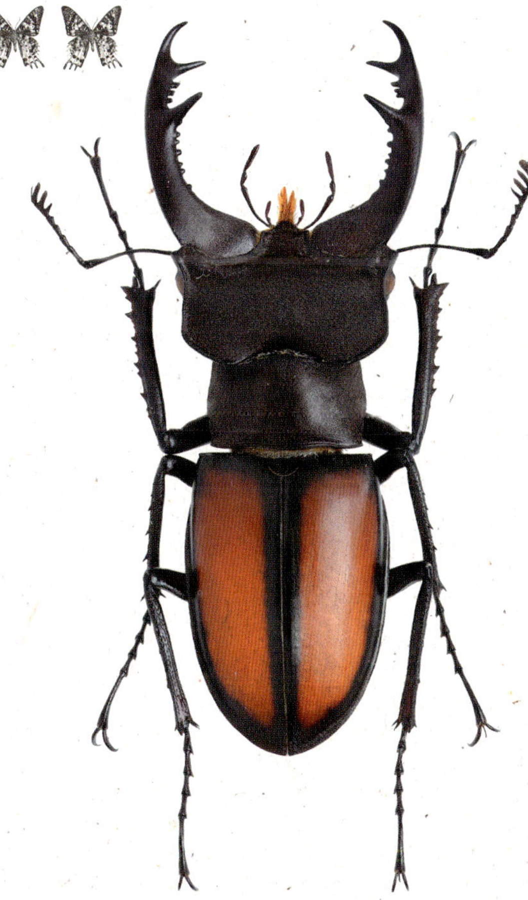

Sketch

Draw the beetle freehand or trace the reference image and transfer it to the watercolor paper of your choice, focusing on the wing covers, legs, and mandible. Spray your paints with water to moisten them.

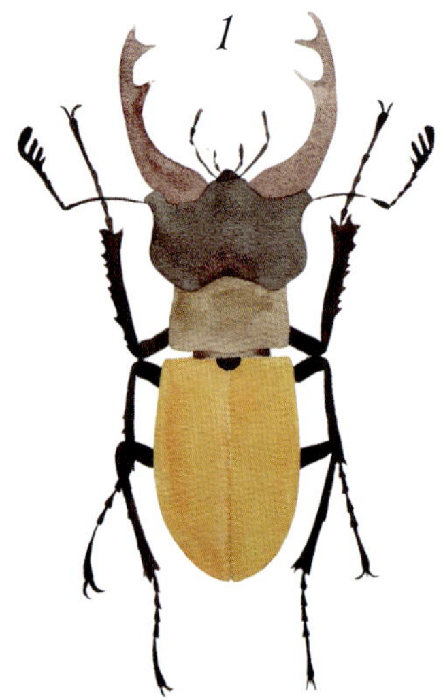

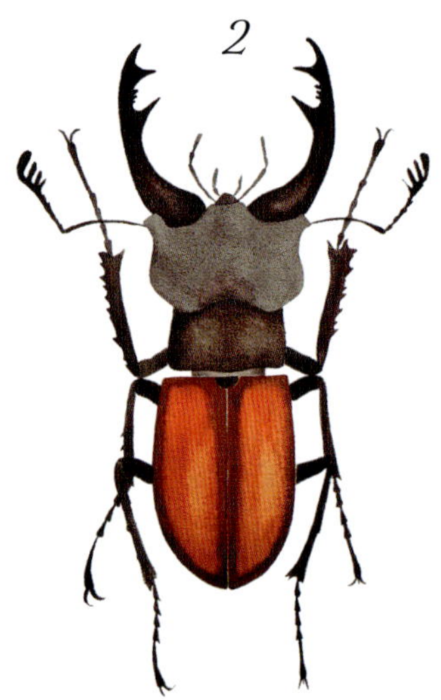

Step 1

Load your medium brush with a medium value of Naples Yellow Deep, and paint a wash on one of the wing covers. Once it's dry, paint the other.

Switch to Raw Umber and create a light wash on the thorax. Once this dries, load your medium brush with a light wash of Ivory Black and paint the head, darkening the value for the top triangle-shaped mark. Before it dries, load your detail brush with Caput Mortuum and dot a bit of color on the lower edge of the head. Keep using your detail brush with Caput Mortuum to paint a medium wash on the mandibles.

Switch to Ivory Black and paint the scutellum with a dark value. Continue painting all six legs and the antennae. Paint the section between the abdomen and the thorax with your detail brush and Raw Umber, adding a bit of Ivory Black to both edges, allowing it to blend to create a gradient.

Step 2

Use a dark value of Ivory Black and your medium brush to paint a wash over the mandibles. Use the lifting color technique (page 14) to get some of the black off the bottom middle of the mandibles, allowing the color underneath to show. Do the same to the thorax.

Switch to French Vermilion and add another wash of color to the wing covers. Paint one side at a time. Lighten the value of French Vermilion as you get to the center, and lift some of the color on the middle if necessary, to be able to see the yellow underneath. Then switch to your detail brush and Ivory Black to outline one wing cover, painting a rather thick line around it. Repeat the process on the other side once the first one is dry.

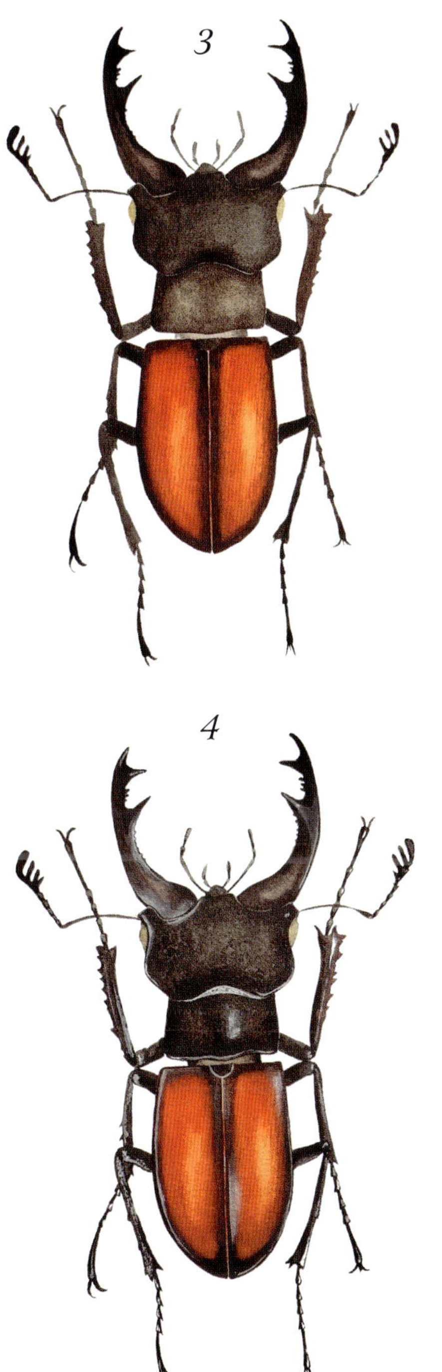

Step 3

Load your medium brush with a dark wash of Ivory Black and paint the head section. Lighten the value as you get to the center. Paint another wash of French Vermilion on the wing covers, adding a darker value on the edges. When almost dry, load your detail brush with Ivory Black and paint the stripe around the wing covers a little darker and more defined. Last, load your detail brush with Caput Mortuum to add a medium value wash on the legs. Let it dry.

Step 4

Add a bit of water to the white gouache, and load your detail brush with it. Have your medium brush clean and ready to soften the needed areas. Start with the mandibles. Paint a line around both outer edges, and soften the line with your medium brush. Paint a light wash over the top right mandible, simulating the light hitting the top of it. Outline the middle section of the inner edge of the left mandible. Moving down to the head, add a highlight line on the left side, top, and outer edge. Paint the area between the head and thorax completely white.

For the thorax, add a smudge in the middle, softening the edges and melting the white into background with a clean medium brush. Next, paint a line down the middle of the wing covers, blend with the clean brush, and outline the edges, leaving some areas untouched. To finish, paint white lines on the legs for highlights, and add little dots to create texture.

This stag beetle is already crawling away!

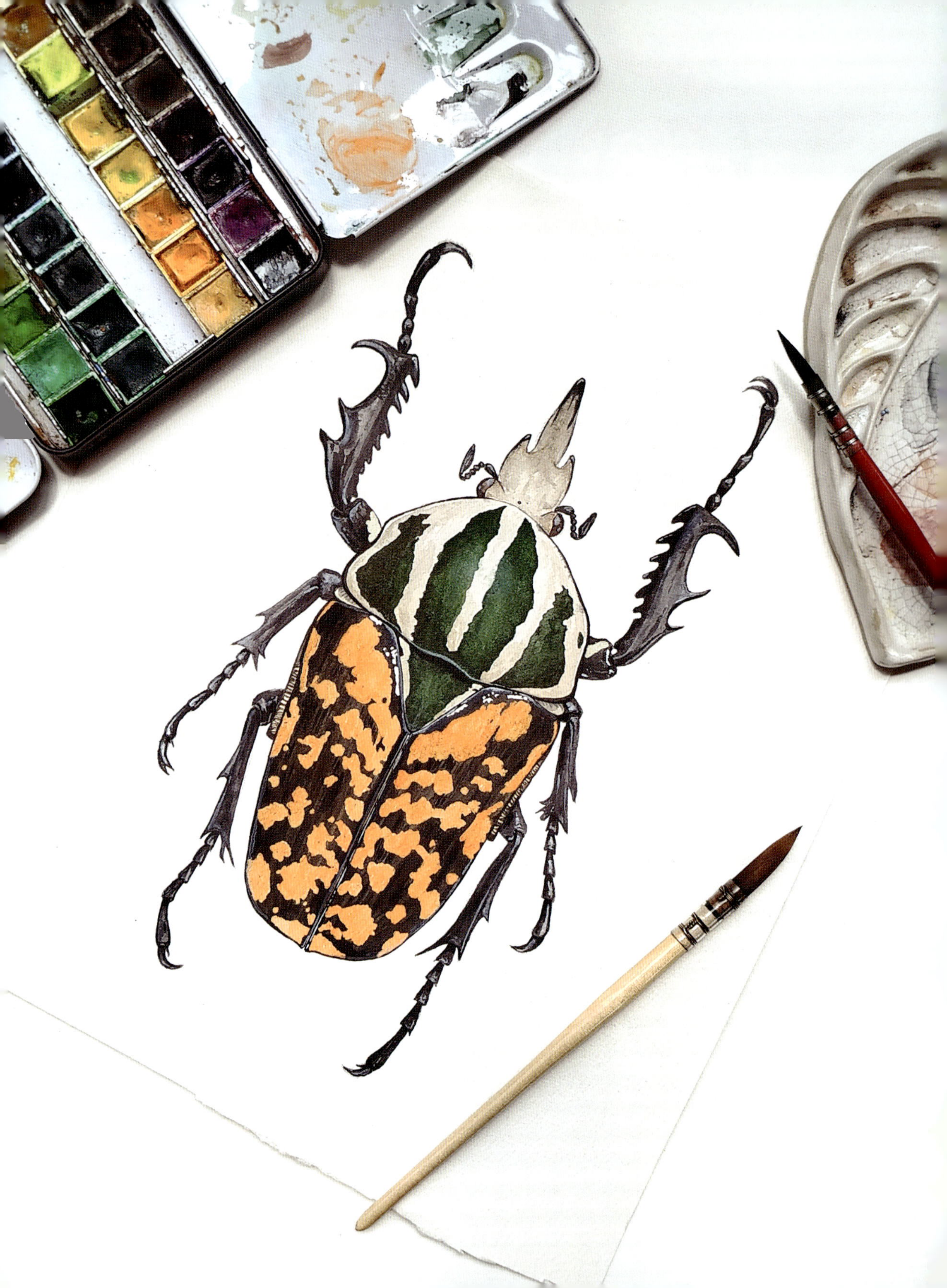

Mecynorhina

Mecynorhina is a large scarab beetle of the sub-family Cetoniinae found in dense tropical African forests. It eats fruits and sap flows from tree wounds. It's very common among beetle breeders for its unique patterns on its wing covers. The specific *Mecynorhina* chosen for this project is a *Mecynorhina oberthuri*. Insects like these are very important to the ecosystem, as they are pollinators, decomposers, and a great source of food for other animals.

Difficulty: Medium

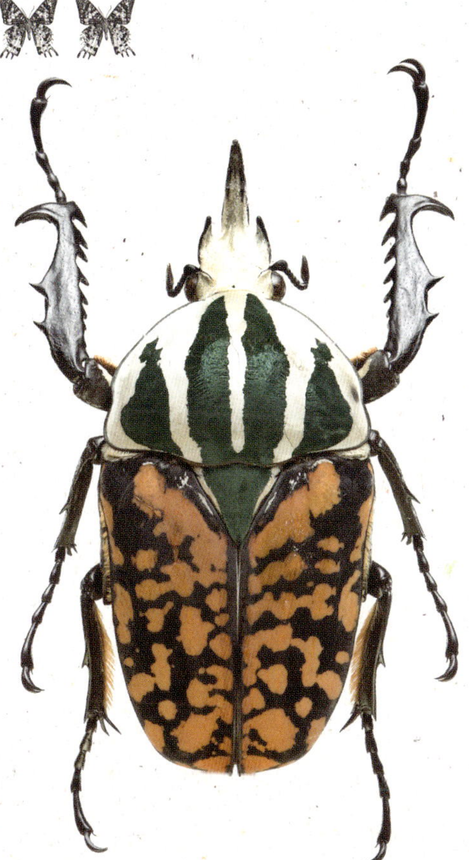

- Watercolor paper of your choice
  - I used a 10 x 10–inch (25 x 25–cm) sheet
- Paints
  - Red Orange, Yellow Ochre, Burnt Umber, Neutral Tint, Hooker's Green, Bright Red, Van Dyck Brown
  - White gouache
- Brushes
  - Old brush for masking fluid (I used a round size 2)
  - Medium round brush (I used size 8)
  - Liner brush (I used size 0)
  - Detail round brush (I used size 2)
- Masking fluid and eraser (to remove)

Sketch

Draw the beetle freehand or trace the reference image and transfer it to the watercolor paper of your choice, focusing on the markings on the wing covers, legs, and antennae. Spray your paints with water to moisten them.

Step 1

Use an old brush to apply masking fluid inside the markings on the upper section of the body (pronotum), little markings on both upper legs, and the lines around the middle section of the scutellum (middle triangle). Once it's completely dry, you can start applying color.

Mix three parts of Red Orange with one part of Yellow Ochre to get an earthy orange hue. Use this with your medium brush to paint a medium/high value wash over the wing covers.

Paint a water wash with the same brush over the upper section of the body and head, then load your brush with just a tiny bit of Burnt Umber. Paint a light wash over the wet area, adding more color to the edges, head, and close to the eyes. Before it dries, switch to your liner brush loaded with Neutral Tint, and outline the upper section of the body and head, allowing it to bleed into the Burnt Umber. Mix Hooker's Green with a bit of Bright Red to darken the color. Load your medium brush and paint the scutellum.

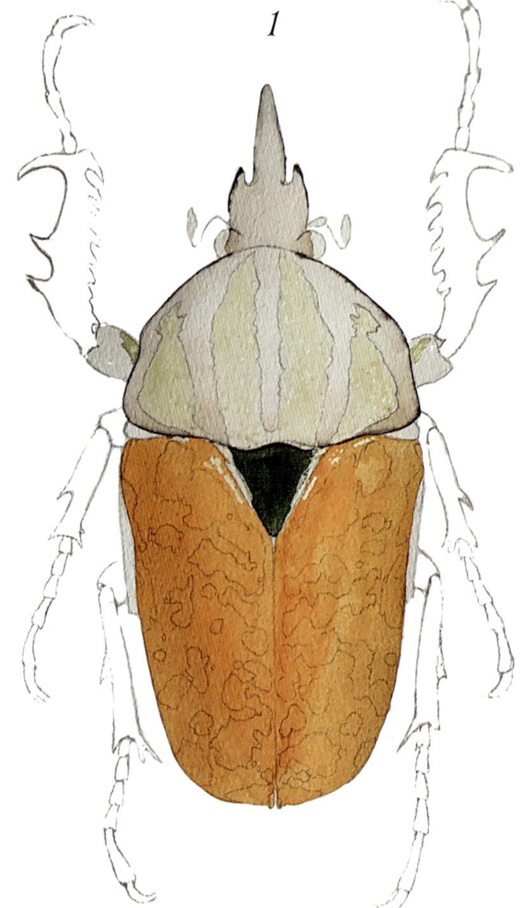

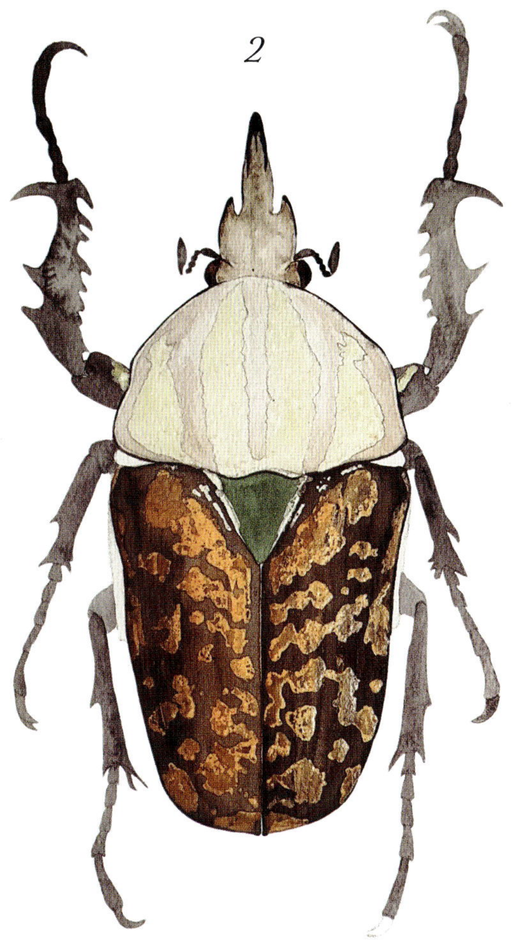

Step 2

Make sure everything is dry before starting this step. Use an old brush to apply masking fluid over the orange area, masking the orange markings. You should be able to see the pattern through the painting. While you wait for this to dry, focus on the legs. Load your detail brush with Neutral Tint to paint a medium wash on all four legs. Switch to the detail brush and Van Dyck Brown to paint the eyes.

Once the eyes are dry, paint a water wash over the head. Load your detail brush with a mix of Van Dyck Brown and Neutral Tint to add texture to the head and upper section of the body, darkening the horn area and around the eyes. Switch to Neutral Tint and outline the horns again—your paper should be damp but not too much. Paint the antennae with Neutral Tint, and once the head is dry, outline the horns again and create the black markings. Last, add little black dots for texture.

The masking fluid on the wing covers should be dry by now. Load your medium brush with Neutral Tint, and paint a wash over the whole area, adding more pigment as you get closer to the edges. This will give the beetle a more rounded shape. Let it dry.

Step 3

Load your detail brush with the mixture of Neutral Tint and Van Dyck Brown to paint the two sections on both sides, under the upper body. Outline them with Neutral Tint and the same brush. Use the same brush and color to start adding depth and texture to the legs. I normally darken the areas where the light would hit (like the inner edges) and the joints.

Now, paint both protuberances on the lower section of the body with your detail brush and the earthy orange mix (three parts of Red Orange with one part of Yellow Ochre). Let it dry, and then apply thin lines (use your liner brush and clean immediately after) of masking fluid across it. Again allow this to dry. Using your detail brush, apply a medium wash of Neutral Tint. Rest your hand, you earned it!

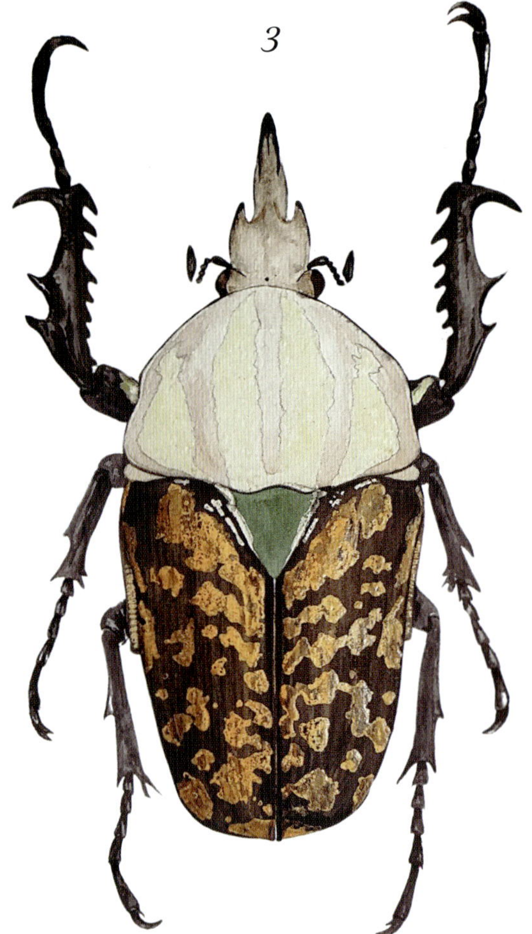

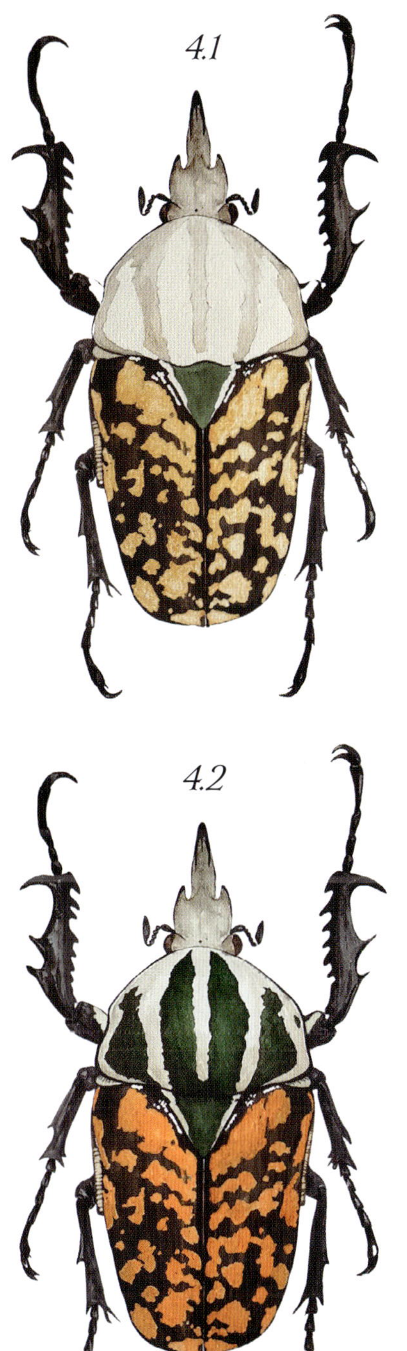

4.1

4.2

Step 4

Once everything is completely dry, use the eraser to gently remove the masking fluid. Mix Burnt Umber with just a dash of Neutral Tint, and use this and your detail brush to paint the marking on the leg joints. (These areas either had masking fluid on them before, or you've left it white.) Do the same with the markings inside the scutellum (middle triangle). Mix Hooker's Green with Bright Red to create a darker shade of green, and have this mixture ready along with just Hooker's Green.

Load your medium brush with Hooker's Green and paint a wash over the markings, adding the darker mix you created on the edges of the markings. The closer to the middle, the lighter the green should be. This will make your bug look like the light is hitting it.

Mix Red Orange with a bit of Raw Sienna, and using your detail brush add texture to the orange markings, leaving spaces untouched so you can see the lighter orange underneath. Switch to your liner brush and outline everything with a darker value of Neutral Tint. For the legs, add some hair-like strokes on both sides under the pronotum. Let your hand flick as you do this to create lines with thin tips. Use your brush and the same color to also add lines along the body—these beetles have what looks like creases on its wing covers.

Step 5

The final step is just add the highlights. Use white gouache diluted with water and your detail brush. Work your way down to avoid touching the wet surface. Start with the antennae and the eyes, thinking about where the light would hit or looking at the reference photo. Then add a line over the scutellum, using a clean brush to soften the line a bit; it'll make it less harsh.

Then work on the upper legs, also adding white lines and softening them with a clean brush and a bit of water. Move to the lower legs, and then outline the scutellum, using either your detail brush or liner brush. Lastly, add a line along the line that separates the wing covers.

Can you feel the power of one of the biggest beetles on Earth!? It's finished!

Tip: If you have a spare brush that's about the same size of the one you're using, it's very helpful to have it clean and ready to soften areas or clean if you spill a bit of color somewhere. If you have to clean your brush every time, you'll be wasting a lot of color.

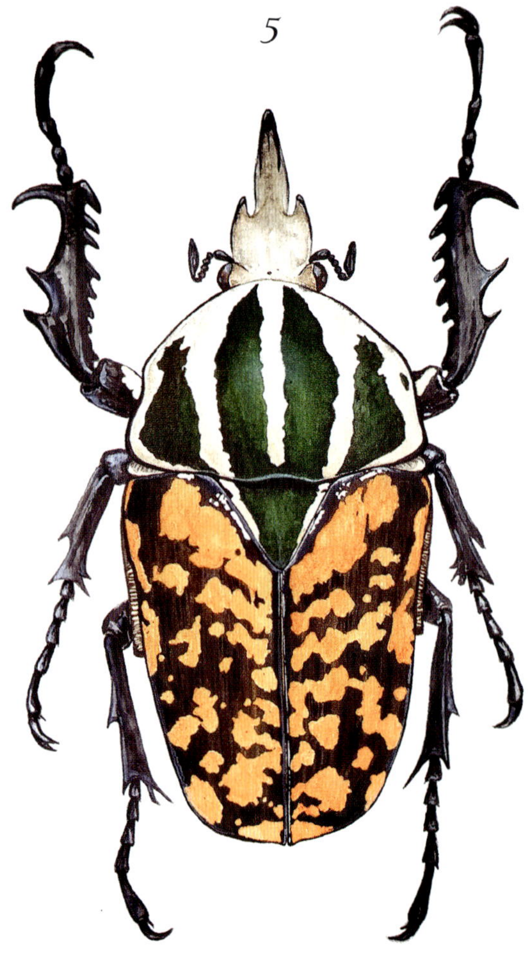

Goliath Beetle

Goliath beetles are considered one of the largest insects in the world. Found in the rainforests of Central and Western Africa, they live in rotting logs and fallen trees.

While an impressive and fascinating creature, the Goliath beetle is facing threats to its survival. The destruction of its habitat due to logging and agriculture is a major concern, as is the pet trade—because of their beauty and impressive stature, Goliath beetles are often collected and kept as a novelty pet.

Difficulty: Difficult

MATERIALS

- Watercolor paper of your choice
  - I used a 12 x 13–inch (30 x 33–cm) sheet, landscape orientation
- Paints
  - Raw Sienna, Neutral Tint, Sennelier Yellow Deep, Brown Pink, Gold Ochre, Van Dyck Brown, French Vermilion
  - White gouache
- Brushes
  - Old brush for masking fluid (I used a round size 2)
  - Medium round brush (I used size 6)
  - Detail round brush (I used size 2)
  - Liner brush (I used size 0)
- Masking fluid and eraser (to remove)

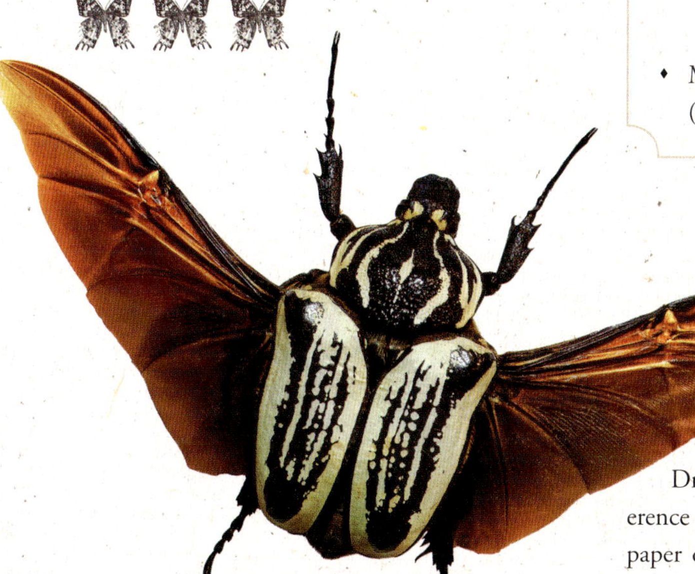

Sketch

Draw the beetle freehand or trace the reference image and transfer it to the watercolor paper of your choice. Spray your paints with water to moisten them.

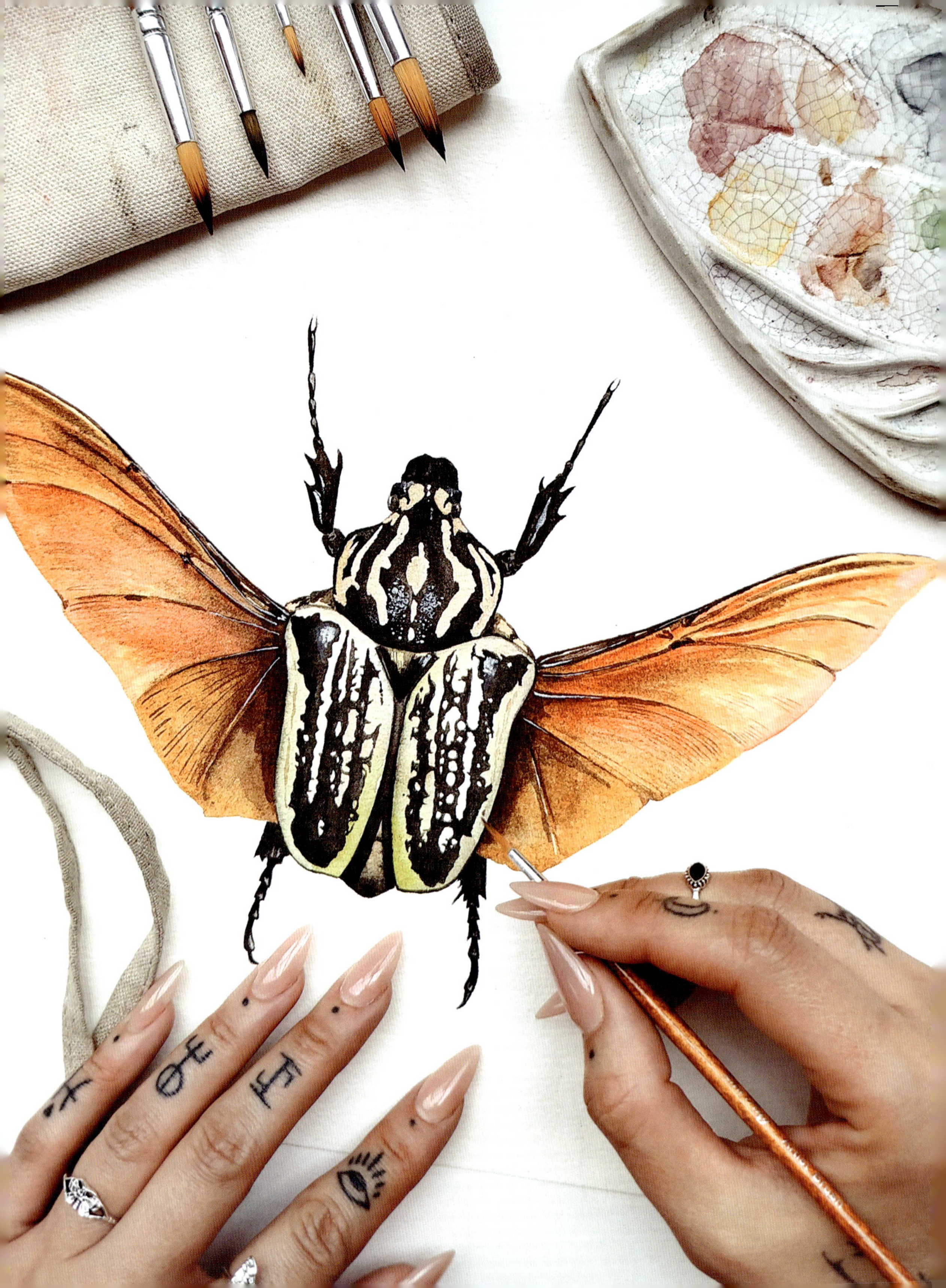

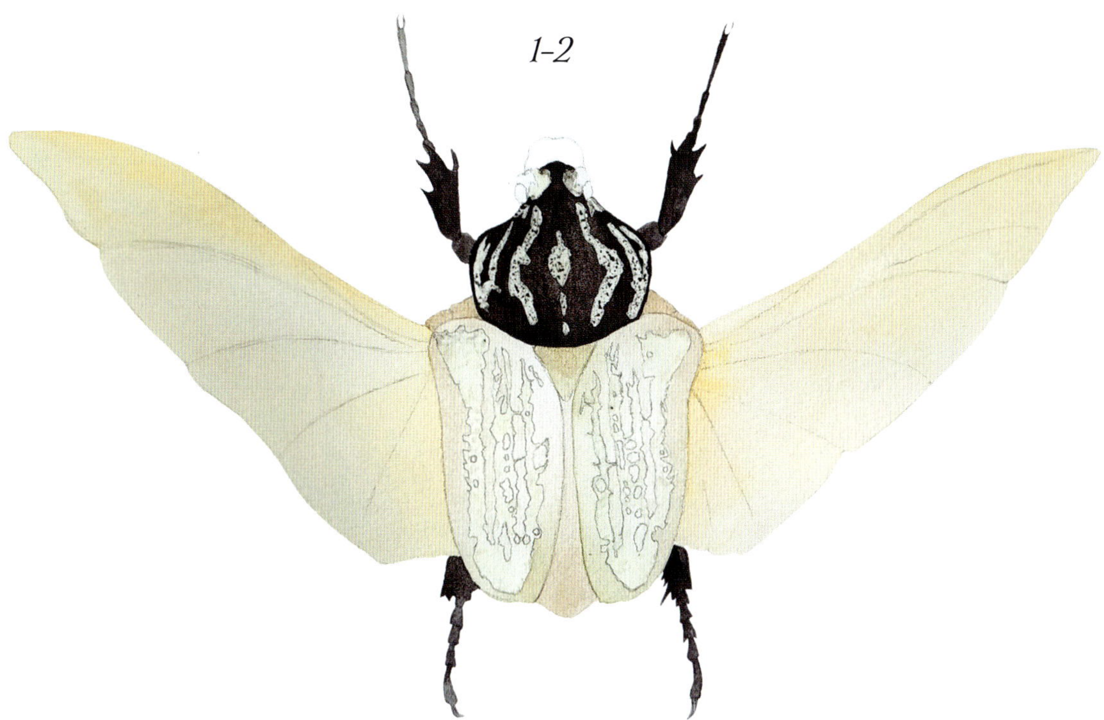

1–2

Step 1

Before laying down any paint, use your old brush to apply masking fluid over the wing covers, thorax, and the area around the eyes. Once the masking fluid is completely dry, load your medium brush with Raw Sienna and paint a medium wash over the wing covers, darkening the value on the top area and the lower section. While you wait for this to dry, switch to your detail brush and a dark value Neutral Tint to paint the legs.

Once the wing covers are dry, switch to your medium brush with Neutral Tint and paint the thorax. Before it dries, add a darker value of the color around it, keeping the middle lighter. Wait for everything to dry.

Step 2

Load your detail brush with a medium value of Raw Sienna and paint the section inside the thorax, add more value to paint the scutellum (middle triangle), and both protuberances over the thorax. Once everything is dry, load your medium brush with Sennelier Yellow Deep and paint a light wash over both wings.

Step 3

Load your detail brush with Neutral Tint and paint the head. Move to the protuberances at the top of the wing covers, and use a dark value of Neutral Tint to paint them, leaving some spaces untouched so you can still see the light brown underneath. Do the same with the scutellum, leaving the top section unpainted. Add some lines over the area, like little hairs coming out of the thorax. Let it dry.

Paint a water wash over the wing covers with clean water, and then load your detail brush with a dark value of Neutral Tint to outline both wing covers. Before it dries, load your medium brush with Brown Pink (very diluted) and paint around both outer sides of the wing covers, as well as the bottom edge, adding darkness to create the impression that it's round. (This happens when you darken the edges of any object.)

Step 4

While you wait for last section to dry, load your medium brush with Gold Ochre to create a wash over the wings. Start with the right wing, and before it dries, darken the value of the color to paint lines along the principal vein. Save the top section of the wing for later. Repeat on the left wing.

Once the thorax is dry, load your detail brush with clean water and paint a wash over the base of the wing covers. Load your brush with a medium value of Neutral Tint and dab color along the bottom edge, allowing the color to run inside. Wait until this is almost dry to paint

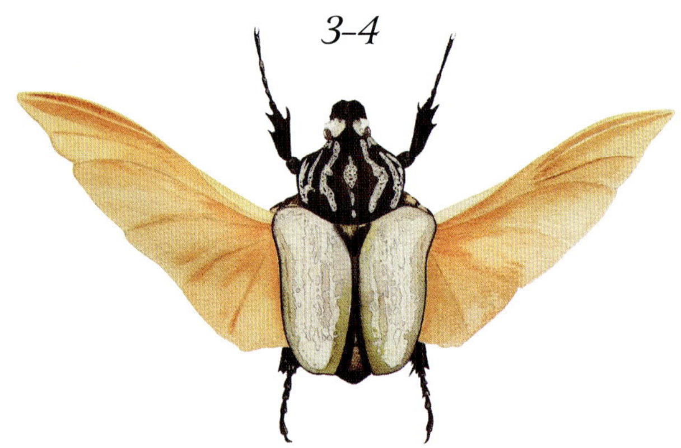

a line across it—exactly over the part where the black stopped bleeding. Let it dry.

Load your detail brush with a dark value of Neutral Tint to paint another wash over the legs. Leave some areas untouched to create the illusion that light is hitting them. Switch to your medium brush and continue using Neutral Tint to paint two black broad strokes inside the wing covers: one on the left side and one on the right, merging them together in the middle. Let it dry. Switch to your detail brush and a darker value of Raw Sienna and paint another wash on the inner space left between the two broad strokes.

Then, paint the eyes with Van Dyck Brown using your detail brush leaving a little blank space in the middle.

Last, load your medium brush with Brown Pink and paint the inner edges of the wing covers, lightening the value as you go inside. Switch to your detail brush and paint an uneven line down the wing covers' outer edges, between the black edge and the masking fluid marking.

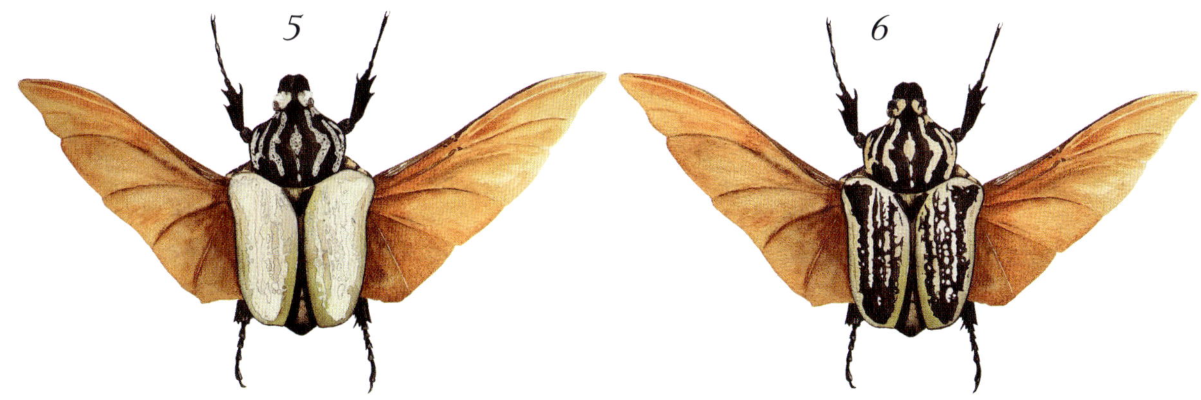

Step 5

Work on the wings now. This part of the process is more intuitive and less precise, so let it flow. First, prepare your palette with the colors you are going to use. These are Gold Ochre, Van Dyck Brown, and French Vermilion. Then, add a water wash over the area with a clean medium brush.

Use your medium brush tip to dot a medium value of Van Dyck Brown where the wings merge with the body, and then drag the pigment, creating lines that fade at the end and blend with the background. Add more pigment on all the inner edges. Mix Gold Ochre with a bit of French Vermilion and add it to the middle of the wing and upper area, dragging the pigment with your brush and moving it as you wish.

When the surface starts drying, switch to your detail brush and Van Dyck Brown to outline the upper edges of one wing, leaving some spaces untouched. Then paint another line right underneath, and another one going towards the middle. Repeat the process on the other wing. Let it dry.

Step 6

Use the eraser to gently remove the masking fluid. Load your detail brush with Neutral Tint and paint inside the markings covering the spaces on the wing covers, and if you feel like it needs a few more lines or dots, just do it. Use your detail brush to redefine the needed areas.

Now for the thorax, switch to a medium value of Raw Sienna and do the same—fill out all the markings. Don't forget the area around the eyes. Paint the part closer to the eyes with Raw Sienna and the outer part with Neutral Tint. Let it dry.

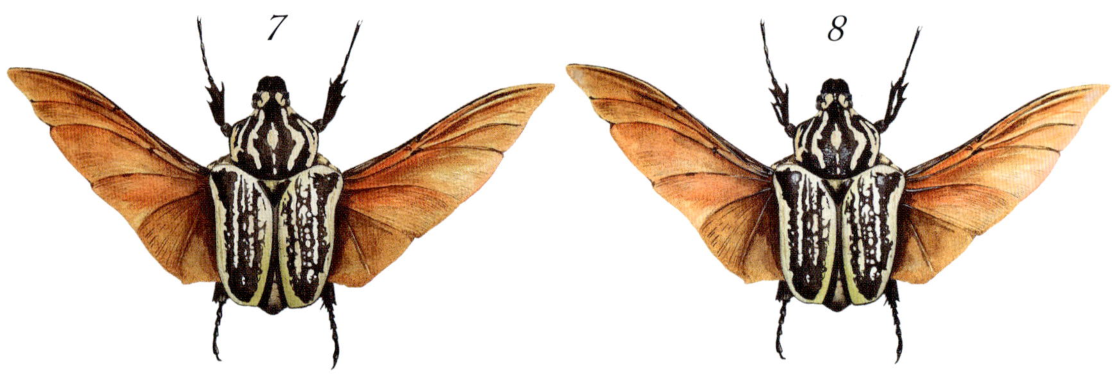

Step 7

Load your medium brush with a mixture of Gold Ochre and French Vermilion and add some color to the upper section of the wing, and then the middle. Create broad strokes with the brush. Let it dry before switching to your detail brush. Load it with Van Dyck Brown and create lines in the upper edge, outlining the whole area, and then mark the veins you created before with the same color. These lines should be uneven and thinner at the end.

Lastly, paint little notches on the end of the wings (the bottom edge) exactly where it curves. Lighten the value of Van Dyck Brown and add thin lines along the wings, changing the pressure and value to create texture. You don't need to paint lines everywhere, just a few.

Switch to your medium brush to paint a dark wash on the wings all around the body area, cleaning the brush immediately after to soften the color getting inside the wing. Don't apply pressure; just let the lines fade a bit to make them less harsh.

Step 8

Add a little bit of water to some white gouache. Load your detail brush and start highlighting the beetle. Start with the head, adding two dots between the eyes, and then go down the thorax. Add dots right in the middle, using a fingertip to soften them.

Then on to the wing covers. Add two big smudges on the upper section of both corners to create light spots. Next comes the wings. Add a highlight over the veins, starting where the wings merge with the body and continue the line until the middle. With a more diluted value of the gouache, add a smudge of white on both tips of the wings. Finally, the legs—just paint a line down both upper legs.

Your Goliath beetle is about to take flight!

Leaf Insect

Also known as walking leaves, these insects belong to the stick and leaf insect order (Phasmatodea), which are known for their unusual appearance: They look confusingly similar to parts of plants such as twigs, bark, or—in the case of leaf insects—leaves. This sophisticated camouflage provides excellent protection from predators.

Note: While these steps are long, they aren't complicated. Instead, this project is all about laying simple details over each other. Please, read through the steps first before diving in to get your bearings! This is a very intuitive project, and though you have these steps to follow, the watercolor blending will make each illustration special and unique.

Difficulty: Medium

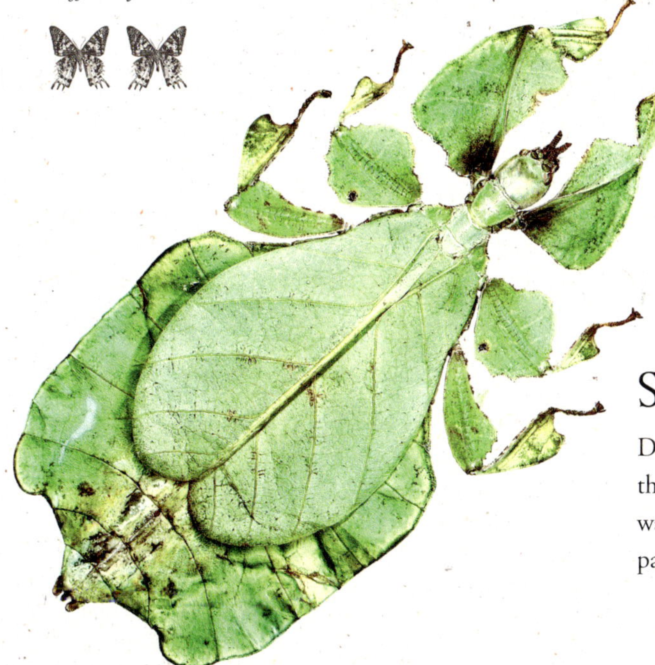

Sketch

Draw the leaf insect freehand or trace the reference image and transfer it to the watercolor paper of your choice. Spray your paints with water to moisten them.

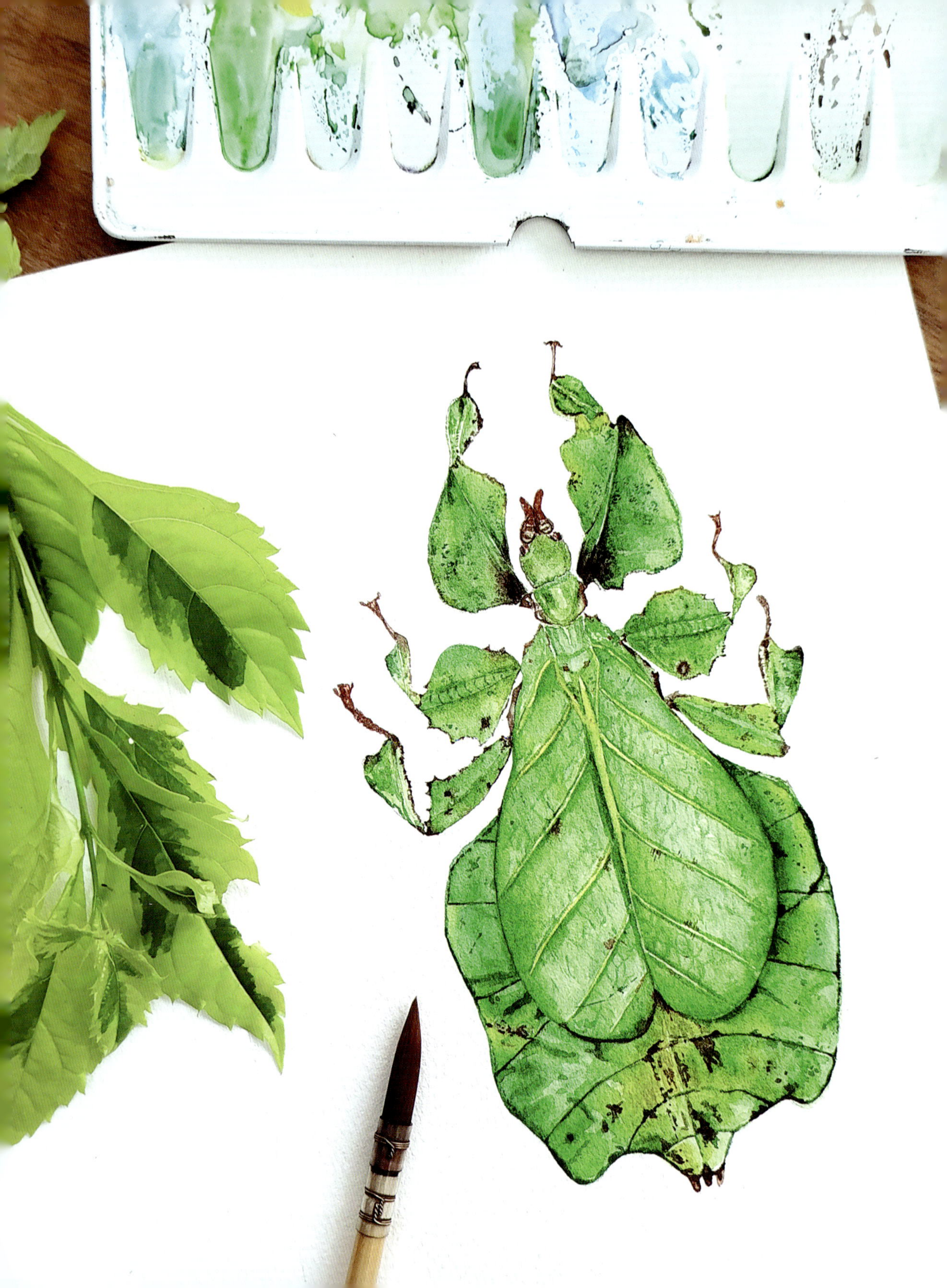

Step 1

Prepare your palette with Primary Yellow, Phthalo Green Light, and Emerald Green. Mix the same amount of Emerald Green and Phthalo Green and have it ready to use.

Using your medium brush, begin by painting a light wash of Primary Yellow on everything but the leg tips and the mandibles. While still damp, switch to Phthalo Green Light and add it to the lower section of the body. Use the tip of your brush to apply the color, and let it blend. Then, switch to the color mix (Emerald Green and Phthalo Green Light) and add it to the lower section of the body. Be intuitive and let the colors flow—it doesn't have to be perfect, but it does have to have the different shades of green.

Step 2

Paint a water wash over the right front leg to prepare the surface area and load your medium brush with a light value of Hooker's Green. Use the tip of your brush to add color to the area. Let it blend with the background. If you need to move the color a bit, keep using the tip of your brush but don't do any brushstrokes—that will ruin the flow of the watercolors. Do the same thing with the left leg.

Keep using Hooker's Green with your detail brush to paint the head and thorax. Leave a space all around the thorax for the yellow to be seen. Paint a water wash over the middle legs,

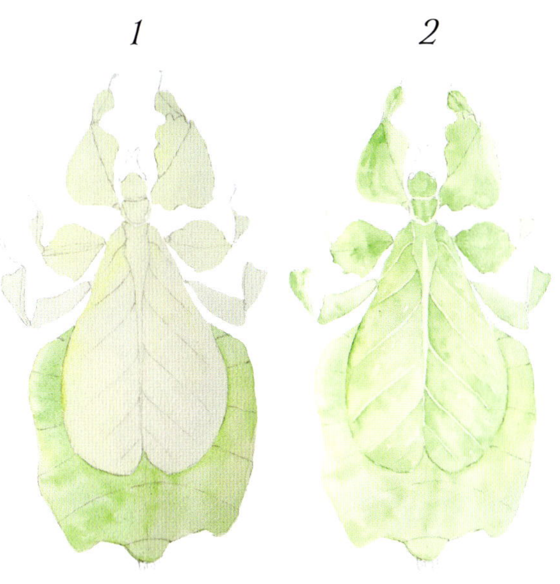

and add Hooker's Green with the tip of your detail brush, letting the color blend. Leave the top section of the legs for later. Repeat the process for the lower legs, leaving the inner edges untouched.

Now for the body area, switch to your medium brush. You are doing a negative painting here. Load your brush with Hooker's Green and paint the area except for the veins—that's why it's called negative painting. You will paint everything but the part where the veins are, to keep those yellow. Add a bit of Phthalo Green Light to the edges of the body, and remember to use the tip of your brush to move the color around. Leave some areas without paint to create some texture.

Step 3

Work on the bottom section of the body. Prepare your palette with Brown Pink and Phthalo Green Deep with the other greens you used in Step 2 (Phthalo Green Light, Emerald Green, and Hooker's Green).

Add another wash to the right side of the lower section of the body. Add Phthalo Green Deep using your medium brush to the area close to middle section of the body. This will make the middle section of the body pop because you're painting a shadow underneath. It's important to work fast to blend all the greens together. Right after you add the darkest green (Phthalo Green Deep), add the Brown Pink to the lower section, and keep adding greens while looking at the photo reference for assistance, if needed. This step is a bit intuitive, and your painting will blend differently than mine. There's no wrong way to do it—just let your inner artist take the lead. Once the right side is dry, paint the left side using the same technique. You can also add drops of water to lighten some areas. Let it dry.

Repeat the process for the middle section of the body using different shades of green and Brown Pink. Use the darkest shades on the edges to create depth. Don't paint over the veins though! Don't forget to leave some spaces blank to create texture.

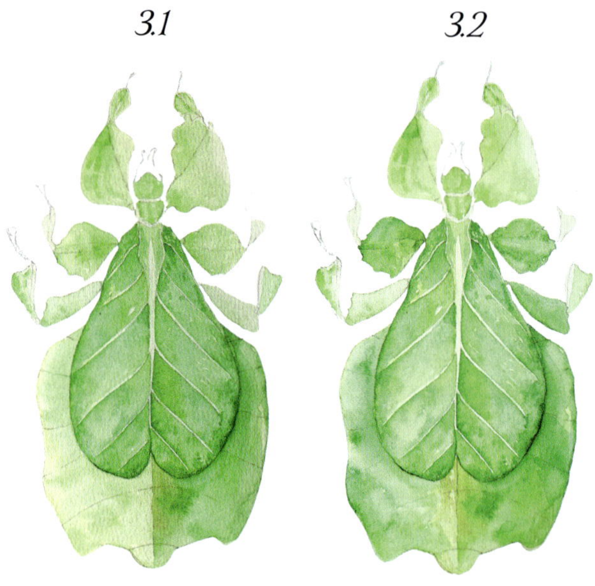

Lastly, paint the middle legs. First, add a clear water wash over the area to prepare the surface. I used Brown Pink for the section closer to the body, and then added Phthalo Green Deep over the top edge and Hooker's Green on the lower edge—but the colors will mix a bit, and that's okay. Repeat on the other leg. It's interesting to paint them a bit differently. These insects try to recreate how a leaf looks, and they're always different.

Tip: Having your colors ready on your palette will make painting so much easier because you won't lose time between transitions, and the colors will blend nicely.

Step 4

Focus on the top legs. Load your medium brush with Hooker's Green mixed with a dash of Phthalo Green Deep and paint another wash over the lower area, leaving little spots untouched. Once it dries, switch to your detail brush and a medium value of Van Dyck Brown to paint the tip of the leg.

Now it's time to add details and be more technical. Load your detail brush with Brown Pink and paint the tips of all of the legs, and then switch to a darker value of Hooker's Green and paint another wash over the area. While still damp, add Van Dyck Brown mixed with Ivory Black to paint the area close to the head and the top corner of the leg. Let it dry.

Once it's dry, keep using your detail brush with Van Dyck Brown to outline the thick vein in the middle of the top leg. Soften the lines with a clean brush. Next, use Phthalo Green Deep to paint a few dots and also lines for the veins—putting just a little pressure. (Don't even touch the paper all the time! This creates a very thin and uneven line.) Paint a line of dots all along the outer side of the leg. For the top section of the leg, use your detail brush with Hooker's Green mixed with a bit of Brown Pink to paint a wash over the area. Let it dry, and switch to Van Dyck Brown to paint a line along the outer side of the thick leg section. In the image on the right, you can see one leg finished. Repeat this process for the other front leg.

Keep using your detail brush to paint the top section of the remaining four legs, combining Hooker's Green and Phthalo Green Deep.

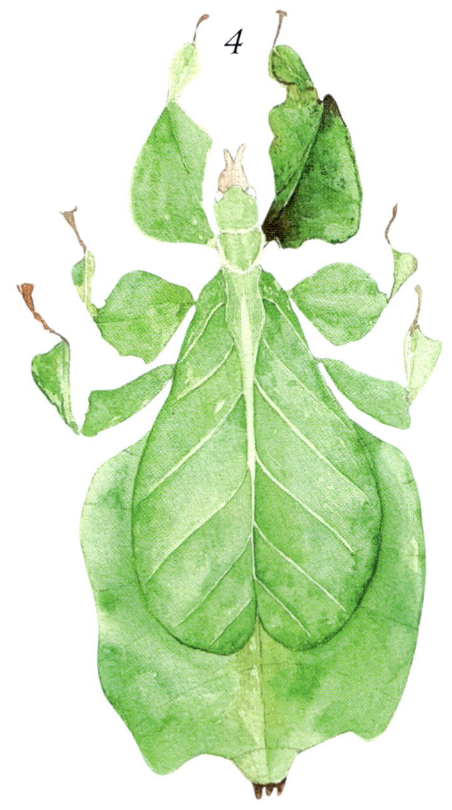

To finish this step, paint a light wash with Van Dyck Brown on the head area (just above the eyes) and the bottom three protuberances. On these, wait until dry to add another layer with a darker value of the same color. Let it dry.

> **Tip:** *If you can't wait for your illustration to dry, you can use a hair dryer to speed up this process, but for some reason, the colors tend to be less bright when you try this trick!*

Step 5

Use your detail brush loaded with Hooker's Green mixed with a bit of Blue Indanthrene to apply the last wash over the top of the upper legs. Leave a space around the edges of this section to keep them lighter. Instead of painting brushstrokes, use the tip of your brush to apply the color. These smudges will create a fantastic texture. Switch to Van Dyck Brown to outline the brown tips on all six legs.

Paint the eyes using a light value of Van Dyck Brown. Let it dry. Then paint the mandible with the same color, just a darker value. Use this to add a dot in the eyes too.

Use the tip of your liner brush to dot a dark value of Brown Pink on both sides of the head. Switch to Phthalo Green Light for the next section of the body right under the head. Paint a half oval shape and switch to Van Dyck Brown to paint the sides where the legs come out of the body.

Now for the second pair of legs. Load your detail brush with Hooker's Green and paint a wash, adding Brown Pink in some areas. Before it dries, add a big dot of Van Dyck Brown on the lower section of both legs—like a dark spot on a leaf. Outline the legs with Van Dyck Brown as well, but not all around; leave some areas untouched. Don't forget to outline the brown tips too. Add lines across the thick vein in the middle of the legs using your detail brush and Phthalo Green Deep. Repeat the detailing process on the lower legs, adding more spikes and brown dots on these than the others. Outline them with Van Dyck Brown, leaving some spaces untouched.

Now let's work on the body. Load your detail brush with Yellow Sophie and paint the veins you carved out in Step 2. Then switch to your medium brush, and use all the previous shades of green to add more texture to the body— again, using the tip of your brush to add the colors. The only requirement here is to use the darkest shade on the edges of the body to create 3D-like dimension. Use Van Dyck Brown and Quinacridone Red to add dots and marks on the body, especially close to the veins and on the bottom edge. Add a stroke on the left side of the central yellow vein to act as a shadow and add dimension. Let it dry.

Once it's dry, use a very light value of Phthalo Green Light to create little veins all over the body. These veins go along and across the body between the yellow veins; they should be very light and subtle. If you feel like the lines are thick or too obvious, wait until they dry, and then use your medium brush with a bit of water to soften the areas that need to be more subtle.

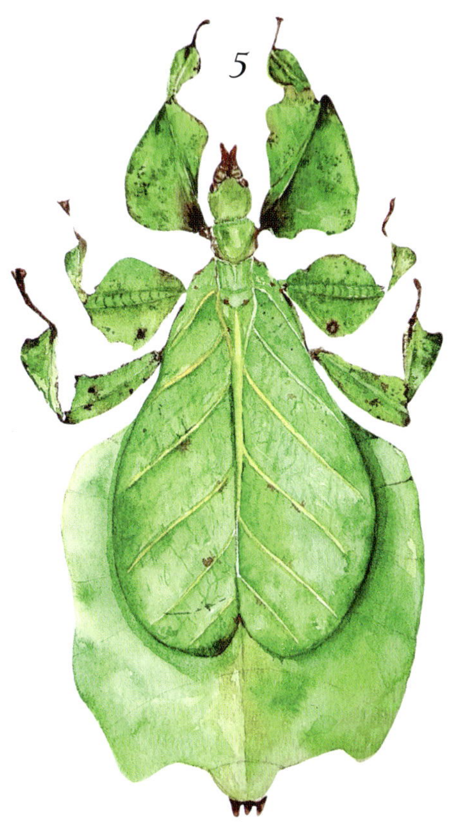

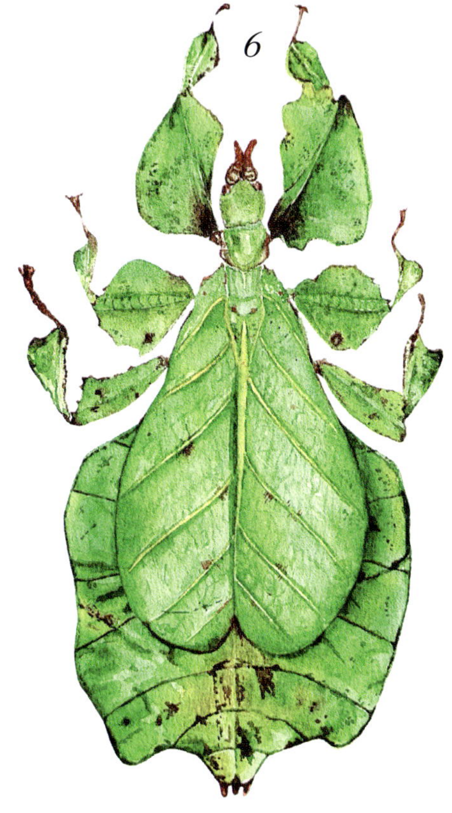

Step 6

You're almost done! It's time to paint the last wash over the lower section of the body. Use your medium brush and the same greens you used in previous steps—just add a darker value over this lower section of the body. Before it's completely dry, work on adding some extra brushstrokes right under the middle section of the body, like creases branching out of the main section of the body.

Switch to your detail brush to outline the lower section of the body with Phthalo Green Deep mixed with Blue Indanthrene. Keep some areas clean without outlining. Next, create the veins using the same color mix of Phthalo Green Deep and Blue Indanthrene. Don't make these lines perfect; add a few dots and lines around it to create more texture. Switch to Van Dyck Brown and add more dots and lines. Concentrate more on the brown markings on the very bottom of this section. Imagine you're painting a leaf that's getting dry or crispy.

This leaf insect is ready to camouflage in the jungle again!

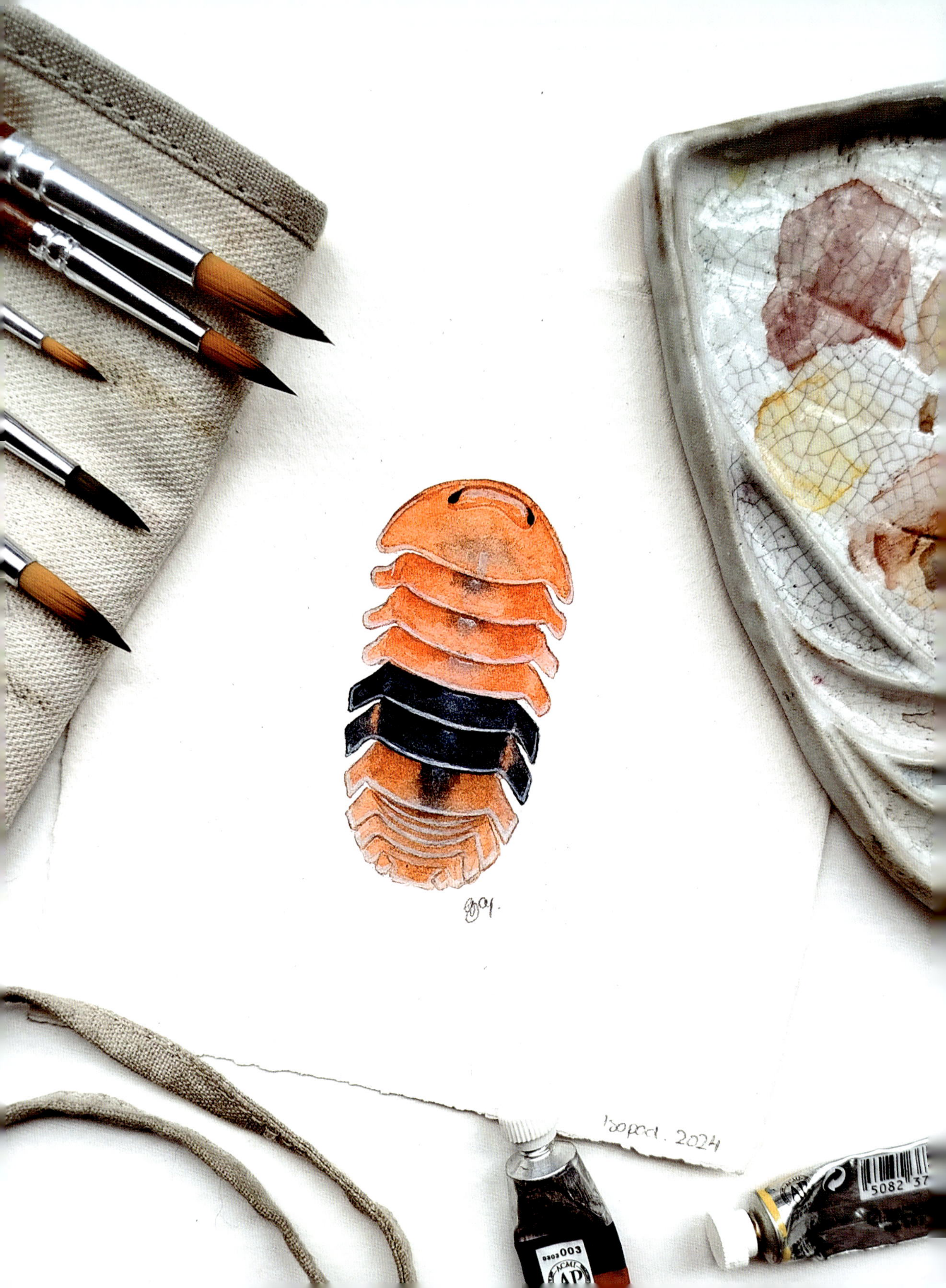

Isopod. 2024

Roly-Poly

"Roly-poly" is the cute name we use to for isopods, pill bugs, or woodlice, tiny creatures that have been on the planet far longer than we have.

Isopods are often treated as pests due to their love of damp places—sometimes in our basement. However, the benefit of woodlice outweighs any damage they could do to our homes and environment. For example, among other things, they ingest mineral soil particles, which are mixed with organic substances in the intestine and excreted as clay-humus complexes. Isopods are significantly involved in improving soil quality.

Roly-polies are often mistaken for insects, but strangely enough, they are crustaceans! And did you know they come in different colors? For this project, I chose the *Cubaris sp.* amber ducky. But there are many other species like the tricolor, scarlet, rosy woodlouse, or even the spiky yellow woodlouse. Maybe after you're done practicing with this tutorial, you can paint some of those!

Difficulty: Easy

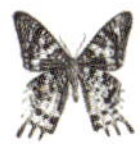

Sketch

Draw the roly-poly freehand or trace the reference image and transfer it to the watercolor paper of your choice, focusing on the thorax and eyes. Spray your paints with water to moisten them.

MATERIALS

- Watercolor paper of your choice
  - I used a 6 x 6–inch (15 x 15–cm) sheet
- Paints
  - Red Orange, Payne's Grey, Carmine
  - White gouache
- Brushes
  - Medium round brush (I used size 6)
  - Detail round brush (I used size 2)

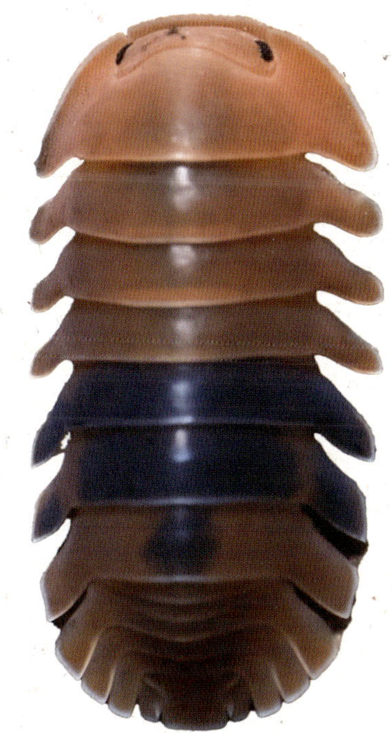

Step 1

Isopods are made of seven segments and a rounded "tail." Load your medium brush with Red Orange and paint a first wash over the head and thorax, skipping the fourth and fifth segments.

Switch to a light value of Payne's Grey and your detail brush to dot a bit of color on the top section of the first three segments, and add more color to the sixth segment, like a line in the middle. Let it dry.

Load your medium brush with Payne's Grey and paint the two remaining segments with a medium wash. Right after, load your detail brush with Red Orange and dot a line of color along the fifth segment on both sides.

> **Tip:** *To keep control over the amount of water and color coming out of brush, dab the tip of your brush onto a paper towel before adding it to the paper.*

Step 2

Make sure the surface is dry before applying the next wash. Mix Red Orange with a bit of Carmine on your palette and load your medium brush to paint a second wash over the orange segments. Paint them one at a time, leaving a blank space right on the bottom of each segment and lightening the value on the sides. Before it dries, add a light value of Payne's Grey to the middle of the head by dabbing some color on with your medium brush. Also, lighten the value of all the colors as you go down—meaning that the head and first three segments should be darker than the bottom ones. Wait for this to dry.

Use a darker value of Payne's Grey to paint a second wash on both darker segments, dotting Red Orange with your detail brush before it dries. Now put eyes on this cute isopod with your detail brush and Payne's Grey. Let this dry.

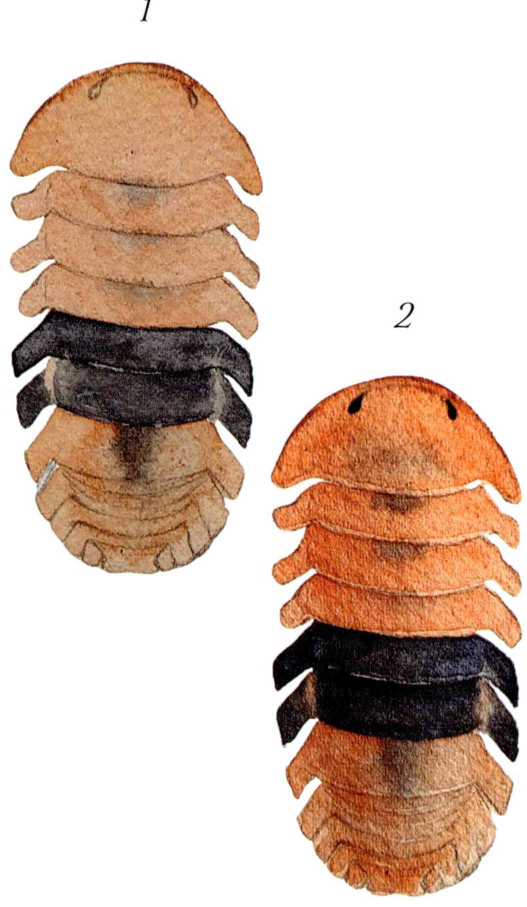

Step 3

Focusing on the head now, load your detail brush with the mixture of Red Orange and Carmine from Step 2 to create the rounded shape around the eyes. If needed, add a darker value of both colors. This line should be bold. Paint a few brushstrokes inside the area to create texture.

Now let's add some dimension. With the same color, outline the head section, leaving about a millimeter of space between outer edge and your new line; this will be your highlight. Load your medium brush with the same mixture and paint another wash over the rest of the segments and tail, adding additional Payne's Grey to the last segments in the same area you did in Step 2; keep the color a line down the center of the seventh section. Wait for this to dry. Load your medium brush with Payne's Grey and paint another wash on the darker segments, adding the Red Orange markings with your detail brush.

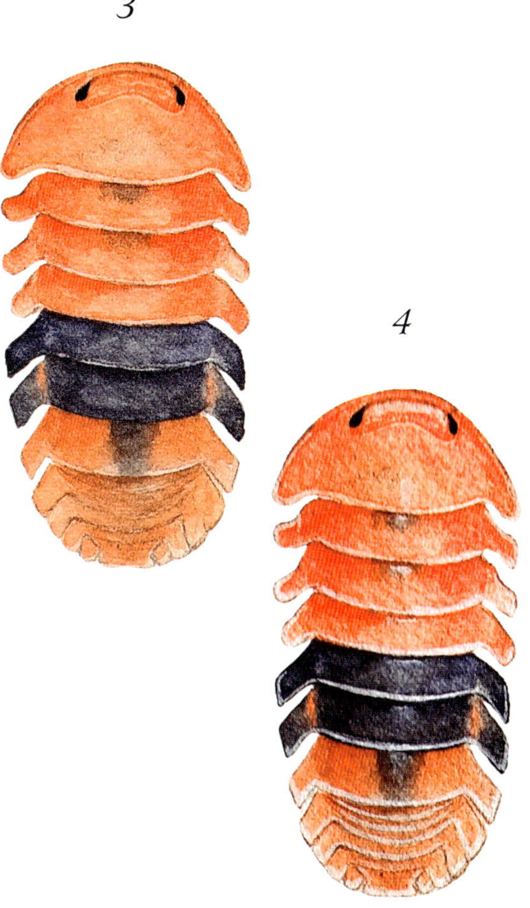

Step 4

Time for the highlights. Load your detail brush with white gouache and paint a line between the eyes, and where you left the space for the highlights in Step 2 (the lower section of each segments), softening the line a little with the same brush with a bit of water.

Next, water down the gouache and add a curving line between the eyes; carefully soften this with the same brush and a bit of water. Then add a little line to the center bottom bit of the head before moving downward—adding a little dot on each segment right at the top, and then softening the smudge with your brush. Finally, keep using your detail brush to define the tail sections. Paint lines with your gouache and outline the top of the square pieces.

This roly-poly is about to curl into a ball and disappear!

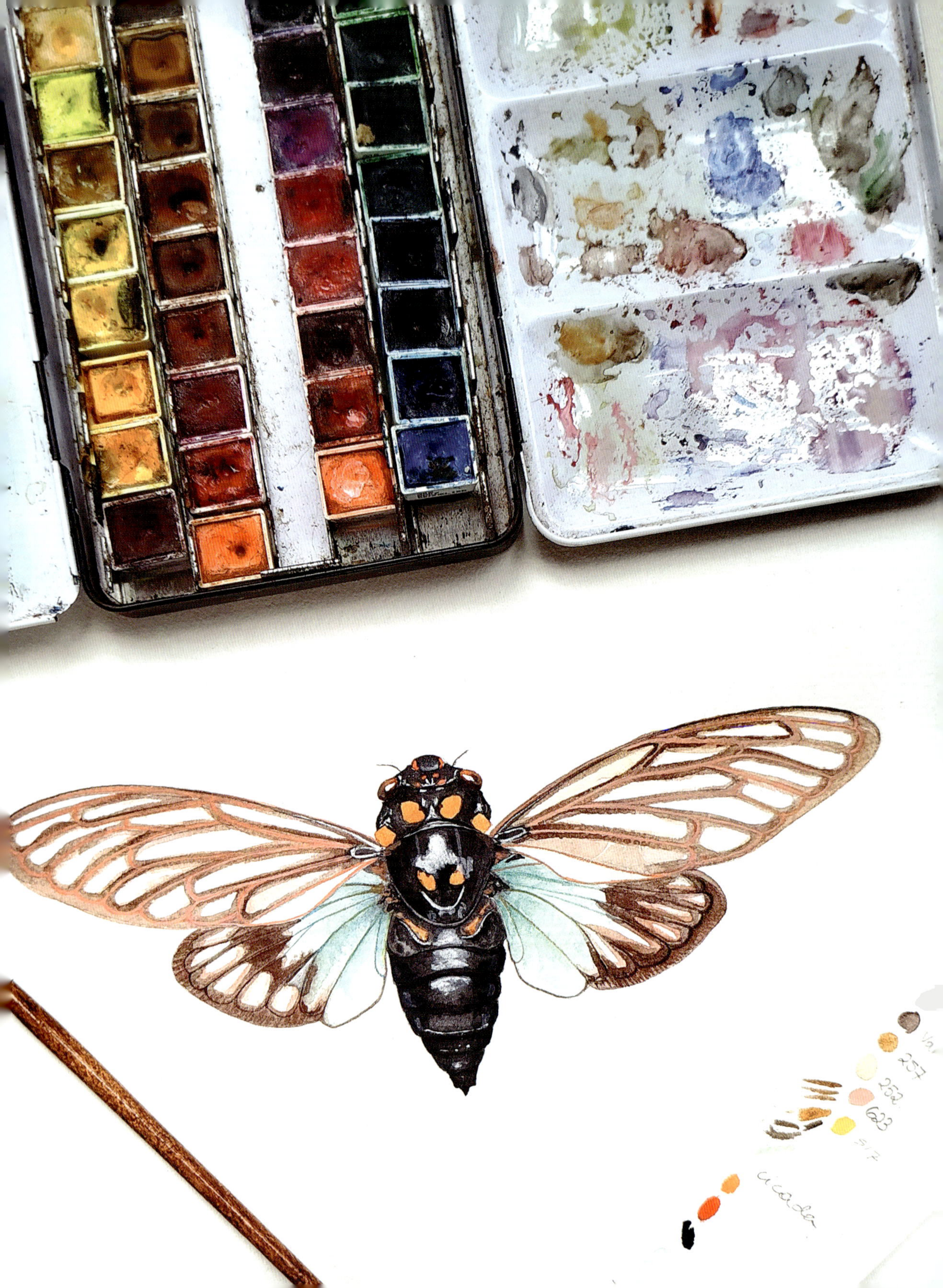

Cicada

While they do die after mating, like most insects, cicadas have some of the longest lifespans of any insect! Some, like the periodical Pharaoh cicada (also known as the 17-year locust), have 17-year long lifecycles! Shortly after hatching, cicada nymphs burrow into the ground where they spend the first 17 years of their lives. Scientists don't know exactly why they wait so long to come up, but they think it might be because it's harder for predators to kill them when there are so many cicadas crawling up at once.

There are many different kinds of cicadas. While the 17-year locusts may be getting all the press, there are actually around 3,400 species of cicadas on earth. *Distantalna splendida*, native to Southeast Asia, is the one you are going to paint in this project.

Difficulty: Medium

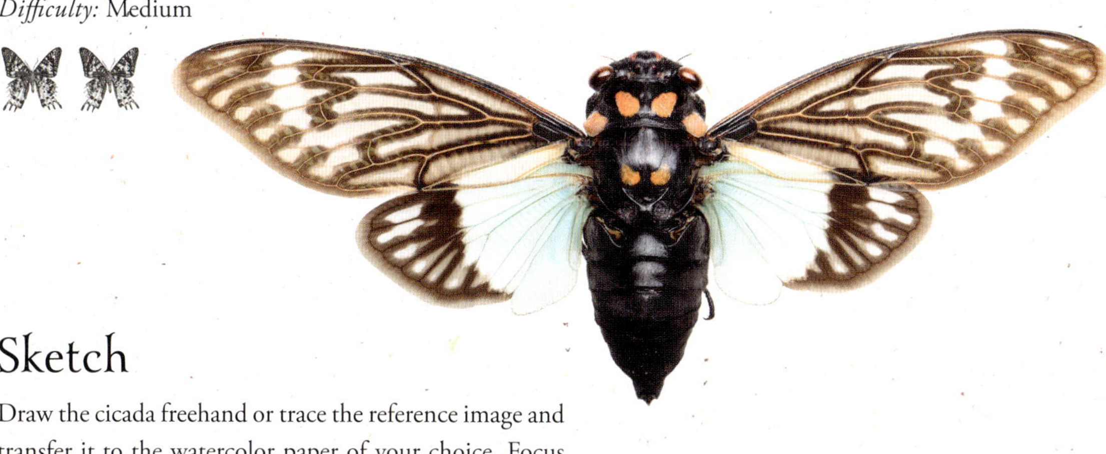

Sketch

Draw the cicada freehand or trace the reference image and transfer it to the watercolor paper of your choice. Focus on the wings' veins and the shape of the body. Spray your paints with water to moisten them.

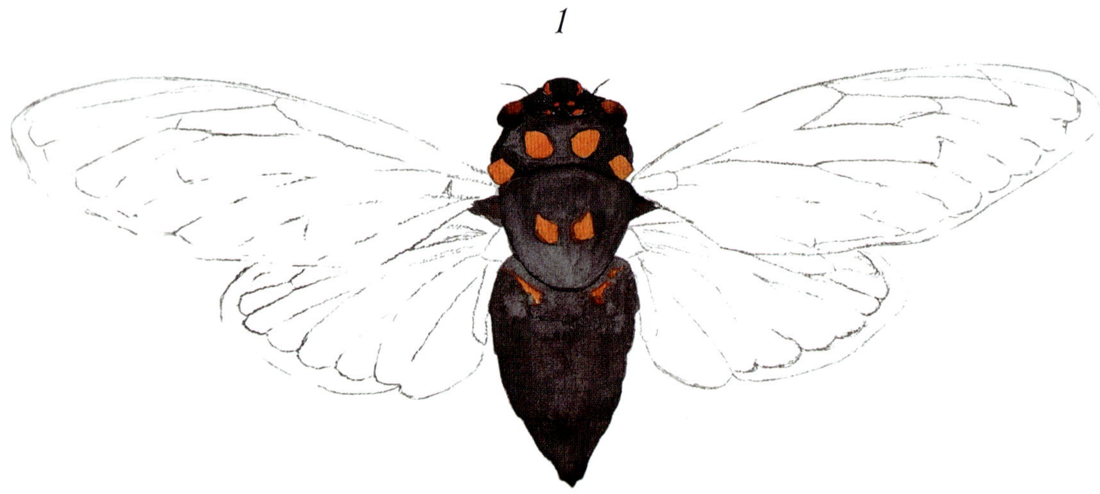

Step 1

Load your detail brush with French Vermilion and start painting the details on the head of the cicada. When painting the eyes, switch to Ivory Black and add a bit of color to the base of the eyes, allowing it to blend. Move to the section right underneath the head and load your detail brush with Red Orange to paint the four markings: the two oval shapes in the middle and the two on the sides. For the bottom section, paint the two marks and the two line markings with the Red Orange. Let it dry.

Load your detail brush with Ivory Black and paint the head, outline the orange markings, and then paint the next section (also omitting the orange markings). Let this dry between each section—this way you'll create a line that marks the separation between sections. Paint the two triangles inside the wings with a dot of Red Orange in the middle. Switch to your medium brush to paint the bottom section of the body, saving the orange markings. Add a darker value on the edges of the body. Use your detail brush with a dark value of Ivory Black to paint the tiny antennae. Let everything dry before moving on.

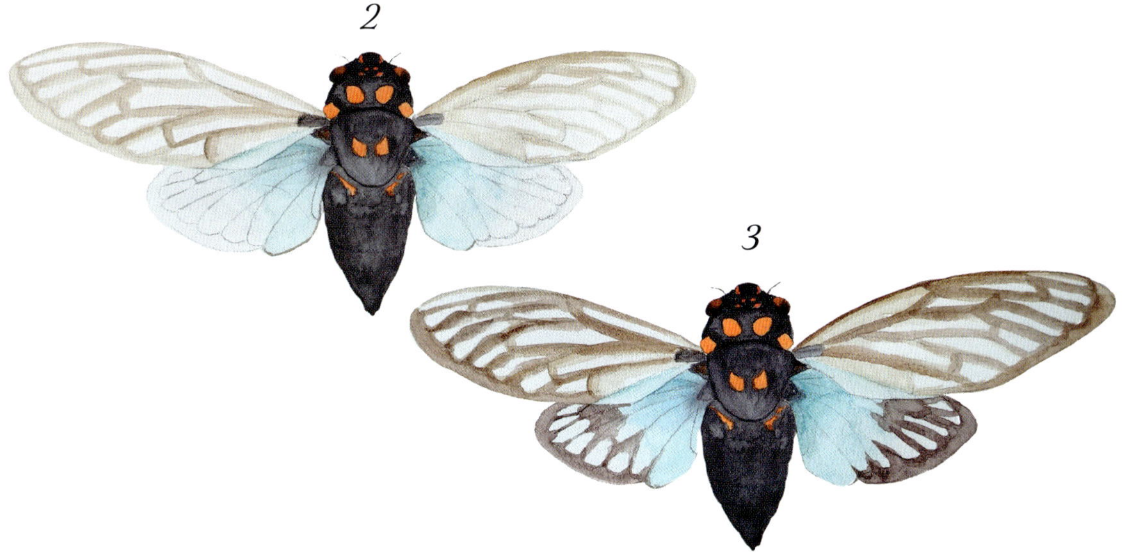

Step 2

In your palette mix two parts Cinereous Blue with one part Emerald Green. Load your medium brush and paint a light wash on the bottom wings that fades towards the middle. To do this, start with a darker value of the mixture and add water as you paint. Before it dries, outline the first section of the wing, the one closer to the body using your detail brush and Yellow Ochre. Also load your detail brush with Ivory Black and paint two more triangle-shaped marks coming out of the body right under the other triangles.

Moving to the upper wings, paint the wings with a very light wash of the Cinereous Blue and Emerald Green mixture, using your medium brush. Then, load your detail brush with Ivory Black and paint the rectangle-shaped marks coming right out of the body. Then, mix Yellow Ochre with a dash of Van Dyck Brown and use this with your medium brush to paint a light wash over all the veins.

Step 3

Load your medium brush with a light wash of Van Dyck Brown and start shaping the lower section of the bottom wings. Paint over the veins with your medium brush, pressing to achieve thicker, uneven brushstrokes. As you get towards the middle of the wing, paint a big smudge—it doesn't have to be perfect; just cover the area as a first layer to work on the details later.

Switch to your detail brush with a light value of Van Dyck Brown and paint over the veins, saving the two lower sections of the wing (the one you painted blue and the following one that should have a light wash of Yellow Ochre and Van Dyck Brown).

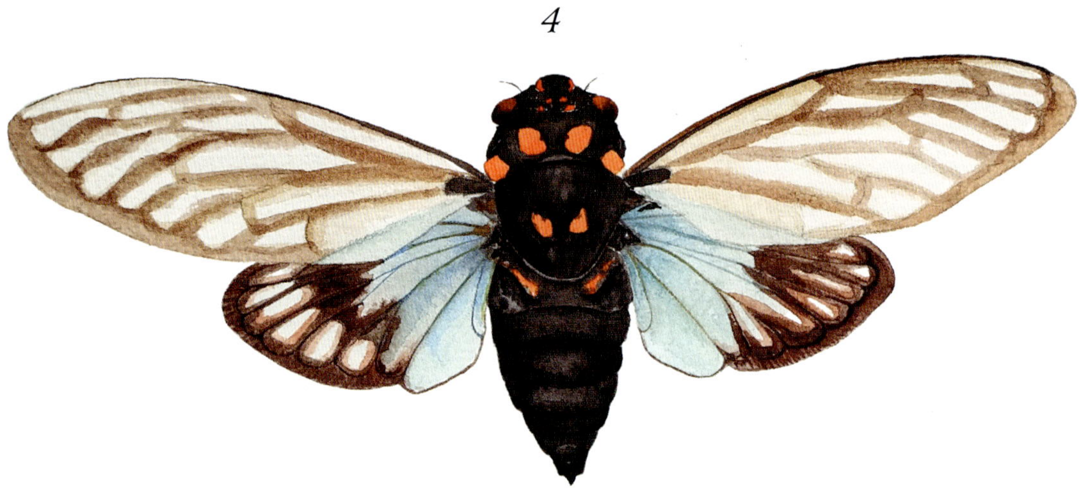

Step 4

Now we'll work on the lower wings to add more details and define the veins. Load your detail brush with a dark value of Van Dyck Brown and paint lines as veins over the pencil markings. (You should still be able to see them through the brown wash.) Outline the blue bottom edge of the wing, and then add a bit of Yellow Ochre to your palette with Van Dyck Brown to keep painting these lines upwards. The three upper veins are going to be painted with a dark value of Cinereous Blue. Load your medium brush with a medium value of your mixture of Cinereous Blue and Emerald Green to create some thick brushstrokes coming out of the middle towards the center to create depth on your wings. Once the brown area is dry, load your detail brush with a darker value of Van Dyck Brown to paint little lines along the bottom edge of the wings.

Work on the upper wings while you wait for the lower wings to dry. Load your detail brush with Ivory Black and create a line from the rectangle-shaped mark outlining the upper edge of the wing. Now that the lower wings are dry, load your medium brush with Venetian Red to paint a light wash inside the white area of the lower wing markings—the space between the veins.

To finish this step, load your medium brush with Ivory Black and define each section of the lower body. Paint one at a time, and let them dry to mark the line in between. Darken the value at the edges and use the lifting color technique (page 14) to create a highlight spot in the middle, as the light would be hitting it.

Move to the middle section, and paint another wash using Ivory Black, leaving about a millimeter of space between the outer edge and your new line; this will be your highlight. Repeat the process on the next section and the head.

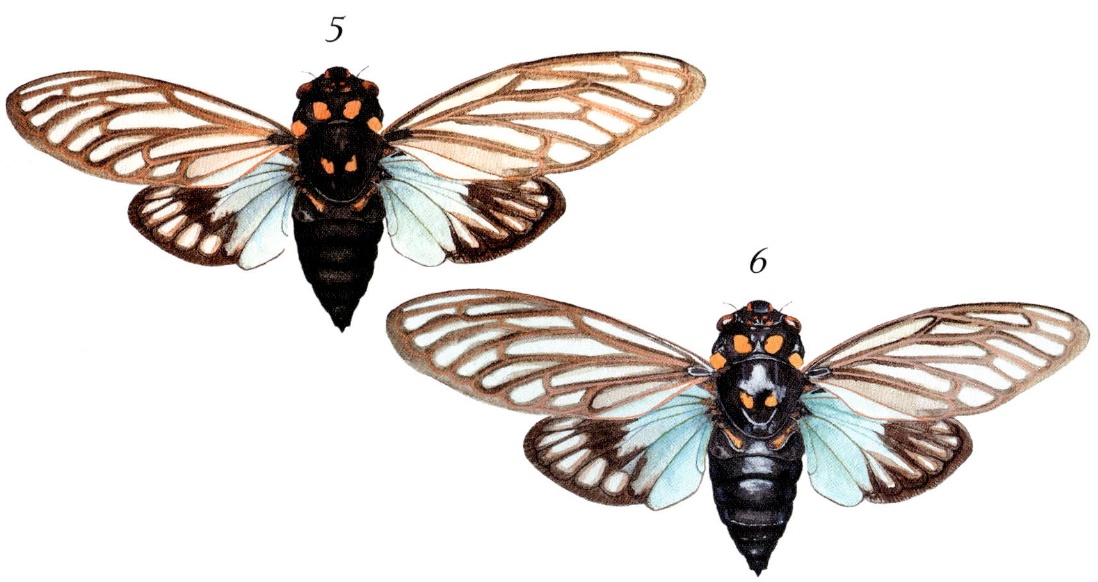

Step 5

Mix Titanium White and Red Orange to create an opaque color to paint over the brown. Load your detail brush and paint over the veins on the upper wings. Switch to your medium brush loaded with a darker value of Ivory Black to define the lower body a bit more. In this case, it depends on how much value you painted on the previous step. You're simply adjusting color now that it's dry. Add more color to the areas where it's needed. The edges should be darker than the middle, and right over each section should be darker too.

Step 6

Time for the highlights. Mix a bit of water with white gouache and using your detail brush work your way down to add the highlights.

First, paint lines right above the section lines over the head area, softening the lines a bit with the tip of a clean medium brush. Then paint a big smudge simulating the light hitting between the orange markings and in the middle of the body paint. Right under the two orange markings, paint a semicircle and paint a line following the shape of the markings right underneath the last orange markings on the sides of the lower body.

In the middle of the bottom section of the body, paint three smudges and soften the edges with your clean brush. Outline the black rectangle markings on the upper wings with white, adding a thin line going over the upper edge of the wing but not all the way—just as a highlight.

This cicada can now emerge from your paper!

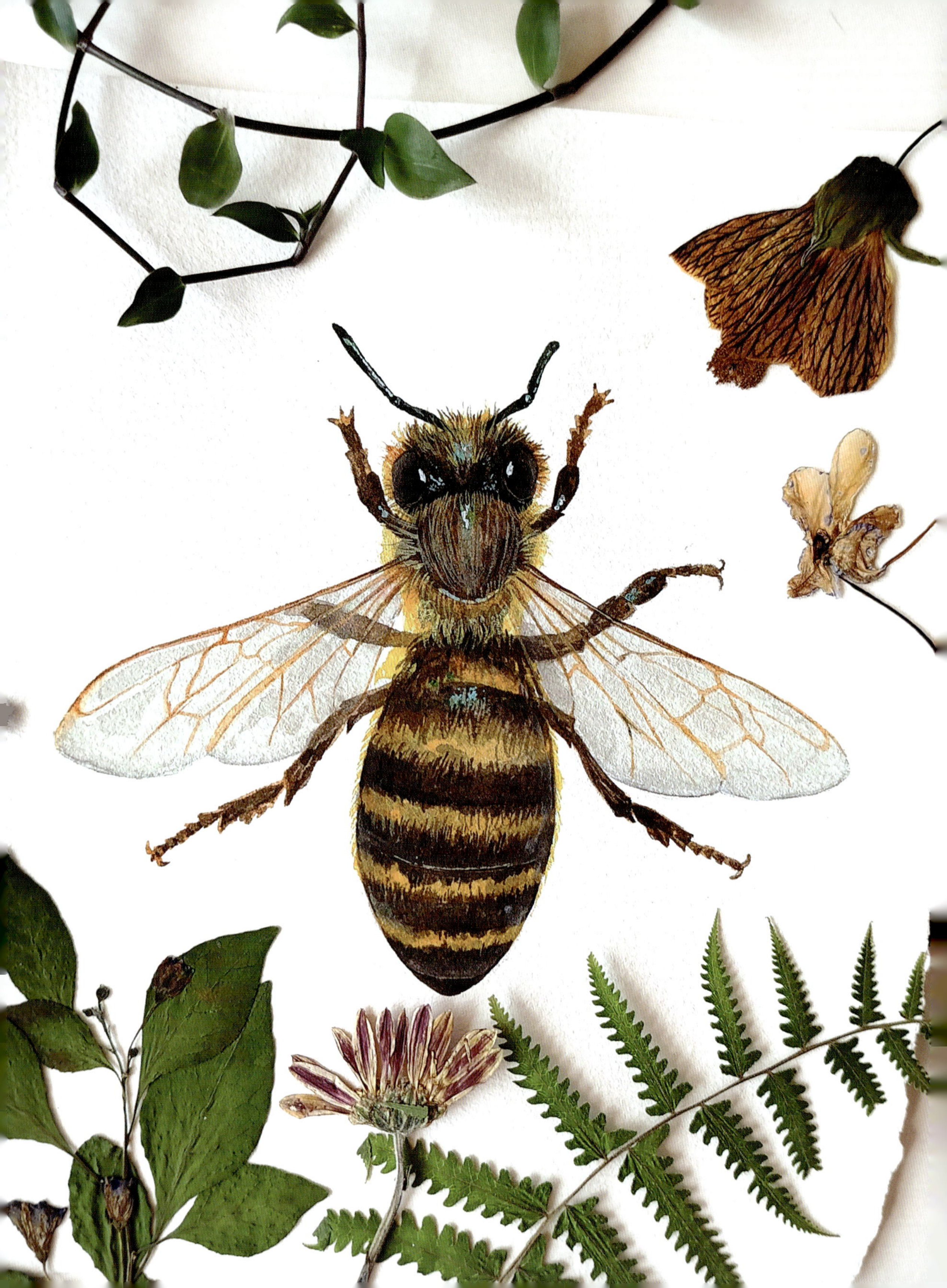

Honeybee

Honeybees live in colonies with one queen running the whole hive. Many of the crops people consume are pollinated by honeybees. Many growers maintain honeybee colonies for this very reason. Without pollination, the plants would not produce fruits and vegetables. Besides pollination, honeybees extract nectar along with the pollen from the flowers. The nectar is transported back to the hive where it is converted into honey.

Although honeybees are one of the most recognizable bees, they represent only a small percentage of bee species!

Difficulty: Medium

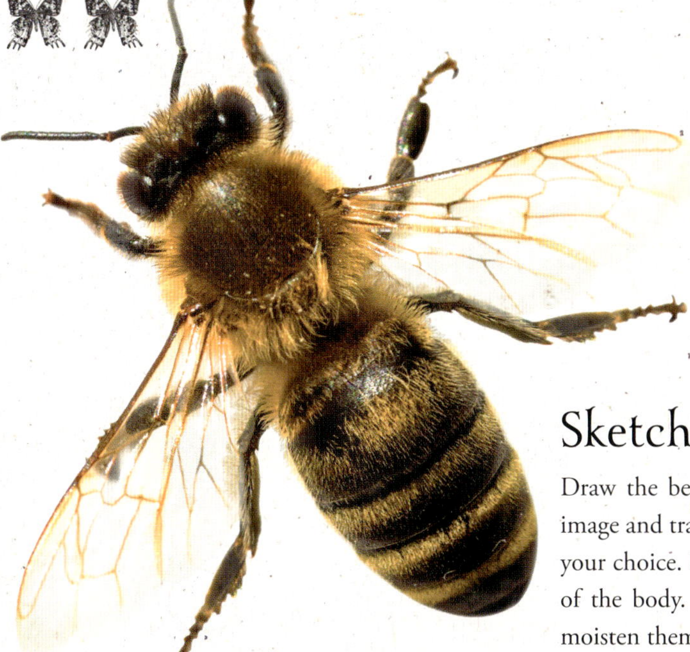

Sketch

Draw the bee freehand or trace the reference image and transfer it to the watercolor paper of your choice. Focus on the wings and the shape of the body. Spray your paints with water to moisten them.

Step 1

Load your medium brush with a light value of Burnt Umber and paint the head, darkening the value at the bottom edge. Before it dries, switch to your detail brush loaded with Emerald Green and paint a little dot between the eyes. Let it dry. Keep using Emerald Green to paint the antennae. Once you are done and before it dries, add a little line on the first section of the antennae with Ivory Black—really thin though! With your detail brush, paint the eyes with a dark wash of Van Dyck Brown. Before they are dry, dot a bit of Ivory Black to the inner edges.

Paint the next section of the body with a medium wash of Van Dyck Brown, and before it dries, paint a line towards the center with Emerald Green, allowing it to blend with the background a bit. Don't use a lot of water—we don't want this fading into the background.

Step 2

The next semicircular section should be painted with a mix of Burnt Umber and a dash of Venetian Red. Add more value over the edges.

For the body, first paint a light wash with the mixture you just created. Use your medium brush for this. When it's almost dry, add five stripes across the body with your medium brush and a medium value of Warm Sepia. The first one should curve upwards, and the next four downwards—to create the effect of roundedness. Add a bit of color over the connection between the sections and another dot of darker

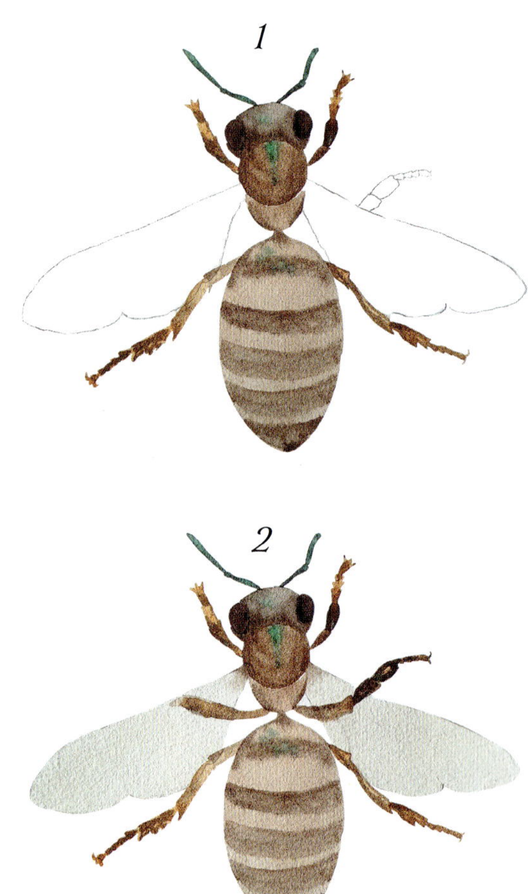

color on the bee's butt. Also dot a bit of Emerald Green over the upper section of the lower body.

Take care of the legs now. First, using your detail brush, paint a wash of Gold Ochre on the legs, and before they dry, use the tip of your brush with Van Dyck Brown to add some color, especially where the joints meet. For the wings, paint a light wash of Yellow Ochre using your medium brush.

Step 3

Load your detail brush with a dark value of Warm Sepia and add value to the head, painting a darker wash on the bottom half of the head. Instead of giving this wash an even layer, use the tip of your brush to dab the painting.

While you wait for this to dry, mix a bit of Ivory Black to your Emerald Green, and paint the antennae with your detail brush—leaving some parts untouched to create highlights, allowing the lighter color to be seen. Moving down to the next section of the body, load your medium brush with Van Dyck Brown, and using the same technique of dabbing the color with the tip of your brush, add a darker value all around this circular section.

> *Tip: By dabbing the paint with the tip of your brush instead of doing brushstrokes, you'll create a nice texture. I do this a lot to create uneven surfaces that look like scales and other things.*

Switch back to Warm Sepia to paint the lower section of the body. Dab a darker value of the color over the stripes and a lighter value of the color on the spaces between. The darkest shade of Warm Sepia should go on the bottom stripes. Since bees are round, this would make your bee look like it's curving downwards. Lastly, paint a dark wash of Warm Sepia on the eyes. Leave a little space unpainted on the tops.

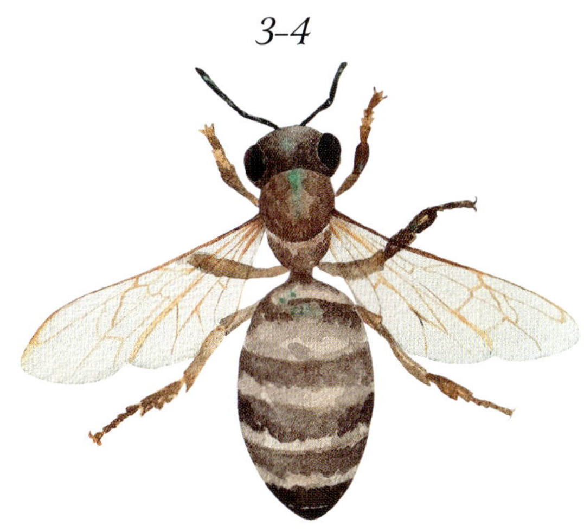

Step 4

Prepare the surface of the wings with a water wash, leaving the paper not so damp. Load your detail brush with a medium value of Ivory Black (don't use much water so you have more control over the process) and outline the bottom of the wings, allowing the paint to blend with the water wash. If it bleeds too much inside the wing, clean and dry your brush and use it as a mop to clean the areas where the black runs. Wait until it dries. Meanwhile, load your detail brush with Van Dyck Brown and outline the upper edge of the wings, thinning out the line as you get closer to the edge.

Switch to Gold Ochre to paint the veins. You should be able to see the pencil markings through the light wash you painted. If not, use the reference photo on page 137. Don't put too much pressure on yourself if these are not perfect. I think it's better if these lines are simple and you don't paint them all.

Step 5

Load your medium brush with a medium value of Indian Yellow and paint a thick line around the middle area of the body. Using the same brush, add color to the lighter sections between the brown stripes. Add the color with your medium brush and dot the painting in smudges, adding more value on the edges. Switch to Warm Sepia and add a darker shade on the third stripe's corners. Let this dry while working on the head. Use your detail brush and a mix of Warm Sepia, Gold Ochre, and Indian Yellow to add hairlike lines coming out of the head.

Step 6

Keep adding hairlike strokes over the head using your detail brush and Warm Sepia. Then add a last wash of Ivory Black over the eyes, leaving the tops untouched. Move to the next section and paint more lines using your detail brush and a darker value of Van Dyck Brown. Switch to Ivory Black to paint a few lines over the Emerald Green mark. Switch to Van Dyck Brown to paint more lines coming out over the yellow area. It's all about creating hairlike strokes over the areas. Move towards the next section with a darker value of Van Dyck Brown, and paint some more lines where the two last sections join.

Switch to Indian Yellow and your detail brush to create more tiny hairs coming out of the bottom section of the body. Once you are happy

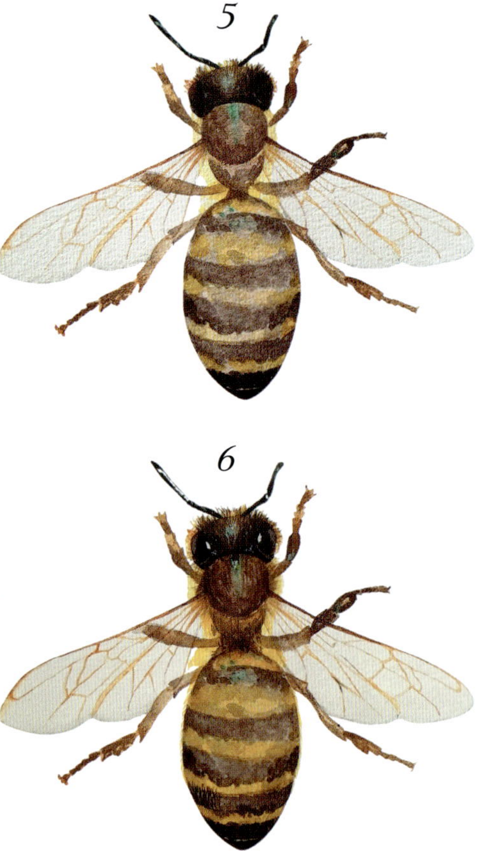

with the look, switch to your medium brush and paint an even wash of Indian Yellow over the yellow areas to even it out.

Once the head is completely dry, mix a bit of Titanium White with Emerald Green and paint some dots right next to the eyes. Add two highlights on the eyes with just Titanium White with your detail brush. Lighten the value of the white with some water to outline the bottom of the eyes.

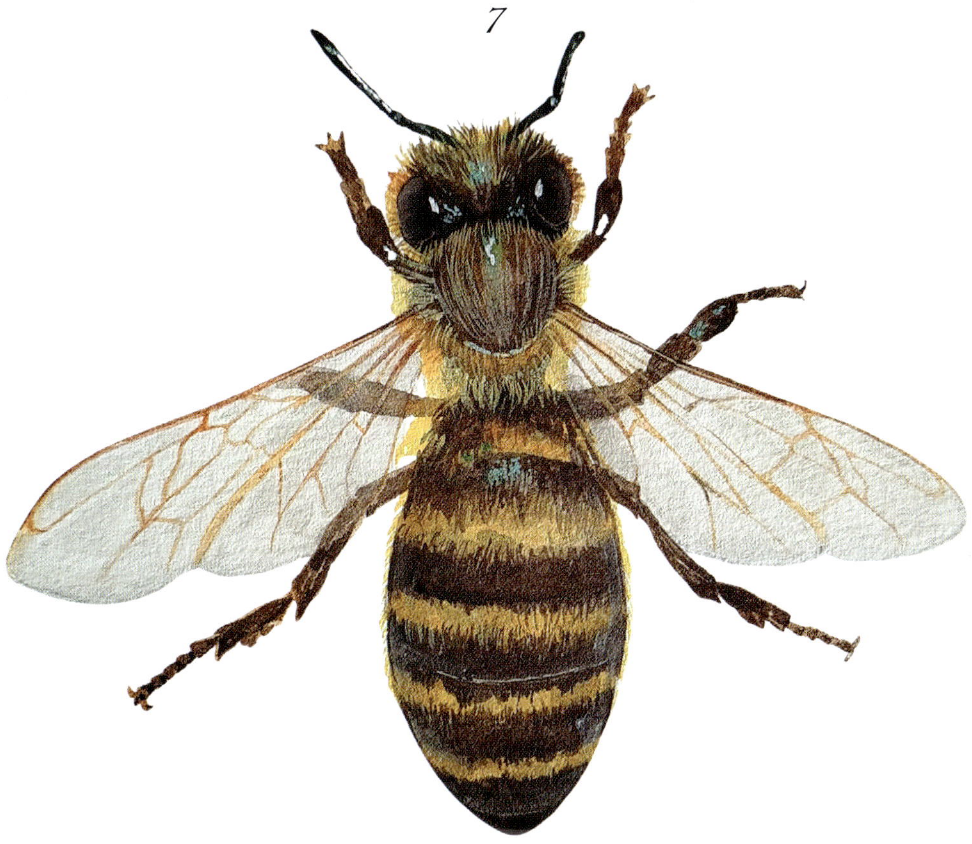

Step 7

Load your detail brush with a dark value of Van Dyck Brown to paint lines over each stripe on the lower section of the body. It's up to you how many lines to paint—just make that bee look fluffy! Mix Yellow Ochre with Titanium White to create an opaque light yellow. Use this and your detail brush to paint more hairlike strokes over the head and the two other sections.

Add another layer of Van Dyck Brown to the legs using your detail brush. When dry, paint some dots of Emerald Green mixed with Titanium White over the head, the lower section of the body, and some of the legs. This is to create a shimmer.

Bzzzz! This bee is already flying to collect some pollen!

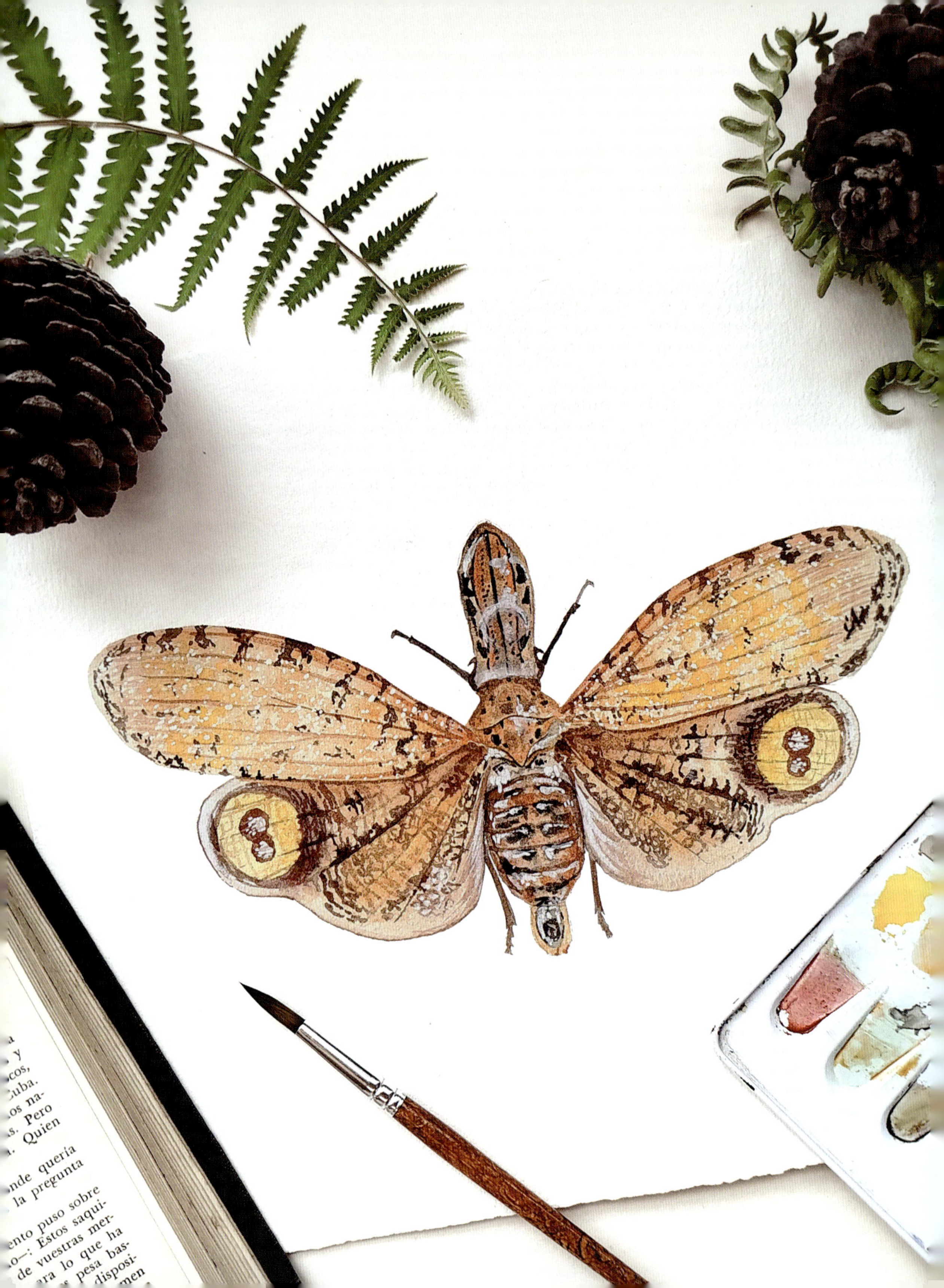

Peanut-Headed Lantern Fly

One of the greatest and weirdest insects in the rainforest, the peanut-headed lantern fly is so named because its head looks like a peanut. It is believed that the head shape changed through natural selection to resemble the head of an alligator. A compelling aspect of this insect is its pair of large, fake eyes on its head. These false eyes serve to deter potential predators by making the insect appear larger and more threatening. Interestingly, these bugs also possess a luminescent feature that can emit light in the dark, adding to their mystique.

Difficulty: Difficult

- Watercolor paper of your choice
  - › I used an 8 x 10–inch (20 x 25–cm) sheet, landscape orientation
- Paints
  - › Yellow Ochre, Gold Ochre, Van Dyck Brown, Red Orange, Yellow Sophie, Ivory Black, Sennelier Yellow Deep
  - › White gouache
- Brushes
  - › Old brush for masking fluid (I used a round size 2)
  - › Medium round brush (I used size 9)
  - › Detail round brush (I used size 2)
- Masking fluid and eraser (to remove)

Sketch

Draw the bug freehand or trace the reference image and transfer it to the watercolor paper of your choice, focusing on the shape of the wings, body, and markings. Spray your paints with water to moisten them.

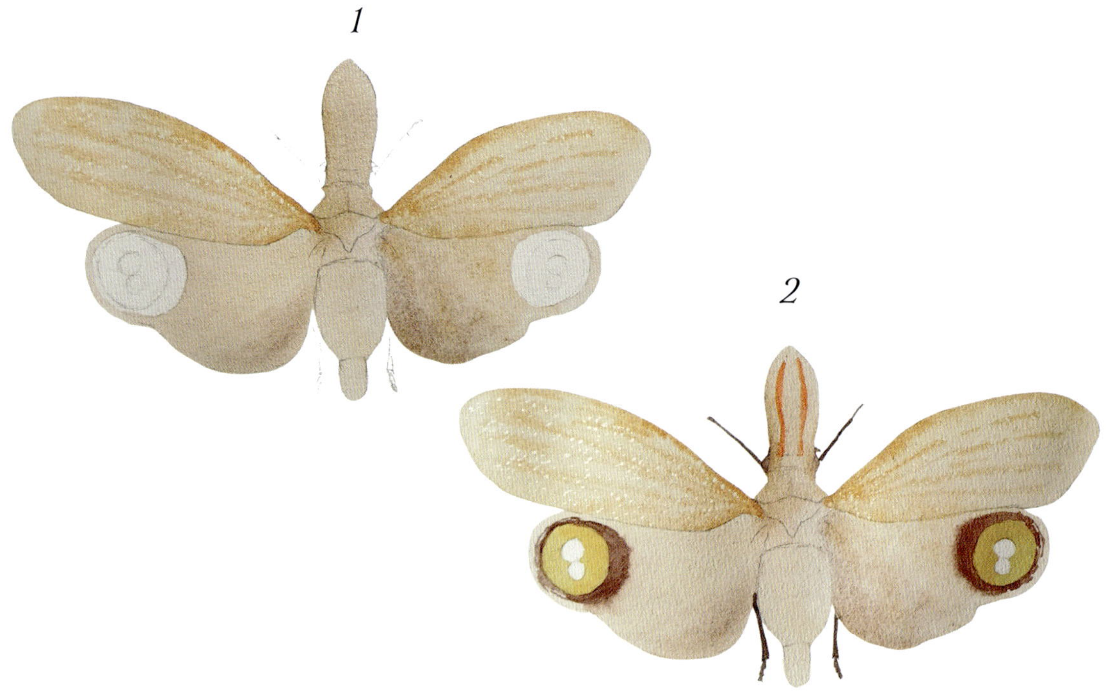

Step 1

Apply tiny dots on the forewing area using your old brush and masking fluid. Once this dries, load your medium brush with Yellow Ochre to paint a wash on the forewings. Before it dries, switch to Gold Ochre and outline the upper edge of the forewings and add veins to the surface. These lines should blend nicely with the background. Let it dry.

Apply a medium wash of Yellow Ochre to the hind wings with your medium brush, saving the eyespots for later. Before it dries, switch to Van Dyck Brown to darken the inner edge. Let it dry. Load your medium brush with Yellow Ochre to add a wash over the body area.

Step 2

Load your detail brush with Van Dyck Brown and paint the legs. Switch to Red Orange and paint the two markings on the head (the two lines with little curves following the shape of the head). Switch to Yellow Sophie and paint the middle of the eyespots. Then, with Van Dyck Brown, paint the outside, softening the edges and blending it into the background. On the outer side, paint a few extra round lines. Paint the eyes and the spike over the eyes using your detail brush and Van Dyck Brown.

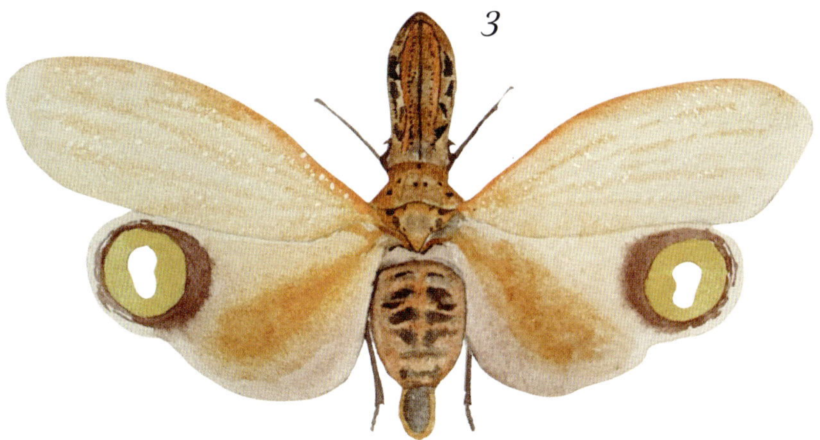

Step 3

Load your medium brush with Gold Ochre and paint a big smudge in the center of both hind wings, softening the edges with your clean brush.

Work on the head now. First, use your medium brush to create a wash with a light value of Van Dyck Brown, then, add a dot of Ivory Black to the base of the head, allowing it to blend with the background. Let it dry. Then, switch to your detail brush and a darker value of Van Dyck Brown to paint the lines on the head: the one in the middle and the other ones surrounding the previous Red Orange lines. In the middle of the lines, paint a line of dots. On the edges of the head, paint the dark markings using your detail brush and a dark value of Van Dyck Brown.

Moving to the thorax, paint a darker wash of Gold Ochre, and in the middle, dot a little bit of Yellow Ochre. Next, while still wet, switch to your detail brush with a dark value of Van Dyck Brown and paint the dots on this section. Let it dry.

The lowest section of the thorax is created by applying another wash of Gold Ochre, darkening the value on the sides and under the upper section of the thorax. Create a thin line with your detail brush, separating both sections. Once this is dry, add the dark markings. Outline the bottom edge with a thin line of Van Dyck Brown and your detail brush. Load your detail brush with a dark value of Gold Ochre and paint two lines on the protuberance right under the thorax. Add another wash over the eyes with Van Dyck Brown and your detail brush.

Work on the abdomen. First, add another wash of Gold Ochre using your medium brush. Switch to your detail brush loaded with Ivory Black and paint the black markings, allowing them to blend a bit. For the bottom section of the abdomen, paint the edge with Yellow Sophie, and once this dries, paint the center with a medium wash of Ivory Black.

Step 4

Load your medium brush with a mix of Yellow Ochre and Gold Ochre. Paint smudges on both forewings—sort of like uneven dots on the first half (the inner half). Do the same for the hind wings. While you wait for this to dry, work on the head.

Load your detail brush with Red Orange and paint the orange markings from Step 3 again to make them bolder. Switch to Van Dyck Brown to add a few subtle markings on the thorax, two on the edges of the top area, and two in the middle bottom section. If necessary, darken the edges with Golden Ochre to create a more rounded effect.

For the abdomen, load your detail brush with a medium value of Van Dyck Brown and paint the lines separating each section. Then switch to your medium brush with Gold Ochre and add color to both sides by applying smudges, especially to the top area.

Step 5

Now that the wings are dry, let's add all those details. Load your detail brush with Gold Ochre and paint a long vein on the top area of one of the forewings. Then switch to a medium

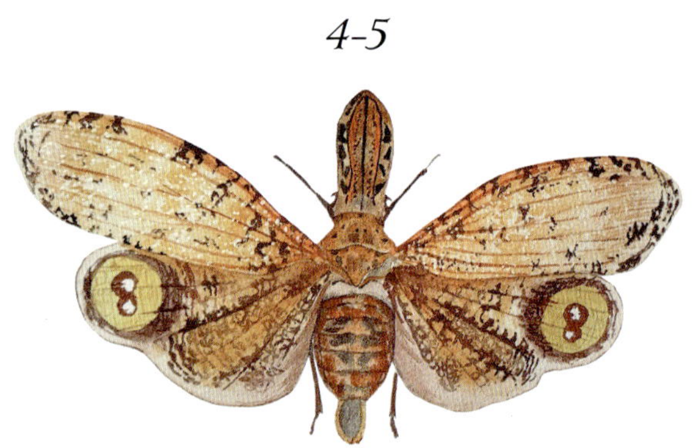

4-5

value of Van Dyck Brown and paint the rest of the veins. Lighten the value as you get to the outer edge. Repeat the process on the other forewing. Keep using your detail brush to paint all the dark markings on the forewings, adding some Ivory Black to darken the color for the markings on the outer edge of the wings.

For the hind wings, load your medium brush with a dark value of Gold Ochre and paint the part of the wings closer to the body. Switch to Van Dyck Brown and your detail brush to create the veins. These veins are a bit different from other insects' because they are across the wing too. Paint some creases on the eyespots using a darker value of Yellow Sophie. To finish, use your medium brush with a light value of Van Dyck Brown to add some thicker brushstrokes on the inner section of the hind wings. Let it dry.

6

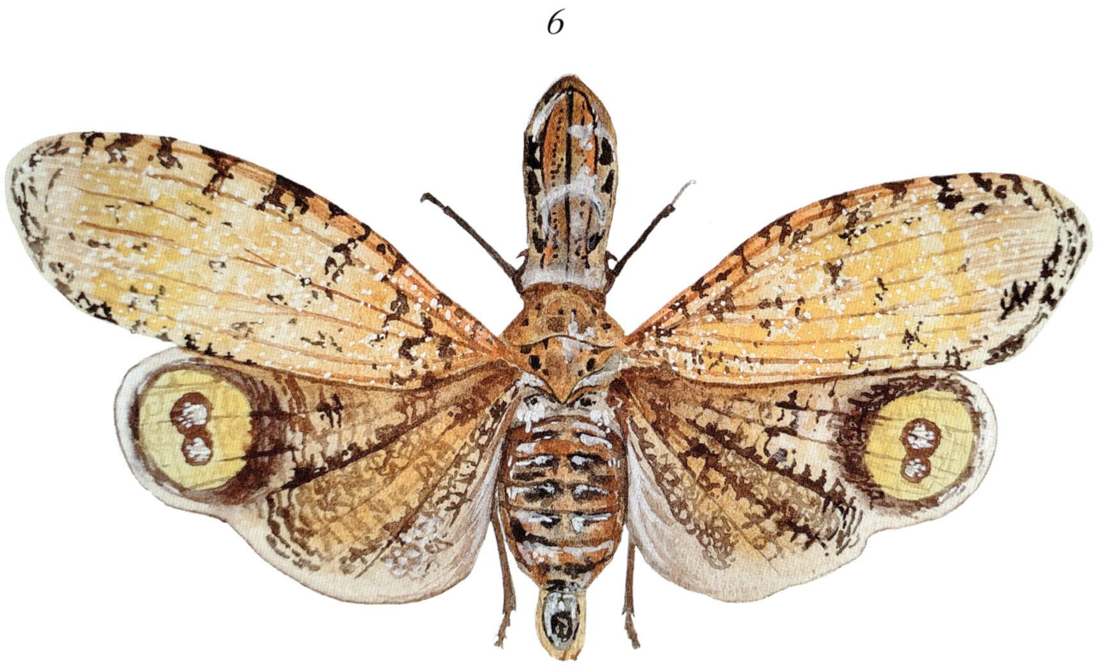

Step 6

Load your medium brush with Sennelier Yellow Deep and create more texture on the forewings, especially in the middle of them. Once dry, use the eraser to gently remove the masking fluid. Prepare your white gouache paint by adding some water to it to activate it. Use it to create the following highlights.

Load your detail brush and start bringing this bug to life. First, the head. Create a semicircle around the area that's more pronounced.

Then add another highlight on the top of the head. Add a light spot on the thorax, and a lot on the abdomen, over each of the black markings. Add a bit of white to the bottom of the abdomen protuberance and paint the inside of it with Ivory Black and your detail brush. On the eyespots' white areas, add a few dots of white gouache to make the area more cohesive. The inner edge of the hind wings should be highlighted too.

And it's done! Watch this planthopper fly away!

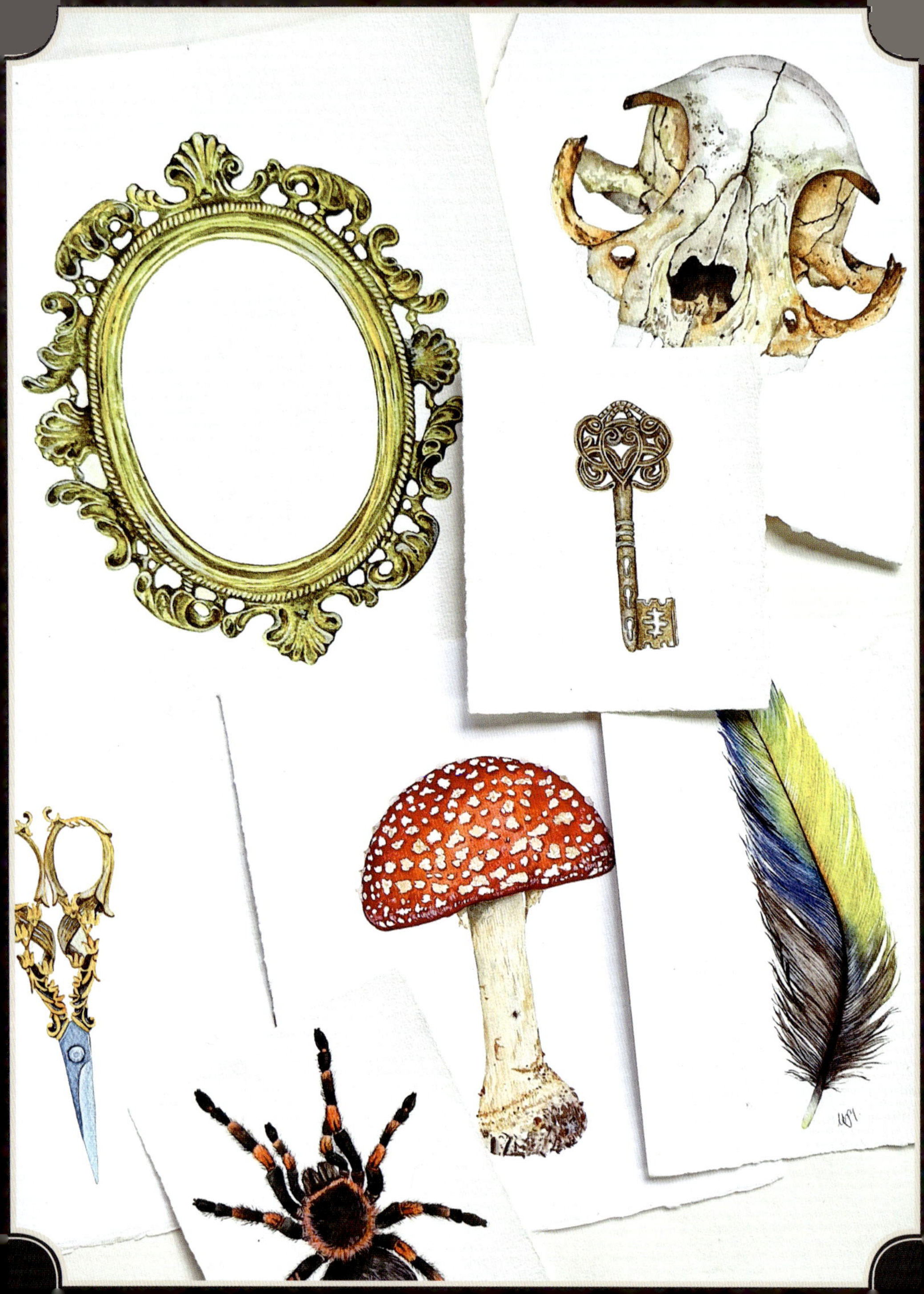

Beautiful Oddities

It's a dream of mine to have a cabinet of curiosities room full of vintage objects, oddities, and skulls. While I wait for this to happen, I've decided to paint my objects, and in this chapter, I bring you some of my favorites!

The Vintage Frame (page 165) is an intricate project that's absolutely beautiful and great for learning about the secret to painting shadows in watercolor to create lifelike objects that pop off the paper. This is the most challenging project in the book, though, so the Old Key (page 171) or the Vintage Scissors (page 155) might be good places to begin before tackling the frame.

You can also find an Amanita Muscaria (page 177), one of the most recognizable fungi in the world. This is another good project to start with in this chapter and learn about color layering. Or try the Tarantula (page 151), which is also an easy one to get you in the mood!

Not everyone likes skulls, but to love a skull or an image of one is to own your own mortality, and spooky things can be beautiful too. With that in mind, I included a Cat Skull (page 159), a medium difficulty project where I'll teach you how to paint in white. If you are not scared of the unknown, this chapter is perfect for you!

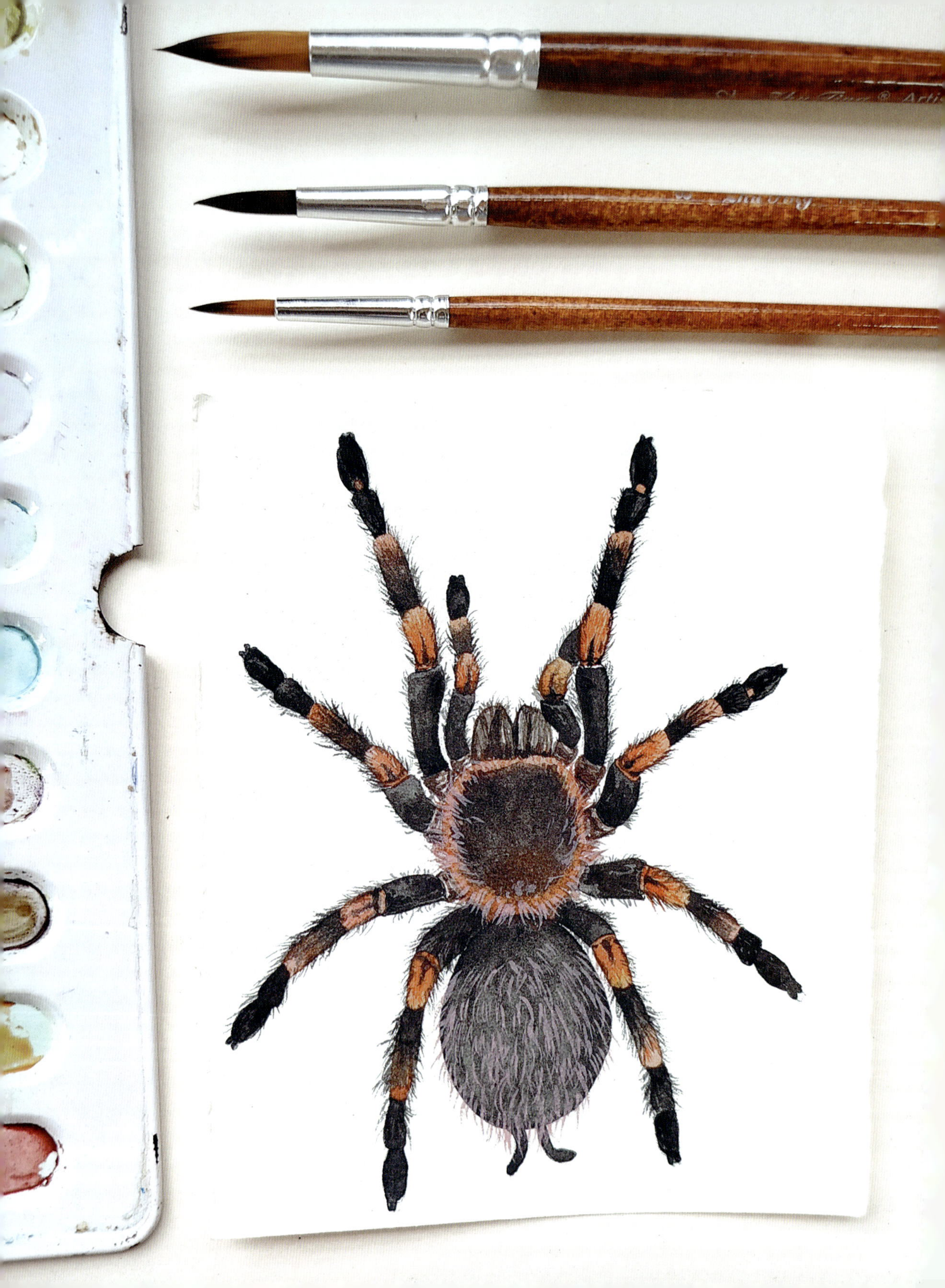

Tarantula

It's safe to say that tarantulas aren't the friend-liest looking of creatures, despite their furry appearance. Like most spiders, tarantulas rarely bite humans and will almost always flee if they have the option. A typical bite from a tarantula is comparable to a bee sting, with only local and temporary pain and swelling. I hope from now on, your fear for these beautiful creatures changes!

Difficulty: Easy

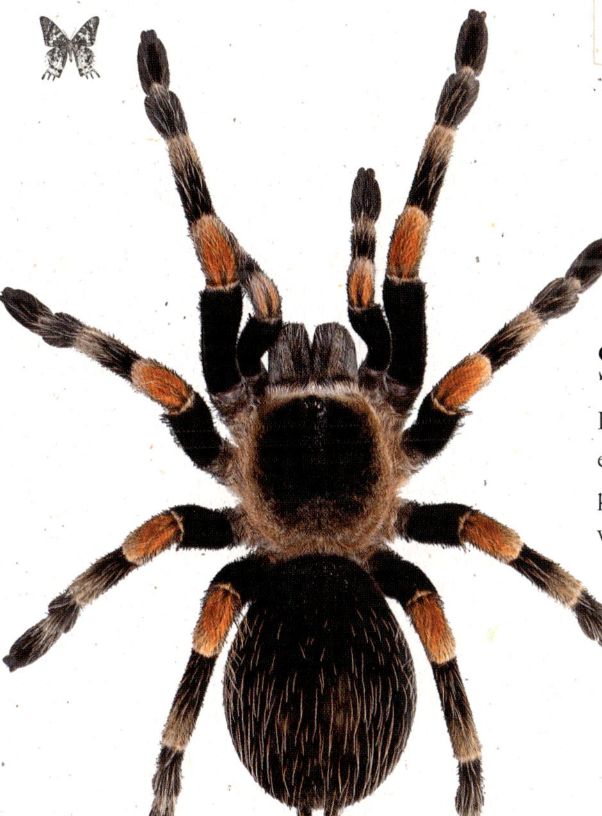

Sketch

Draw the tarantula freehand or trace the reference image and transfer it to the watercolor paper of your choice. Spray your paints with water to moisten them.

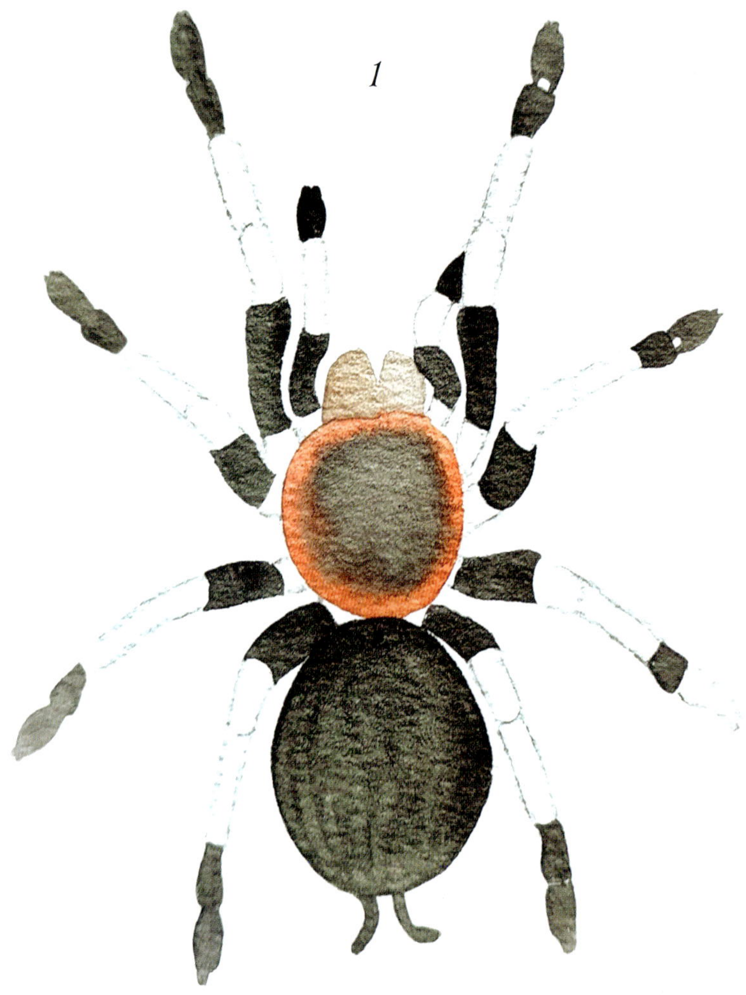

Step 1

Load your medium brush with Ivory Black and paint the abdomen, starting from the top and lightening the value of the color as you go down. Then, paint lines along the abdomen with the same color to create texture. Paint the spinnerets (the two little protuberances coming out of the bottom of the abdomen) with a medium value of Ivory Black and your detail brush.

Next, paint the cephalothorax (middle section of the tarantula) using your medium brush and Ivory Black, leaving a space all around it where you are going to add the first wash of Red Orange. Allow the colors to blend. Move to the mandibles. For these, use a light wash of Van Dyck Brown and your medium brush. Lastly, paint the sections of the legs that are completely black—use your medium brush and Ivory Black.

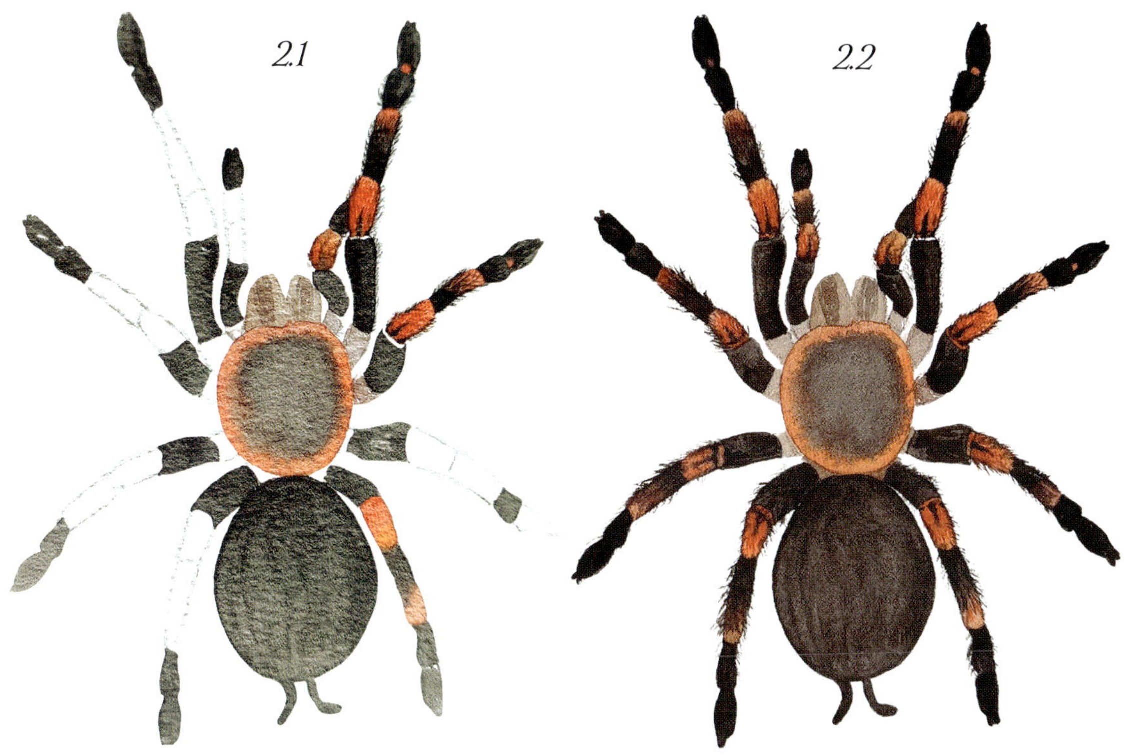

Step 2

Prepare your palette with Quinacridone Red, Bright Red, Ivory Black, and Van Dyck Brown. Having your colors ready in your palette will make working on the painting much easier. Use your detail brush throughout this whole step.

Working on one leg at a time, paint the first section of a leg with a very light wash of Van Dyck Brown and a dash of Quinacridone Red. Wait until it's dry. For the second part of the leg, just paint a dark wash of Ivory Black. For the next section of the leg, create a wash of Red Orange, then once it's almost dry, add a line of Ivory Black in the middle and outline the section with a very thin line. Load your brush with Bright Red and dot a bit of color around the black line you just painted to add a more reddish color that creates depth. Create hairlike lines coming out of the section with Ivory Black and Bright Red.

The fourth section has a gradient of Ivory Black and Quinacridone Red. Once the section is dry, add hairlike strokes coming from the black over the red. Also add more hairs coming out of the leg section. For the last section of the leg, paint a dot of Quinacridone Red right in the middle. Repeat the process for all the legs.

Switch to Van Dyck Brown and paint a few lines in the middle of the jaws.

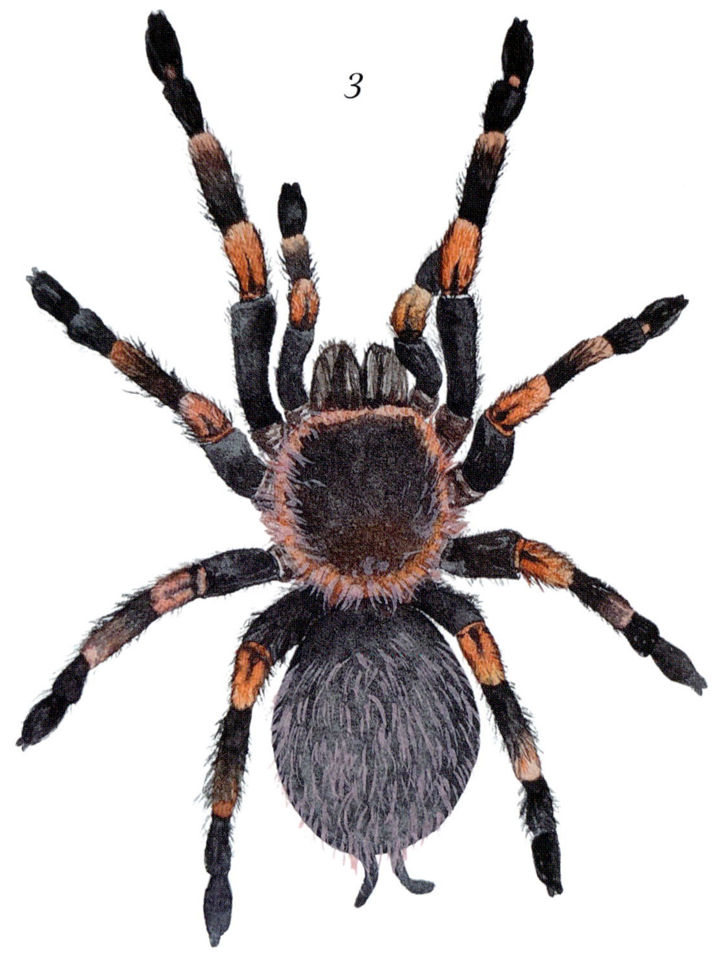

Step 3

Keep using your detail brush and Van Dyck Brown to complete the jaw area. Darken the value to paint more lines along the jaws, adding more value closer to the head. Outline them with a dark value of Van Dyck Brown. Use the same brush and color to outline the first section of each leg and add some creases on them too. Create these lines very unevenly and change the value of Van Dyck Brown to create texture.

Use your medium brush to add a dash of Quinacridone Red to the lower section of the cephalothorax. Before it dries, add a clear water wash to the top of the cephalothorax to blend with the red you just painted. The last step is mixing Bright Red with a bit of white gouache to create a light, opaque value of red. With this mixture loaded on your detail brush, create the fluffy texture of the abdomen. On the cephalothorax, paint only hair over the orange area, towards the outer edge.

Your beautiful tarantula is finished!

Vintage Scissors

To me, vintage tools look like treasures.

One of my fondest childhood memories is my dad's workshop. He had a pair of very old scissors. You always knew where to find them, and God forbid you forgot to return them to their correct location! I always found vintage objects precious, and I had to include a pair of beautiful vintage scissors in this book to honor that memory.

Historians believe the earliest form of scissors were developed in prehistory and would have looked something like modern sheep shearers. But the first trace of scissors as they are known today can be found in an illustration in a Latin Bible dating from the 10th century.

I learned while preparing this tutorial that scissors measuring 8 inches (20 cm) or longer should technically be referred to as shears, but shears have a thumb hole and a larger finger hole.

This is one of the easiest tutorials you'll find in this book, yet its intricate design will give you a taste of using a tiny brush to achieve all those details.

Difficulty: Easy

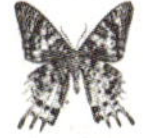

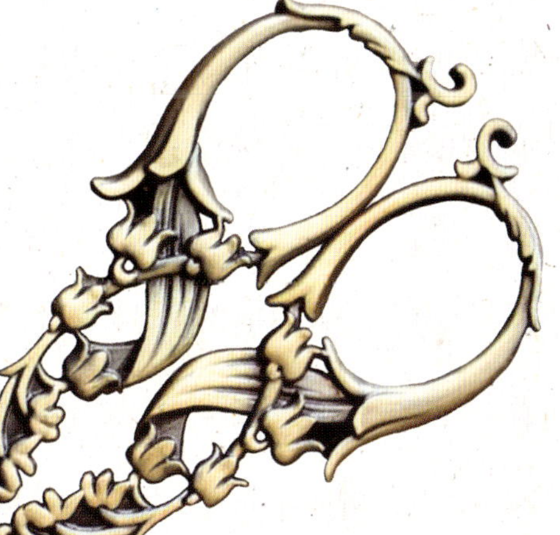

Sketch

Draw the scissors freehand or trace the reference image and transfer it to the watercolor paper of your choice. Focus on the filigree on the handles. Spray your paints with water to moisten them.

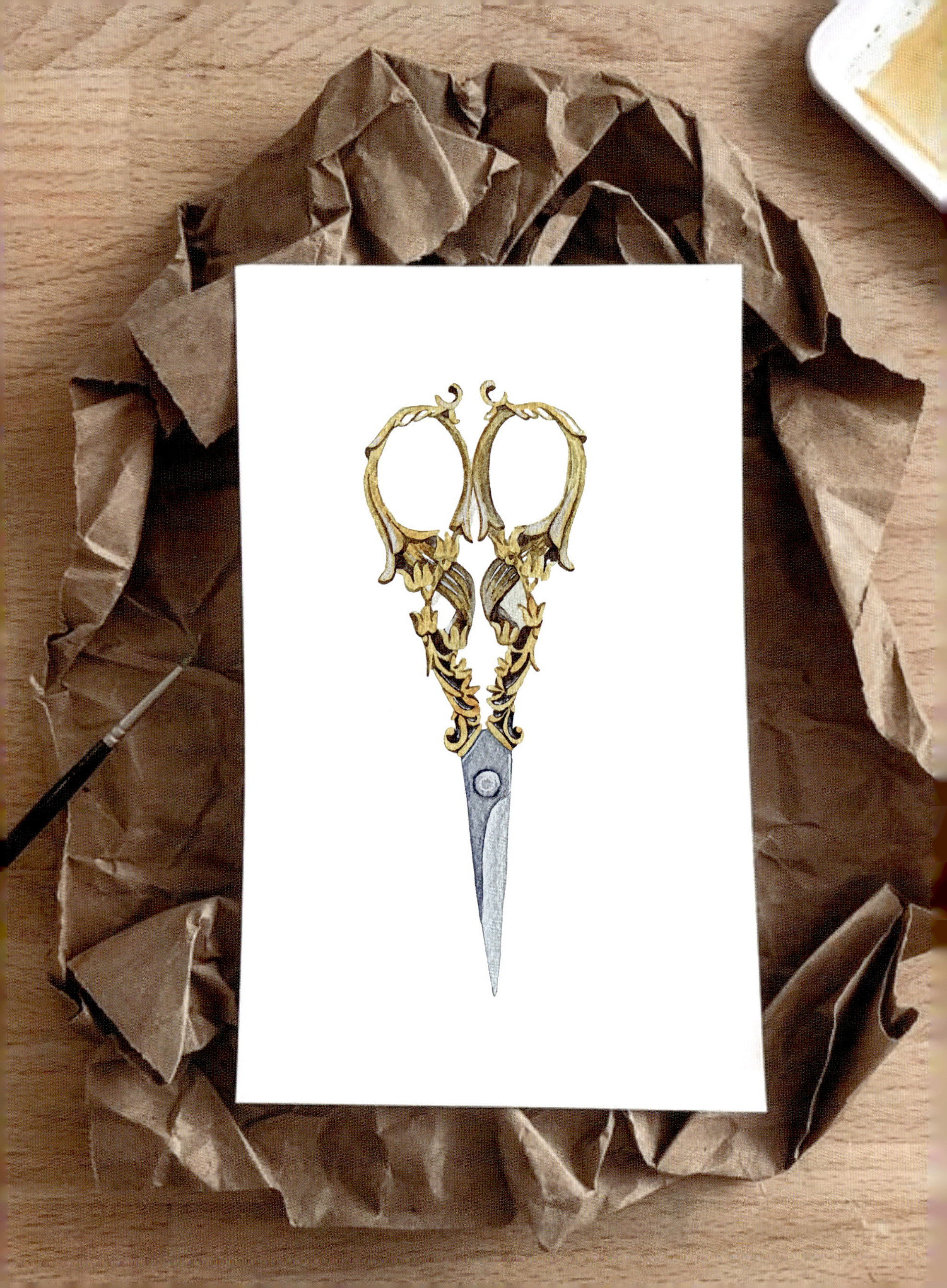

Step 1

If you feel confident that you can keep the paint inside the intricate design, use the medium brush to paint a wash of Raw Siena over the handles. (Otherwise go ahead and use the detail brush to ensure you can create sharp lines.)

Step 2

While you wait for the handle to dry, take care of the blades. Using your palette, mix three parts of Ash Blue to one of Payne's Grey—creating a metal-looking color. Add enough water to paint the first wash. Swatch it, and once you are happy with how it looks, paint the blade with the color very lightly.

Once it's all dry, with your detail brush and the same colors, but more saturated, add a thin line around the pivot screw and the handle border. This starts creating depth and gives 3D dimension to your scissors. Use your medium brush that's just a bit wet to smooth the edges of these new lines.

The last step here will be to use the wet-on-dry technique to sharpen the cutting edge of the scissors—add fine lines on the blade with the same color mixture you made before in Step 2 but just a little bit more saturated. These lines give even more texture to the blades.

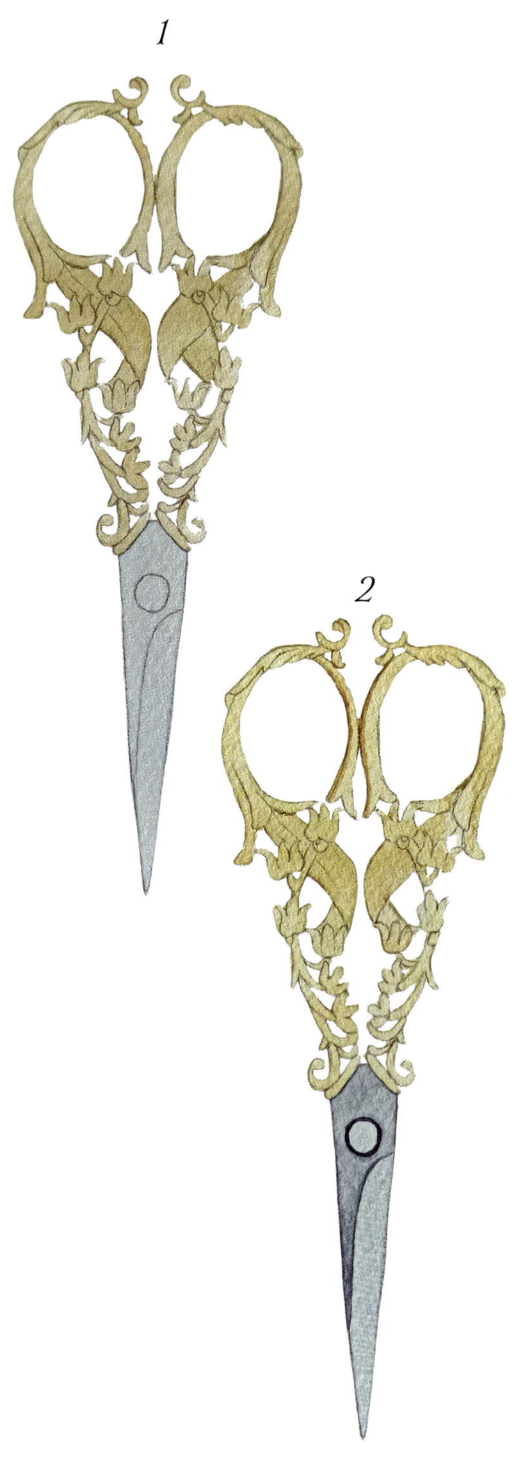

Step 3

Using your medium brush, add another wash of the mixture to the blades, skipping the cutting edge and adding a darker value to the edges. This creates the illusion that the cutting edge is shiny and sharp.

Step 4

Now let's add more dimension and depth to the scissors. With the Ivory Black and the detail brush, paint a black line around the pivot screw as thinly as you can. With the same brush and color, start filling out all the insides of the filigree. Leave this to dry, and rest your eyes! It takes a lot of concentration to paint all those little nooks—think about it as a meditation, like painting mandalas.

Step 5

Use your detail brush and Sepia to create the shadows. For this step, you need to paint around the filigree shapes with a darker color to recreate the shadows of the curve, as well as under the corners and joints. You can look at the photo reference on page 155 or be intuitive! Paint the marks on the handle, under the first filigree line with your detail brush. Wait until it's dry to keep these details bold.

Step 6

Once it's all dry, highlight some of the filigree with white gouache and the liner brush. Think about where the light could be hitting, and add a fine line in the same direction as the drawing.

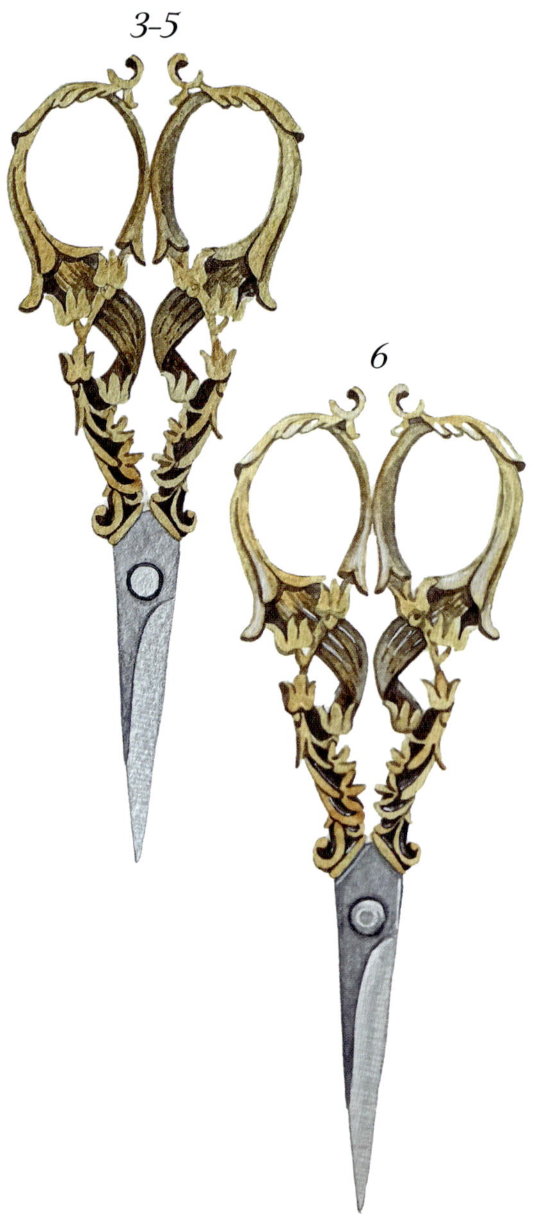

Also add a circle to the pivot screw and a little line to the cutting edge for a final shiny touch, and your vintage scissors are ready to be framed!

Cat Skull

A cabinet of curiosities room wouldn't be complete without a skull. Enveloped in mystery and steeped in ancient lore, the cat skull serves as a captivating symbol that transcends time and culture. In diverse cultures around the globe, cats hold deep symbolic significance. Ancient Egyptians revered cats as sacred beings, associated with protection and guidance by the goddess Bastet. In Japanese folklore, the beckoning cat or "Maneki-neko" is a symbol of good fortune and prosperity, believed to bring luck to its owner.

Note: While these steps are long, they aren't complicated. Instead, this project is all about laying simple details over each other.

Difficulty: Medium

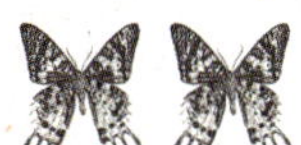

Sketch

Draw the cat skull freehand or trace the reference image and transfer it to the watercolor paper of your choice. Spray your paints with water to moisten them.

MATERIALS

- Watercolor paper of your choice
  - › I used an 8 x 10–inch (20 x 25–cm) sheet, vertical orientation
- Paints
  - › Payne's Grey, Raw Sienna, Gold Ochre, Van Dyck Brown, Brown Pink, Caput Mortuum, Raw Umber
- Brushes
  - › Medium round brush (I used size 9)
  - › Detail round brush (I used size 2)

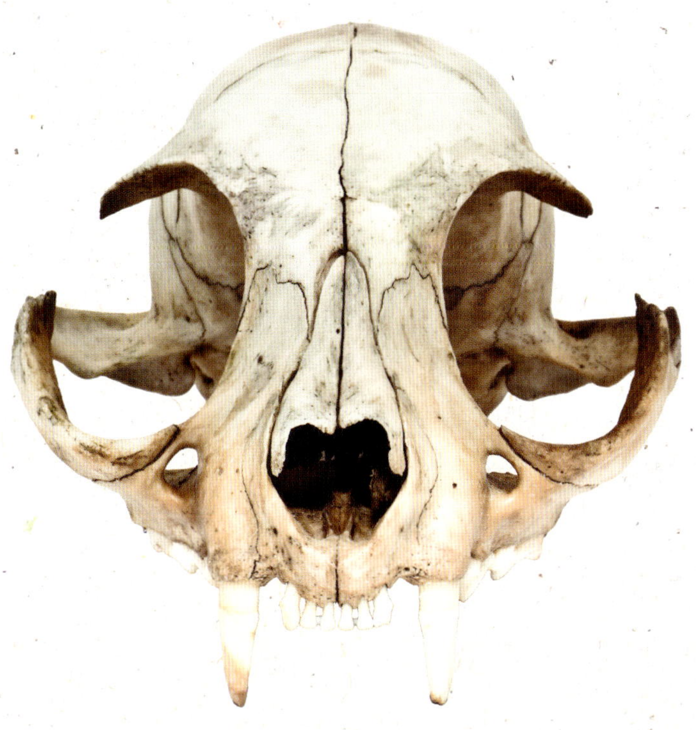

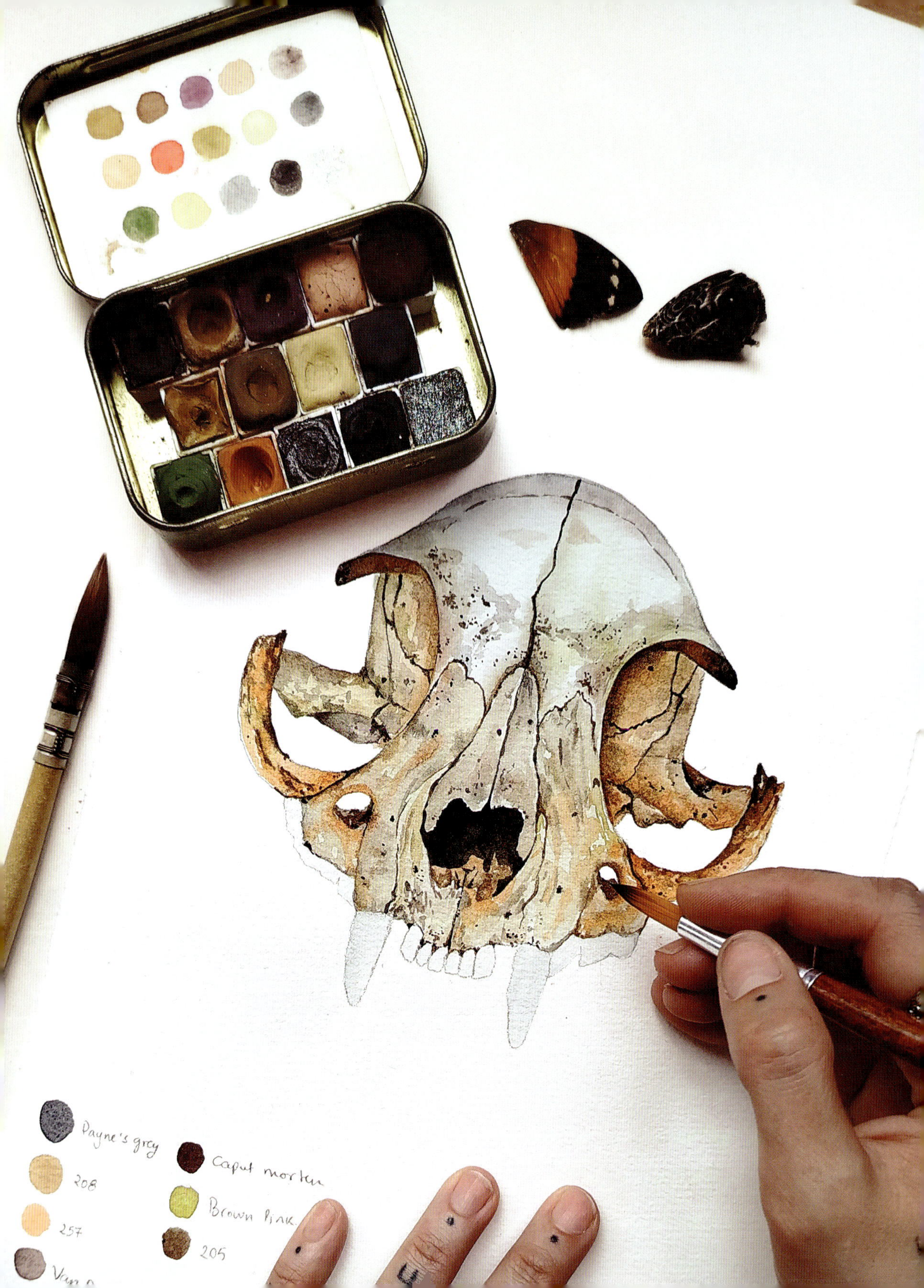

Payne's grey
208
Caput mortuu
257
Brown Pink.
205
Van

1

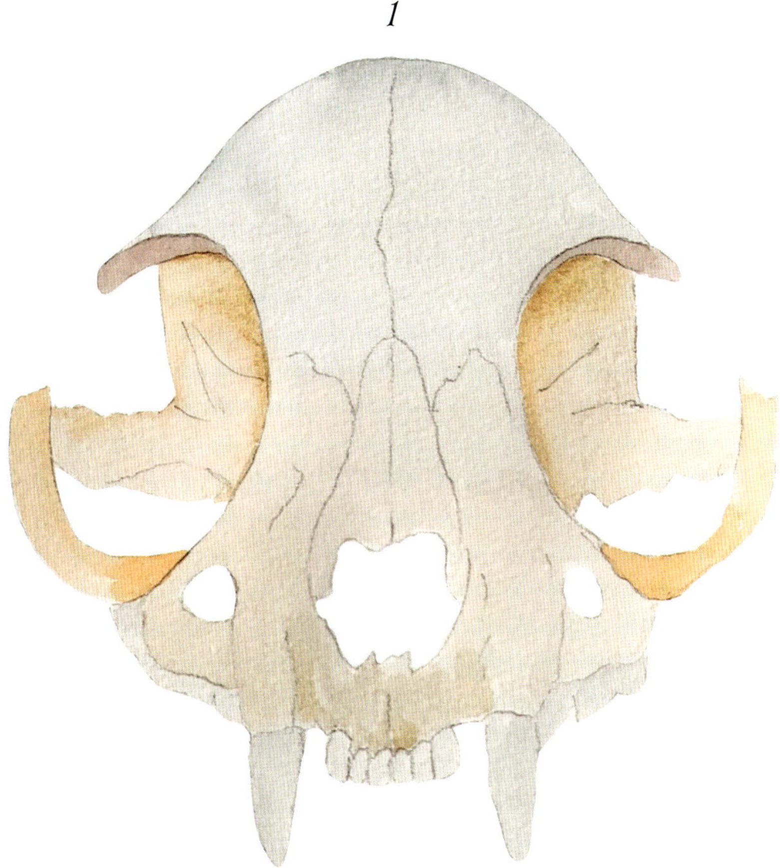

Step 1

Begin by preparing your palette. Separately mix Payne's Grey and Raw Sienna with enough water to paint the first wash. Load your medium brush with a very light wash of Payne's Grey and start painting the skull from the top. When you get to the part between the eye sockets—where the nose bones start—switch to a very light wash of Raw Sienna. Don't paint inside the nose hole or the holes on the sides of the skull.

Once the first layer is dry, load your medium brush with a light wash of Gold Ochre and paint inside the eye sockets, adding more value on the edges and the front bone. Let this dry. For the teeth, use a very light wash of Payne's Grey and your detail brush. Lastly, load your detail brush with a medium value of Van Dyck Brown and paint the little section above the eye sockets.

Step 2

Wet the surface above the eye sockets carefully with your medium brush—don't press down as you don't want to lift any color. Load your medium brush with a medium value of Brown Pink and add some color to the area by dabbing it with your brush and letting the watercolor do its thing!

Once that's dry, switch to your detail brush loaded with a dark value of Van Dyck Brown and paint the lines of the skull—the one that's going across the center and all around the nasal area. Paint these lines a bit unevenly—thicker in some areas and thinner in others. With a clean medium brush with a bit of water, soften the edges and drag the paint towards the outside of the nose, fading into the skull. Also paint a sort of semicircular line right at the top of the skull about 1 centimeter from the edge.

Now let's work inside the nose. For the top section, paint a light wash of Van Dyck Brown using your medium brush. Let it dry. Next, load your medium brush with a dark value of Van Dyck Brown with a dash of Payne's Grey to darken the color and paint the nose hole, except for the bottom section, where you will paint a dark wash of Raw Sienna when the black part is dry. In this lower section, add a bit of Van Dyck Brown using your detail brush and adding it to the bottom edge. To finish, load your detail brush with Van Dyck Brown and add dots and lines over the nose skull area to create texture and the look of something "rotten."

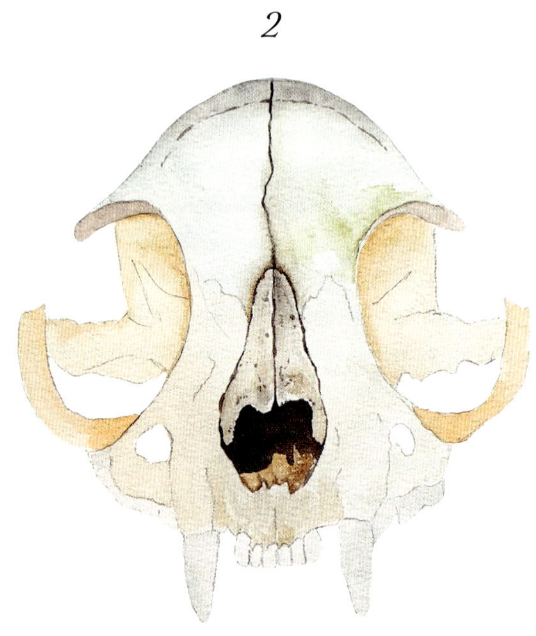

Step 3

This is a very intuitive painting, and for this step, it's a matter of adding smudges and texture over the area. And although I'm going to explain how I painted this, you can take the lead and experiment, letting your creativity take over. I also advise that you read through this step before diving in, so you understand what's happening!

Load your medium brush with Caput Mortuum to add some smudges on the skull. I added a few over the eye sockets and in the middle of the top of the skull. Switch to a light value of Payne's Grey and add more smudges between and on top of the eye sockets and on the top edge of the skull. Switch to your detail

3-4

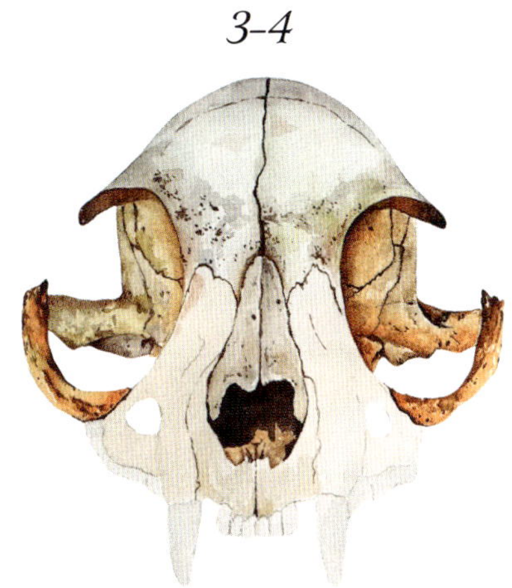

brush and Van Dyck Brown and continue painting the lines that separate each section of the skull: the two lines that go from the nasal area towards the eyes, the line that goes down the center form the nasal area towards the teeth, and the two lines on the sides marking the bone that holds the fangs.

Step 4

Work on the eye area now. Load your detail brush with a dark value of Gold Ochre and paint the little sections above the eye sockets (the ones that you painted the Van Dyck Brown wash over in Step 1). Before it dries, load your detail brush with Payne's Grey and paint the outer edges and the inner edges to create depth.

Move to the lower bone of the right eye socket. Load your medium brush with Gold Ochre and paint a medium wash, and then switch to Raw Umber and dot some paint with the tip of your brush over the upper edge of the bone. Let it blend with the Gold Ochre. The surface will start drying as you paint, and this is fine. It will

make the next brushstrokes more defined, and this is perfect. Paint the inner top edge all the way to the top with your detail brush loaded with Raw Umber. Switch to Van Dyck Brown and paint another layer of lines on the tip of the bone. Outline the bottom edge where this bone touches the rest of the skull. Add little dots and lines all over the area.

Once dry, move to the inside area of the eye socket. Load your medium brush with Gold Ochre and paint a medium wash, switching to Raw Sienna for the outer edge. Add more value on the inner corner, creating a shadow. Once it's dry, load your detail brush with Van Dyck Brown and paint lines, creating the different parts of the bone structure. Add dots and little lines all over the area, especially on the areas that bend or are closer to the edges.

For the other eye, the process is similar for the upper and lower bones—so paint those areas—however, the inside is a bit different.

For the inside part of the left eye socket, load your medium brush with Raw Sienna and paint a medium wash, adding smudges of Brown Pink before it dries. Switch to your detail brush loaded with Van Dyck Brown and paint the lines between each bone and dots to create more texture. I also added a little section right on the bottom edge, painting it just with a light wash of Van Dyck Brown and adding value on both edges. Paint dots over the eyes, using the same brush and Van Dyck Brown. Also add some dots on the area. Rest your hand, and take a break! You earned it. Plus, it's good to take your eyes off your painting for a moment so when you go return it's like seeing it with different eyes.

5

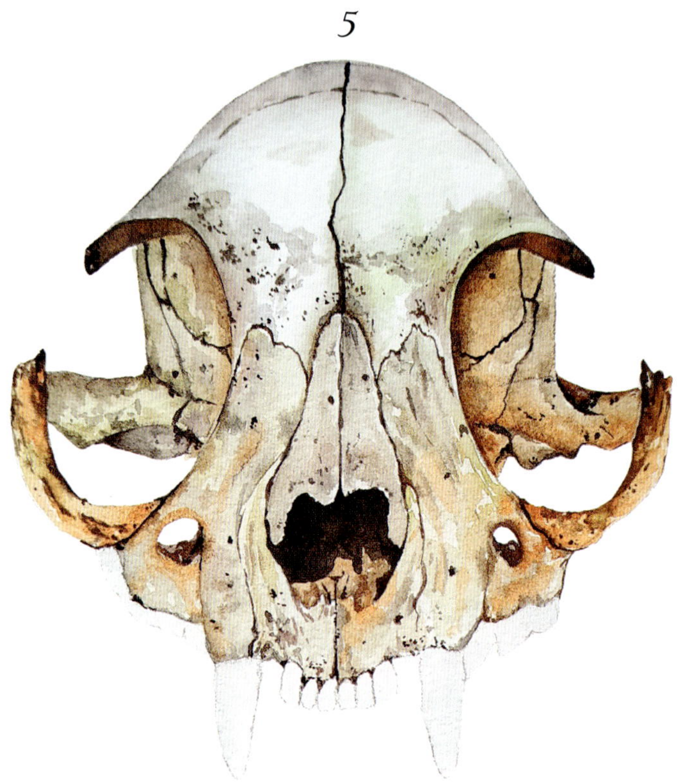

Step 5

First, paint a water wash over the lower section of the skull (around both sides of the nasal area) with clean water using your medium brush. Load your medium brush with Gold Ochre and paint brushstrokes along the section on both sides. Concentrate on the sides over the hole section especially, darkening the value. Paint around the holes, outlining them. Switch to Brown Pink and do the same—paint a few brushstrokes along the area, but less than what you did with the Gold Ochre. Change to Raw Sienna and add some color. You can even add a few brushstrokes of Van Dyck Brown.

Load your detail brush with a dark value of Payne's Grey to add more dots. Move to the teeth area and paint the parts between each tooth. Paint the inside area of the holes on both sides of the skull with Van Dyck Brown and your detail brush, outlining the edges.

This cat skull is ready to be part of your oddities collection!

Vintage Frame

Frames can hold just about anything, but this one feels like it would hold something more mysterious, like a portrait of a Victorian woman with a knife in her hand or a ghostly visage in a dark hallway. We can only imagine!

Note: This piece requires patience. Basically, the ornament shapes are created through a combination of carefully controlled layering and detailing using light and dark tones to build depth—making a flat painting look more dimensional and intricate.

Difficulty: Difficult

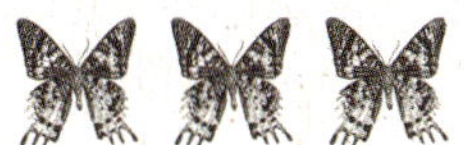

Sketch

Draw the frame freehand (if you dare!) or trace the reference image and transfer it to the watercolor paper of your choice. Focus on the intricate flourishes surrounding the edges to help guide the painting process. Spray your paints with water to moisten them.

MATERIALS

- Watercolor paper of your choice
    - I used a 9 x 12–inch (23 x 30–cm) sheet, vertical orientation
- Paints
    - Yellow Lake, Van Dyck Brown, Ivory Black, Brown Pink, Gold Ochre, Sennelier Yellow Deep
    - White gouache
- Brushes
    - Medium round brush (I used size 6)
    - Detail round brush (I used size 2)

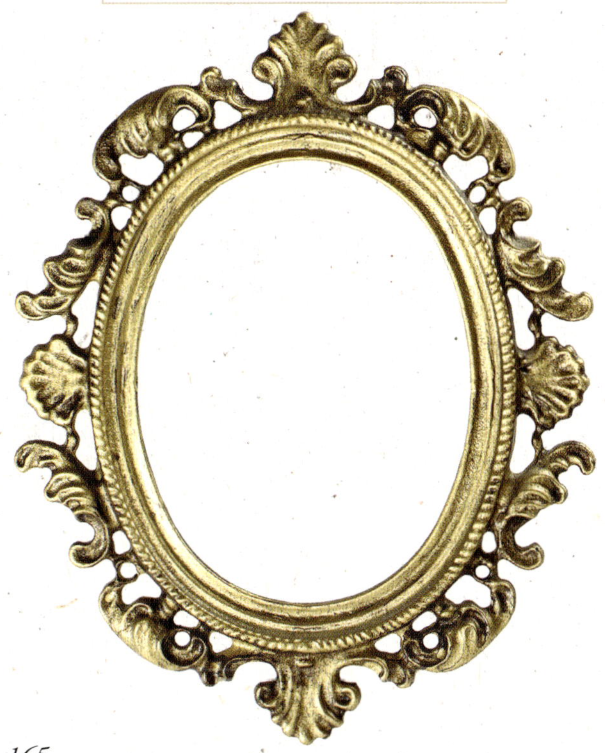

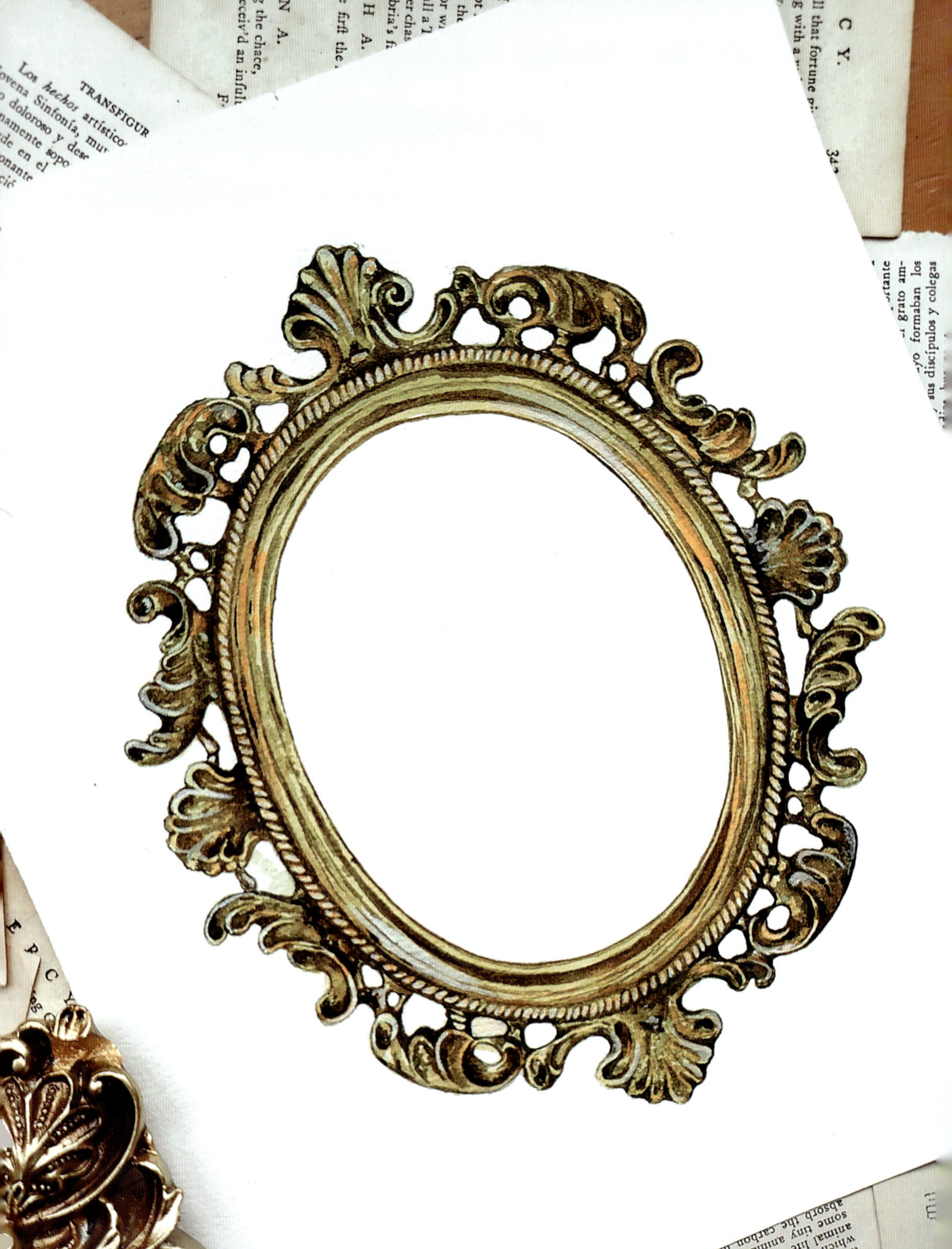

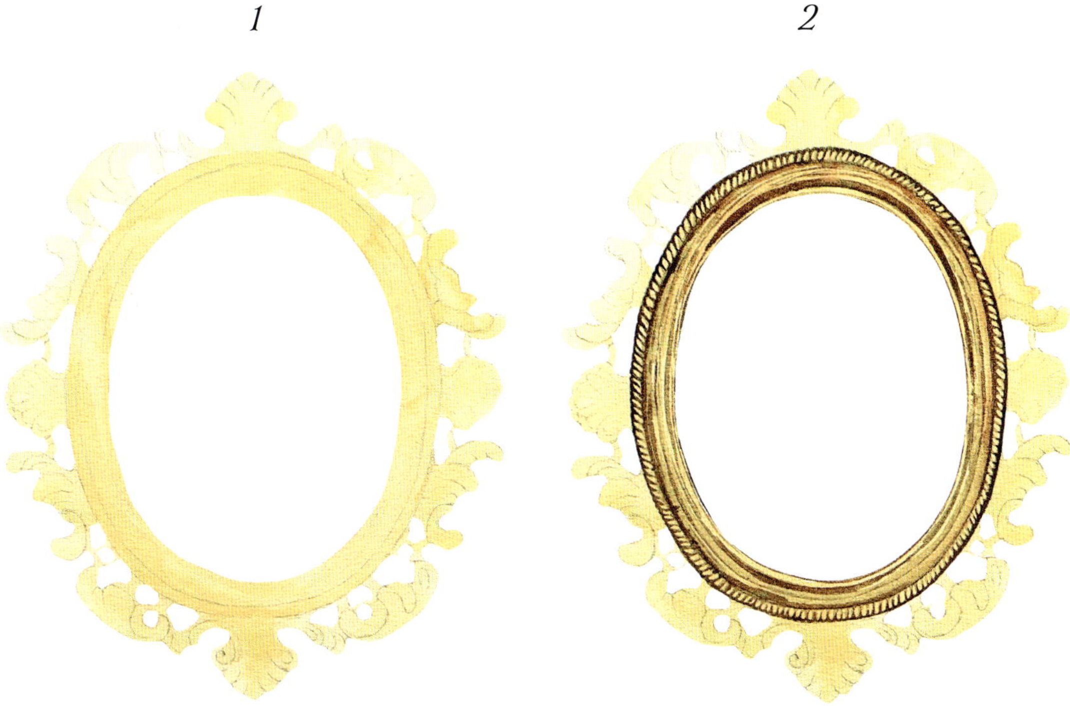

Step 1

Load your medium brush with Yellow Lake and apply a first wash covering the entire surface to give the frame its overall color. It's really important here to be careful not to paint outside the ornamental shapes.

Step 2

To give the frame dimension and structure, we'll start with the center oval. Load your detail brush with Van Dyck Brown and outline the inner edge of the frame. Then paint another line following the shape of the oval but leaving a space between this line and the inner edge. This line has to be uneven—thick in some places and thin in others—to make the frame appear more three-dimensional. Keep painting oval-shaped lines in different thicknesses and variations of the same color until you get to the border where the ornaments are. Mix Yellow Lake with a bit of Ivory Black to add some shadows between the lines.

Load your detail brush with a dark shade of Van Dyck Brown and outline each of the little ovals, carefully adding the darker color to mimic the shadows and contours of the ornaments. Let this dry.

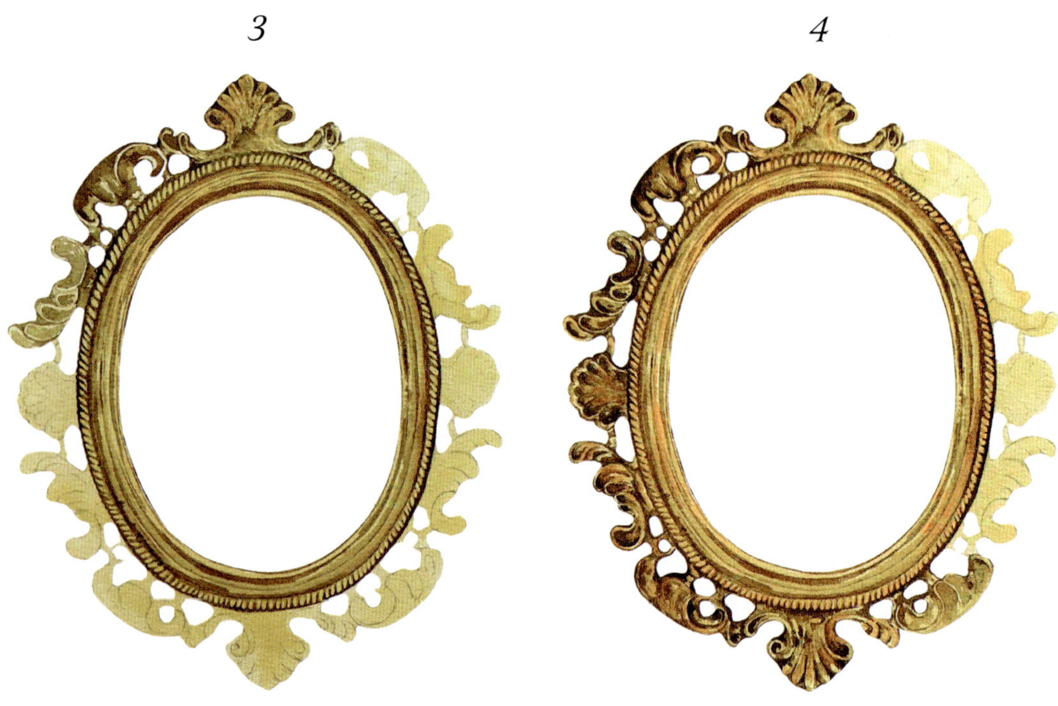

Step 3

Load your detail brush with the mix of Yellow Lake and Ivory Black from Step 2. You are going to gradually add layers of this color to define the curves and ornamental details. Start creating the lines that define the top shell (at 12 o'clock). Refine the edges and contour each shape by reinforcing the border with a darker shade. Soften the edges by blending wet paint into the surrounding areas to create a smoother transition, especially on the rounded flowing parts. At the base of the second ornament (near 11 o'clock), leave four little circular shapes untouched to add depth.

Step 4

You are going to use your detail brush for this entire step. Keep adding a darker value of the mix of Yellow Lake and Ivory Black to the areas that would be in the shadows—that don't have dimension, such as in the grooves and indentations.

Create a first wash with a lighter value, and then start darkening the areas that need it. Go back and forth over the filigree, adding more details as it dries, and you can see how it's turning out. Load your detail brush with Brown Pink and add some lines on top of the already painted area that will blend everything together.

Focus on the shell-shaped area on the left side (9 o'clock). Paint each groove, starting with a darker value on the rounded area and lightening the value as you paint down. Switch to Gold Ochre and add a few brushstrokes of this color in the grooves.

Once you figure out how to paint one section, you'll be able to paint them all! It's about paying attention to where the light hits, or where the ornament shape is more prominent, giving that area the lightest value of the color, and from there adding depth to the surrounding area. Mark the outline with the darkest shade of Van Dyck Brown.

I advise you to look at the reference photo on page 165, but also dive into the painting and let your intuition guide you. Once what you've completed is fully dry, paint a light wash of Sennelier Yellow Deep over the entire frame now that it's completely dry to soften all the lines.

Step 5

Continue working your way around the frame, repeating the process from Steps 3 and 4 to paint the ornaments.

Add a few darker lines between those previous lines to create subtle variations in the gold tones using your medium brush and Sennelier Yellow Deep. Switch to your detail brush and add some of this color throughout the entire frame, creating more variations of the golden tones. Switch to Brown Pink to create dots and smudges as if the frame is a little rusty.

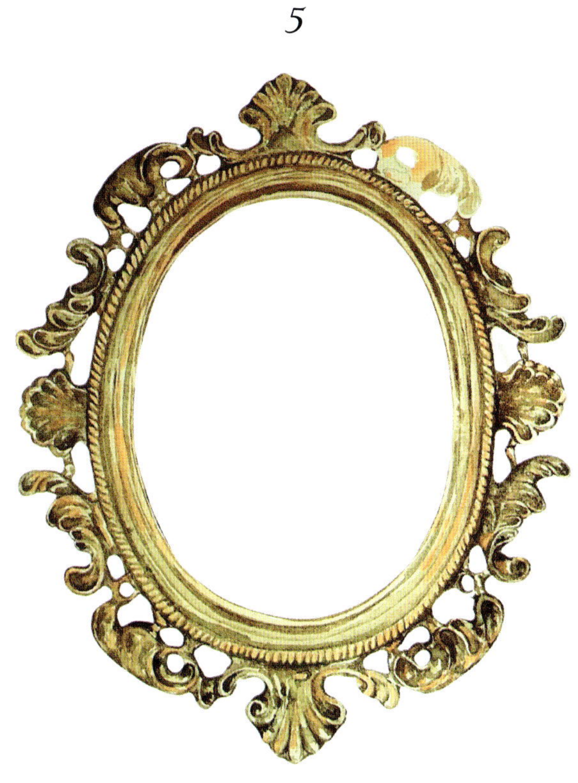

Load your detail brush with Ivory Black and paint darker shades to create more depth, but avoid the highlighted areas where the lighter shade of yellow is painted. Keep in mind to use darker shades for areas that would naturally fall into shadow. Once the main shapes are outlined, let it dry.

6

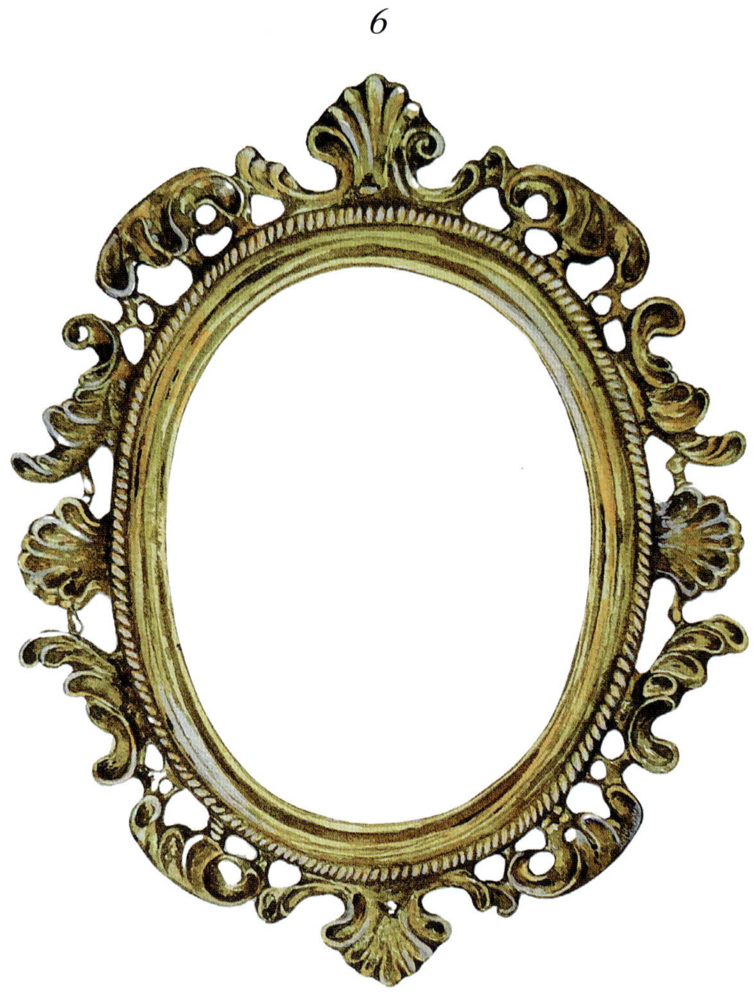

Step 6

Prepare white gouache in your palette to create the final highlights. Load your detail brush, and add a dot of white on all the little oval shapes around the frame. Then paint two thick lines over the inner section on the top right side and on the left bottom side.

Then choose the areas where the light should hit the most and add white there. For example, on the part of the ornamentation that protrudes more. Add a few dots to some other areas as you see fit, and now this beautiful vintage frame is ready to hold your memories or a taxidermied bug!

Old Key

It's time to unlock the mystery behind old-fash-
ioned skeleton keys! The earliest skeleton keys
date back to ancient Egypt and Rome, and they
were particularly useful during the medieval
period. But a key can be something more than
just a key. I come from Spain, where once upon
a time, the people who lived there (the Moors)
were banished from their homes. To this day,
some people cherish and keep their old house
key as a reminder and a treasure.

Difficulty: Medium

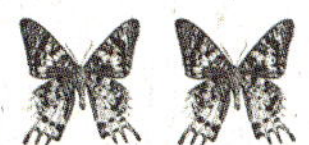

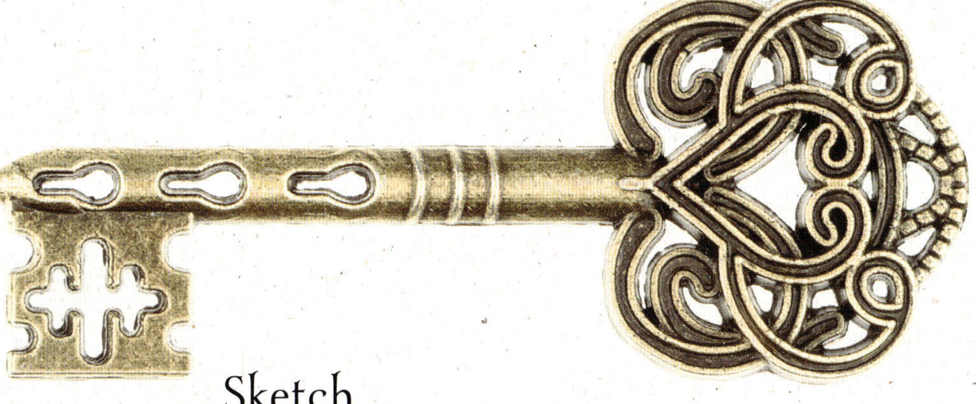

Sketch

Draw the key or trace the reference image and transfer it to the
watercolor paper of your choice. Focus on the intricate top area to
help guide the painting process. Spray your paints with water to
moisten them.

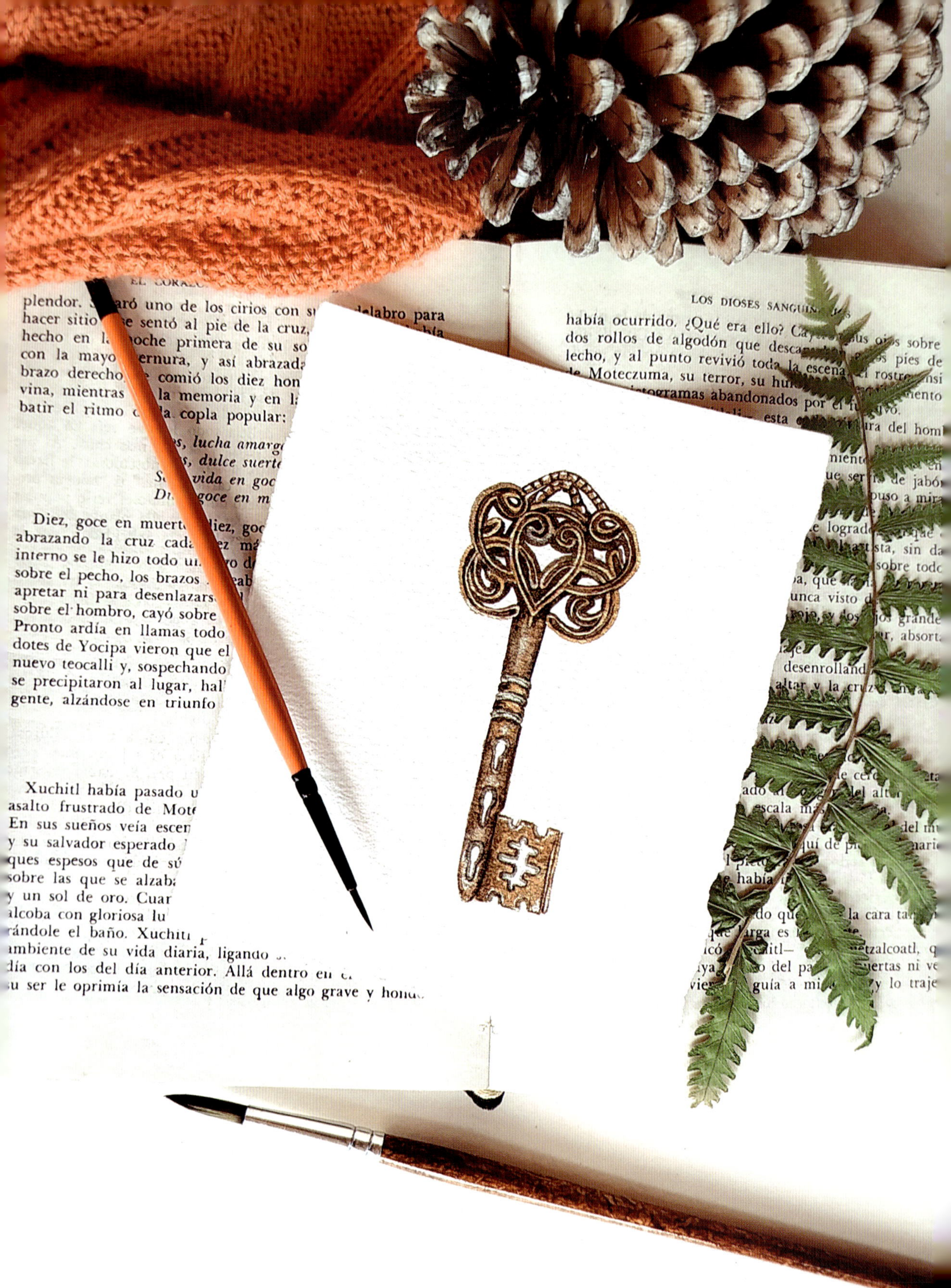
EL CORAZ...
plendor. ...aró uno de los cirios con s...
hacer sitio ...e sentó al pie de la cruz,
hecho en l... ...oche primera de su so...
con la mayo... ...ernura, y así abrazada
brazo derecho... ...e comió los diez hon...
vina, mientras ... la memoria y en l...
batir el ritmo ... la copla popular:

...s, lucha amarg...
...s, dulce suerte
S... vida en goc...
D... goce en m...

Diez, goce en muert... ...iez, goc...
abrazando la cruz cad... ...ez má...
interno se le hizo todo u... ...o d...
sobre el pecho, los brazos ... ...eab...
apretar ni para desenlazars... ...
sobre el hombro, cayó sobre ...
Pronto ardía en llamas todo ...
dotes de Yocipa vieron que el ...
nuevo teocalli y, sospechando ...
se precipitaron al lugar, hal...
gente, alzándose en triunfo

Xuchitl había pasado u...
asalto frustrado de Mote...
En sus sueños veía escen...
y su salvador esperado ...
ques espesos que de sú...
sobre las que se alzab...
y un sol de oro. Cuar...
...lcoba con gloriosa lu...
...rándole el baño. Xuchiti ...
...mbiente de su vida diaria, ligando ...
...día con los del día anterior. Allá dentro en ...
...u ser le oprimía la sensación de que algo grave y hond...

LOS DIOSES SANGUIN...S
...rrido. ¿Qué era ello? Ca... ...us oi...s sobre
...de algodón que desca... ...es pies de
...l punto revivió toda la escena... ...l rostr... ...nsi
...uma, su terror, su hu... ...miento
...ogramas abandonados por el f...vo.
...di... esta ... ...ra del hom...

...mient...
...ue ser... ...a de jabó...
...ouso a mir...
...e logrado... ...que ...
...artista, sin da...
...sobre todo
...a, que ... ...
...unca visto d...
...oje, y dos ...jos grande
...r, absort...
...aje ...
desenrolland...
...altar y la cruz ...
...di...
...e cerc... ...ta
...ado a... ...r del alt...
...escala m...
...del m...
...quí de p... ...ari...
...habia ...
...do que ... la cara ta...
...que larga es ...
...licó ...itl— ...tzalcoatl, q...
...ya... ...o del pa... ...uertas ni ve...
...vie... ...guía a mi ... y lo traje...

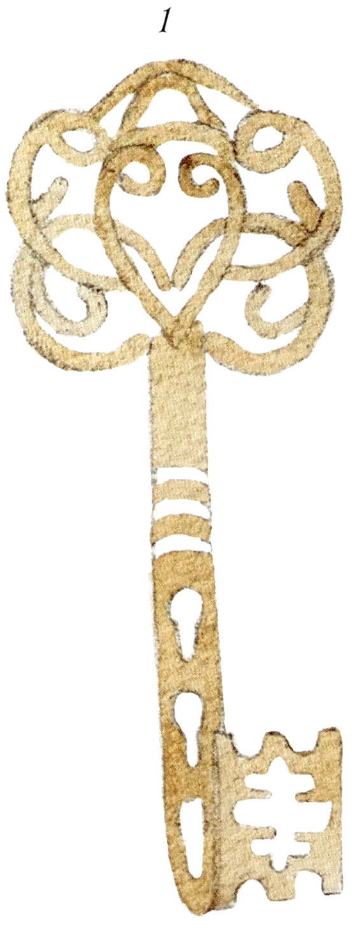

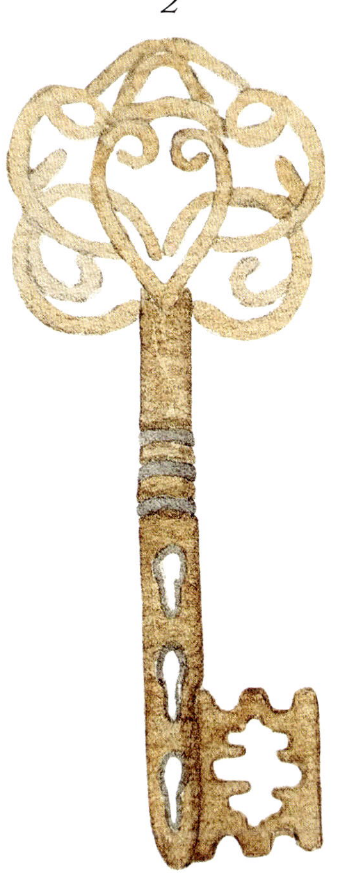

Step 1

Load your medium brush with Raw Sienna and paint a wash over the entire surface of the key body, except for the three lines that cross the key.

Step 2

After the base wash has dried, switch to your detail brush and Cinereous Blue with a bit of Neutral Tint to create a gray tone to paint the three lines while adding more value to the edges. Use your detail brush to add another layer to the lines with a dark value of Raw Umber. This creates a sense of depth and subtle shading. Add a line around the edges of the lines, and soften the lines by dragging the color towards the middle. Switch to your previous mix of Cinereous Blue and Neutral Tint and outline the inside of the three holes on the bottom part of the key.

Step 3

Load your detail brush with Van Dyck Brown and paint the inside of the head of the key, keeping in mind the direction of the lines and the position. For example, the heart-shaped section is on the front, so you can paint the brown line without any interruption. But the lines behind that have to stop right where the other line crosses.

Move to the key's stem. Using your detail brush and a dark value of Van Dyck Brown, paint the area where the filigree of the key ends. Drag the color with a clean brush towards the edges. Keep painting the edges with a darker value of Van Dyck Brown, dragging the color towards the center. This creates a darker shade over the area. Paint each section between the gray stripes by adding more color around the edges.

Moving to the bottom area, outline it with a dark value of Van Dyck Brown, and again soften the edges by dragging the color towards the center. Finally, paint a medium value wash of Van Dyck Brown over the area, leaving about a millimeter around it without paint as a highlight.

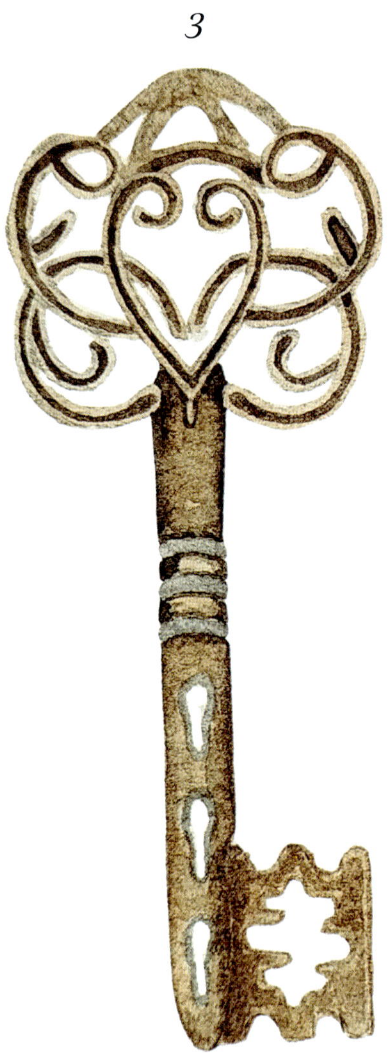

4

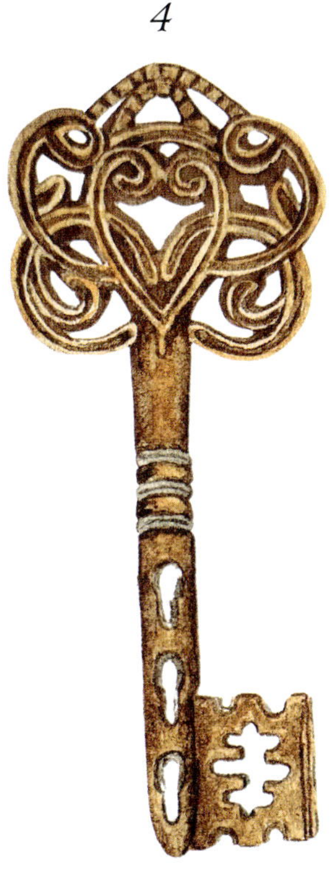

5

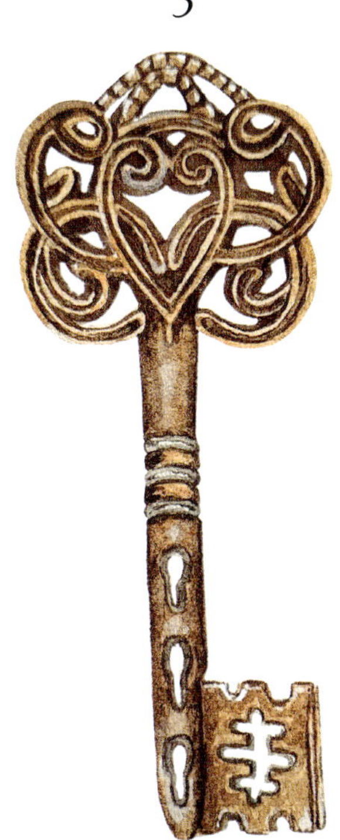

Step 4

Once everything is dry, paint a medium value wash of Gold Ochre over the entire surface of the key. Next, load your detail brush with Van Dyck Brown and add a shadow inside the filigree. Then add little lines over the two top swirls. Switch to your mixture of Cinereous Blue and Neutral Tint and paint a line inside the gray stripes. Use Van Dyck Brown to outline the key again, adding an extra dark line where the key bit fits with the handle. Also paint two lines creating the wards.

Step 5

Time to add the highlights with white gouache. Load your detail brush and add a dot in the space created between each line on the top of the key handle. Then add a few more brushstrokes on some of the swirls. Next, paint a light line with your detail brush down the handle from top to bottom. Smooth the line with a clean brush.

Switch to your mix of Cinereous Blue and Neutral Tint to paint the inside area of the bit, outlining the whole inside about a millimeter around it. Switch again to gouache and paint the last highlight on the top of the bit.

Your key is finished!

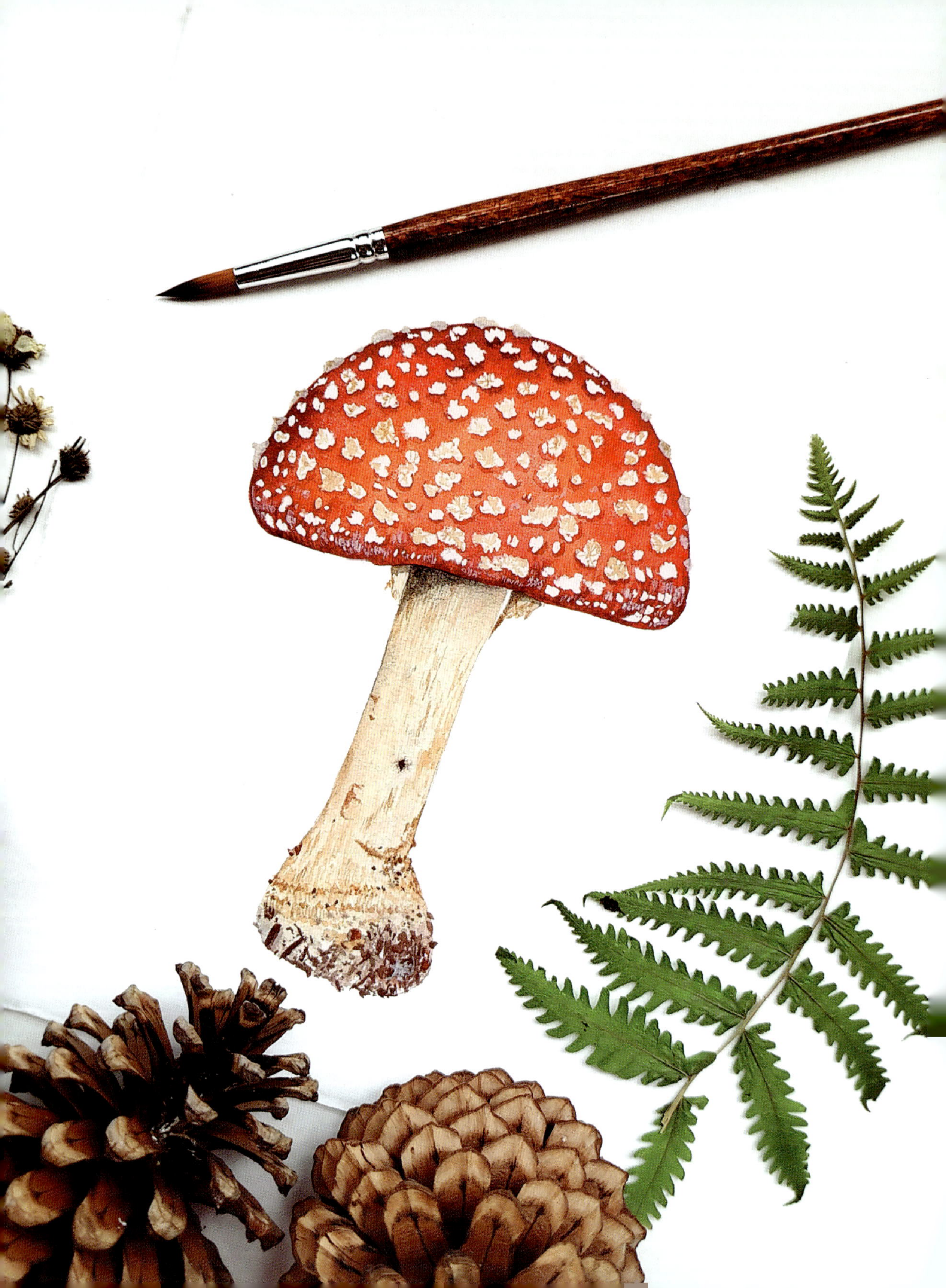

Amanita Muscaria

Well known for its red and white-spotted cap, the fly agaric (*Amanita muscaria*) is one of the most instantly recognizable mushrooms. Noted for their hallucinogenic properties, they were once used as a fly poison—thus the origin of its name! The red and white-spotted toadstool is rife in popular culture. So much so that garden ornaments and children's books often depict them as homes for gnomes and fairies. Perhaps this explains its global recognition. There are even rumors of Santa Claus's flying reindeers using this mushroom to get their running start! Whatever its legends, it's a beautiful 'shroom and a great place to start painting botanical art.

Difficulty: Easy

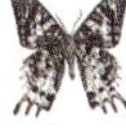

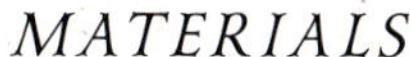

- Watercolor paper of your choice
    - I used a 7 x 8–inch (18 x 20–cm) sheet, vertical orientation
- Paints
    - Yellow Sophie, Bright Red, Raw Sienna, Van Dyck Brown, French Vermilion, Alizarin Crimson, Red Orange, Venetian Red, Payne's Grey
    - White gouache
- Brushes
    - Old brush for masking fluid (I used a round size 2)
    - Medium round brush (I used size 8)
    - Detail round brush (I used size 2)
- Masking fluid and eraser (to remove)

Sketch

Draw the mushroom freehand or trace the reference image and transfer it to the watercolor paper of your choice, focusing on the cap markings. Spray your paints with water to moisten them. Let's start painting!

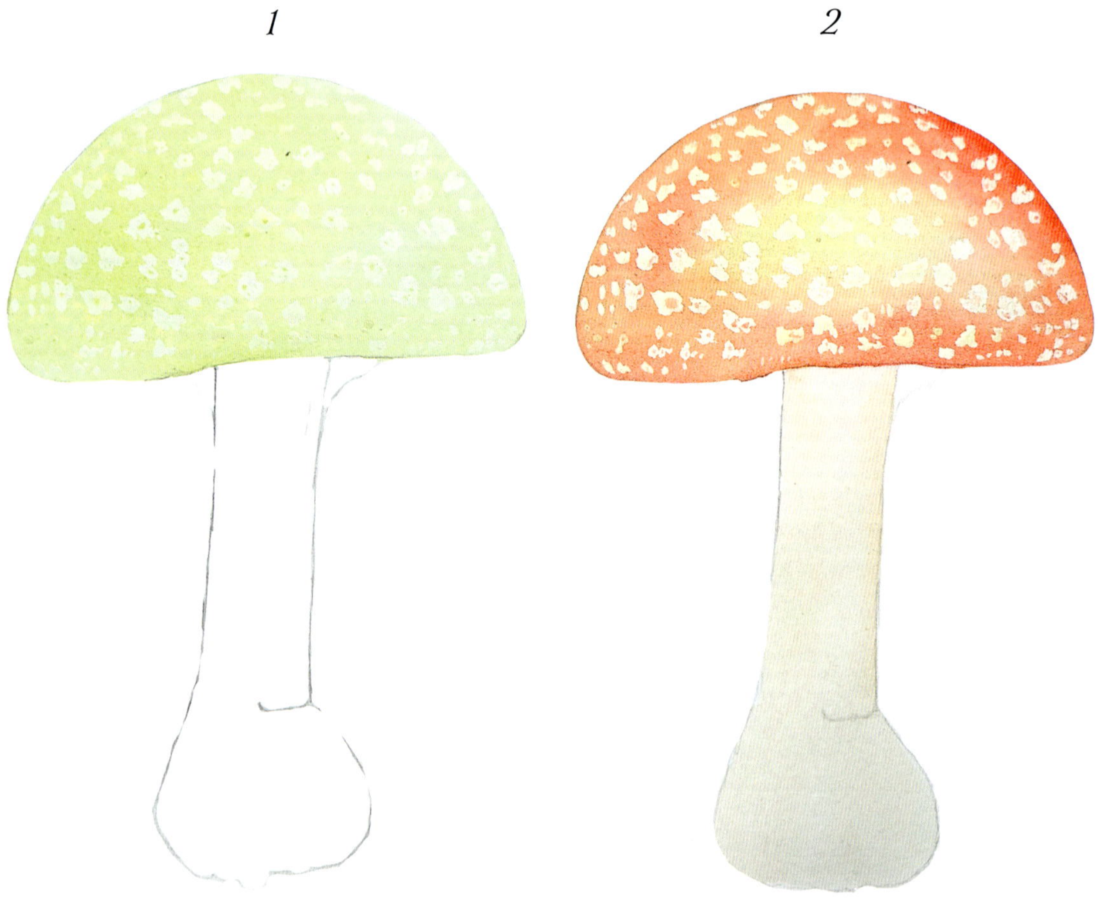

Step 1

Before laying down any paint, use your old brush to apply masking fluid to create the little white scales on the cap. The masking fluid makes it easier to paint big, colorful brush marks while shielding the white paper underneath. Once it's dry, with your medium brush, fill in the cap of the mushroom with a first light wash of Yellow Sophie.

Step 2

The paper should be still damp for this second wash over the cap. Use your medium brush and a medium value of Bright Red. Lighten the value as you get closer to the middle and keep the yellow in the center. Allow the colors to blend a bit. Let it dry. Switch to Raw Sienna to paint the stalk of the mushroom. Just give it a light, even wash.

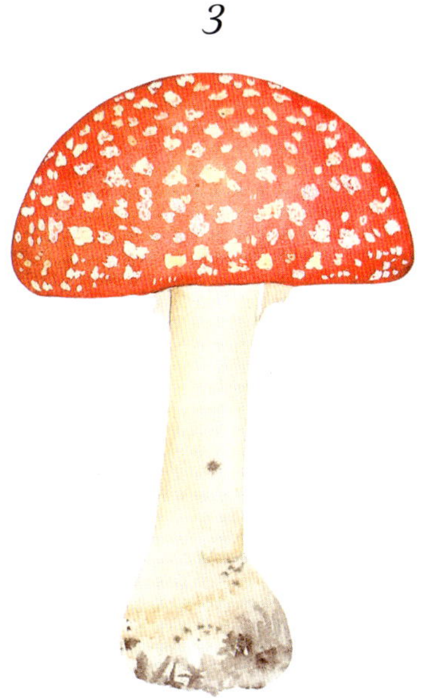

3

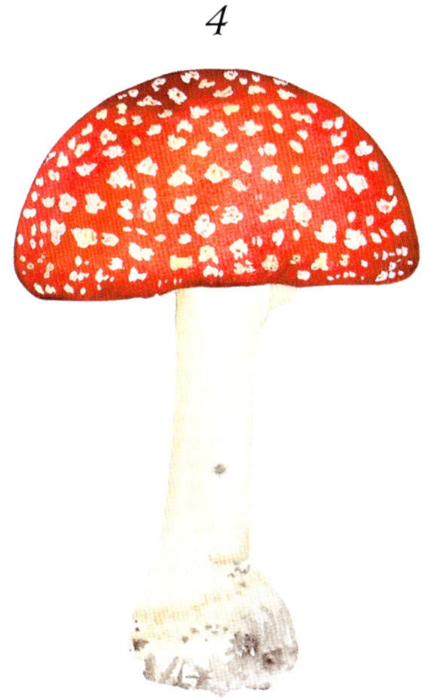

4

Step 3

Switch to your detail brush to add some texture and details while the stalk is still damp. To do this, load your brush with Van Dyck Brown and add a dot with the tip of your brush around the middle of the stalk. Then paint lines on the volva (the bottom of the stalk). Don't worry if these lines mix with the background—this is just the first layer, and watercolors can look unpleasant on the first stage of the painting process. Switch to Raw Sienna to paint the ring skirt with a light evenly painted wash. Add some darker value of Raw Sienna over the crease on the bottom, painting little lines across the volva. Now paint a thick line down the right edge of the stalk, and soften the inner edge with a clean brush and just a bit of water. This is done to create the impression that the stalk is rounded. Repeat on the other side. Let it dry.

Load your medium brush with French Vermilion to paint another wash over the cap area. Start on the edges with a medium value of the color, lightening the value as you get closer to the center of the cap.

Step 4

Keep adding layers to the cap. This time, load your medium brush with Alizarin Crimson and paint another wash, darker at the edges of the cap and lightening the value of the color as you get closer to the center. Before it dries, switch to Red Orange and paint the center of the mushroom cap, covering the yellow area you left before. Leave everything to dry completely before moving on.

Step 5

Use the eraser to gently remove the masking fluid. Load your detail brush with Raw Sienna and paint some of the insides of the little scales. Just paint some lines and smudges and don't fill them in completely.

While you wait for the scales to dry, move down to the stalk. Switch to your detail brush with a medium value of Raw Sienna to create lines along the stalk. Keep in mind the direction of the light. Rather than painting the same vertical lines all over the stalk, leave out the middle to keep the highlight area, so that the brighter part of the stalk is untouched. Paint lines on the ring skirt with a darker value of Raw Sienna to show the shadow of the cap. Add a few darker lines of Raw Sienna on the stalk to create different textures.

Now paint the volva area. Use your detail brush with a mixture of Raw Sienna and Venetian Red to create three lines of small brushstrokes across the area and over the crease of the stalk. Switch to Van Dyck Brown to paint more lines and dots on the bottom volva using different values of the color. Imagine you just took the mushroom out of the ground and it's covered with dirt.

Once the cap is dry, it's time to add shading and shadows. These new shadow shapes won't cover all of the mushroom, but only some select areas where we want to deepen the colors. Load your medium brush with Alizarin Crimson and

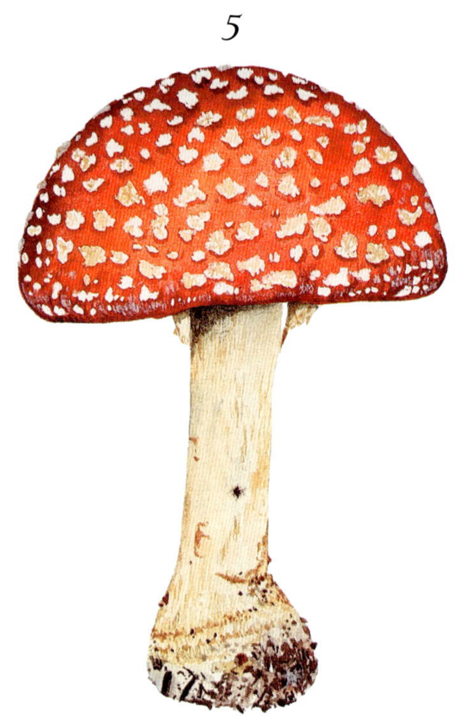

add color to the top of the cap and the bottom edge. This will make your mushroom look more rounded. Also add a bit of color right down each of the scales.

Switch to the white gouache and add some more tiny white scales where you think the cap looks empty, and especially at the bottom of the cap. Add a few lines exactly where the cap curves down. Also paint a few more scales on the top. Switch to Payne's Grey and add the shadow under the cap. It's kind of like a triangle-shaped form on the stalk.

With that, your mushroom is finished!

Feather

Feathers, like hair, fur, fingernails, whiskers, quills, scales, and so much more, are made of keratin—the very same protein that helps provide structure in our own epidermis. Beautiful and seemingly delicate, feathers are also strong and aid a bird in flight.

This is a macaw feather. Macaws are king-sized members of the parrot family. They are also famous for their bright colors, like the ones you can appreciate in this feather. Since ancient times, macaws have been popular as pets. Their colorful plumage, large size, and ability to talk have made them show birds and "attention-getters" around the world. Unfortunately, trapping for the pet trade is a major factor in the macaw's population decline. Chicks can often bring in thousands of dollars from collectors to the trappers, giving them incentive to continue this practice.

Difficulty: Easy

MATERIALS

- Watercolor paper of your choice
  - › I used a 5 x 7–inch (13 x 18–cm) sheet, vertical orientation
- Paints
  - › Van Dyck Brown, Neutral Tint, Primary Yellow, Ultramarine Blue, Red Orange
  - › White gouache
- Brushes
  - › Medium round brush (I used size 9)
  - › Detail round brush (I used size 1)

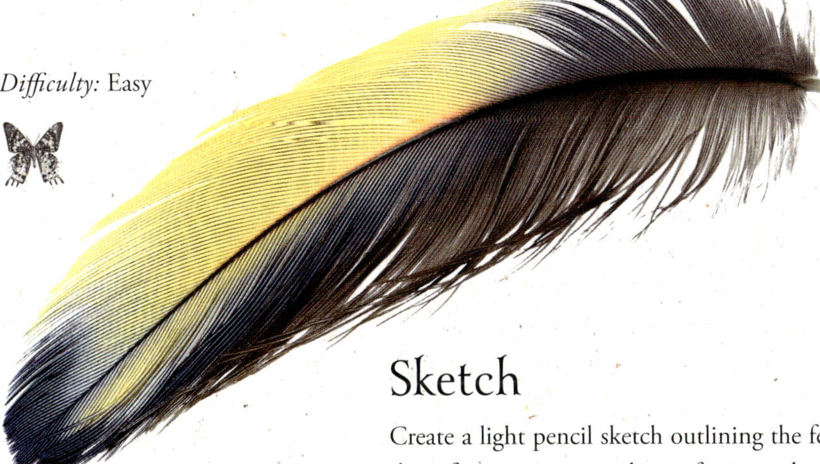

Sketch

Create a light pencil sketch outlining the feather shape or trace the reference image and transfer it to the watercolor paper of your choice. Spray your paints with water to moisten them. Let's start painting!

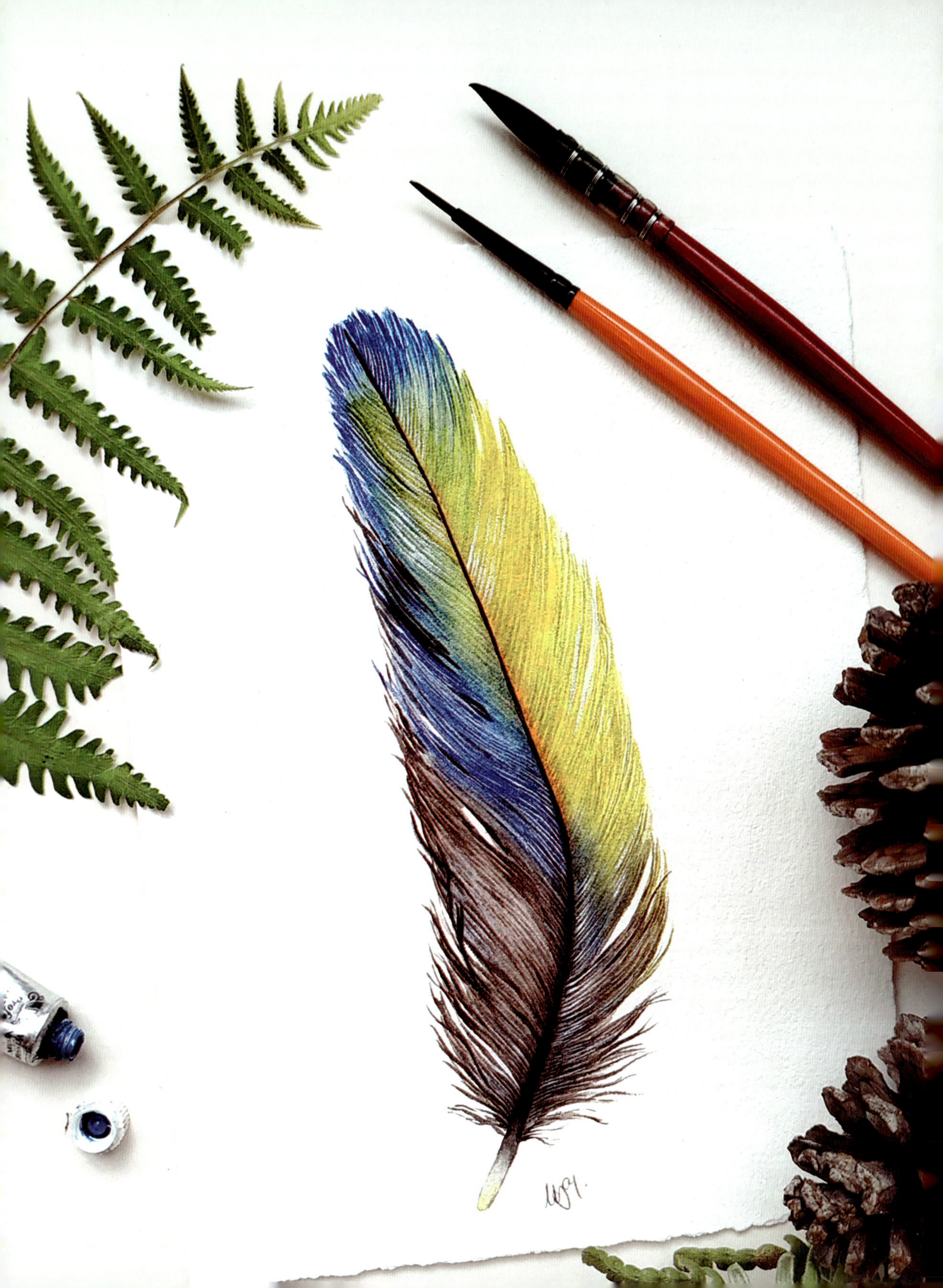

Step 1

Mix Van Dyck Brown with a bit of Neutral Tint to darken the tone. Load your medium brush and start applying a base wash starting from the bottom right side. When you get close to the middle, switch to Primary Yellow and paint the wash all the way up, except for the tip, where you'll use Ultramarine Blue.

Switch to the left side, load your medium brush with the mixture of Van Dyck Brown and Neutral Tint, and paint a light wash towards the center, switching to Ultramarine Blue towards the center. Leave a space close to the central vein to add Primary Yellow.

Step 2

After the first layer is dry, load your detail brush with Van Dyck Brown and paint lines with a light/medium value on the right. Create these lines, keeping the movement of the feather shape. As you go up the feather, switch to the color base. For the yellow area, mix a bit of Ivory Black with Primary Yellow to darken the color. Use this to paint more lines and add texture.

Then, switch to Red Orange and your medium brush to paint a line on the middle right side of the central vein. Clean your brush and soften the line towards the center.

Paint the central vein using a dark value of Neutral Tint and your detail brush. Leave a space untouched on the base of the vein to show the quill. Once you are done with the vein, clean your brush and soften the edges with a little clear water. Finish with a dash of Primary Yellow at the end of the quill.

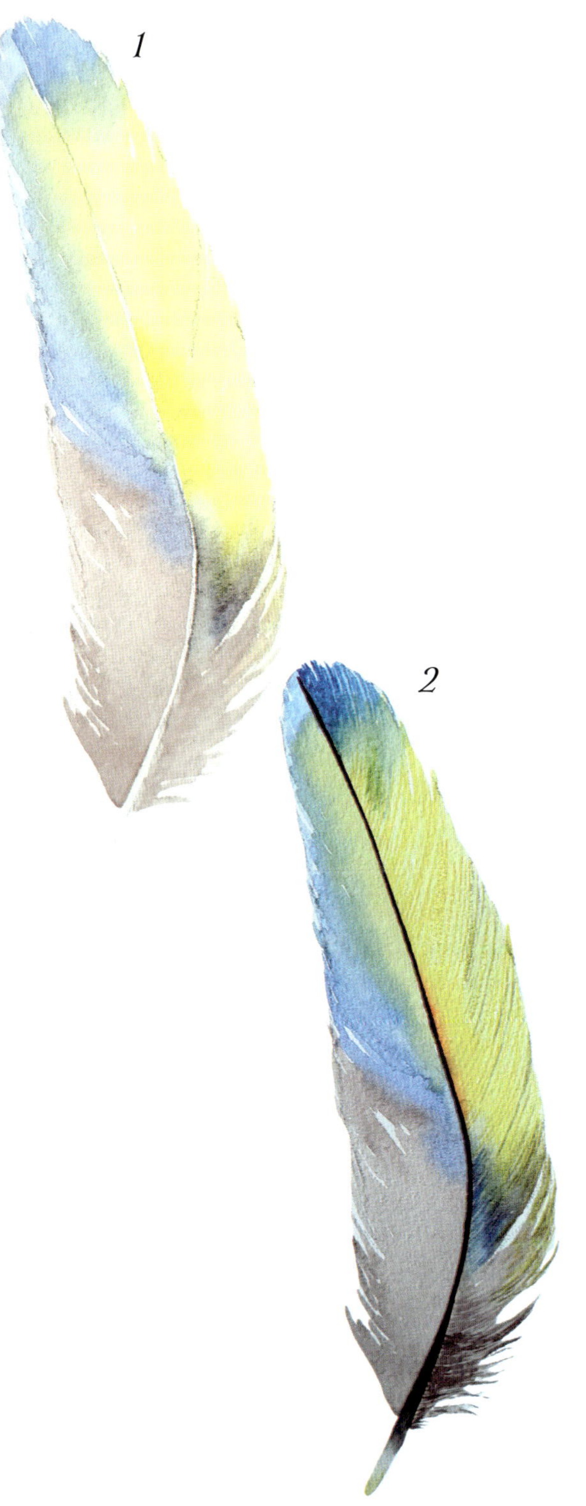

Step 3

Work on the left side now. Load your detail brush with a light value of Van Dyck Brown and paint more lines, again following the shape of the feather, switching to Ultramarine Blue as you get to the blue area. Paint a few blue lines over the yellow wash.

Darken the value of Van Dyck Brown and paint more lines over the feather, using the pressure of your brush to paint thicker lines. Paint some lines out of the wash to create the fluffy texture as if the feather is a bit ruffled.

Step 4

Continue painting lines, changing the value of the color as needed, and smooth out the color transitions with a few lines of the color next to the one you are going to switch to. For example, you're painting Van Dyck Brown lines in the brown area, and as you get to the blue area, paint some thin lines over the blue and then switch to Ultramarine Blue. Repeat this throughout the whole feather. The only difference here is that you'll be painting a few thicker Van Dyck Brown lines on the blue left side of the feather. Take your time creating these lines. The more the better, and use different line thicknesses. I personally like to paint the thicker lines with a lighter value and the thin ones with a darker value, and I prefer to use a very dry brush—almost like using a pencil. Let it dry.

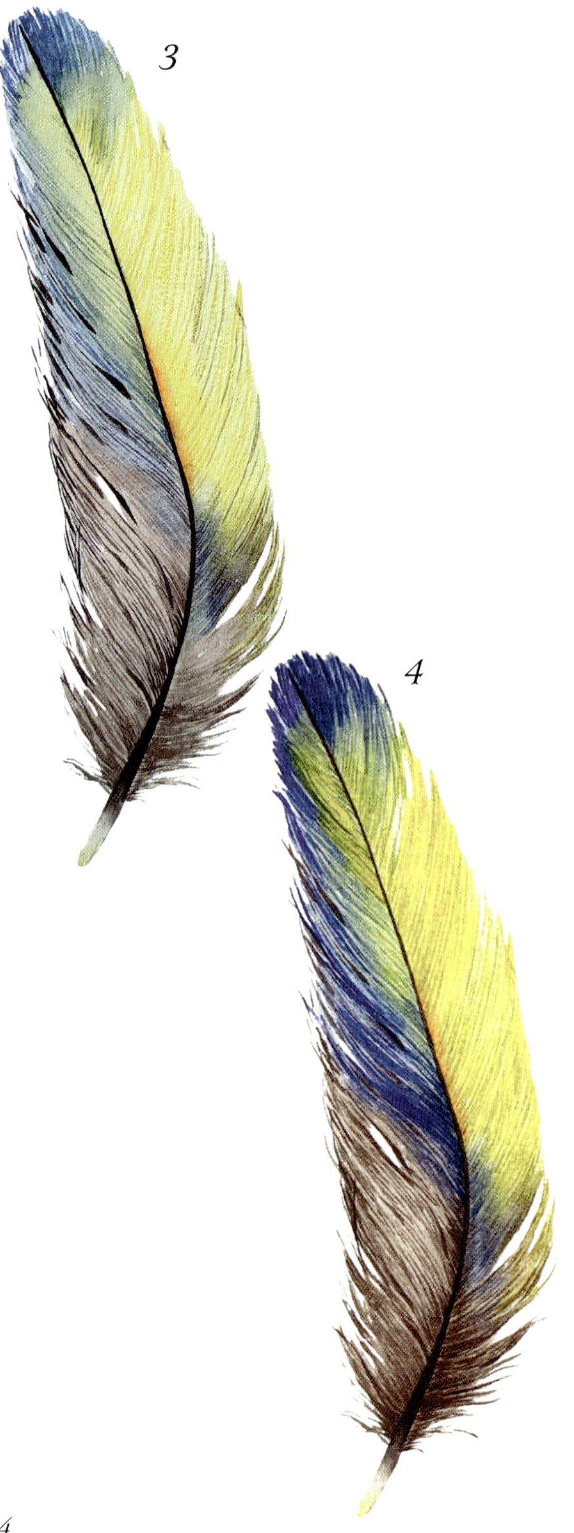

Step 5

Load now your medium brush with a medium value of Van Dyck Brown and paint a thick line on all brown areas touching the central vein with the tip of your brush and pressing the belly of the brush onto the paper. Then soften the edges with the same clean brush.

Load your medium brush with a medium value of Primary Yellow and paint a wash on the yellow area. This will soften the lines you painted and make your illustration look more homogeneous. Do the same in the blue areas by loading your brush with a medium value of Ultramarine. Let this dry. Prepare your white gouache in your palette, and using your detail brush, paint some white lines on some areas, closer to the central vein.

The feather is finished!

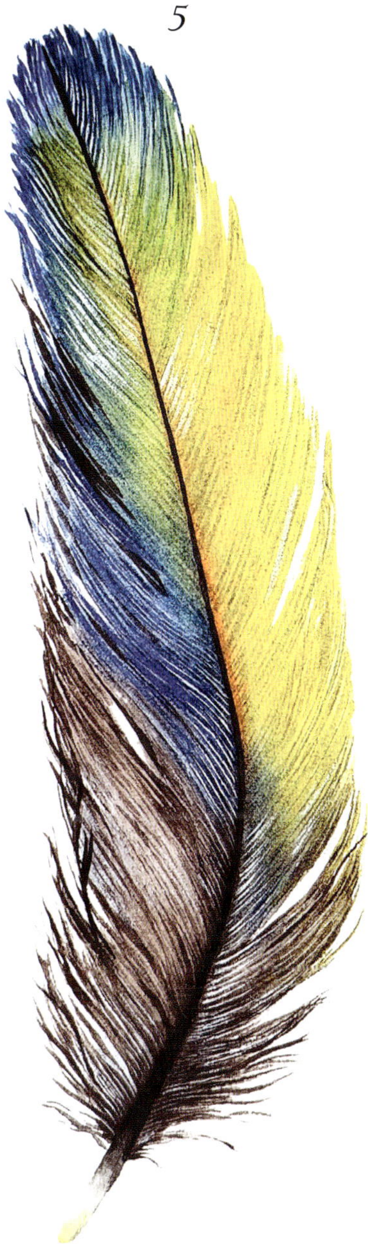

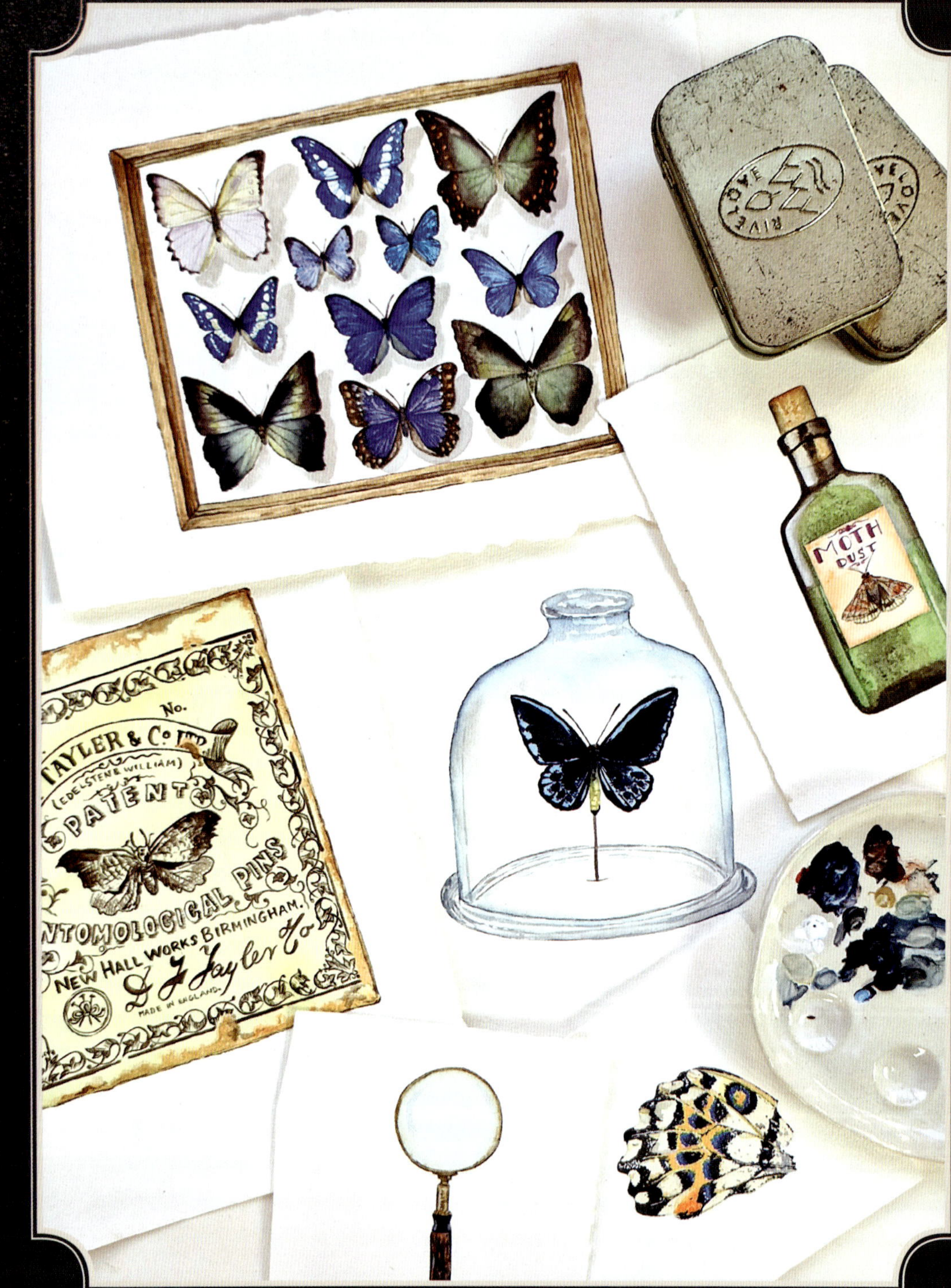

RIVE LOVE
MOTH DUST
No.
TAYLER & Co LTD
(EDELSTEN & WILLIAM)
PATENT
ENTOMOLOGICAL PINS
NEW HALL WORKS BIRMINGHAM.
J. & J. Tayler
MADE IN ENGLAND.

Entomology Drawer

Are you ready to look into this drawer and find out what's inside?

I have collected a variety of projects for you to learn different techniques and to dive into this amazing world of science. Each project in this chapter will teach you different techniques and challenge your inner artist! You can either paint these separately, or create a beautiful collection of entomology items that all go together.

The Moth Dust Bottle (page 199) would be a great project for getting used to painting wings. If you feel adventurous though, you can flip to the Insect Taxidermy Box (page 205) — our most challenging project in this book. With it, you'll learn the power of composition, among other things!

When starting out, it's best to have room to play with your brush. So, instead of forcing yourself to paint miniatures, use a larger sheet of paper to give yourself the room to explore all the details. I recommend using paper that's at least 5 x 6 inches (13 x 15 cm). Alternatively, if you're going for a composition with all the subjects on one sheet, I recommend using a piece of paper that is at least 11 x 10 inches (28 x 25 cm).

I hope you enjoy this chapter and feel the magic once you start doing these projects. Be patient with yourself, and remember that watercolors are meant to do their own thing, and that's the most beautiful part of this medium.

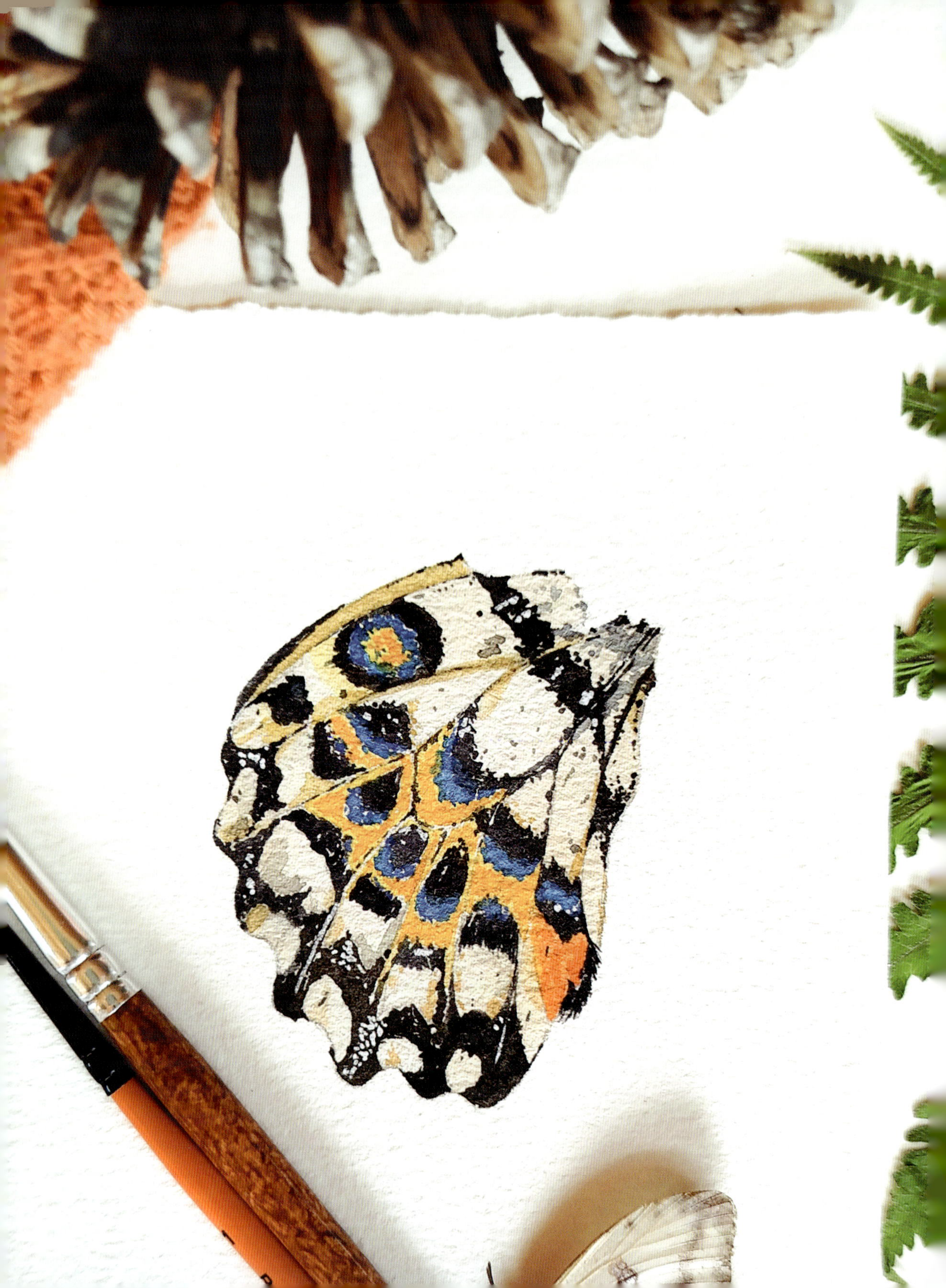

Butterfly Wing

I have a little box full of butterfly wings I have found in nature. I imagine fairies using these wings to craft ballgowns, and they are real treasures to me. I have to include painting one in this book because focusing on just the wing of a butterfly, you realize how incredibly beautiful and detailed they are. Plus, it's easy to become familiar with the patterns when working on a smaller scale.

Difficulty: Easy

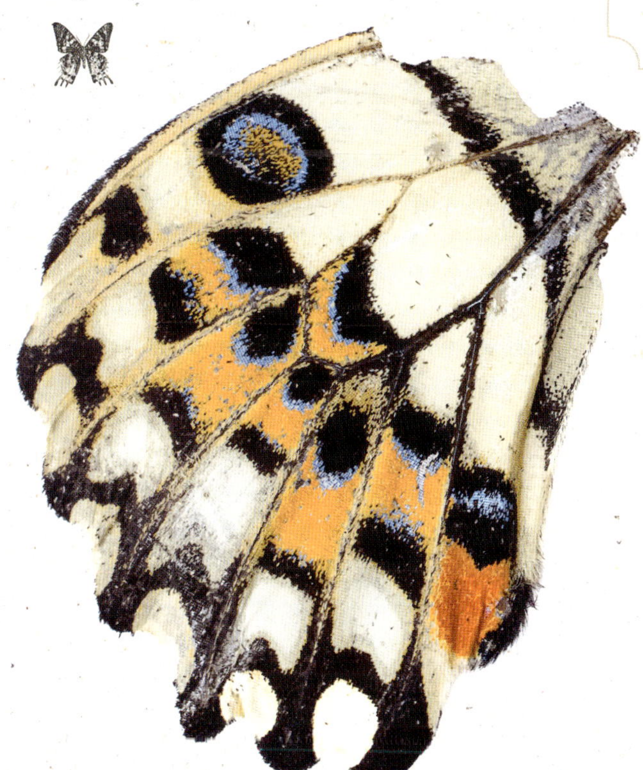

Sketch

Draw the butterfly wing freehand or trace the reference image and transfer it to the watercolor paper of your choice. Focus on all the patterns to make the painting process easier later. Spray your paints with water to moisten them.

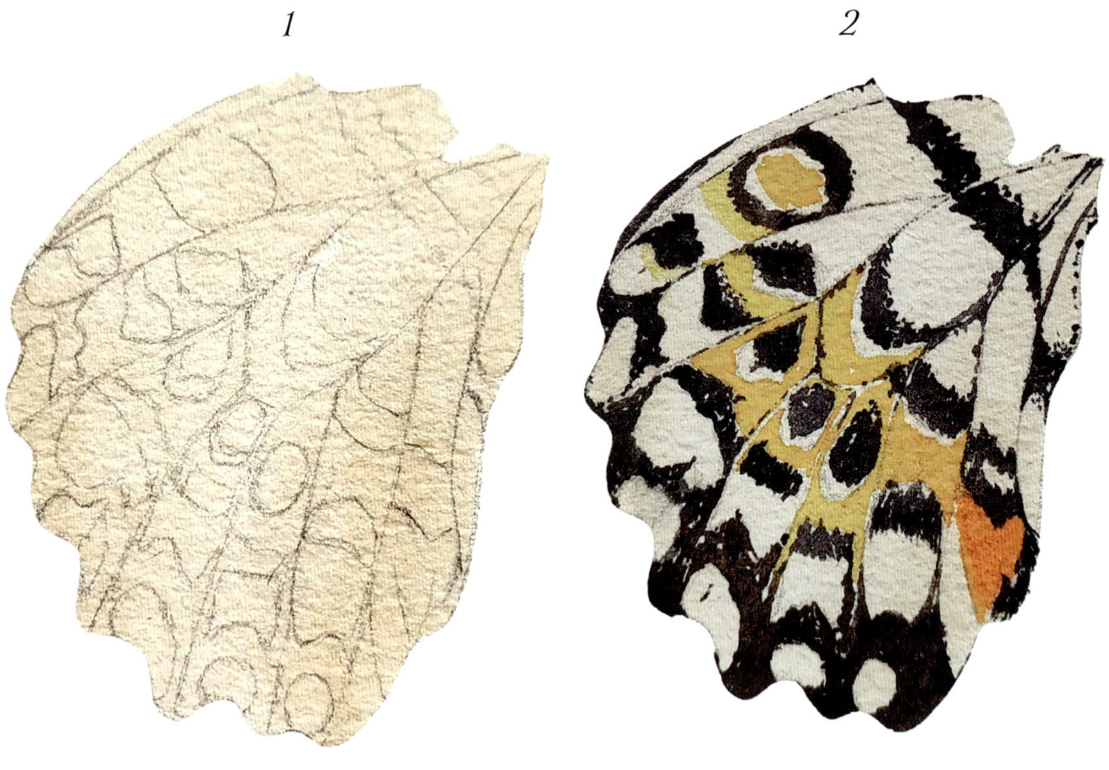

Step 1

Load your medium brush with a medium value of Raw Sienna and paint a wash over the whole wing. Let it dry.

Step 2

Using Ivory Black and your detail brush, paint all the black markings, but instead of painting just brushstrokes, use the tip of your brush to add the color in little dots until you've completed the shape of the marking. This technique makes the marking look like it's full of little scales. What I normally do is first paint a light wash of the color I'm using, and then I start adding dots on top of it, leaving some tiny spaces blank. Let everything dry before adding the next layer of color. For the lines between the markings, use your detail brush with Ivory Black to paint them, but don't paint long lines. Instead, paint very thin little lines that fade a bit. Load your detail brush with a mix of Red Orange and Indian Yellow to fill out the spaces in the middle section of the wing. (Use the photo on page 189 for reference.) For that one orange marking on the right side, use just Red Orange. Let it dry.

Step 3

Load your detail brush with Sennelier Blue mixed with a bit of Ivory Black and Titanium White to create an opaque gray. Use it to paint dots on the torn part of the wing—some dots can go over the black paint. Switch to Raw Sienna and paint a thick line on top of the previous black lines that separate the different markings. On the upper edge of the wing, paint the inside of the section with Raw Sienna.

To add some texture to the areas that are lighter, add a darker value of Raw Sienna just on the edges (where the black markings start). You can also use a light value of Ivory Black and paint some smudges, but just in a few of the markings. Lastly, add dots on the spaces that seem empty to you—for example, the markings right down the torn part of the wing.

Load your detail brush with Sennelier Blue to finish the wing. Paint the eyespot on the left top edge with the blue, between the orange and the black. Use the same technique we used earlier by first applying a light wash, and then painting little dots with the tip of your brush. Finish all the areas where it's blue. Switch to a darker value of Red Orange to add the last wash on the bottom edge, making sure that it's darker than the rest. Also add some lines over the orange area.

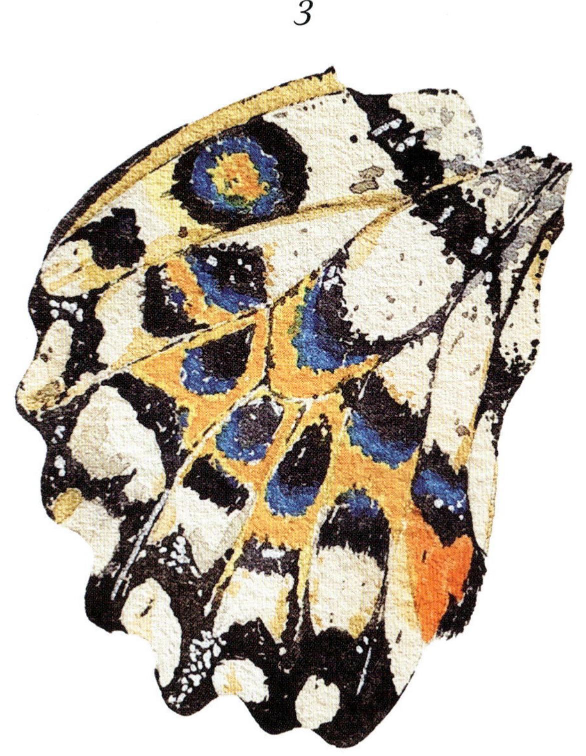

3

Time to use your white gouache to create some highlights. Load your detail brush with gouache diluted with water and paint dots on the bottom section of the wing. Continue highlighting the vein lines in the same area. Paint a few more dots on the black and blue markings.

The delicate wing is finished!

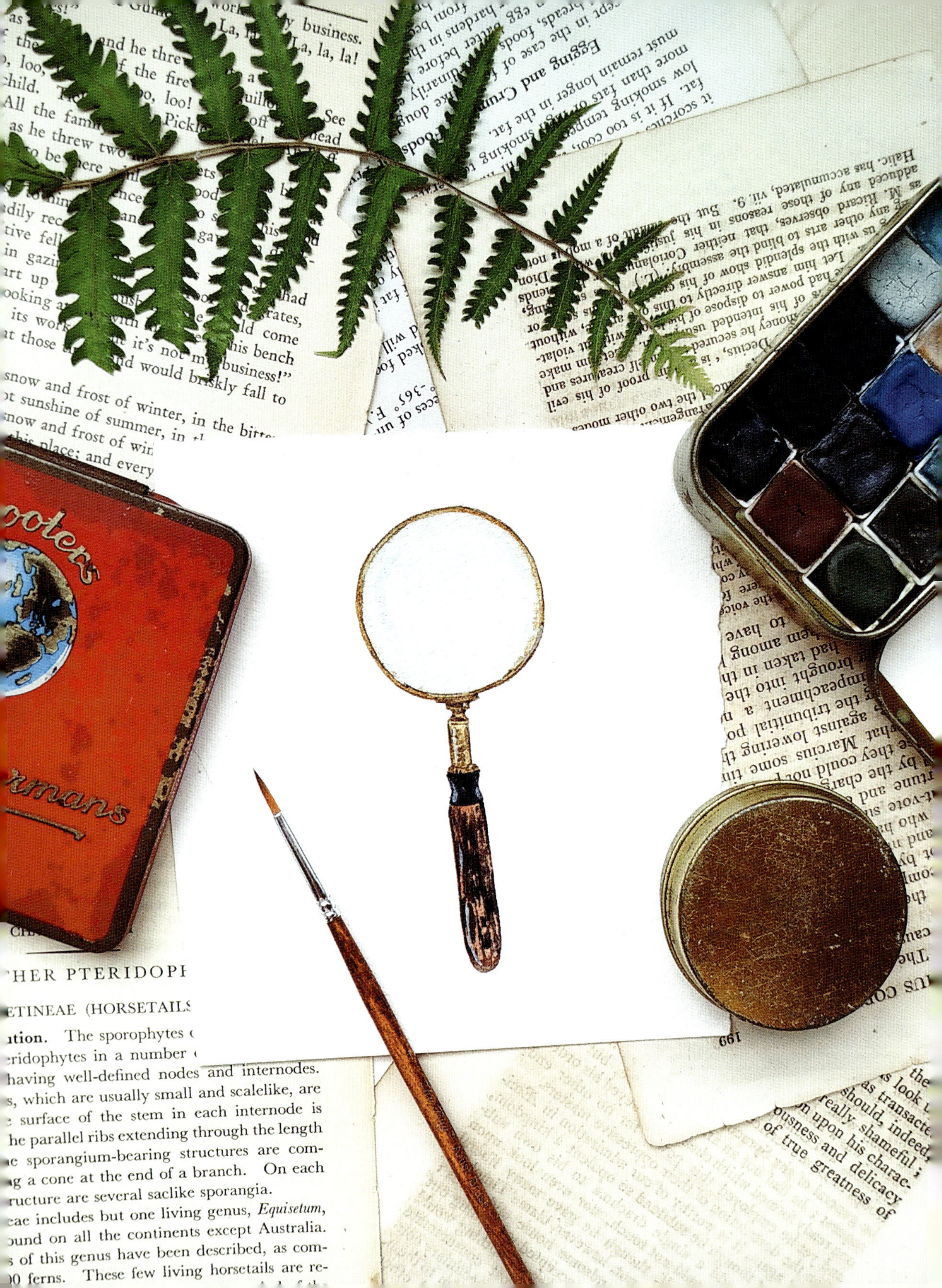
HER PTERIDOPH
ETINEAE (HORSETAILS
tion. The sporophytes
eridophytes in a number
having well-defined nodes and internodes.
s, which are usually small and scalelike, are
e surface of the stem in each internode is
he parallel ribs extending through the length
e sporangium-bearing structures are com-
g a cone at the end of a branch. On each
ructure are several saclike sporangia.
eae includes but one living genus, Equisetum,
ound on all the continents except Australia.
s of this genus have been described, as com-
0 ferns. These few living horsetails are re-

Antique Magnifying Glass

An antique magnifying glass is more than a functional tool that makes objects appear larger. From the elaborate Victorian *repoussé* designs to the sleek lines of those from the Art Deco era, each magnifying glass represents a historic treasure from years past that needs to be properly cared for and preserved!

Difficulty: Easy

Sketch

Draw the magnifying glass freehand or trace the reference image and transfer it to the watercolor paper of your choice. Spray your paints with water to moisten them.

Step 1

Load your medium brush with Venetian Red and paint a wash on the wooden section of the handle. Wait for this to dry. Switch to Cinereous Blue and paint a light wash on the glass area. Let this partially dry before moving on. Then, load your medium brush with Raw Sienna, and paint a wash on the top section of the handle. Then outline the glass part with the same color, switching to your detail brush so you have more control over the amount of color that bleeds inside the blue area. Once everything dries, use your medium brush and Neutral Tint to paint the black area.

Step 2

Load your medium brush with a darker value of Venetian Red to create another wash on the wooden handle. Let it dry. Switch to your detail brush loaded with Raw Sienna and outline the glass again with a darker value. Add a little shadow on the right side inside the blue area. Then add another wash on the top handle section.

Now that the wooden handle section is dry, use Neutral Tint to create the pattern on the wooden area by adding brushstrokes all over. For the black section right over this, darken the value on the edges. Switch to Van Dyck Brown to create the aged effect on the handle's top section by adding dots, and outline each part separating them with a thin line. Outline the frame around the glass with Van Dyck Brown and your detail brush. Let everything dry.

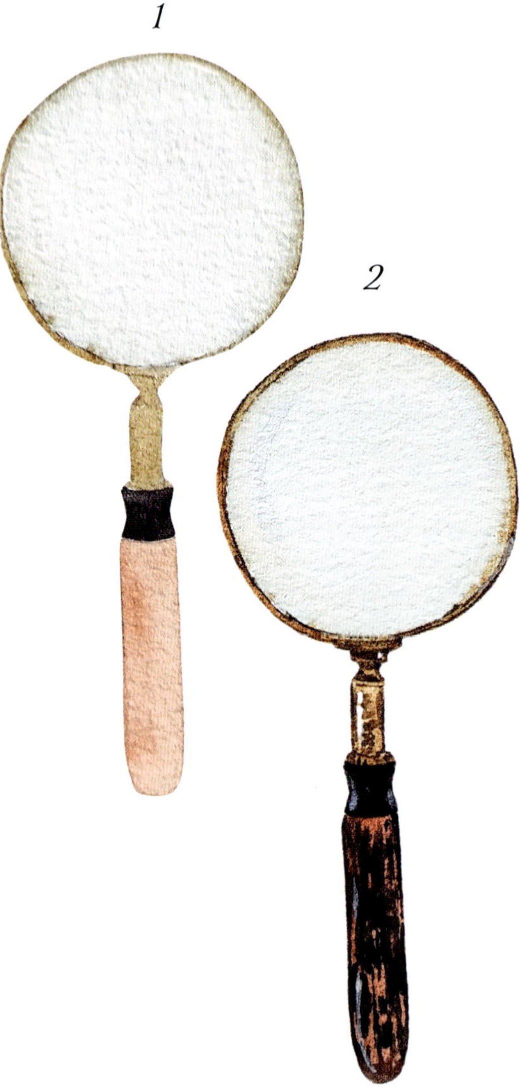

To finish your magnifying glass, load your detail brush with white gouache diluted with water. Add highlights to the left side of the handle and a thin line on the right inside part of the frame around the glass. I also added two circular highlights on the bottom edge of the glass and the top middle left side.

Your magnifying glass is ready to be used!

Glass Dome Insect

Glass domes are magical things, like little fairy worlds inside glass. This way of keeping insects is very popular because you can appreciate the specimen at all angles. In this project, I have chosen a blue birdwing butterfly. And here, I'll be teaching you how to create a composition with two different elements.

Difficulty: Easy

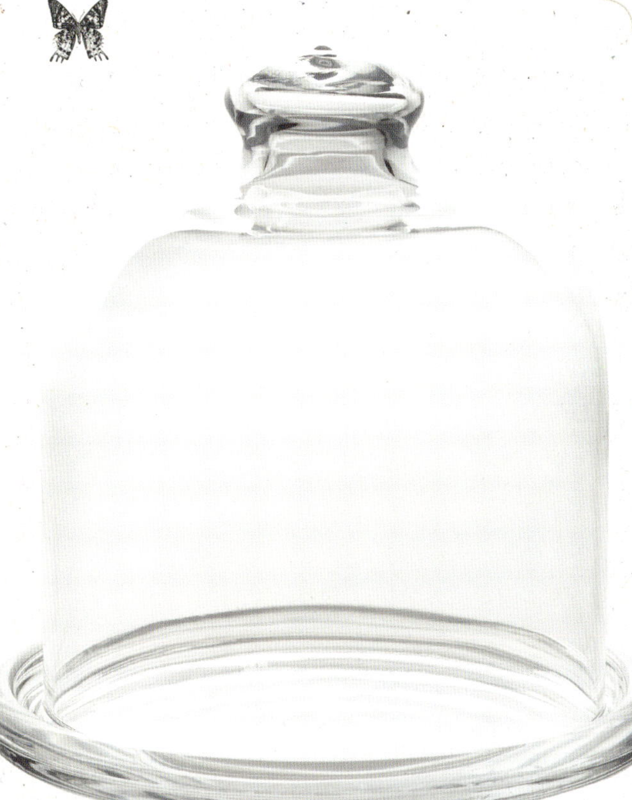

Sketch

Draw the glass dome freehand or trace the reference image and transfer it to the watercolor paper of your choice. Then do the same with the butterfly, calculating the middle of the dome and painting a line from the abdomen of the butterfly to the middle of the dome base. Spray your paints with water to moisten them. Let's paint!

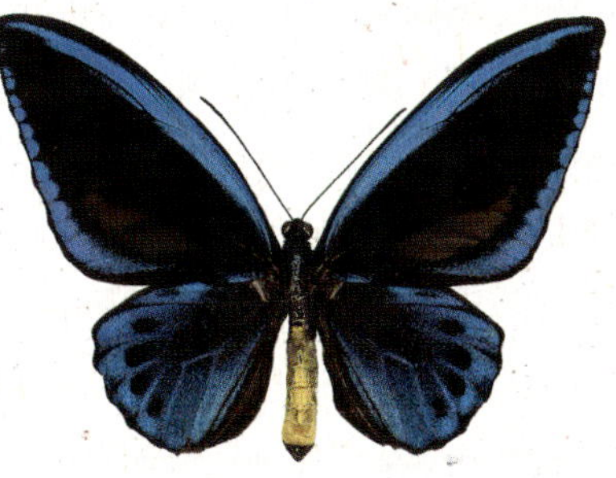

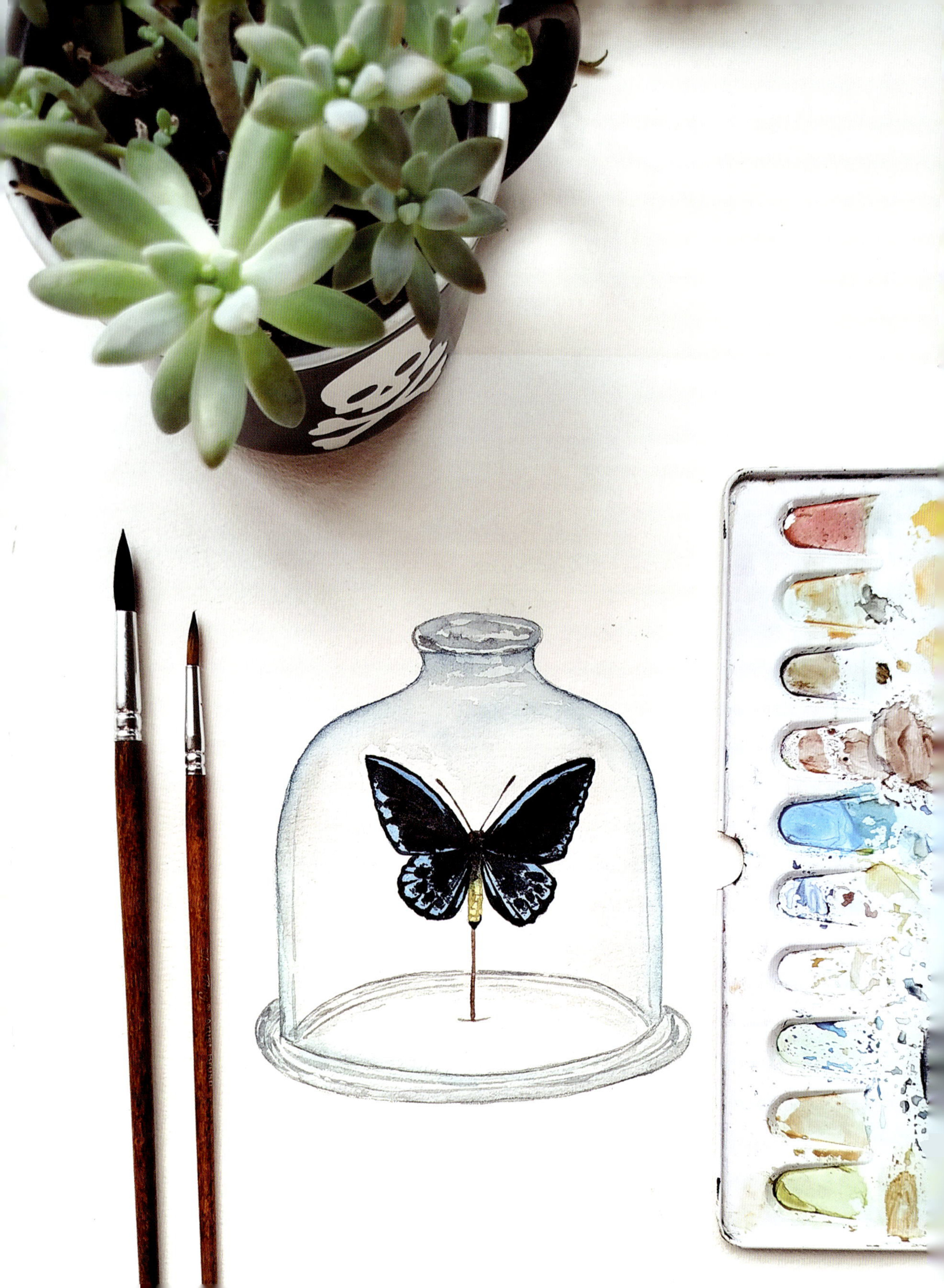

1

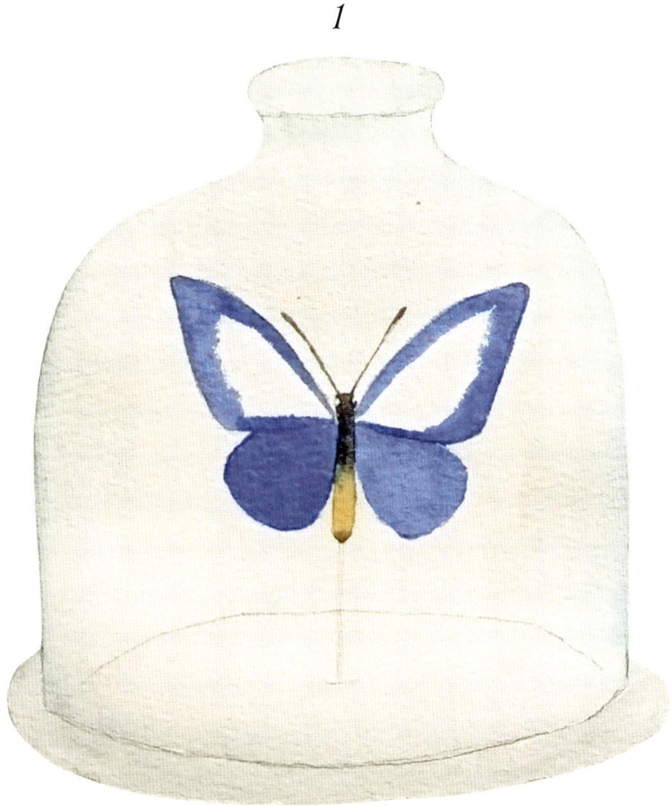

Step 1

Start with the butterfly. Load your medium brush with Phthalocyanine Blue and paint the hind wings with a medium wash, and then paint the forewings, leaving a space for the black markings. Once this dries, use your detail brush to paint the body, first using Yellow Sophie for the abdomen, and then the Payne's Grey for the head and thorax (except the tiny eyes). Allow the colors to blend, and then add a little touch of Payne's Grey to the bottom of the abdomen and the antennae. Allow to dry.

Prepare the surface of the dome by creating a water wash over the area, stopping before touching the butterfly. Load your detail brush with a medium value of Cinereous Blue and start applying the color to the line of the dome—the color will start blending into the water. Do this all around the dome, and use your medium brush to move the color or clean the areas where too much pigment settles by lifting it with a clean brush. For the dome base, create a light wash of Payne's Grey. These two washes are really light!

Step 2

Load your detail brush with Payne's Grey and paint the space you left on the forewings in Step 1, adding some veins on the side edges coming out of the black and merging on the outer edges. Outline the forewings.

Move to the hind wings, load your detail brush with Payne's Grey, and paint the black markings inside the blue area. Add four dots on the bottom edge of each wing. Outline the hind wings and paint the veins coming out of the bottom edge. Load your medium brush with a mix of Cinereous Blue and a bit of Payne's Grey. Use this to add another wash to the glass dome's sides and the top, but darker this time. Then soften the edges with a clean brush.

Switch to a medium value of Payne's Grey and paint another wash on the base of the dome (the plate), creating the light reflection. Use your detail brush to paint a thin line separating the dome from the plate area, and paint the circle inside the dome (the inside part of the plate). Switch to your medium brush to paint a shadow right under the line you just painted to act as a reflection.

Step 3

Use Van Dyck Brown and your detail brush to paint the butterfly holder stick. Next, use Cinereous Blue to create another wash for the top of the dome and the sides. Then soften the edges with a clean brush. Mix a bit of Payne's Grey with your Cinereous Blue to darken the color and outline the sides of the dome and the top using your detail brush, and then switch

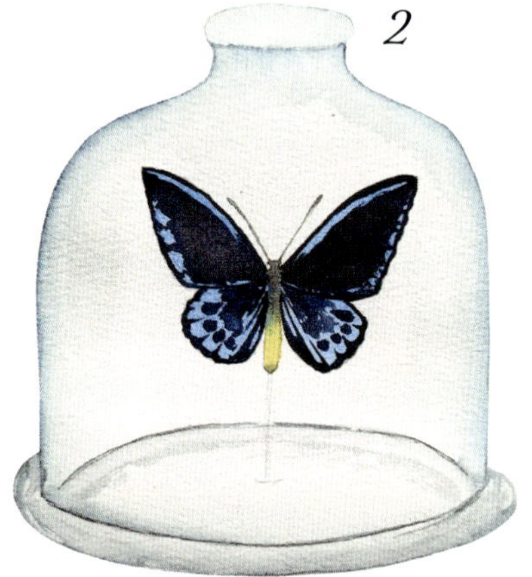

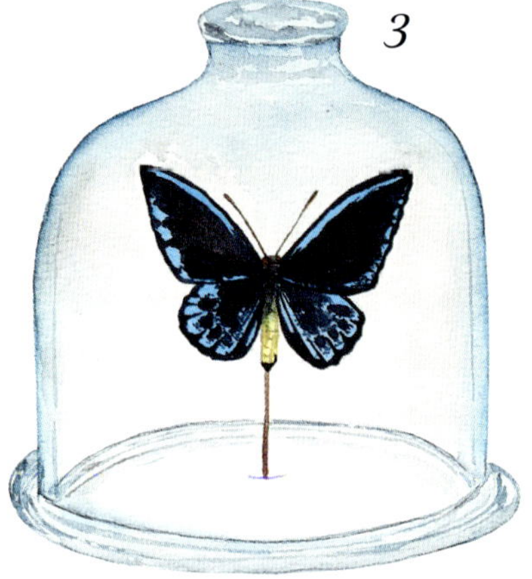

to your medium brush to create the shadows. Instead of using just the tip of your brush, use the "belly," putting pressure on the brush and changing the pressure to create thicker or thinner lines. Paint the reflection on the top of the dome with an uneven circle inside the dome. Load your detail brush with a medium value of the mixture of Cinereous Blue and Payne's Grey to paint two lines on the sides of the dome and the base.

Your glass dome is done!

Moth Dust Bottle

This is the most whimsical project in the book. As a child, I cherished old objects such as bottles or tins, but in my imagination, these were not old objects but magical things. Remembering those times, I created this painting: a mini bottle filled with the dust of moth wings, an enigmatic powder to create spells!

Difficulty: Medium

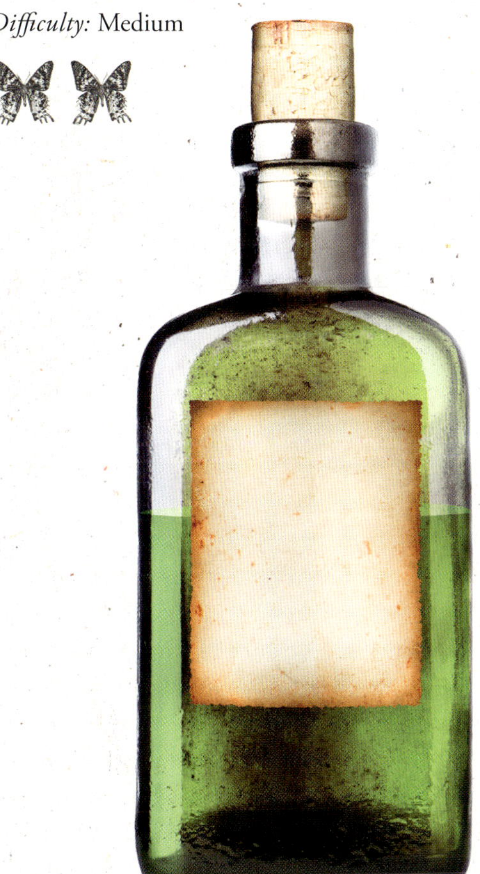

MATERIALS

- Watercolor paper of your choice
  - I used a 5 x 7–inch (13 x 18–cm) sheet, vertical orientation
- Paints
  - Hooker's Green, Van Dyck Brown, Yellow Ochre, Brown Pink, Gold Ochre, Permanent Magenta, Raw Sienna, Venetian Red
  - White gouache
- Brushes
  - Medium round brush (I used size 8)
  - Detail round brush (I used size 2)

Sketch

Draw the bottle freehand or trace the reference image and transfer it to the watercolor paper of your choice. Do the same with the moth on the label, and add the lettering "moth dust." The lettering style is up to you! Spray your paints with water to moisten them.

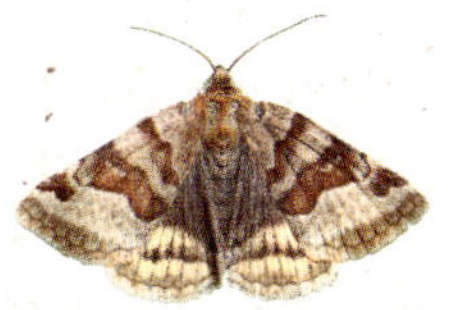

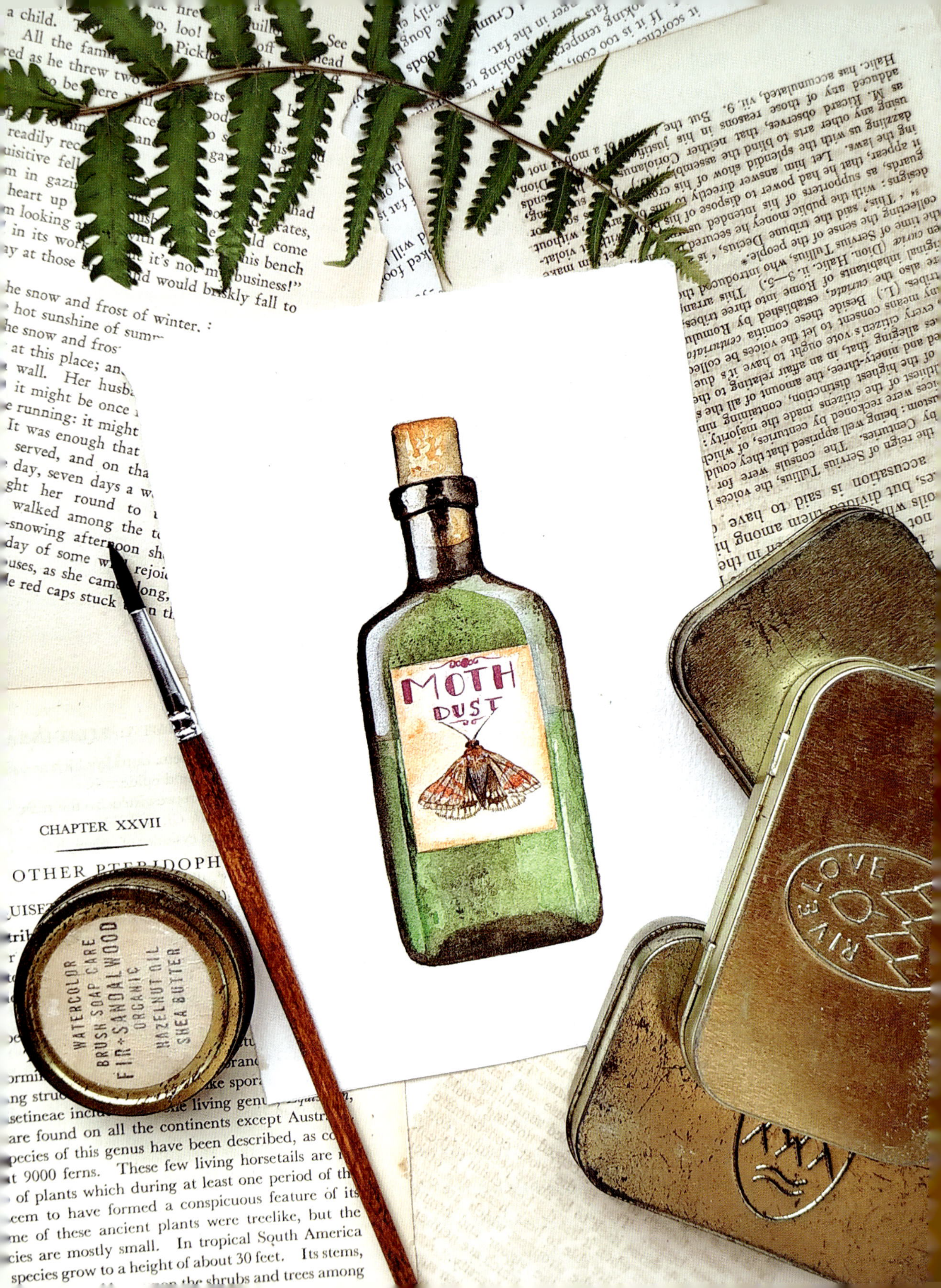
MOTH
DUST
WATERCOLOR
BRUSH SOAP CARE
FIR + SANDALWOOD
ORGANIC
HAZELNUT OIL
SHEA BUTTER
LOVE

Step 1

Load your medium brush with Hooker's Green and paint a medium wash on the bottom section of the bottle (about half of the bottle). Once dry, switch to Van Dyck Brown and paint the other half, keeping the cork unpainted. Load your medium brush again with Hooker's Green and add color to the section above the label, allowing the colors to blend. Use your brush to direct the Van Dyck Brown to the corners and the Hooker's Green right above the label. Once this is dry, paint the cork with a light wash of Yellow Ochre.

Step 2

Load your medium brush with a darker value of Hooker's Green and paint another wash, making a line a few millimeters off the label all the way down to the bottom. Repeat on the other side, and then fill in the area below the label. Directly above the label, paint a semi-circular wash of Hooker's Green. Switch to Brown Pink and blend some of the color to the bottom middle and top of the bottle.

Then, load your medium brush with Van Dyck Brown and paint the bottom section of the bottle, blending the color with the green background. Then outline the left side of the bottle, and when you get to the top, paint a line across the neck and on the right—just outline a little bit of the curved area. Last, outline each side of the bottle top section using your detail brush and Van Dyck Brown. Let it dry.

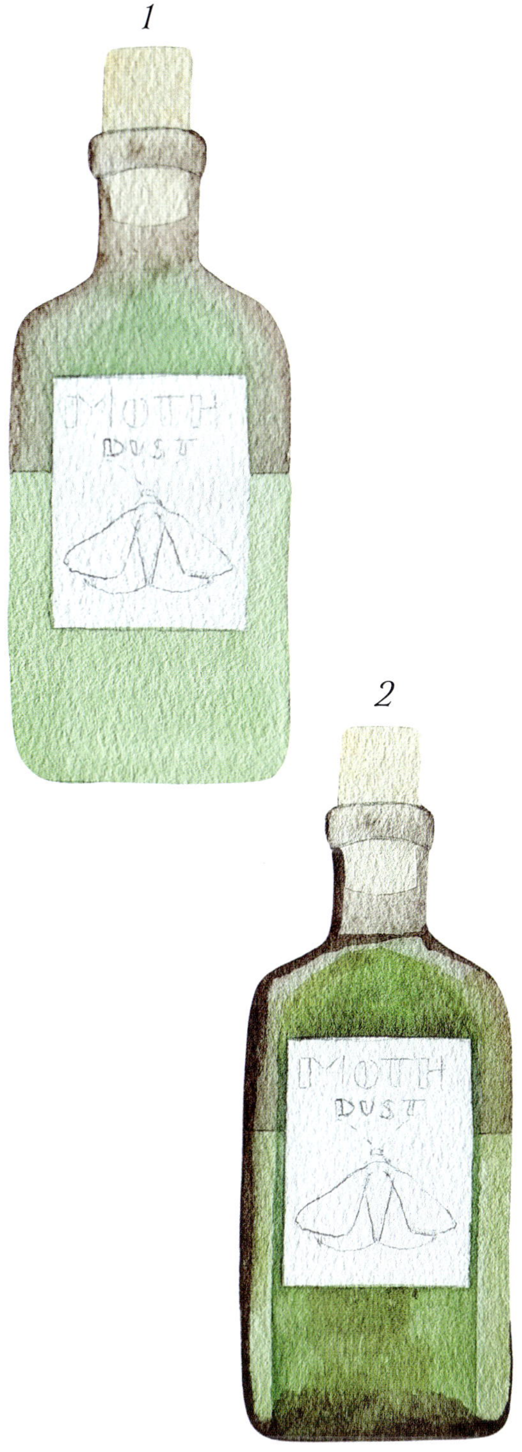

Step 3

Load your medium brush with Gold Ochre and paint some dots and smudges on the cork. While you wait for this to dry, work on the label. Paint your lettering with Permanent Magenta using your detail brush; I also added some ornaments on the top and bottom of the lettering.

Now for the moth. Load your detail brush with Raw Sienna and paint a wash on the forewings. Let them dry. Then paint a wash on the hind wings. Use Venetian Red to paint the body—it doesn't matter if the color bleeds over the wings as it will give it a more cohesive look. At the middle of the body, switch to Van Dyck Brown. Let this dry.

Once the wings are dry, paint the markings on the forewings using your detail brush and Venetian Red. Switch to a darker value of Raw Sienna to add the veins. On the hind wings, paint the top area with a medium value of Van Dyck Brown. At the middle of the wings, start creating the veins coming out of the brown; at this point, also paint the brown markings on the bottom section of the forewings right before the wings end. Last, add little hairlike strokes on the bottom edge of the hind wings. With a medium value of Van Dyck Brown, finish the moth. Paint the antennae and eyes and make some of the veins a bit darker with a second wash of this color.

Switch to your medium brush and use Van Dyck Brown to finish the bottle's neck. Add a thick stripe in the middle of the neck all the way to the top. Paint this line with little touches of your brush instead of painting a clean brush-

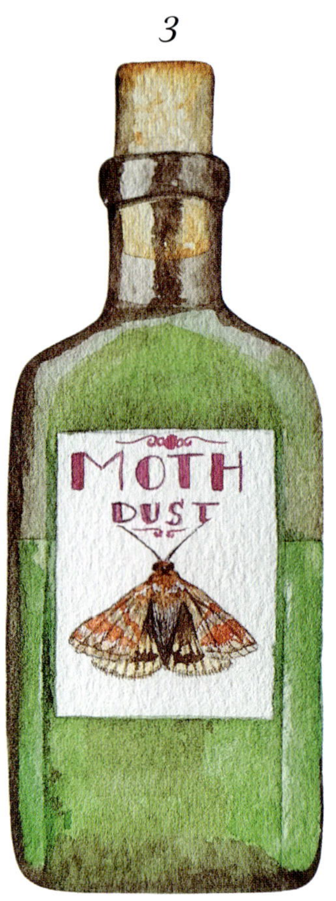

stroke. It's supposed to be a reflection of the light, and it looks more realistic if it's uneven. Outline the lip area, adding a thicker line to both sides. Outline the cork too, and soften the edges with a clean brush.

Switch to Hooker's Green and paint the sides of the label area with a darker value, adding smudges to this section instead of applying an even wash. Add a few smudges with a darker value of Brown Pink and Hooker's Green mixed together on the right side, close to the label. Let it dry.

Step 4

Load your medium brush with a dark value of Van Dyck Brown and outline the bottle again. Using a clean brush, soften the edges of the color inside the bottle area, blending it with the background. Paint a light wash of it right under the cork. On the bottom, emphasize the dark area using the same brush and Van Dyck Brown. Do the same on the middle stripe on the neck—adding more value there and on the line that crosses the neck.

Then paint a medium wash of Brown Pink all over the green area using your medium brush. Before this dries, switch to your detail brush and Van Dyck Brown to add dots all over the area, creating the effect that the bottle is dirty inside. Vary the shape of these dots. Create more texture on the cork with your detail brush and Venetian Red. Once the green area is dry, load your medium brush with Yellow Ochre and paint the label. Then switch to Venetian Red to create some smudges as if the label is old. Let it dry.

Load your medium brush with white gouache diluted with water and create the highlights on the bottle. Paint a highlight on the left side of the bottle, and then do the right side. For the neck, paint a line on the left side. Soften the edges of the inner sides of the white markings, fading them a little.

You can create spells now with your dust!

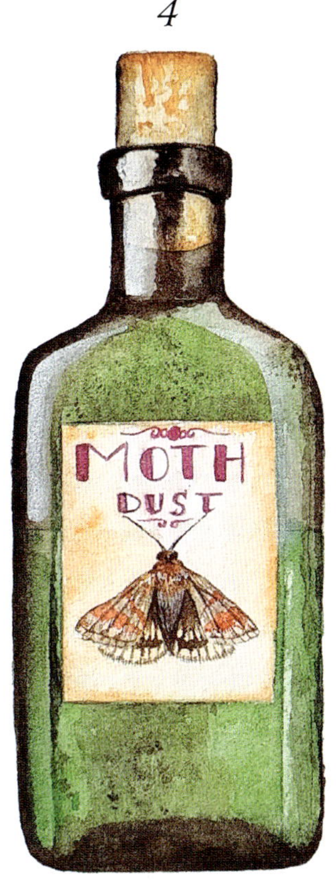

> **Tip:** *Painting glass can be challenging, but most of the time you don't need to worry about painting the glass itself but focusing your attention on painting the distorted shapes and reflection of the light. Don't even think at all—just paint what you see. Be sure to paint what you actually see, and not what you think you see. Part of what makes painting glass tricky is that your brain tries to dictate what the painting should look like, and that interferes with the visual information that is actually in the photo reference.*

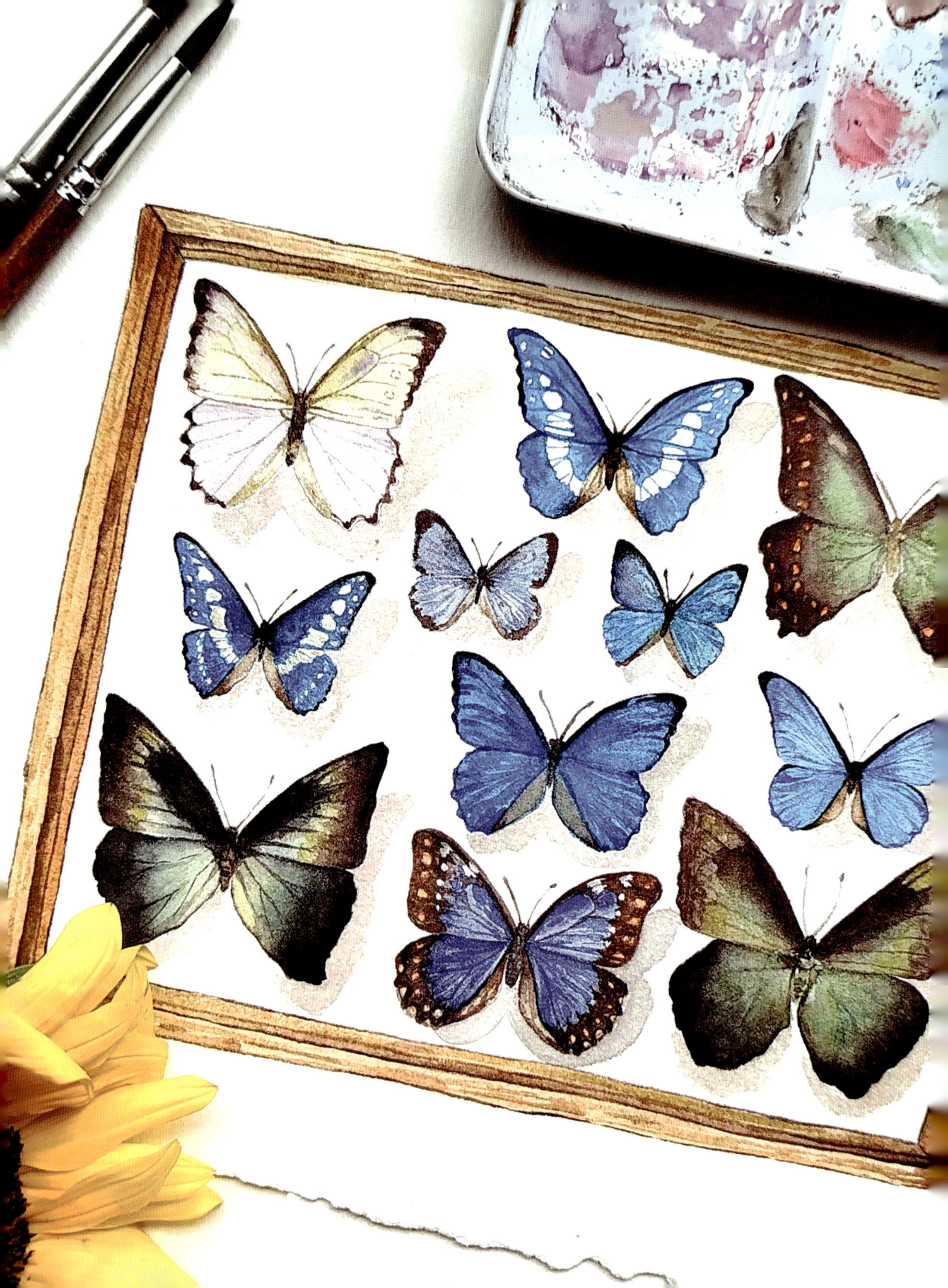

Insect Taxidermy Box

As I have said before, it's a dream of mine to have an entomological collection, and while I wait, I love painting those kinds of treasures! This particular butterfly taxidermy box includes different morphos and other tropical butterflies.

Because of all the individual layers of paint for each butterfly, this piece may take you a bit more time than some of the others. I suggest grabbing a nice beverage and turning on some music to enjoy both the painting and drying processes.

Note: The complexity of this illustration is more about the number of elements rather than the elements themselves, since morpho butterflies are pretty simple.

Difficulty: Difficult

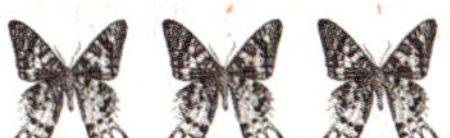

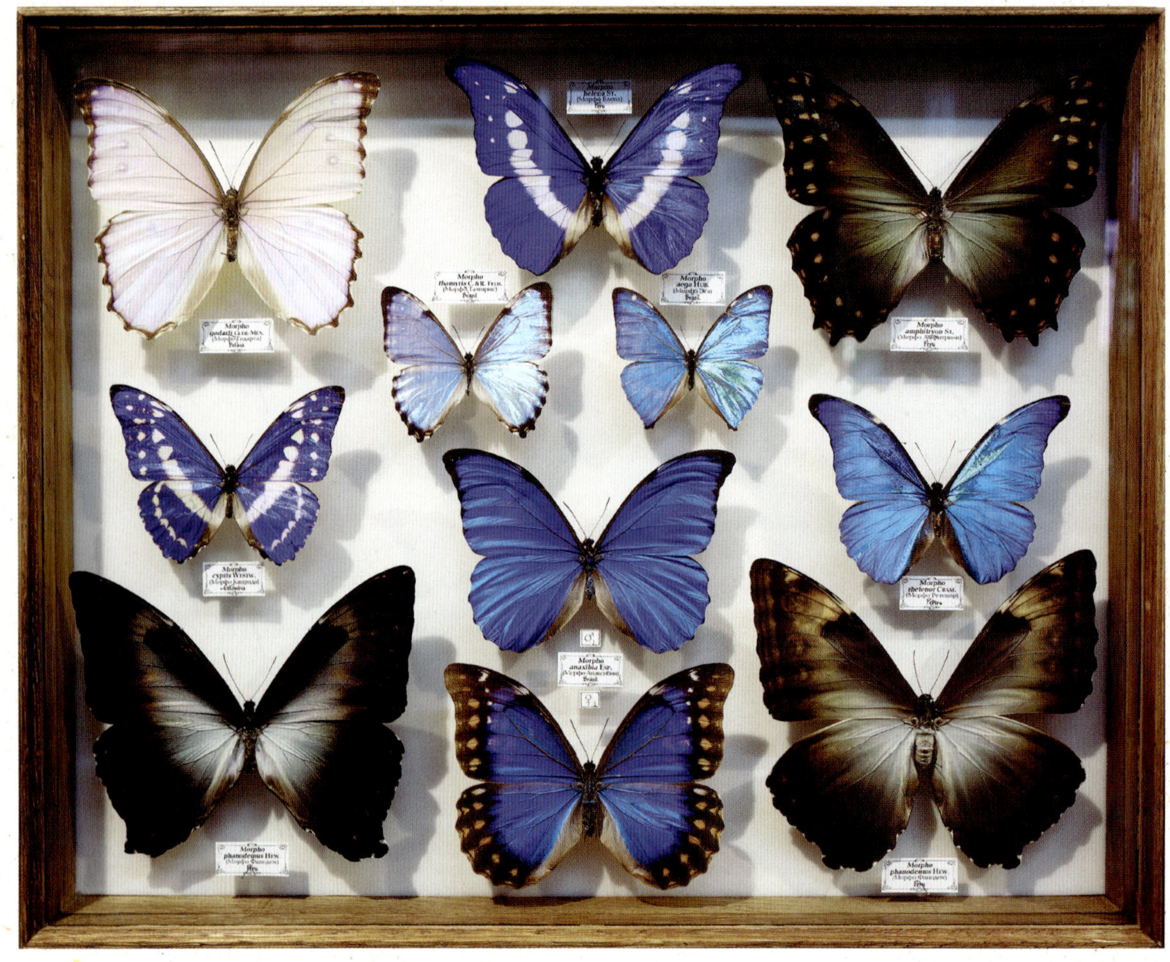

Sketch

Draw the butterflies freehand or trace the reference image and transfer it to the water-color paper of your choice, focusing on the shape of the wings and the frame around them. Spray your paints with water to moisten them. Let's paint!

1

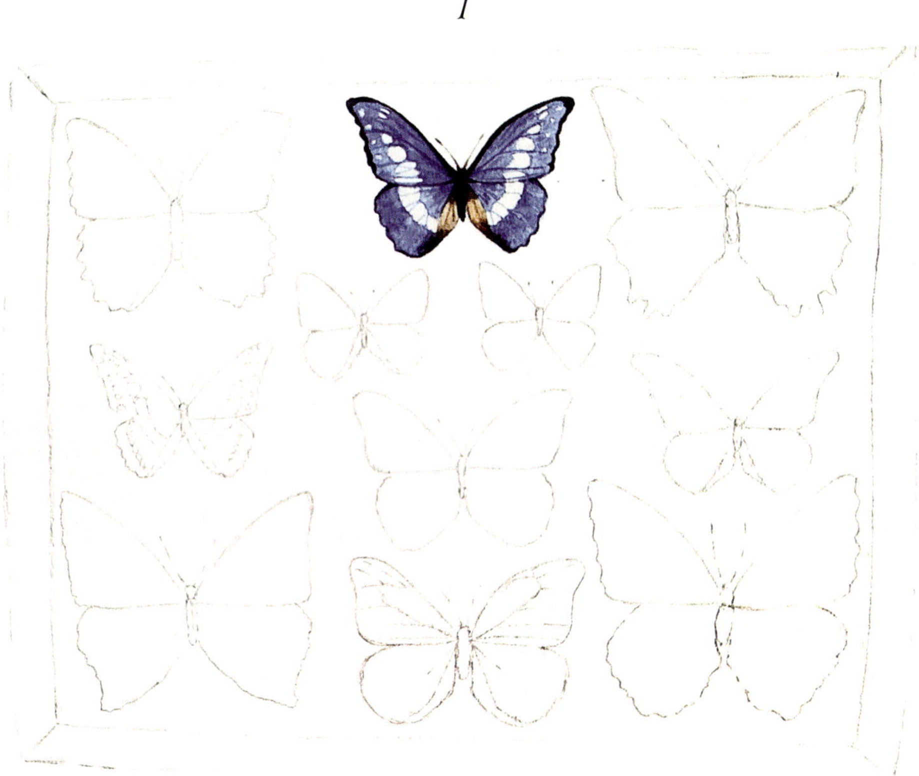

Step 1

Start with the top-center butterfly. Load your detail brush with a medium value of Ultramarine Blue and paint the forewings except for the white areas. Let it dry. Move to the hind wings, and paint a medium wash of the same blue, except for the white areas and the bottom edge. Let it dry.

Switch to Raw Sienna and paint the lower edges of the hind wings. Before this dries, load your detail brush with a dark value of Payne's Grey to add color to both corners of this section. Also, paint the body and antennae and outline all of the butterfly wings with this color, making the line thicker on the forewings. With a darker value of Ultramarine Blue, paint the veins on all four wings—even on the white areas too, dividing the sections. Use Van Dyck Brown and your detail brush to add two lines coming out of the black area on the corner of the hind wings.

2

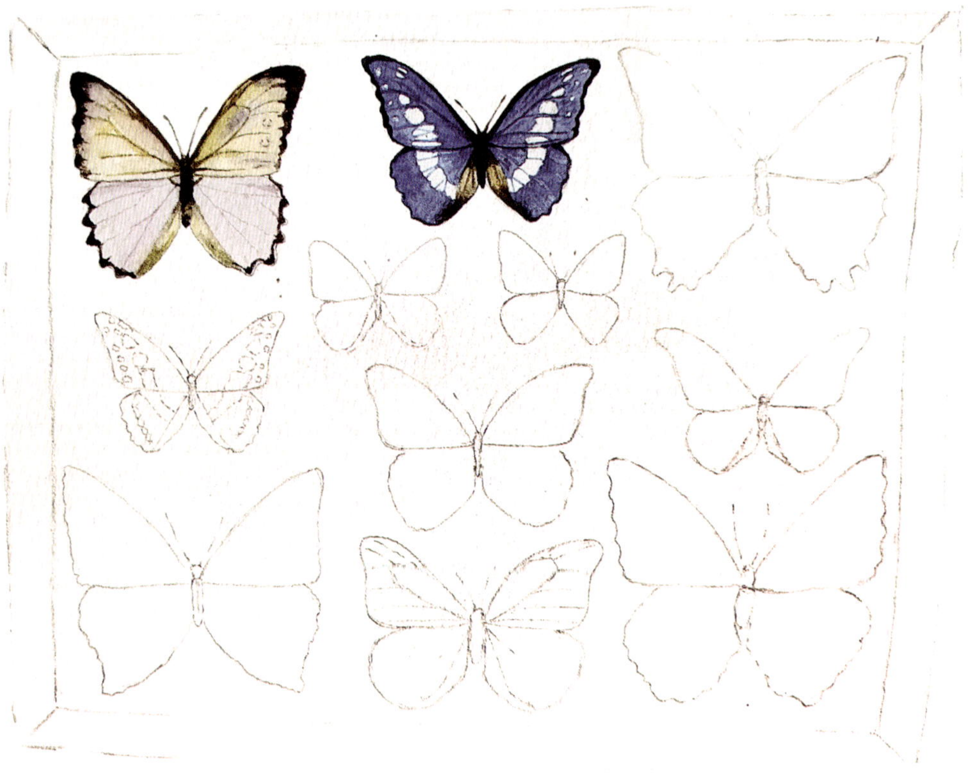

Step 2

Now paint the top-left butterfly. Start with the forewings. Use your detail brush to paint a light wash of Brown Pink, and on the top corner of the forewings paint a wash of Dioxazine Purple. Add two brushstrokes of Brown Pink that are a bit darker on the top edge of the wings. Let it dry.

Now paint the hind wings. Create a light wash of Dioxazine Purple over them, and switch to Brown Pink for the bottom edges, darkening the value on the lower parts. Let this dry. Load your detail brush with Van Dyck Brown and paint the body and antennae with a dark shade. Outline the forewings, getting a bit inside the wings to make it look like the beginning of the veins. Switch to Brown Pink and paint the veins.

Moving to the hind wings, use a darker value of Dioxazine Purple, and with your detail brush create the veins. Switch to Van Dyck Brown for the veins that are closer to the body. Keep using your detail brush and Van Dyck Brown to outline the lower edge of the hind wings.

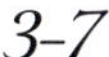

3-7

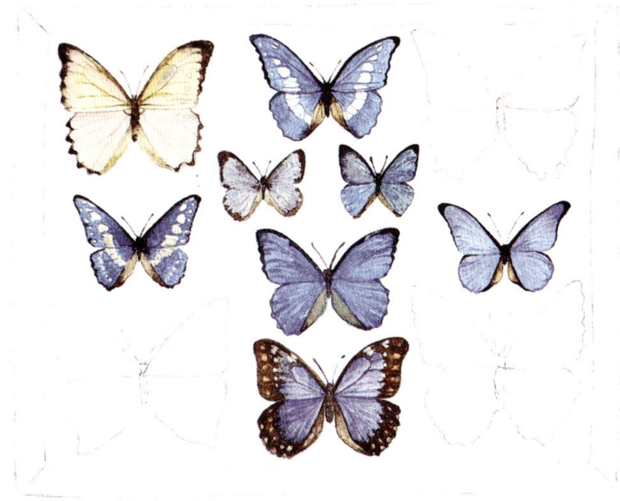

Step 3

Repeat Step 1 for the blue butterfly on the center-left. To add a little point of difference, paint a few lines inside the white markings with your detail brush and a light value of Brown Pink.

Step 4

Now paint the two little butterflies under the first one you painted. Mix Dioxazine Purple with a bit of Ultramarine Blue for the one on the left. Use your detail brush to paint a light wash over the wings, leaving a space on the bottom of each hind wing. Everything will dry pretty quickly as it's a small butterfly, but keep in mind that the surface should be almost dry to paint the next step. Switch to Payne's Grey to outline the wings and create the markings on both forewings and hind wings. The color is going to blend a bit with the background, and that's exactly what we want. As the wings

continue to dry, paint the body and antennae with Payne's Grey.

Add a bit of Dioxazine Purple to Payne's Grey, and with the detail brush, darken the value of the inner corners of both the hind and forewings where they merge with the body. Load the same brush with a light wash of Payne's Grey and paint the lower section of the hind wings, adding Brown Pink to the bottom corner. Let it dry. Use a darker value of the Dioxazine Purple and Ultramarine Blue mixture to paint a few veins on the wings.

The other tiny blue butterfly is an easy one. Mix Ultramarine Blue with Dioxazine Purple, but with less purple this time, and paint a wash on the four wings, leaving the space on the bottom edge untouched. Once dry, darken the value to paint some veins—do this very lightly (barely touching the paper with the tip of your brush)—on both hind wings and forewings.

Switch to Payne's Grey to outline the upper edge of both forewings, thickening the line on the top edge, allowing it to blend with the background. Keep outlining the forewings all around and a bit on the top of the hind wings. Paint the body and antennae with Payne's Grey. Switch to a light value of Warm Sepia and paint the bottom edge of the hind wings, darkening the value on the corner bottom edge.

Step 5

Now paint the morpho right under the two little ones you just finished. Load your medium brush with a medium value of Cinereous Blue and create a wash on all four wings. Switch to your detail brush to create the veins with the same color with a dash of Ultramarine Blue. On the hind wings, shape the curves on the edge of the wings at the end of the veins. Use Payne's Grey to outline the forewings, shaping the curves on the sides. Paint the body with Payne's Grey as well. To finish, lighten the value and paint the bottom inner edge of the hind wings, darkening the value on the bottom corner.

Step 6

Paint the butterfly underneath the morpho you just painted. Load your medium brush with Ultramarine Blue and create a light wash over the four wings, leaving space, especially on the edges of the wings, to create the other markings.

Switch to Red Orange to paint the markings on the edges—six on the forewings and five on the hind wings. Just a dot of color! Load your detail brush with Van Dyck Brown and outline these dots on the forewing as you paint the outer area, to look like the beginning of the veins. Continue making the veins on the top section, and use a darker value of Ultramarine Blue to create the lower veins. Add a darker shade of Van Dyck Brown between the orange markings.

For the hind wings, the process is similar, but with the detail brush, use a darker value of Van Dyck Brown to outline the orange markings, create the wavy shapes on the outer edge, and switch to a darker value of Ultramarine Blue to create the veins. Once everything is dry, paint a light wash of Red Orange on the spaces between the waves of the edge, and paint a thin line with Van Dyck Brown to close the hind wings' outer edge.

Use Payne's Grey to darken the top edge of the forewings a bit and paint the body and antennae. Paint the lower inner section of the hind wings with a light wash of Yellow Ochre, and outline it with Van Dyck Brown, painting a few smudges inside the area and darkening the part where the wings meet with the body. Oh! And once dry, don't forget to add some highlights on the top of the forewings using your white gouache.

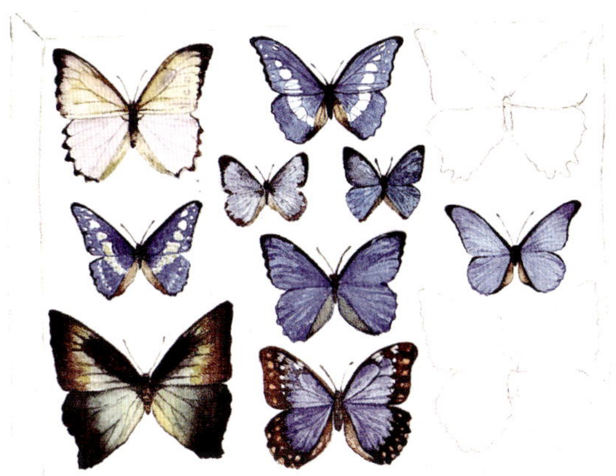

Step 7

Now paint the Morpho butterfly in the center-right position. Load your medium brush with a medium value of Cinereous Blue and create a wash on the four wings. Switch to your detail brush to create the veins with the same color with a dash of Ultramarine Blue. Outline the hind wings with a dark value of Payne's Grey, and outline the top edge of the hind wings separating both wings. Once dry, use Yellow Ochre for the lower section of the hind wings, outlining the area with Payne's Grey and adding a bit of Van Dyck Brown to the part between the black line and the Yellow Ochre to make the transition less harsh.

Step 8

For the bottom-left butterfly, load your medium brush with a light value of Phthalo Green Deep and paint the inner section of the forewings. Switch to Brown Pink and create a gradient of these colors. Then use both Van Dyck Brown and Payne's Grey for the outer edges of the forewings. It should look like a gradient of the four colors blending a bit into each other. You want to have a bit of control over what's happening on your paper, so for this, use just enough water so the colors will blend but won't mix into a puddle of shades and create muddy wings. Let this dry.

Switch to the hind wings, creating a gradient of Brown Pink, transitioning into Phthalo Green Deep, and then Payne's Grey. Before it dries, add a dot of Van Dyck Brown to the top edge of the hind wings. Let this dry.

Switch to your detail brush and paint the body with Van Dyck Brown. Add some lines in the abdomen with Payne's Grey. Keep using Payne's Grey to create a big strip on the upper section of the forewings, and from there, paint the veins. Also darken the areas where the wings meet the body.

9

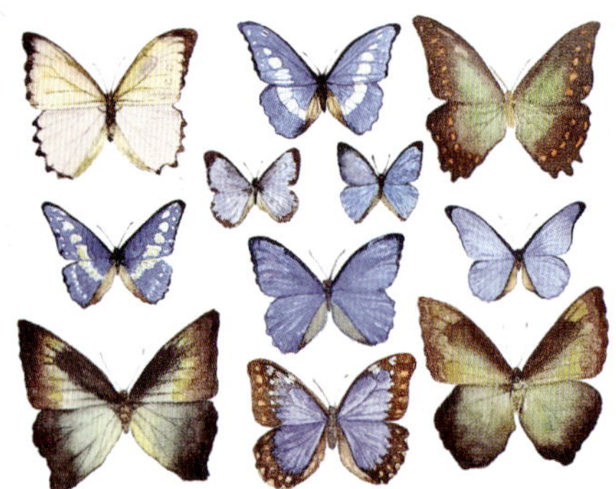

10

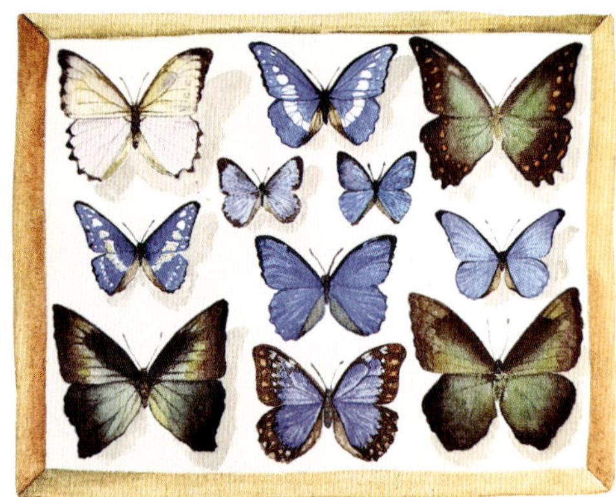

Step 9

Now on to the top-right butterfly. Mix Phthalo Green Deep with a bit of Brown Pink, and using your medium brush, paint a light wash on the four wings. Around the middle of the wings, switch to Van Dyck Brown and keep painting, leaving the markings for the orange untouched. Before the green area dries, paint the outer top edge of the forewings, letting it blend with the background. On the hind wings, outline the bottom inner edge. Switch to your detail brush to paint the body with a wash of Brown Pink. Paint the antennae too. Once everything is dry, paint the orange markings with your detail brush and Red Orange.

With a darker value of the mixture of Phthalo Green Deep and Brown Pink, very lightly paint the veins on the hind wings.

Moving down to the last butterfly, you'll be returning to a similar process as in Step 8. But change out the Payne's Grey on the forewings for Van Dyck Brown.

Step 10

Use your medium brush to paint the frame using a medium value of Yellow Ochre for the color base. Add Burnt Sienna to the top left side where the two pieces of wood meet and to the bottom right corner. Here you can play a bit and mix different shades of brown to create wooden texture. I used Brown Pink and Warm Sepia. Let this dry. To paint the shadows under the butterflies, I mixed all the colors I have used throughout the painting process to create a grayish shade, and with a very light value of this mixture, I painted the shape of the wings, on the right side of the butterflies creating the illusion that they're pinned and projecting a shadow.

11

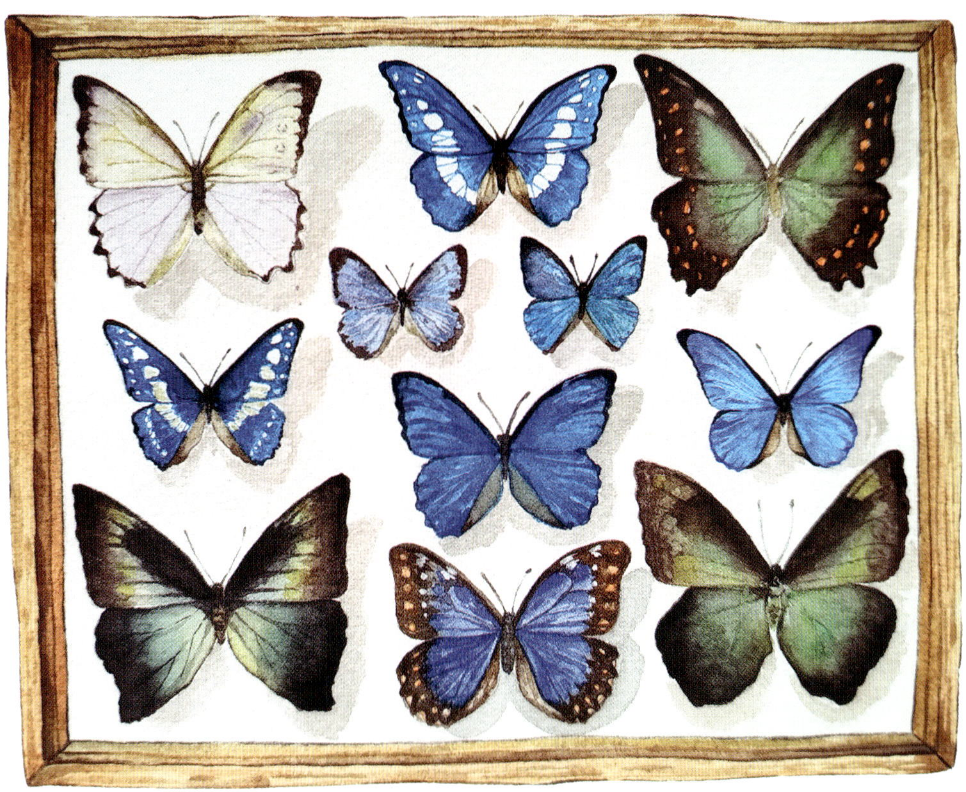

Step 11

Give yourself a pat on the back if you made it to this point! You're about to finish the longest project in this book! Using your detail brush loaded with Van Dyck Brown, add a line right in the middle of the wooden frame, separating it into two sections. Next, outline the inner edge and the outer edge of the frame.

On the inner section of the frame (if we are painting a wooden box, the lid would be the outer section, and the inner section is what you are working on now), paint thin uneven lines using your detail brush and Van Dyck Brown. On each corner add more value of the brown you've used before or the darkest shade to create a dark shadow. Paint a few more lines on the lid area, using a lighter shade of brown where the wood creases.

Your beautiful butterfly taxidermy box is ready to be hanging in your cabinet of curiosities room! Don't you love it?

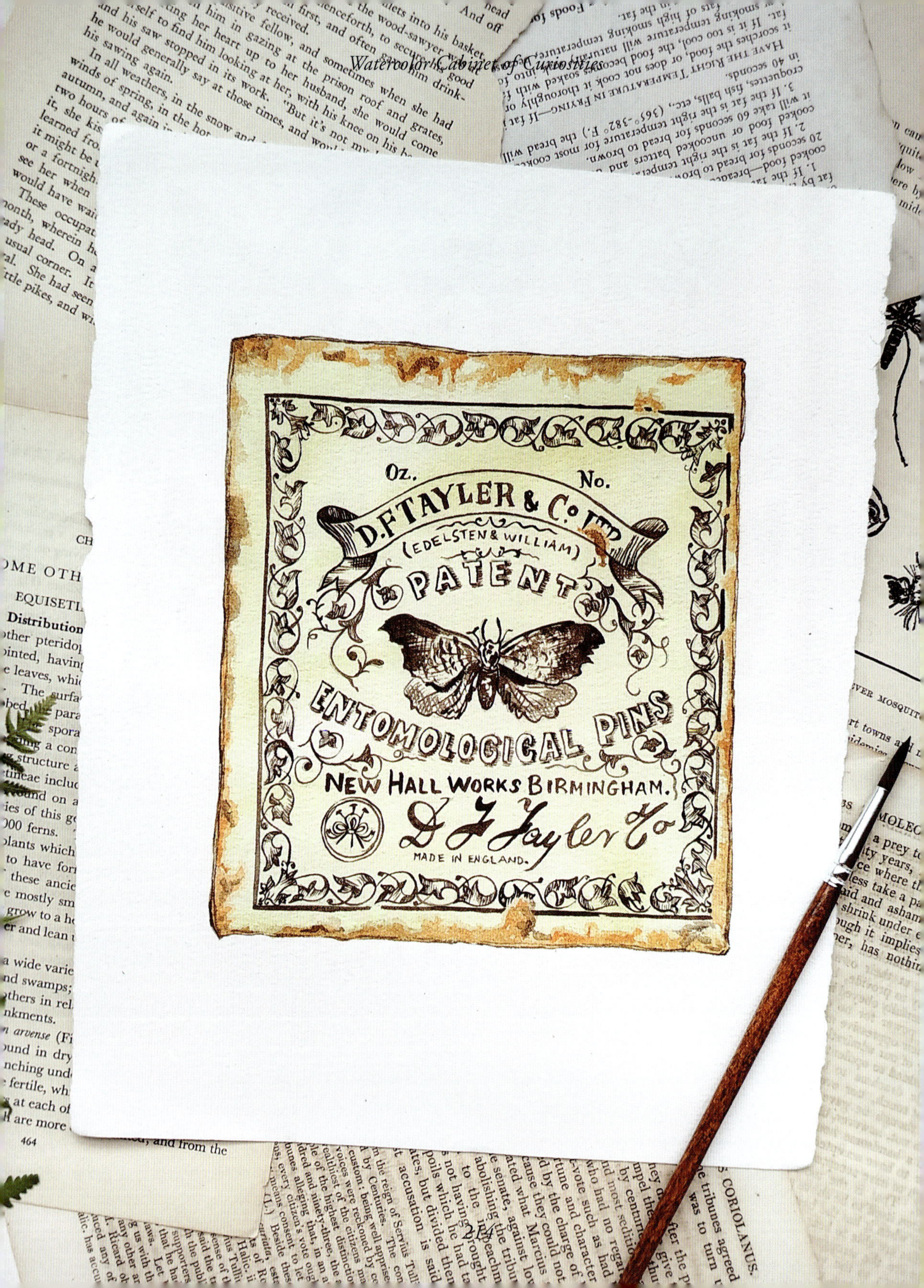

Oz.   No.

D.F. TAYLER & Co. LTD.
(EDELSTEN & WILLIAM)
PATENT
ENTOMOLOGICAL PINS
NEW HALL WORKS BIRMINGHAM.
D. F. Tayler & Co.
MADE IN ENGLAND.

Old Entomology Flyer

Before the internet gave us all the answers, books, zines, and flyers were really important tools. The science of entomology began with the founding of the Academy of Nature Sciences in Philadelphia in 1812. They began a tradition of traveling around the world in search of insects. Artists like Lucy Way Sistare Say became an important part of the expeditions, illustrating the insects as true to life as possible for others to study. That would have been my dream job!

Note: This piece is about practicing your lettering and precision skills. With this project, you'll get better at painting tiny details and creating a worn-out look through using washes.

Difficulty: Easy

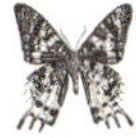

Sketch

Draw the flyer freehand or trace the reference image and transfer it to the watercolor paper of your choice, focusing on the intricate details like the borders, text, and moth illustration. Spray your paints with water to moisten them.

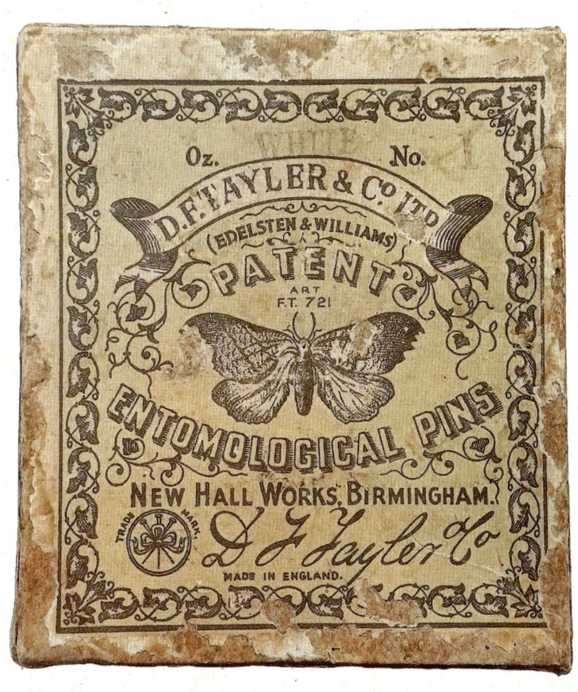

Step 1

Load your medium brush with a medium value of Brown Pink and paint a wash on the flyer. It doesn't need to be an even wash; it looks even better if you add more water to some areas and create marks on the surface as if the paper is aged.

Outline the cover with Van Dyck Brown using your detail brush. Then, once the surface is dry, load your medium brush with a light value of Van Dyck Brown and paint the edges with smudges to create torn edges. Switch to Gold Ochre to create more texture on the aged areas.

Step 2

Load your detail brush with a dark value of Van Dyck Brown to paint all the decorative flourishes around the edges. Add thin lines inside each of them, creating shadows—as you can see in the photo reference. Then, paint a border. Keep in mind that the paper is old, and some parts of the pattern are faded. In these areas, don't draw any lines or flourishes; instead, create a smudge.

Step 3

Keep using your detail brush and Van Dyck Brown to paint the banner and the lettering. Some of the letters inside the banner are not complete due to the flyer's age. Paint just the top part of the last three letters inside the banner. To create depth on the banner corners, paint lines across it, and paint a light shadow on the top section of the banner were it folds backwards.

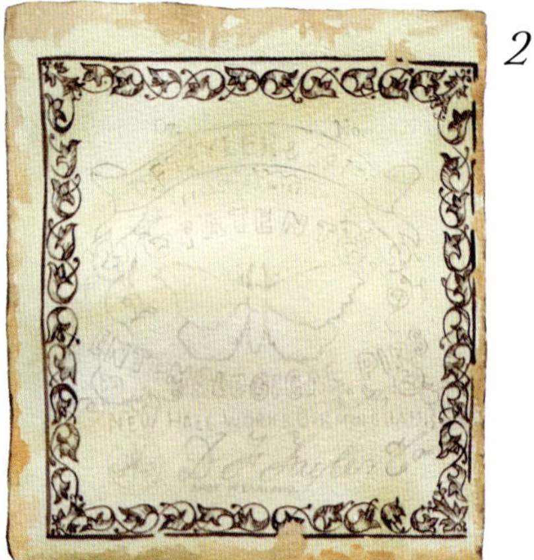

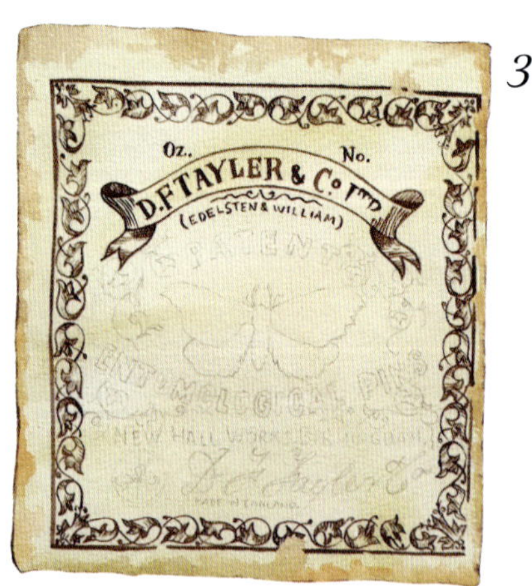

4

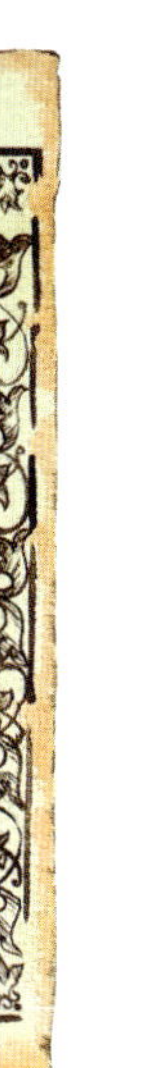

5

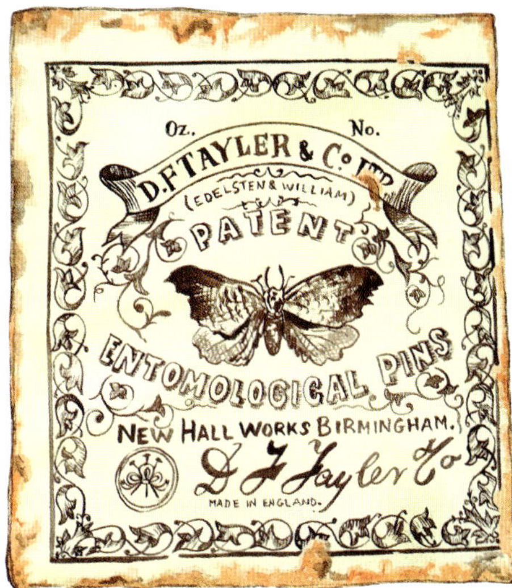

Step 4

Keep using your detail brush and Van Dyck Brown to paint the rest of the flourishes around the banner area, saving the moth for later. Add lines for shadows right under the capital letters, creating a 3D effect. Once you're done, it's time to focus on the moth.

Outline the wings and body using your detail brush and Van Dyck Brown. Switch to your medium brush to darken the tips of the fore-wings. Create a transition from these dark tips to the veins. Create texture by adding wavy lines across the wings, simulating scales. Add a few lighter smudges on the center of the forewings.

Use your detail brush to paint a shadow of a darker Van Dyck Brown value underneath the hind wings. This will immediately make your forewings pop! Lighten the value, and keep using your detail brush to paint the veins and some crossed lines on the bottom section of the hind wings.

Step 5

It's time to emphasize the worn-out look. Load your medium brush with a medium value of Gold Ochre. Use your brush to create smudges, using more of the belly of the brush than the tip. Play with your hand, and let it flow around the painting. It's really fun and relaxing. Switch to Van Dyck Brown, and with a medium value create a few more smudges. Switch to your detail brush again, and with a darker value of Van Dyck Brown, create a few thin lines on the edges, especially in the corners.

Your vintage flyer still has a lot of life ahead!

Reference Image Credits

> Hodecek, Jiri. 6 December 2014. Shutterstock, https://www.shutterstock.com/image-photo/blue-morpho-isolated-235903942. (page 23)

> Ultrashock. 11 October 2008. Shutterstock, https://www.shutterstock.com/es/image-photo/giant-emerald-birdwing-o-priamus-poseidon-18795487. (page 27)

> P_vaida. 21 December 2018. Shutterstock, https://www.shutterstock.com/image-photo/great-tiger-moth-arctia-caja-1264709866. (page 31)

> Zheltyshev. 24 May 2022. Shutterstock, https://www.shutterstock.com/image-photo/large-white-pieris-brassicaebutterfly-family-whiteflies-2160400937. (page 37)

> LMPark Photos. 28 April 2024. Shutterstock, https://www.shutterstock.com/es/image-photo/green-luna-moth-on-sidewalk-near-2455821079. (page 41)

> Boldina, Alina. 26 January 2020. Shutterstock, https://www.shutterstock.com/es/image photo/sphingidac-moth-acherontia-atropos-isolated-on-1627446067. (page 47)

> Vladfotograf. 29 December 2018. Shutterstock, https://www.shutterstock.com/es/image-photo/natural-yellow-butterfly-isolated-on-white-1270220995. (page 51)

> catocala7. 14 June 2024. Shutterstock, https://www.shutterstock.com/es/image-illustration/green-red-colorful-butterfly-urania-ripheus-2476062407. (page 55)

> Hondow, Brett. 22 April 2018. Shutterstock, https://www.shutterstock.com/es/image-photo/common-buckeye-butterfly-junonia-coenia-rest-1074832586. (page 59)

> Standbridge, Sandra. 19 April 2021. Shutterstock, https://www.shutterstock.com/es/image-photo/stunning-male-emperor-moth-saturnia-pavonia-1958901136. (page 67)

> Attentive, Simia. 18 June 2018. Shutterstock, https://www.shutterstock.com/es/image-photo/male-giant-atlas-silk-moth-attacus-1116066590. (page 73)

> Super Prin. 13 July 2016. Shutterstock, https://www.shutterstock.com/es/image-photo/indian-orange-oakleaf-dead-leaf-butterfly-452121067. (page 79)

> Wirestock Creators. 18 May 2023. Shutterstock, https://www.shutterstock.com/es/image-photo/insect-collection-rhinoceros-beetles-specimen-isolated-2305294999. (page 87)

> Klejdysz, Tomasz. 24 November 2017. Shutterstock, https://www.shutterstock.com/es/image-photo/cetonia-aurata-called-rose-chafer-green-762399658. (page 93)

> Proskurina, Valentina. 6 July 2013. Shutterstock, https://www.shutterstock.com/es/image-photo/ladybug-isolated-on-white-145029469. (page 97)

> Wirestock Creators. 13 January 2024. https://www.shutterstock.com/image-photo/insect-collection-stag-beetle-specimen-isolated-2412577335. (page 103)

> Ultrashock. 7 November 2008. Shutterstock, https://www.shutterstock.com/es/image-photo/top-view-colorful-flower-beetle-mecynorrhina-20213944. (page 107)

> photomaster. 21 April 2024. Shutterstock, https://www.shutterstock.com/es/image-photo/giant-goliath-isolated-on-white-background-2452786845. (page 113)

> will_dupratt. 18 February 2022. Shutterstock, https://www.shutterstock.com/es/image-photo/grays-leaf-mimic-phyllium-bioculatum-2126130344. (page 119)

> Creative Stock Studio. 21 August 2021. Shutterstock, https://www.shutterstock.com/es/image-photo/isopod-cubaris-amber-ducky-on-bark-2029009643. (page 127)

> bluehand. 18 January 2013. Shutterstock, https://www.shutterstock.com/es/image-photo/green-brown-cicada-tosena-splendida-on-125203298. (page 131)

> Prudek, Daniel. 27 January 2024. Shutterstock, https://www.shutterstock.com/es/image-photo/detail-bee-honeybee-latin-apis-mellifera-2418453905. (page 137)

> smspsy. 9 November 2015. Shutterstock, https://www.shutterstock.com/es/image-photo/close-fonarnitsa-laternariya-laternaria-tingo-maria-337531466. (page 143)

> van Holten, Nynke. 22 October 2020. Shutterstock, https://www.shutterstock.com/es/image-photo/top-view-mexican-redknee-tarantula-aka-1839345166. (page 151)

> Dakos, Alana. Etsy, https://www.etsy.com/listing/1205777235/tulip-garden-embroidery-scissors-antique. (page 155)

> Aleksandrov, Vasilii. 18 October 2016. Shutterstock, https://www.shutterstock.com/es/image-photo/skull-domestic-cat-on-white-background-500773639. (page 159)

› kmarka. 8 March 2018. Shutterstock, https://www.shutterstock.com/es/image-photo/picture-frame-old-bronze-1041895627. (page 165)

› azure1. 20 February 2016. Shutterstock, https://www.shutterstock.com/es/image-photo/old-key-isolated-on-white-background-379870594. (page 171)

› Magnusson, Roland. 3 November 2016. Shutterstock, https://www.shutterstock.com/es/image-photo/fly-agaric7amanita-muscaria-isolated-on-510017887. (page 177)

› MustafaNC. 27 February 2014. Shutterstock, https://www.shutterstock.com/es/image-photo/real-macaw-bird-feather-natural-colors-173710484. (page 181)

› Gh07. 14 July 2024. Shutterstock, https://www.shutterstock.com/es/image-photo/beautiful-detail-part-butterfly-wing-2489209213. (page 189)

› Militarist. 1 October 2022. Shutterstock, https://www.shutterstock.com/es/image-photo/retro-vintage-magnifying-glass-isolated-on-2209240893. (page 193)

› BestPix. 11 May 2021. Shutterstock, https://www.shutterstock.com/es/image-photo/small-glass-stand-cake-lemon-isolated-1972427030. (left on page 195)

› Kachkovskyi, Iurii. 20 February 2019. Shutterstock, https://www.shutterstock.com/es/image-photo/butterfly-ornithoptera-urvilianus-frame-isolated-on-1319523317. (right on page 195)

› Caridad, Pablo. 29 September 2010. Shutterstock, https://www.shutterstock.com/es/image-photo/old-fashioned-drug-bottle-label-isolated-62031373. (left on page 199)

› Brix, Matthias. 17 November 2021. Shutterstock, https://www.shutterstock.com/es/image-photo/burnet-companion-moth-owlet-moths-2077013809. (right on page 199)

› Savina, Galina. 4 December 2018. Shutterstock, https://www.shutterstock.com/es/image-photo/moscow-russia-11262018-morpho-collection-tropical-1249920802. (page 206)

› Protasov AN. 26 July 2024. Shutterstock, https://www.shutterstock.com/es/image-photo/tel-aviv-israel-july-7-2024-2494683239. (page 215)

Acknowledgments

I'd like to extend a big thank you to my friends Colleen and Bel, who helped me when I was stuck with my English.

To Sadie, my editor, for being such a sweetheart and guiding me through the process.

To all my friends who supported me and understood when I was MIA!

To my husband, Wukong, who's always been there to give me ideas.

But my biggest thank you is to my kids—Luqman, Harun, Sammy, and Ivy—for inspiring me to always be better.

About the Author

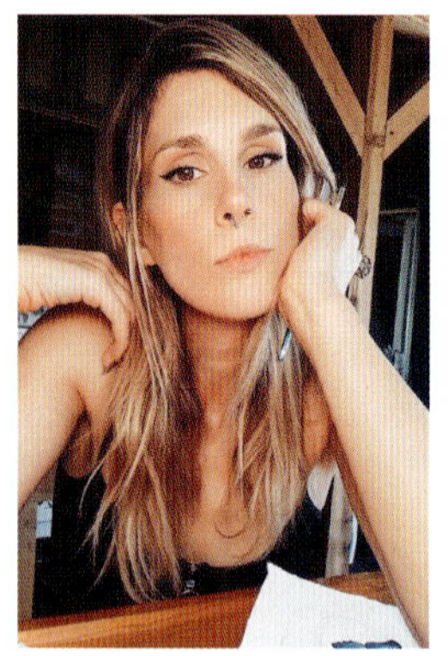

Nassybah Touriño is the artist behind Nussay Art.

She was born in Granada, Spain. While she has always had a passion for art, it wasn't until she moved to Madison, Wisconsin, that she started creating on a regular basis and sharing her illustrations on Instagram. She then took the chance to quit her regular job to fully follow her dream of becoming a freelance illustrator. She began her business, Nussay Art, and her work has since been featured in product design, stationery, and textiles, as well as wholesale and private commissions.

In 2019, Nassybah was diagnosed with Hodgkin lymphoma and had to move back to Spain to be closer to her family and get treatment. After this difficult period, she decided to move to Mexico for a slower life, and she started leading watercolor workshops in the magical forest of Chiapas. Now she finds inspiration in the beautiful nature of Chiapas' biodiversity, and creates lush watercolors inspired by the views from her home in San Cristóbal de las Casas.

When not painting, Nassybah enjoys seeking quiet moments for hiking, making small bouquets of flowers and herbs, or reading. She loves exploring new places, and enjoys anything that includes the forest, friends, and food!

Index

A

Amanita Muscaria, 177–180

anatomy guide, 17–18

Antique Magnifying Glass, 193–194

Arches, 10

Atlas Moth, 73–77

B

beetles

anatomy guide, 18

Flower Chafer, 93–96

Goliath Beetle, 113–118

Hercules Beetle, 87–91

Stag Beetle, 103–105

blending, 13, 49

Blick Studio Tracing paper, 10

Blue Morpho Butterfly, 23–26

butterflies and moths

anatomy guide, 17

Atlas Moth, 73–77

Blue Morpho Butterfly, 23–26

Butterfly Wing, 189–191

Cabbage Butterfly, 37–40

Common Buckeye Butterfly, 59–65

Death's-Head Hawkmoth, 47–50

Emerald Birdwing Butterfly, 27–30

Emperor Moth, 67–71

Glass Dome Insect, 195–198

Luna Moth, 41–45

Monarch Butterfly, 51–54

Orange Oakleaf Butterfly, 79–83

Sunset Moth, 55–58

Tiger Moth, 31–35

Butterfly Wing, 189–191

C

Cabbage Butterfly, 37–40

Canson, 10

Cat Skull, 159–164

Cicada, 131–135

clear water wash, 12, 48

cold-press paper, 9–10

color mixing, 14–15, 33

color theory, 14–15

color wheel, 14

colors

bleeding, 88

complementary, 15–16

making darker, 16, 53, 100

making lighter, 16

pastel, 96

primary, 14–15

secondary, 14

tertiary, 14

Common Buckeye Butterfly, 59–65

complementary colors, 15–16

D

Death's-Head Hawkmoth, 47–50

difficult projects

    Atlas Moth, 73–77

    Common Buckeye Butterfly, 59–65

    Death's-Head Hawkmoth, 47–50

    Emperor Moth, 67–71

    Goliath Beetle, 113–118

    Insect Taxidermy Box, 205–213

    Orange Oakleaf Butterfly, 79–83

    Peanut-Headed Lantern Fly, 143–147

    skill level, 19

    Vintage Frame, 165–170

E

easy projects

    Amanita Muscaria, 177–180

    Antique Magnifying Glass, 193–194

    Butterfly Wing, 189–191

    Cabbage Butterfly, 37–40

    Emerald Birdwing Butterfly, 27–30

    Feather, 181–185

    Glass Dome Insect, 195–198

    Hercules Beetle, 87–91

    Ladybug, 97–101

    Luna Moth, 41–45

    Monarch Butterfly, 51–54

    Old Entomology Flyer, 215–217

    Roly-Poly, 127–129

    skill level, 19

    Tarantula, 151–154

    Vintage Scissors, 155–158

Emerald Birdwing Butterfly, 27–30

Emperor Moth, 67–71

entomology drawer

    Antique Magnifying Glass, 193–194

    Butterfly Wing, 189–191

    Glass Dome Insect, 195–198

    Insect Taxidermy Box, 205–213

    Moth Dust Bottle, 199–203

    Old Entomology Flyer, 215–217

F

Fabriano, 10

Feather, 181–185

Flower Chafer, 93–96

G

Glass Dome Insect, 195–198

Goliath Beetle, 113–118

gradient, 13

H

Hercules Beetle, 87–91

Honeybee, 137–141

hot-press paper, 10

I

Insect Taxidermy Box, 205–213

insects. See also butterflies and moths

    Cicada, 131–135

    Flower Chafer, 93–96

Goliath Beetle, 113–118

Hercules Beetle, 87–91

Honeybee, 137–141

Ladybug, 97–101

Leaf Insect, 119–125

Mecynorhina, 107–112

Peanut-Headed Lantern Fly, 143–147

Roly-Poly, 127–129

Stag Beetle, 103–105

L

Ladybug, 97–101

layers, 13, 70, 100

Leaf Insect, 119–125

lifting colors, 13–14

Luna Moth, 41–45

M

masking fluid, 10, 53

Mecynorhina, 107–112

medium projects

Blue Morpho Butterfly, 23–26

Cat Skull, 159–164

Cicada, 131–135

Flower Chafer, 93–96

Honeybee, 137–141

Leaf Insect, 119–125

Mecynorhina, 107–112

Moth Dust Bottle, 199–203

Old Key, 171–175

skill level, 19

Stag Beetle, 103–105

Sunset Moth, 55–58

Tiger Moth, 31–35

Monarch Butterfly, 51–54

Moth Dust Bottle, 199–203

moths. See butterflies and moths

mushrooms

Amanita Muscaria, 177–180

anatomy guide, 17

O

oddities

Amanita Muscaria, 177–180

Cat Skull, 159–164

Feather, 181–185

Old Key, 171–175

Tarantula, 151–154

Vintage Frame, 165–170

Vintage Scissors, 155–158

Old Entomology Flyer, 215–217

Old Key, 171–175

Orange Oakleaf Butterfly, 79–83

P

paintbrushes, 9, 33, 112, 128

Panart brushes, 9

Peanut-Headed Lantern Fly, 143–147

pencils, 10

primary colors, 14

R

Roly-Poly, 127–129

S

secondary colors, 14
Sennelier professional palette, 8
skill levels, 19
Stag Beetle, 103–105
Sunset Moth, 55–58

T

tarantulas
    anatomy guide, 18
    Tarantula, 151–154
techniques
    blending, 49
    clear water wash, 12, 48
    color mixing, 14–15, 33
    dabbing paint, 139
    letting dry between sections, 99
    lifting colors, 13–14
    organic markings, 40, 44
    painting glass, 203
    tracing lines, 38
    transferring sketches, 14
    washes, 12–13
    wet-on-dry, 12–13
    wet-on-wet, 12–13, 24
tertiary colors, 14

Tiger Moth, 31–35
tools for watercolor painting
    masking fluid, 10
    paintbrushes, 9
    pencils, 10
    tracing paper, 10
    watercolor paints, 8–9
    watercolor paper, 9–10
    white gouache, 10
tracing paper, 10
transferring sketches, 14

V

vellum paper, 10
Vintage Frame, 165–170
Vintage Scissors, 155–158

W

washes, 12–13
watercolor paints
    color palette, 8–9
        preparing enough colors, 54, 76, 122
watercolor paper, 9–10
wet-on-dry watercolor painting, 12–13
wet-on-wet watercolor painting, 12–13, 24
white gouache, 10, 96
Winsor & Newton, 10